ATTLEE

ATTLEE

A Life in Politics

NICK THOMAS-SYMONDS

BLOOMSBURY ACADEMIC
LONDON · NEW YORK · OXFORD · NEW DELHI · SYDNEY

BLOOMSBURY ACADEMIC
Bloomsbury Publishing Plc
50 Bedford Square, London, WC1B 3DP, UK
1385 Broadway, New York, NY 10018, USA
29 Earlsfort Terrace, Dublin 2, Ireland

BLOOMSBURY, BLOOMSBURY ACADEMIC and the Diana logo
are trademarks of Bloomsbury Publishing Plc

First published in Great Britain 2010
This edition published 2023

A catalogue record for this book is available from the British Library.

A catalog record for this book is available from the Library of Congress.

ISBN: PB: 978-0-7556-3613-6
ePDF: 978-0-7556-3615-0
eBook: 978-0-7556-3614-3

Printed and bound in Great Britain

To find out more about our authors and books visit
www.bloomsbury.com and sign up for our newsletters.

FOR MY GRANDPARENTS, MY PARENTS, REBECCA, MATILDA OLWYN, FLORENCE ELIZABETH MARY, WILLIAM NICKLAUS AND PIPPA

CONTENTS

ILLUSTRATIONS

ACRONYMS AND ABBREVIATIONS

BMA	British Medical Association
CH	Companion of Honour
FBI	Federation of British Industries
ILP	Independent Labour Party
NATO	North Atlantic Treaty Organization
NEC	National Executive Committee
NBG	no bloody good
OM	Order of Merit
PM	prime minister
PPS	parliamentary private secretary
SEAC	Southeast Asia Command
SDP	Social Democratic Party
SPGB	Socialist Party of Great Britain
TUC	Trades Union Congress

ACKNOWLEDGEMENTS

I would like to thank my three excellent researchers: Mr Phil Alderton for all his painstaking work, Mr Thomas Braithwaite for his excellent efforts and also Mr Maximillian Krahé, like Attlee an old Haileyburian. I would also like to thank Mr Toby Parker, Archivist at Haileybury and Mr John O'Brien at the India Records Office. Mr John Dunbabin, Emeritus Fellow of St Edmund Hall, Oxford, read the first draft in great detail, and I am grateful for all his insightful feedback. Miss Gillian Peele of Lady Margaret Hall also read the text and gave me some very useful comments. I had a very interesting conversation with the current Earl Attlee (Clement Attlee's grandson), and Anne, Countess Attlee (Clement Attlee's daughter-in-law) was very generous with her time, giving me access to very useful papers in her possession, which she has kindly given me permission to quote (from material for which she is the copyright-holder). I would also like to thank Tony Benn for taking the time to give me an interview, and Sir Gerald Kaufman MP for his letter dealing with my queries. Of course, any inaccuracies in the work are my responsibility.

PREFACE

The debate generated by the publication of *Attlee: A Life in Politics* has highlighted Attlee's enduring relevance to modern politics. The book itself concluded with a lament: if there was no place in modern politics for a taciturn, non-charismatic 'chairman' leader like Clement Attlee – understated and unemotional in public, modest and practical – then that would say more about the modern political system and media than it would about him. Yet I did not underestimate the many lessons for modern politics found in the political life of Clement Attlee.

Prima facie, the situation that Attlee faced when he became leader of the Labour Party in November 1935 has similarities to the situation that the Labour Party faces today. Attlee was opposite a coalition government containing both Conservatives and Liberals. That government was grappling with the economic aftermath of a worldwide financial crisis brought about by the Wall Street Crash of 1929. The economy was the central domestic issue. Attlee's leadership has deeper significance too. Harrying the government in the House of Commons – even with its commanding majority – by consistently highlighting the misery caused by high unemployment was of course very important. And, whilst Attlee may not be remembered as a particularly successful leader of the opposition, he was able to change his party's position on the major foreign policy issue of the day. Labour's stance on defence moved towards one of favouring rearmament in view of the threat posed by Hitler's Germany, culminating in Attlee opposing Prime Minister Neville Chamberlain's famous 'Munich Agreement' of October 1938.

The two central principles of Attlee's leadership style – exhibited most obviously when he was prime minister – were allowing a number of colleagues of great ability to carry out their jobs without undue interference; and that constructive achievement is ultimately more important than presentation.

These are enduring political lessons, relevant to any era. Prime ministers can set the direction of their governments and demand excellence from their departmental ministers without interfering in the work of colleagues on a daily basis. Voters may be impressed by style and presentation, but ultimately they judge governments on what they achieve. Modern prime ministers would also be well served by developing Attlee's ability to compartmentalize. Attlee showed this quality not just in his personal life (for example, his brother Tom's decision to conscientiously object during the First World War whilst Attlee himself served left their relationship unaffected), but also repeatedly in his ability to deal with a variety of issues demanding instant responses that came across his desk in Number Ten.

None of the critical assessments of *Attlee: A Life in Politics* have changed my mind about the overall conclusion: 'Clement Attlee bestrides the twentieth-century history of the Labour Party. Its greatest constructive achievements are his government's achievements.' To my surprise some reviewers saw *Attlee: A Life in Politics* as a negative biography.[1] To a certain extent this may be a product of the organization of the book's chapters: the extraordinary achievements of national insurance, national health and nationalization were packed into 14 pages in Chapter 16. It is certainly not my view, to quote Lord Hattersley, that 'dumping ... [Attlee] ... would have improved Labour's chances of becoming "the natural party of government"'. Neither do I think, as is alleged by Francis Beckett, that Attlee 'was not much to write home about', nor that Herbert Morrison would have made a better Labour leader or prime minister had he been chosen by the Labour parliamentary party in 1935. Rather, my difficulty with that particular election is the paucity of direct evidence about why Attlee won. Certainly one piece that escaped my attention was William Golant's 1970 journal article on Attlee's emergence as leader in 1935.[2] Yet even this detailed study runs into the same difficulty. Quoting A. L. Rowse, Golant states as follows:

> One observer closer to events suggests that 'Bevan directly influenced the 1935 election for the leadership by pressing trade union MPs to vote for Attlee. The action of either Morrison or Greenwood would have alienated one-third of the party. Attlee alienated none'. Though there is *no corroboratory evidence* [my emphasis] of Bevan influencing MPs the general point is valid ...

Historians are inevitably left in danger of relying to too great an extent on the diaries of Hugh Dalton; given the later significance of the 1935 leadership election – producing, as it did, the Labour Party's first prime minister of a majority government – it is a shame that little further direct evidence exists.

The book's central purpose was a study of the Attlee leadership style. It was never my intention to produce a 'hero worship' biography; rather, it was to subject the Attlee leadership style, particularly as prime minister, to sustained analysis. My aim was to produce a positive, but not uncritical, biography. Of course, some of my analysis has proved controversial, not least in respect of my assessment of Attlee's role in Indian independence, one area of policy where he did depart from his chairmanship model of leadership and, along with Stafford Cripps, exercised a direct influence.[3]

One quotation I had not come across is cited by Francis Beckett in his review of *Attlee: A Life in Politics*. Beckett once put the criticism of Attlee giving India independence too quickly to Lord Healey, who responded: 'Have you ever tried crossing a precipice in two bounds?' My point, however, was not so much that independence required two moves but that the *jump itself* was undertaken a little too quickly. This assessment is based upon the effect of a withdrawal from India in such a short period coupled with a 'hands-off' approach. There was a great human tragedy, with what we would today call ethnic cleansing taking place in villages as majorities attempted to drive out minorities to ensure that they fell on their preferred side of the so-called 'Radcliffe' lines. Violence continued daily, with thousands evicted from their homes, creating a major refugee crisis. *The Times* reported on 5 September 1947 that over 1 million, and perhaps as many as 2 million, people were on the move in the Punjab due to communal massacres. The 'Mountbatten Plan' was approved by the British cabinet on 27 May 1947, with independence a mere 80 days later on 15 August 1947. What I argued for was a slight delay once the problems became clear, or taking more active steps either side of independence to assist the native populations. I am not for a moment suggesting that these problems could have been averted completely given their scale, but I do believe that their effects could have been mitigated. I give one example of a decision that could have been different: India and Pakistan were left to police their own borders, meaning that British troops could only protect refugees if their line of march or overnight encampment *happened* to overlap. A more strategic approach could have helped alleviate the crisis.

I also felt that the lack of time contributed to problems over the princely states, particularly Kashmir, where I questioned the effect of a personal Attlee effort with the maharajah. Philip Ziegler, in his review of *Attlee: A Life in Politics*, is very critical of my suggestion that Attlee should have intervened at all after Mountbatten had spent four days attempting to persuade the maharajah to accede to either India or Pakistan and failed.[4] However, my point is that there *was* an opportunity for Attlee to intervene and that, whilst he may well not have succeeded where Mountbatten had failed, what would have happened had he intervened remains an unanswered question. All this is not to say, however, that I do not praise Attlee very positively for his role in Indian independence. The achievement was a staggering feat of statesmanship. Yet my conclusion on India, that 'With partition, Attlee found the only viable solution, but implemented it too quickly. His navigation of the difficult channel towards an agreed form of independence still deserves great credit' is one that I still regard as fair on consideration of the evidence.

Attlee the man has an enduring popularity with people, the reasons for which have become clear to me from meeting readers at book promotion events and through the many letters I have received. Attlee is well known and highly regarded because his government left so many visible and lasting monuments. The National Health Service remains the greatest British institution, so cherished by the people that, even in a modern-day general election, no major British political party would dare to argue against the principle of healthcare provided on the basis of need, not wealth, free for all at the point of delivery. The welfare state may be subject to periodic proposals on reform, and child benefit may now be non-universal, but the postwar 'cradle to grave' welfare state implemented under Attlee certainly remains the governing model. People also relate to Attlee not simply because he was so authentic ('a sheep in sheep's clothing' as Winston Churchill famously put it), but also because he was a man of staunchest ethics and unblemished character, beyond any form of personal criticism.

The laconic Attlee may not have been suited to the modern 24-hour media. And Attlee's leadership model was context specific. With a set of less-talented colleagues, it would not have worked as it did. Without the very personal, charismatic leadership styles of Ramsay MacDonald, his predecessor as Labour leader, and Winston Churchill, his predecessor as prime minister, neither his party nor his country may have been ready for such a leader. Yet Attlee should not be dismissed easily. Lessons from his political life would serve twenty-first century statesmen well.

Nick Thomas-Symonds
Abersychan, Torfaen, 31 October 2011

FOREWORD TO THE 2023 EDITION

Clement Attlee is one of only three postwar Labour leaders, alongside Harold Wilson and Tony Blair, to have been elected Prime Minister.

This book is a reminder of what Labour, at its best, in power, can achieve. It's also a reminder of Labour's enduring mission, today, as in 1945, to change people's lives and to build a better, fairer society.

It is my pleasure to provide a Foreword to this book. Nick is not only a good friend and valued member of the shadow cabinet, but, as this book shows once again, he is also a thorough, balanced and persuasive historian.

Nick is right to be critical and analytical, as the best historical writing always is. This book will spark debate about the past. It also contains lessons for the next Labour government.

Nick argues – powerfully – that 'Clement Attlee bestrides the twentieth-century history of the Labour Party. Its greatest constructive achievements are his government's achievements'. So he does. It is extraordinary that the Attlee government accomplished so much in so little time – and in such inauspicious circumstances.

Even in the rubble of the aftermath of the Second World War, Attlee's administration managed to create the modern welfare state, build new council homes for families across the land and expand state education, pensions and national insurance for millions of working people. In the NHS, Attlee's government built the finest achievement of postwar Britain – and the clearest example of the difference Labour can make in power. On the world stage, Attlee's government created enduring structures for our national security, including NATO in 1949.

Nobody would argue that there is a direct parallel between the recent Covid-19 crisis, in which humanity faced the common threat of the virus, and the experience of the Second World War. Yet there are points of comparison, not least in the sense that both were times of national, collective sacrifice. The heroism of our frontline workers was, and is, an inspiration. Both periods were also followed by a difficult phase of financial challenge. Yet it is here that the comparison breaks down.

In 1945, as Nick sets out, Attlee's incoming ministers faced what the economist John Maynard Keynes called a 'financial Dunkirk' that was the result of running the economy for years on a war footing. Today's financial issues are the product of Conservative incompetence: over a decade of anaemic growth under successive chancellors of the exchequer, including Rishi Sunak, and Liz Truss's disastrous premiership with its catastrophic mini-budget. Today, working people are paying the price of a crisis made in Downing Street.

Our UK is being let down by its current government at Westminster. That's why we should take inspiration from the scale of Attlee's ambition for change to realize our country's potential. He set out a vision of how Labour could rebuild: to leave behind the injustice and unfairness of inter-war Britain and to make it, in his words, 'a place where men and women can live finely and happily … free citizens of a great country'.

As Attlee showed in 1945, at times like this, the Labour Party does not look back; it looks only to the future. Our task – and our duty – is to build a better Britain with a government on the side of the people working in partnership with trade unions and businesses. I want this to be a country committed to a building a greener, fairer society; and I want us to – once again – be an active force for good in the world, admired and respected by other countries. We should be leading by example in defending human rights and fighting the climate emergency. It was the hope that a better future was possible that underpinned Attlee's great government. Labour's mission under my leadership is to restore that optimism today.

Then, as now, it needs a transformative Labour government to glimpse the future and to set out a transformative programme that can change lives and change Britain.

That is the key lesson that Attlee leaves us.

It is the task that I, Nick and the whole Labour Party now have ahead of us: to build a brighter future for our country.

To do that, we need to fully understand the vital role past Labour governments have played in bringing about change – and I am grateful to Nick for his important contribution to that task.

Rt Hon Sir Keir Starmer KC MP, Leader of the Labour Party
February 2023

INTRODUCTION TO THE 2023 EDITION

When writing the introduction to the first edition of this book thirteen years ago, I cited a University of Leeds/Ipsos MORI poll of university academics in 2004 that rated Clement Attlee as the twentieth-century's greatest prime minister.[1] Having been elected to parliament in 2015, and seen – at close quarters – successive Conservative prime ministers take office and leave in failure, I can only conclude that Attlee's achievements seem even more impressive as time passes.

Of course, the UK has changed dramatically since Attlee held the highest political office in the land. When his minister of health and housing, the great Aneurin Bevan, walked into Park Hospital, Manchester,[2] on 5 July 1948 to launch the National Health Service, the greatest single accomplishment in postwar British politics, the polio vaccine was still eight years away, whilst, today, our brilliant scientists discovered more than one vaccine for Covid-19 barely more than eight months after the first UK national lockdown in March 2020.

Yet the National Health Service's founding principle remains intact, and with great public support: that people should receive healthcare of a universally high standard, based on their medical need, not ability to pay. Over seventy years since its foundation, the National Health Service, with its magnificent, committed staff and our care workers working alongside it, has once again, through the Covid-19 pandemic, shown its value to our society. It is not an outdated institution from our past; it is a living example of how socialism in action can improve people's lives for the better.

That the finest achievement of his governments remains so central to our national life is crucial, but it is not the only reason why Attlee is so important today. His governments shaped the postwar era in the most challenging of circumstances. John Maynard Keynes described the economic inheritance of 1945 as a 'financial Dunkirk'. As is set out in *The Scale of the Challenge, July-November 1945*, Attlee had to manage the mass demobilization of those serving in the armed forces whilst avoiding high unemployment: a great failure of the post-1918 government, under which unemployment soared to over two million in the early 1920s. The very physical fabric of the UK needed to be rebuilt. There was wartime damage across vast swathes of the country: industries were taken into public hands, and there was an urgent need for repaired and newly built homes.

Attlee succeeded for two reasons: first, his core belief in the kind of society he wanted to create, and, secondly, through his focus on getting things done. His experience as a social worker in London's East End in the years before the First World War never left him. He rejected the Victorian idea that poverty was the fault of the individual. Instead, he drew a firm conclusion that poverty could only be addressed through systemic political change and legislation. He rejected the notion of limited government leaving people abandoned with nobody to help them but themselves. Governments should not stand to one side; they should act to make people's lives better.

That central principle guided him, and his determination to translate it into concrete action made his governments a success. Reflecting on the qualities a prime minister needs, Attlee said: 'A sense of urgency, of dispatch. A sense of the time and the occasion and the atmosphere of the country'.[3] What a stark contrast that is with some who have held the office since.

Attlee told his newly appointed government ministers in 1945 that they would be judged on what they succeeded at, not on what they attempted: his administrations focussed on constructive achievement for people. No whiff of personal scandal ever touched Attlee, and he always expected the highest standards from the ministers he appointed. He was a person of few words who chaired cabinet with efficiency, and was impatient of long, rambling discussions. He ensured that ministers reached a conclusion, a set of actions that could be taken forward. Speaking to the Oxford University Law Society in 1957, he offered this reflection: 'Democracy means government by discussion but it is only effective if you can stop people talking.'[4]

When he died in 1967, the then prime minister, Harold Wilson, who had served in Attlee's cabinet as President of the Board of Trade, paid tribute in the House of Commons:

> Woe betide … the Minister who submitted a paper that was sloppy in
> its expression, or who was not on top of his job, or who relied on civil
> servants to do his thinking for him. His rebukes – whether in Cabinet,

or in private meetings at No. 10 when he summoned the Ministers to his presence – were fierce and devastating. But, equally, when understanding and help were needed, Clement Attlee never failed.[5]

Attlee was a true chair of cabinet who brought the best out of others and knew how to manage a team effectively.

Attlee's obituary in *The Times* read: 'Much of what he did was memorable; very little that he said.'[6] As a person of few words, Attlee would have rather liked that. He was a prime minister who made change happen. In his autobiography, *As It Happened*, published in 1954, he reflected on the impact his governments had made and the different path that would have been taken had the Conservatives won the 1945 General Election: 'Unless there had been a Government with a clear policy and a resolute will we might well have slipped back to the evil conditions of the past.' Instead, the result of his governments maintaining full employment and developing social services was that the 'great mass of abject poverty has disappeared'.[7]

None of this is to suggest that Attlee did not make mistakes, or that we should look at his views and actions uncritically. The intention of this biography is to recognize Attlee's monumental achievements but also to be balanced. Readers can make their own judgments on Attlee: political history should always be a debate about *all* aspects of leaders' contributions. One proposition, however, is difficult to contest, and that is that Attlee's governments had an impact on the UK for decades after the general election defeat of October 1951.

Similarly, the recent Covid-19 crisis will have consequences that will be felt for many years to come. We will never forget all those whose lives have been lost and the families for whom life will never quite be the same again. Our frontline workers have put themselves at risk day after day, putting themselves in danger to help others and keep people safe. They have been there when they were needed. Trade unions have shown their enduring importance, pressing for health and safety provisions in workplaces and the furlough scheme; the campaigning of the whole Labour Movement has saved lives and livelihoods.

Yet, unlike the Attlee government in 1945 that sought to improve the lives of generations of people, the Conservative chancellors of the exchequer since 2010, including Rishi Sunak, generated little in the way of economic growth. Our public services were left in a weakened state going into the pandemic, putting them under intolerable pressure. Since then, Liz Truss's catastrophic mini-budget has, once again, meant that working people are paying the price of Conservative incompetence.

So we know that – as in 1945 – our country's future success cannot be taken for granted. We need an active UK government that recognizes, and acts upon, the huge challenges that people face in their everyday lives.

The work of Clement Attlee and his governments teaches us, above all, that a national crisis should be followed by an ambition from leaders that meets the challenge of the moment. Attlee shaped the postwar UK and made it a better place. Let us take inspiration from that as we approach the great challenges of the years ahead.

Rt Hon. Nick Thomas-Symonds MP
Abersychan, Torfaen, February 2023

INTRODUCTION

In 2004 a University of Leeds/Ipsos MORI poll of university academics rated Clement Attlee, 37 years after his death, the twentieth-century's greatest prime minister with an average mark of 8.34 out of 10; Winston Churchill was second on 7.88.[1] Attlee's governments of 1945–51 unquestionably represented the high point of twentieth-century constructive achievement for the Labour Party. Manifesto promises were fulfilled quickly and efficiently: at home, the government created the welfare state and the National Health Service; abroad, it decolonized vast swathes of the British Empire, including India, and cemented Britain's relationship with the United States. The Attlee governments' approach of maintaining high levels of employment with major industries under public ownership became the orthodoxy in postwar British politics until Margaret Thatcher's 1979–90 Conservative government. Yet, Attlee the man is frustratingly hidden. During his career there was a characteristic reticence to open up to others. According to his obituary in *The Times* he was 'devoid of those external marks which Aristotle thought necessary for men of consequence – sincere and quietly impressive was the most that could be said of his public personality'; with Attlee, 'much of what he did was memorable; very little that he said.'[2]

Attlee became prime minister in July 1945 as the leader of a Labour Party that had won a landslide victory with a majority of 144 seats. Only Tony Blair in 1997 (179) and 2001 (167) had more impressive Labour victories. With 47.8 per cent of the popular vote, Attlee seemed to have achieved the platform for Labour to dominate postwar British politics. He had apparently united the working class and the middle class around the common goal of improving society around collective provision. His government represented one answer to what the historian David Marquand has termed the 'Progressive Dilemma': how the Labour Party can successfully appeal to enough non-Labour voters to win an election without losing its core working-class vote. The free market orthodoxy of pre-1939 Britain seemed to be truly dead and buried. Yet, just six years and three months after the 1945 victory and despite all that Attlee's governments had appeared to achieve, Labour was out of office, condemned to opposition for a further 13 years. At the time of writing, in 2009, Labour has governed for only 23 of the 57 years since Attlee lost the general election of 1951. His government therefore presents one of the great paradoxes of twentieth-century British history: why it achieved so much, but lost power so quickly; why it framed the terms of political debate for so long, yet led to the Labour Party being in opposition for so long. Perhaps the greatest paradox was, however, Attlee himself.

Attlee led the Labour Party for 20 years, from 1935 to 1955. No other leader of a major political party in twentieth-century Britain held the reins for so long. His longevity was the result of a number of factors – timing being key. Had the Second World War not broken out in 1939, Labour would almost certainly have lost a 1939 or 1940 general election, and Attlee would have been deposed. Labour's catastrophic defeat in the 1931 general election – reduced to a mere 52 parliamentary seats – left it a generation away from power, barring a seismic political event, which duly happened in the form of the war. His two closest rivals for the leadership, Ernest Bevin and Herbert Morrison, never agreed on replacing him. Bevin, the first general secretary of the Transport and General Workers' Union, wartime minister of labour from 1940, and then Attlee's foreign secretary after 1945, and Morrison, leader of the Labour Group on the London County Council in the 1930s, wartime home secretary from 1942, and Attlee's deputy after 1945 before a brief period at the Foreign Office after Bevin's death in 1951, were political enemies. Attlee survived plots against his leadership in 1939, while he was ill, and in both 1945 and 1947, when Bevin stood loyally by him.

Attlee represented a deliberate departure from the deeply personal leadership style of Labour's first prime minister, Ramsay MacDonald. When, on the collapse of the second Labour government in 1931, MacDonald abandoned the Labour Party and formed the national government, the party yearned for a leader who listened to and consulted his MPs. When Attlee told the 1953 Labour Party conference that he was there to carry out the party's wishes, it was more than rhetoric. His public speeches were designed not to affect government policy or persuade reluctant colleagues to accept his point of view, but to speak *for* the agreed policy or strategy. He saw himself more as a facilitator than a positive force in the decision-making process. Particularly in government, his role was to find consensus among his colleagues with minimum fuss:

> The essential quality of the PM is that he should be a good Chairman able to get others to work. He must be able to decide in the last resort

between competing policies. He must have the architectonic sense. He must see the whole building not the bricks. ... I would sum up the essence of the Premiership by saying that there must be someone to take a decision. The decision that he must take is not that a certain course should be followed but that a decision must be come to.[3]

That quotation captures the essence of the leadership style Attlee applied. The principal enemy of such an approach is stasis, a failure to reach a conclusion: the Attlee method allowed discussion, but discussion *with a purpose*. 'Democracy means government by discussion, but it is only effective if you can stop people talking.'[4] For Attlee, the prime minister was not generally meant to be an active contributor of policy, only an arbitrator between competing policies if absolutely necessary. Policy ideas should come from the departmental ministers. He applied this theory throughout his time at Number 10, through good times and bad. The Public Record Office contains the Attlee government papers, and they proceed through the production of 'Memoranda' – documents a minister or ministers had prepared for discussion to form the basis of discussion in a particular committee or in the full cabinet. Attlee 'Memoranda' are very rare indeed. Attlee's own papers – the documents his civil servants prepared for him – are annotated with the minimum number of words. In red pencil, Attlee generally wrote 'Agreed'; or 'Yes' or 'No'; or asks for the views of relevant departmental ministers. Morrison's comment that 'his attitude to his colleagues was strangely like Ramsay MacDonald in that there was a remoteness about him so that it was quite impossible to approach near enough to get inside his mind'[5] is an indication of success in implementing his leadership style, rather than a sign of failure. Such was his technique: he wanted the machinery of government to move efficiently and not be delayed by a prime ministerial spoke in the wheels.

This is not to say that Attlee did not depart from his central idea of chairmanship. He was happy to take on a greater responsibility in certain policy areas: independence for India and the development of Britain's nuclear weapons were two examples. He could also intervene in matters, question his ministers and search for answers, as he was to do in the early part of 1947 when the coal shortage was at its worst. He was willing to lecture his ministers on performance if necessary. In March 1948, he circulated a memorandum to his government ministers and junior ministers about their delivery in the House of Commons: 'I have noticed that junior Ministers, and even some seniors, are exposing themselves to justifiable criticism by reading their speeches in the House. ... Mr Churchill always has his speeches written out in full, but does not appear to be reading.'[6] Attlee's choices of *which* areas he intervened in proved to be the most controversial aspect of his leadership style.

His limitations were clear: he failed to *mitigate* the damaging coal shortage in the winter of 1946–47; he failed to find an agreement on public control of the iron and steel industry; he was unable to find a compromise between the conflicting personalities of Aneurin Bevan and Hugh Gaitskell in March 1951, causing the resignations of three government ministers; and in the government's major crises – particularly the economic difficulties of 1947 and 1949, he gave no lead. He knew little about economics and was quite open about this deficiency. As Gerald Kaufman sums up:

> Clement Attlee did not win the 1945 election. The 1945 election won Clement Attlee. … It is true that he presided over the greatest reforming government in modern times. However, these reforms were all in the Labour Party 1945 manifesto and were steered through parliament by Herbert Morrison. When it came to a real crisis, namely the clash between Gaitskell and Bevan, Attlee mishandled it, with the result that Labour lost office for 13 years in 1951.[7]

The ultimate fascination of Attlee is both his extraordinary success *and* his apparent failure. This book is principally a study of his leadership style, of what Attlee's successes owed to that style and whether the failures were a result of that style or the failure to apply *any* style at all. Drawing on primary evidence, first-hand interviews, and new material,[8] I seek to show that Attlee's approach to leadership was an authentic reflection of his personality, experiences and background. He *was* a moderate, sensible, well-grounded man with few insecurities; he did not adopt a persona to project an image. He was the antithesis of a charismatic leader; there is in fact the argument that he had no significant personality at all. The story, often attributed to Churchill (but denied by him), about the empty taxi drawing up in Downing Street from which Attlee emerged, became legend. Just a few months after he became prime minister in 1945, the king's principal private secretary, Sir Alan Lascelles, noted: 'Attlee at 6 p.m. The King's complaint that he can never get anything out of A. is well-founded. He is agreeable and friendly, but closes every subject with a snap of the jaws, and if you don't try to launch a new one yourself, the rest is silence.'[9] Penetrating that silence is the major challenge of this biography: it is to show that, while he may have been a man of few words, there is in fact much to get out of Clement Attlee.

Chapter 1
GROWING UP IN VICTORIAN ENGLAND, 1883–1901

In a romantic view of the history of the Labour Party the first Labour prime minister of a majority government should have been a determined member of the working class who had surmounted the obstacles of his background to occupy the highest political office in the land. Yet, Clement Attlee stubbornly refused to be categorized that way, for he was not born into poverty in a one-roomed house on a coalfield as the 'man in the cloth cap' Keir Hardie had been. Unlike Hardie, or even the first Labour prime minister, Ramsay MacDonald, who were illegitimate, Attlee was born into a professional middle-class family on 3 January 1883 and his childhood was very conventional. Attlee did not come from an aristocratic background as did, for example, Winston Churchill, born to a son of the seventh Duke of Marlborough at Blenheim Palace. In fact, the only link between the Attlee and Churchill childhoods was a governess, Miss Hutchinson, who taught both Churchill and Attlee's sisters. However, Attlee's background was undoubtedly privileged in the context of late Victorian England, with a heritage in law, medicine and art.

Attlee's father, Henry Attlee, had been articled to Claridge Druce solicitors in London at the age of 16, and rose to become president of the Law Society. His mother Ellen was the eldest daughter of Thomas Simons Watson, who was descended from doctors. Watson had been educated at Cambridge and became secretary of the Art Union, 'a semi-commercial show which published reproductions or rather prints of pictures by well known artists'.[1] The Attlees had four children (two boys and two girls) before moving to Westcott, Portinscale Road, Putney. There they had four more, another girl and three boys – Tom, Clement and Laurence. The 1881 census had confirmed the total population for Great Britain and Ireland\ at just over 35 million. Of these, it has been estimated that around five million had no means whatsoever beyond their weekly wage.[2] Many millions of the adult population still did not have the vote. The 1884 Franchise Act increased the electorate from 3 million to 5.75 million, around 59 per cent of the adult male population.[3] As a householder, Henry Attlee would have had the vote. He also had significant means. He developed Westcott by extending the nursery and servants quarters and by adding a billiard and smoking room. The house was on two floors, but with a semi-basement containing the kitchen and scullery, 'which looked out on the yard on ground level'. There was 'plenty of room for the whole family and a spare room'. The garden was about half an acre, 'just big enough for tennis', and the Attlees employed four servants – a cook, parlourmaid, housemaid and boot boy who came in by day. None of the children did any housework 'except perhaps a little mild dusting'.[4]

Attlee had a traditional Victorian childhood. He was brought up a strict Anglican. Every morning Henry Attlee said prayers before breakfast to the whole family and servants; after breakfast, psalms were read with Ellen Attlee presiding. Sundays were strictly observed: 'no games were allowed and only Sunday reading'. The children went to church, to 'a children's service in the afternoon and in later years to evensong'.[5] Attlee was instilled with an enduring sense of Christian values – his personal life was entirely without scandal and he was scrupulously honest and courteous in his dealings. He was not, however, left with a lifelong belief in the existence of God, captured in his famous phrase that he believed in the ethics of Christianity but not in the 'mumbo jumbo'. He was also introduced to imperialism and acquired a strong attachment to the British Crown. His earliest memory of a public event was Queen Victoria's Golden Jubilee in 1887 when, at the age of just four, he placed a flag on the house porch. Yet, Ellen never encouraged political discussion[6] and political events of the 1880s and early 1890s had no major impact on the Attlee family.

For reasons that remain unclear, Attlee did not attend school until he was nine years old. Several explanations have been suggested – a lengthy illness, possibly chicken pox; or, according to his younger brother, Laurence, the fact that he was physically under-sized; or his marked shyness. Laurence, in fact, was physically larger, and gave the older brother his cast-off clothes.[7] However, Attlee had a happy, stable childhood. Prior to 1892, when he went away to Northaw Place preparatory school in Potters Bar, he had been taught by his mother, and he had read widely, developing a particular interest in poetry. Later, he recalled that 'Tennyson was an early love. ... How well I recall the shock of his death in 1892, for to a nine-year-old he appeared as immortal as W. G. Grace or Queen Victoria.'[8] When he did eventually attend school, his older brother Tom, with whom he developed a lifelong political discussion preserved in a series of letters, was already a pupil there. As a younger child, Attlee was brought up 'with a great reverence for … [his] … seniors … [who] … had … attained a standard of virtue which … [he] … could never hope to approach'.[9] His respect was long-lasting; he later declared that Tom, who lived in Cornwall after being a conscientious objector during the First World War, 'was a keen churchman and served on many diocesan things … [arguing for] … a genuine and practical Christianity. Many consider him to have been a saint'.[10] Northaw was a small school, with only 30 to 40 boys. It was there that Attlee was endowed with his lifelong love of cricket. He also cared for William Jowitt when he was a new boy, who went on to serve as lord chancellor throughout Attlee's time as prime minister.

In the Easter term of 1896, Attlee sat his entrance examinations for Haileybury College. He passed and was placed in the top form of the lower school. Ironically, therefore, the British prime minister who presided over independence for India attended a public school with origins in a training college for civil servants for the raj. The Attlee family's link with Haileybury was very strong. Attlee recalled: 'We were all [the Attlee sons] destined for Haileybury because an old family friend was master of Lawrence House.'[11] Yet, Henry Attlee was also a governor of the school and nominated pupils to join it. Haileybury records show that in January 1896 he recommended a boy from Kent and even after Attlee had left in Easter 1903 Henry Attlee was still using his influence to nominate a pupil from Temple Gardens in London.[12]

Haileybury's headmaster during Attlee's time was Edward Lyttelton, who had held the post since 1890. Interestingly, in the microcosm of Haileybury, Lyttelton was something of a social reformer. By 1905, when Lyttelton left to become headmaster of Eton, new boys had their teeth inspected; a new sanatorium was provided and there was a medical officer actually living within the school itself.[13] However, to say that Lyttelton influenced Attlee directly would imply that they had more direct contact than they actually did. Beyond one term's teaching at the start of 1901 when Attlee was in the sixth form,[14] there is nothing to suggest that Attlee either spoke regularly to Lyttelton or indeed felt inspired by any of his actions. He was, however, caned by him. The relief of the British at Ladysmith on 28 February 1900 brought out the young Attlee's patriotism. Lyttelton refused to give pupils a holiday for the relief of Ladysmith, so most pupils took part in a demonstration in nearby Hertford. Attlee was one of 72 who were punished: 'Prefects were too old and the Lower and Middle Schools too young and perhaps too numerous to be punished, so we of the Upper School expiated the sins of the rest.'[15]

Attlee also played games, though without distinction. He did, however, have significant involvement in school societies. From the third term of 1898, when he was in *The Taming of the Shrew*, he regularly appeared in plays the Shakespeare Society performed. Over the following three years, he appeared in *The Merry Wives of Windsor*, *Much Ado About Nothing*, *King Lear*, and, in the second term of 1901, *Hamlet* and *Love's Labour's Lost*. He often played a number of parts, being, for example, the Duke of Burgundy, Regan (one of Lear's daughters) and a knight, in *King Lear*.[16] Leading parts seem to have eluded him, but there is no doubt that he was a leading and active member of the society: Tony Blair was not the only Labour prime minister to have acted in his youth. By the third term of 1900,[17] he was a member of the Literary and Debating Society, but he resisted becoming a regular speaker. Issues such as a tax on coal, professionalism in sport, placing the railways under state control, and press freedom largely passed him by.[18] He also took his first steps towards a military career, joining the Lawrence House Company in his final years: in the house records for 1901 he appears as a private in the first term, later becoming a lance corporal.[19] Even at this early stage, his organizational skills shone through. In his role in charge of a tent at a cadet camp, one of his charges saw Attlee as a 'quiet, self-contained young man' for whom there was 'no special respect but who, nevertheless, ran things with unobtrusive efficiency': at the end of the camp Attlee's team carried off the prize for the 'best kept tent'.[20] Lady Attlee, his daughter-in-law, puts it like this: he organized things 'so that everyone could give of their best. ... People liked working for him'.[21] His organizational skills were one of the 'great secrets' of his later political success.[22]

It is odd that Attlee remained very shy. His final school report suggested that he was a confident young man: 'I believe him a sound character and think he will do well in life. His chief fault is that he is very self-opinionated, so much so that he gives very scant consideration to the views of other people.'[23] He had every reason to be confident. His comfortable background had given him the opportunity of not just an education, but also of travel. There had been no annual seaside holidays after 1896 because his father had purchased a country house in Thorpe-le-Soken, a small village in Essex. Attlee was visited there by, among others, the Birmingham Quaker Joseph Sturge, who had taken him on his first trip abroad, to Switzerland, in 1899. As he was so well-organized, and able to read quickly, he found time to finish around four books a week.[24] Later, he remembered reading Thackeray 'in great gulps at school'. His earliest Robert Browning poetry collection, *Men and Women*, was the gift of a master at Haileybury. His mind became 'stored with poetry'.[25] There was also leadership potential in Attlee's teenage years. Staying at the school for five years until the age of 18, he became a prefect in his final year, which involved responsibility for a dormitory of 42 boys. Of the six prefects listed for Lawrence House in the second term of 1901, it was noticeable that Attlee was the only one not in the house team for any kind of sport.[26] This serves to enhance the achievement. His behaviour and activities around the school, as opposed to on the sporting field, had obviously impressed. Lyttelton would have had to have sanctioned Attlee's appointment, and the honour would not have been given easily.[27]

At this time, his mind must also have turned to applying to Oxford University, for, having been joined at Haileybury by his brother Laurence in 1898, his brother Tom had left for Corpus Christi College. His older brothers had been to Oriel College and Merton College. History was his passion, and he tried for a place to study it at University College where he sat and passed the entrance examination, 'Smalls', to start in 1901. Appropriately, therefore, Attlee came of age in the year of Queen Victoria's death. His Victorian childhood ended as the Edwardian age began. Attending a public school such as Haileybury undoubtedly had a significant impact on his view of society. His first published poem, *Lines on the Cab Strike*, was published in the *Haileyburian* on 8 March 1899. The strike is presented as an inconvenience to the upper classes, who might be tempted to move elsewhere:

No! Stay in London a little.
Their wives and bairns must eat;
In a little they'll be more humble
And beg for a fare at your feet.[28]

It was not that he was a public schoolboy who fervently defended his class and his upbringing and frowned upon any socialist, or, indeed, alternative, views to which he had been introduced. The reality was that he had simply never been properly introduced to a sustained criticism of the capitalist society in which he had grown up. His childhood, as with a number of later aspects of his life, was extraordinarily compartmentalized. Outside events did not intrude on his basically happy existence and, in 1901, while Attlee did not quite have the world at his feet as Haileybury's most outstanding scholar, he had in place the platform upon which to build a secure career, whether in public life or in another sphere. He had a secure financial background, a good education, family contacts and the opportunity of an Oxford education.

Chapter 2
FROM OXFORD
TO THE EAST END, 1901–14

In the years before the First World War, Attlee underwent his life's major conversion. Having had little interest in social issues, he became a socialist. In doing so, he took full advantage of the opportunities his comfortable background provided. He completed his degree and, through his father's connections, began a career as a barrister. He did not remain at the Bar, but financially he did not need to. He was able to spend his time on social work in the East End of London. He became manager of the Haileybury-supported Stepney Boys' Club, which assisted local poor children, and was also secretary of another socio-educational establishment, Toynbee Hall. He joined the Independent Labour Party and campaigned on the Poor Law. He was an official 'explainer' for Lloyd George's ground-breaking National Insurance Act of 1911 and, in 1912, became a lecturer at the London School of Economics, teaching students who were themselves about to enter social work. Had he needed to hold down a regular, well-paid job, many of these activities would not have been possible.

Working with the poor did not seem a likely career path when, in autumn 1901, Attlee went up to University College, Oxford. He loved the university and thoroughly enjoyed his time there. It was an extension of both his family life and school. His brother Tom was at Corpus Christi and he would often go for a walk with him on a Sunday, take lunch and visit another brother, Bernard, who was the vicar of Wolvercote. He continued to read widely, and retained his interest in poetry and general reading: 'My bent at the time was wholly romantic. I delighted in poetry and in history. ... I did not read for "schools" with any great assiduity, being beguiled into all kinds of miscellaneous reading not strictly germane to the course which I was studying.'[1] As at Haileybury, he did not excel at sport, but did achieve a half-blue in, of all things, billiards.

Attlee did not follow the route of so many aspirant politicians by seeking the presidency of the Oxford Union. He felt he was too shy to speak there, and his only foray into debating was in the college debating society against fellow undergraduate Basil Blackett, later a civil servant with expertise in finance, who served on the Indian Viceroy's Council in the 1920s. Attlee spoke in favour of protectionism, while Blackett defended free trade.

It is not entirely clear why Attlee was persuaded of this view. This was of course the time of the start of the great divergence of opinion in the Conservative Party between free traders and protectionists, led by the Liberal Unionist Joseph Chamberlain, who held the post of colonial secretary in the Conservative–Liberal Unionist coalition of 1895–1905. Chamberlain advocated a system of import tariffs for goods entering the British Empire, thereby consolidating the empire as a single entity, and providing the funds for social reform at home. This view challenged the free trade orthodoxy that had dominated British politics since Sir Robert Peel repealed the Corn Laws in 1846. Attlee was clearly persuaded, whether for patriotic reasons of protecting the empire or for finding money to spend on social reform is not apparent. There was no shortage of evidence in respect of the need for social reform. Joseph Rowntree published his study of poverty in York in 1901 and Charles Booth published the last of his 17 volumes on life and work in London in 1903. Yet, Attlee, by his own admission, as a Conservative who was neither politically active nor politically ambitious, had given 'no real thought to social problems'.[2] He saw Oxford as predominantly Conservative, save for the likes of R. H. Tawney and William Temple, who were both at Balliol. Joseph Chamberlain was seen as the 'dynamic leader'.[3] On this basis, Attlee's sole foray into political debate might just as well have been out of admiration for Chamberlain as of patriotism.

Certainly, it was Attlee's views on protectionism that brought him into conflict with his history tutor, Arthur Johnson, a free trader whom Attlee did not find very inspiring. The only tutor to whom he ascribed much of an influence was Ernest Barker, who taught Attlee in his third year. Barker was 29 when Attlee went to him and, while he did not enter public life as such, he was a brilliant academic, becoming the first holder of the Rockefeller-endowed chair of Professor of Political Science at Cambridge in 1928. He may well have had an impact on Attlee's career thinking at the time, for Attlee later said that if he had been able to choose a career for himself in 1904, it would probably have been as a don. However, Attlee obtained a second-class degree, so an alternative had to be found – the Bar.

That Attlee was ever a barrister is surprising given his personal characteristics. There was his shyness and his scant record of debating or immersing himself in any of the major issues of the day, let alone mooting on points of law. Yet, he did have one major asset that still often seems to help in a legal career – the family connection of his father, whose influence over both the career choice and the direction of learning was all-pervasive. Attlee did not accept this, claiming that his father 'brought no pressure to bear on his children in the choice of a profession'. Yet, even he seems to concede an underlying influence at least: 'My father was a solicitor and, therefore, I might look to some help at the start.'[4]

Nowhere is his father's influence more obvious than in terms of the existing barristers to whom Attlee went for training – his pupil masters. Wisely, Attlee seems to have started reading for the Bar in 1904 in a Lincoln's Inn chambers with Sir Philip Gregory, a leading conveyancing barrister. The generally non-contentious law of transfer of property is unlikely to have involved many court appearances, and it is probable that this was seen as the first step towards an all-round introduction to the types of work available, including more conten-tious work. Having passed the Bar examinations in 1905 and been called to the Bar in March 1906, Attlee moved to widen his experience, and became a pupil to Theobald Mathew, a friend of the family. That Attlee went as a pupil to Mathew at 4 Paper Buildings demonstrated both the scope of his father's influ-ence in London legal circles and the scale of the opportunity he was given to pursue a career at the Bar. Mathew was 'much sought after as a pupil master',[5] and his later pupils included Sir Stafford Cripps, a significant figure both in the Labour Party and in Attlee's political career; Quintin Hogg (Lord Hailsham), who served in various cabinet posts in the 1950s and 1960s before becoming lord chancellor under both Heath and Thatcher; and Peter Thorneycroft, who rose to become chancellor under Macmillan, 1957–58, and chairman of the Conservative Party under Thatcher in 1975. Attlee seems to have enjoyed his time with Mathew without being enthused about work at the Bar. 'Theobald Mathew was a great character, full of humour – as all who have read his *Forensic Fables* will agree – and I had an enjoyable time working with him.'[6]

Mathew was, however, thought of as 'no great advocate (albeit a superb after-dinner speaker)' but 'a lawyer of great distinction in a distinguished gener-ation of learned lawyers'.[7] Whether a more outstanding persuasive orator would have been inspiring is unknown. Certainly, Attlee does not seem to have been considered as a potential future advocate. It is no surprise that his first pupil master, Gregory, proposed Attlee for a conveyancing job during his period with Mathew: 'I should probably have got it had it not been found that I lacked some months of standing at the Bar.'[8] Yet there were opportunities at 4 Paper Buildings to have aroused the interest of even a half-hearted potential barrister. The King's Counsel, or senior barrister at the chambers was no less than Lord Robert Cecil, son of three-time prime minister the third Marquess of Salisbury. Attlee worked for him on the Norfolk earldom case (a 1907 case emphasizing, among other things, the central legal feature of peers, namely their right to sit in the House of Lords) and reviewed a book on peerage law. Indeed, these were also highly political chambers. The final member of 4 Paper Buildings was Malcolm Macnaghten, who became an Ulster Unionist MP in 1922. Mathew was a great admirer of Gladstone,[9] and Cecil entered the House of Commons as Conservative MP for Marylebone East in the Liberal landslide of 1906. Yet this event passes without even a mention in Attlee's memoirs. Politics was clearly still far from his mind.

When Attlee completed his pupillage, he moved to chambers where Sir H. F. Dickens, son of the novelist Charles Dickens, was the King's Counsel. To succeed at the Bar, first and foremost a barrister needs work. Attlee could not take cases directly from members of the public; he had to rely on solicitors to instruct him and build a reputation. However, he simply did not get sufficient work. In London, he only had two or three briefs; further out on the legal circuit he managed just one.[10] He continued to attend chambers, but his 'heart was not in the job' and he tried, unsuccessfully, to apply for other jobs.[11] In the autumn of 1908, his father died and, in 1909, Attlee finally stopped practising. His brief, unsuccessful stint at the Bar was most likely brought about by his father and his own respect for his father's wishes. Later, he joked: 'Perhaps I didn't entirely fail in law. ... I did appoint the Lord Chancellor!'[12]

Attlee's focus from as far back as 1904 had not been his legal career. After leaving Oxford, he lived back at home, often playing billiards, and he joined his brother Tom's literary club, which included in its membership young civil servants such as E. G. V. Knox, who was later editor of *Punch* (1932–49). His life was, however, changed in October 1905, when, as he put it, 'an event occurred which was destined to alter the whole course of my life.'[13] One might think that it was seeing the world in a different way, visiting and appreciating different cultures, drawing different lessons from the political systems of other countries, or perhaps seeing a major event or taking time for a period of deep reflection. However, Attlee was not well-travelled in the sense that, say, Winston Churchill (who had been a war correspondent in South Africa during the Boer War) was, though during his Oxford days as an undergraduate he had been to the south of France, Belgium and the Netherlands.

Such destinations were not the locations of the conversion. Attlee's road to Damascus was in fact in East London. He first visited the Stepney Boys' Club with his brother Laurence in October 1905. The club catered for the needs of boys in a poor area and also formed a battalion of the Cadet Corps. The poverty of the East End was a different world from the one in which Attlee had grown up. 'Few members of the club wore collars and ties and not many had any other than their working clothes.'[14] He found a distinct set of values: generosity was rated above the middle-class virtue of thrift.[15] In 1907, he took over as manager: the minutes show that on 2 August 1907, the decision was taken to appoint him to the post with effect from 1 November of the same year.[16] The well-organized Attlee was in his element. His grappling with political concepts was mixed with practical problems: one of his earliest tasks was to provide a ventilation system.[17] He felt there was 'no better way of getting to know what social conditions are like than in a boys' club. One learns much more of how people in poor circumstances live through ordinary conversation with them than from studying volumes of statistics.'[18] In many ways this quotation is an indication of how Attlee came to socialism, and a view that the capitalist system had to be reformed to ensure that all classes of society could have an acceptable standard of living. Clearly, there is a better way of knowing how 'people in poor circumstances' live – living among them and having the experiences yourself. Alternatively, Attlee could have visited the boys' families and seen their home conditions for himself, but his experience is clearly one of sympathy with what the attendees at the club told him. Yet, his conversion to socialism was complete. 'From this it was only a step to examining the whole basis of our social and economic system. … I understood why the Poor Law was so hated.'[19]

There is a question of how genuine the conversion was given how easily and rapidly it took place. Christian ethics had, however, been a central part of Attlee's childhood, so serving others was nothing new. Indeed, the greater significance of the conversion is not that its nature has been overstated but that it actually happened, which is an indication of how extraordinarily compartmentalized the first 22 years of his life had been. When he was exposed to how the poorer classes lived, he responded and adjusted his views accordingly. These views also found expression in his poetry. He penned *Socialism* in 1908:

> Surely some day we'll make an ending
> Of all this wretched state of want and greed.[20]

Writing *Limehouse* in 1910, it was the plight of the poor that troubled him:

> Poor, tired mothers trying
> To hush the feeble crying
> Of little babies dying
> For want of bread today.[21]

The ability, however, to compartmentalize, remained. While his work with the poor was very much a feature of his time at the Stepney Boys' Club, it was a place to which old Haileyburians continued to be invited: Attlee, as had been the case with previous managers, continued to advertise in *The Haileyburian* that 'dinner and a bed' could be obtained by someone from his old school by writing to him.[22]

As a socialist, an obvious group to join in Edwardian Britain was the Fabian Society. At his first meeting, Attlee, while noting that all the platform speakers seemed to have beards, was impressed with George Bernard Shaw and Sidney Webb, but unimpressed with H. G. Wells. A few days later a Welshman, Tommy Williams, who was very unhappy about the right-wing Charity Organization Society's action, visited him at Haileybury House. Attlee told him he was a socialist and Williams invited him to come on the following Wednesday to join the local branch of the Independent Labour Party. There were around 12 members, who were often afraid of admitting their membership due to the risk of losing their jobs. However, there were three or four meetings a week in the open air. Attlee's average week in 1907 involved four evenings a week at the club, one night at the Independent Labour Party branch before refereeing football matches for boys at the Haileybury Club on Saturdays, and open-air speaking on Sundays. He was also able to travel abroad occasionally. In September 1907 he visited America for the only time prior to the Second World War. Sent to escort his sister Mary home from a cousin's house in Canada, Attlee sailed from Liverpool to meet her in Montreal. He went ashore at Quebec and, finding that his sister would not be arriving at Montreal for three days, he went to Boston and New York before meeting her at Niagara Falls.

Attlee undoubtedly enjoyed his time at the club and formed a deep attachment to it. Indeed, in his earliest weeks as prime minister in 1945, he found time to write to members of the club: 'I never forget that almost forty years ago I took the first step which has led me to my present position by going down to visit the Haileybury Club that started my connection with Limehouse which has continued to the present day.'[23] As late as 1965, when he was in his early eighties, he was still a member of the guild council for the Stepney Boys' Club.[24] As far as the cadet element was concerned, there was banter with the cadet officers, one of whom, Charles Phillimore, a banker, called him 'Keir 'Ardie'.[25] Attlee later recommended Major Bennett, another officer who had been at the club since 1885, for an award for lifelong service.

The year 1909 marked a change in Attlee's life when his interest in the poor of the East End found practical political expression. A cause was readily available in terms of what the Liberal government's response should be to the report of the Royal Commission on the Poor Laws and Relief of Distress. The Conservative–Liberal Unionist coalition government set up this commission in 1905 and it reported in 1909. To appreciate the significance of its recommendations, it is necessary to consider the background. For centuries, the

Elizabethan Poor Law of 1601 had set the framework for how to deal with the country's poor. It provided for both 'indoor' and 'outdoor' relief – that is, a place in the poorhouse or help outside such institutions, including food, clothing and money. With the Poor Law Amendment Act of 1834, the Whig government led by Earl Grey shifted the balance in terms of how relief was provided. The act was based on the work of a poor law commission that included the utilitarian Edwin Chadwick. Its philosophical inspiration was therefore a policy of the 'greatest happiness for the greatest number'. The government accepted its recommendations and organized the poor law system into poor law unions, each of which had to provide a workhouse; it discouraged the unions from providing outdoor relief, which poor law guardians, boards that made decisions for those within their local union, distributed.

To many on the left, the Poor Law was both harsh and undignified in that it blamed the poor themselves for the condition in which they found themselves. Aside from those like the Local Government Board, which essentially argued for the efficacy of the current system, the 1909 commission produced a split between the 'majority report' and the 'minority report',[26] neatly embodying the left–right division on the issue. By stating that the poor law should remain, that *too much* outdoor relief was provided and that poverty was due to moral factors, the majority report was a great disappointment to progressive reformers. The minority report, signed, among others, by Beatrice Webb and the future Labour leader George Lansbury, under whom Attlee served as deputy from 1931 to 1935, clearly stated that the poor should not be blamed for their condition; the Poor Law should be ended and education and health improved. Most poor people were not to blame for their condition, and society as a whole should take responsibility through the state. Attlee passionately supported the minority report, and opposed the Victorian attitude to poverty enshrined in the majority report in the form of self-help, limited government intervention and distinguishing clearly between the deserving and undeserving poor. Beatrice and Sidney Webb decided to form a campaign for the minority report and Attlee became its lecture secretary. Attlee enjoyed it: while it was a left-wing campaign, there were those from the other parties who supported it, including Robert Harcourt of the Liberals and Sir Gilbert Parker of the Conservatives.

In 1909, with J. J. Mallon who had, among other things, organized an exhibition in London to draw attention to conditions, Attlee looked closely at work in the various 'sweated' industries. This contributed to the passing of the Trade Boards Act in 1909 by Winston Churchill, then president of the Board of Trade in the Liberal government. The act set up boards in a limited number of industries to which both representatives of employers and employees were nominated, with powers to set minimum wage rates. Building on this, in 1910 Attlee became secretary of Toynbee Hall, set up in 1884 and named after the

Oxford historian Arnold Toynbee. Graduates of the hall engaged in social work with the poor in deprived areas. Attlee took up residence there, but left at the end of the year to return to Stepney and Limehouse.

In 1911, Attlee became an 'official explainer' for the National Insurance Act that the Chancellor of the Exchequer Lloyd George passed that year. The act is widely regarded as one of the foundation stones of the welfare state and it brought the concept of national insurance into British politics where it has since remained. In some senses it is odd that Attlee ever took on this task. Fabians, and indeed, members of the Independent Labour Party, opposed it on the basis that it took contributions from the workers themselves. This principle flowed naturally from the minority report: the scheme should not ask for a contribution from the workers; Attlee had argued for recognition that poverty was not the individual's fault and that the burden of helping should fall on society as a whole. The act did not reflect that view. Part 1 provided for health insurance in the form of sickness benefit from the fourth day of illness for 13 weeks, then another 13 weeks at a reduced rate before a period of disability benefit, which could continue indefinitely. There was a right to consult a general practitioner, treatment for tuberculosis in a sanatorium and maternity benefit. It was estimated that around 15 million people would benefit. To square private companies providing health insurance, Lloyd George allowed such bodies to become 'approved societies' and to manage funds. The employee was to contribute 4d a week, the employer 3d and the state 2d.[27] Part 2 of the act provided unemployment insurance for 15 weeks within any 12-month period. The employee was to contribute 2½d a week, the employer 2½d and the state 2d. However, it was experimental and covered only industries where unemployment was 'cyclical' rather than 'chronic' – shipbuilding, mechanical engineering, iron-founding, vehicle manufacture and construction.[28]

However, there was a more practical approach on the left. The chairman of the Parliamentary Labour Party, Ramsay MacDonald, sought some amendments to the bill and, while he failed to alter the balance in contributions away from the employee in respect of the health insurance, he did manage to improve provision for married women, to approve trade unions as friendly societies and to have the proposals for low-paid workers 'simplified'.[29] Subject to these points, he was broadly in favour: 'On two fundamental points ... he had no misgivings ... the state had at last accepted a responsibility to protect the wage earner against the accidents of life. ... As for the contributory principle ... it was a positive advantage.'[30] Attlee's position, therefore, is a portent of his attitude on many occasions in the future: he did not reject a practical method of improvement in order to retain the purity of his beliefs.

The position Attlee took on the National Insurance Act did not damage his relationship with the Webbs. He continued to campaign for the Independent

Labour Party and against the Poor Law. He lived briefly with his brother Tom in Limehouse before the latter married the secretary of the Wandsworth Labour Exchange, Kathleen Medley. Then, in 1912, thanks to the influence of Sidney Webb, Attlee became a lecturer and tutor at the London School of Economics. He was appointed on the basis of his practical knowledge of social conditions to the Department of Social Science and Public Administration. He lectured on local government and dealt with students about to go into social work. He also became a member of a school care committee for Trafalgar Square School and, in that role, supervised meals for poor schoolchildren. The Liberal government had passed the Education (Provision of Meals) Act in 1906, which empowered local authorities to provide meals. The London County Council was then Conservative and had, according to Attlee, provided meals through pressure of public opinion 'very grudgingly'.[31]

Yet, for all his political activism, Attlee had a peripheral involvement with the great political issues of the prewar period. He was able to hear the shooting and view the scene of the then home secretary Winston Churchill's decision to open fire on Latvian criminals (and potential political revolutionaries) who had hidden in Sidney Street, East London in 1911. In the London dockers' strike of the same year he played a part in serving meals to dockers' children, and he collected money for the Irish transport and general workers' strike in Dublin in 1913. He worked for his own union, the National Union of Clerks (which he had joined when he joined the Independent Labour Party), and also for the London Carmen's Trade Union, speaking at one point in the Mile End Road from the back of a cart. It says a great deal about Attlee's involvement with political issues that he drew the following conclusion about prewar events. 'Looking back on those days, one is inclined to think of them as quiet and peaceful compared to the present time, but they were, in fact, filled with controversy.'[32] The constitutional struggle between the Lords and Commons, Irish Home Rule, and the increasing international tension evidently passed him by. There is understatement, and there is personal experience divorced from deep emotions about events. In the Edwardian era, Attlee was certainly hands-on in terms of experiencing social problems. But the abiding impression is of a man who was passionate about his beliefs but retained a sense of objectivity. Attlee enjoyed immersing himself in the causes he had chosen on the basis of his experience, but he was clearly neither blinded by them nor emotionally dependent on them.

By 1914 Attlee had both political experience and political ambitions. He never had to make great personal sacrifices to pursue his interests, unlike, for example, George Lansbury, who in 1912 resigned his parliamentary seat of Bow and Bromley to force a by-election on the issue of women's suffrage, which he lost. Attlee claimed that his ambition was limited to 'working as a member of the rank-and-file and perhaps getting on a local council',[33] but his activities suggested wider ambitions than that. He was secretary of the Stepney branch of the Independent Labour Party from 1908 and spoke publicly on its behalf; he also began to speak at other London branches. He was branch delegate to the Labour conference in Edinburgh in 1908, twice stood for Stepney Borough Council, and twice for the Limehouse Board of Guardians. He was also twice runner-up for the representation of London on the national administrative committee of the Independent Labour Party. His profile would have put him in a strong position to seek selection as a parliamentary candidate. Yet, how his career might have progressed had there been a general election in 1915 cannot be known. Instead, his life was changed by the outbreak of the First World War in August 1914, the news reaching him while on holiday in Seaton with his brother Tom and his wife.

Chapter 3
THE FIRST WORLD WAR, 1914–18

Attlee's experience of the First World War reflected entirely the attitudes he had developed both growing up and since he left Oxford in 1904. His deep sense of duty drove him to join the army and to risk his life in service of his country. His direct experience in the conflict – serving in appalling conditions in Gallipoli before being part of the evacuation and being wounded in Mesopotamia – changed him. Later, as Lady Attlee pointed out, he 'rarely talked about his war experiences'.[1] For the first time he became a genuine leader of men, with responsibility on the front line for the morale of his troops in life and death situations. He was also struck by the harshness of life. After Gallipoli, he continued to write poetry, but romantic themes became rarer; his later writing was lighter and often satirical. Yet, he retained his sense of objectivity, perhaps, above all, his ability to compartmentalize, and he bore no ill will towards his brother Tom, who was a conscientious objector throughout the conflict.

Britain declared war on Germany with effect from 11 p.m. on Tuesday 4 August 1914. The Labour movement, with its strong strands of socialist pacifism, was almost inevitably going to find it difficult to remain united. However, in the initial days before and after the declaration it did achieve a sense of unity in opposition to the potential conflict. George Lansbury, then editor of the left-wing *Daily Herald* (which became *The Sun* in 1964) criticized the war as a capitalists' conflict and organized a rally at Trafalgar Square on 2 August 1914, which around 20,000 people attended.[2] Attlee, in Devon with Tom, did not attend. However, the German invasion of neutral Belgium (prior to the British declaration of war) changed the view of many on the left who had initially opposed the conflict. On 7 August 1914, Ramsay MacDonald, who was not in favour of the war, resigned as chair of the Parliamentary Labour

Party; Arthur Henderson, who supported the war, took his place and entered the cabinet in the newly formed coalition government in 1915.

Attlee was determined to do his duty and fight, so immediately sought to join the army. He was turned down initially on grounds of age (he was 31 and the maximum age was 30) and then because he still held a volunteer commission in the cadets. Not to be deterred, he joined the Inns of Court Regiment Officer Training Corps (on the advice of a Mr Bond, an adjutant in the cadets) as an instructor, as a potential route to a commission in the regular army. After some time on a waiting list, mostly spent instructing new arrivals, he was drafted into the corps and performed drills in Temple Gardens. Such was his commitment that, still concerned about his age, he asked a former pupil of his at the London School of Economics to ask her brother-in-law (who had command of one of the new Kitchener battalions) to apply for him and subsequently received a letter ordering him to report to the 6th South Lancashire Regiment at Tidworth as a lieutenant.[3] He was put in command of seven officers and 250 men. The existing adjutant, Captain Marsh of the Indian Army, went to serve in France and Attlee was appointed in his place. This was now the ultimate expression of Attlee's patriotism – voluntary war service in a position of responsibility.

Attlee's training continued at Winchester and Chobham until, in the first week of June 1915, he was issued with maps of France and Flanders. He thought he would first see active service there, but when orders came to equip with tropical kit he guessed it would be Gallipoli or Mesopotamia. On 12 June he marched down to Frimley station in Surrey, travelling by night to Avonmouth, where he boarded the *Ausonia* for Gallipoli. On the way, the ship stopped at Malta, where he purchased a fly net and found time for a game of billiards.[4] He continued to write poetry; while he did not keep a daily diary he did produce, mainly from memory, written records of his experiences.[5] After calling in at Alexandria, Attlee sailed through the Greek islands, stopping at Lemnos, when he penned a poem named after the island, illustrating the bittersweet experience of travelling through the beautiful surroundings, with 'sweet thyme-scented breezes':

> Many a time I've longed these ways to go …
> Right willingly all these would I exchange
> To see the buses throng by Mile End Gate
> And smell the fried fish shops down Limehouse way.[6]

Gallipoli still marks one of the most tragic episodes in British military history. Winston Churchill, then First Lord of the Admiralty, had been pressing for some time to open another line of attack in order to free up a supply route to Russia and threaten Austria from the Balkans. Churchill's idea was simple: invade the Gallipoli peninsula, place a fleet of ships in the Sea of Marmara, putting Constantinople under threat, and force the Turkish government to sue for peace. Greece, Bulgaria and Romania would then be brought into the war on the Allied side.[7] The major question was how to make this possible. A solely naval operation on 18 March 1915 failed to make any inroads; troops were therefore moved onto the peninsula on 25 April 1915. One set of landings was made around the southern toe of the peninsula, Cape Helles; another set was made at Anzac Cove on the western side. Attlee set off for Helles from Mudros harbour at Lemnos at 6 p.m. on 1 July. Two destroyers carried the troops up to the *River Clyde*, which was in use as a pier to disembark on the peninsula. The military situation was poor. The Turks, commanded by the later first president of modern-day Turkey, Mustafa Kemal, were in a strong defensive position. The high ground of Achi Baba, five miles from the landing areas at Helles, was never taken.

Attlee knew that he might never return home, and wrote 'Before Action' in the knowledge that he had not left his own family behind to mourn him:

> If I should die before another day,
> I shall not leave a child behind to say
> 'My father fought and died in Freedom's fight.'[8]

There was death all around in the dreadful living conditions. There were 'billions of flies feeding on thousands of unburied corpses.'[9] Attlee recalled that 'water was obviously the difficulty and we were on an allowance of half a waterbottle a day – not much considering the intense heat.' Despite the insanitary conditions, Attlee's background and status as an officer still counted for something. He accepted an invitation to dinner from the commanding officer and enjoyed a four-course meal one evening. But the front line was not far away. He recalled a 'long tramp through apparently endless communication trenches with occasional notices of "Duck your heads, lads" and eventually reached the firing line' to relieve the 29th division Lancashire Fusiliers. Attlee stayed there for six or seven days. The Turks were so close that Attlee's men could draw their fire by firing up into the air themselves.[10] He began to develop signs of dysentery: 'most of our insides were upset with the sandy water and the flies. These simply swarmed.' He went down for a rest to the beach but then returned to his regiment and tried to carry on, but the 'dysentery got worse, bully beef and biscuits, salt bacon and strong tea not suiting it'. He passed out, was taken back to the beach and transported away on the *Devanha*, a hospital ship. Attlee was still determined to serve and did not take the easy option of going home: 'They asked me whether I'd go to England or Malta and, wanting to join the battalion, I said Malta.' Attlee was duly transferred to Hamrun Hospital before moving on to Dragonera, 'a very stately mansion lent for the use of convalescents by the Countess Scicluna.'[11]

The dysentery was timely. Attlee missed the Allied attack of 6 and 7 August 1915, which sought to take the high ground of Sari Bair Ridge above Anzac, together with new landings at Suvla Bay just along the coast, and a further attack at Helles. His division sustained thousands of casualties. While convalescing, his mind turned to broader political issues. On 27 August 1915, he wrote to Tom: 'The papers as you say are vile, especially *The Times* who are … for conscription … they must know that at this stage conscription will not be of any service.'[12] For once, Attlee perhaps allowed sentiment, and his own desire to serve his country, to trump practical considerations. If the war were to be sustained with heavy troop losses, conscription was almost inevitable at some stage, and Asquith's coalition started to introduce it in January 1916.

Within weeks of sending this letter, Attlee was granted his wish to return to Gallipoli. He went first to Alexandria, where he saw his older brother Bernard, now a navy chaplain, and then rejoined his battalion at Suvla. He arrived on a small Clyde river steamer on a Sunday night but could not land and lay there all night. Now in the autumn, the weather was a major problem. There was a storm in early December and Attlee recalled a 'rushing torrent' before the rain turned to snow. He commanded a rearguard to protect the troops who were all evacuated from the Anzac/Suvla area on the night of 19 December 1915. In what had become typically brave fashion, Attlee left with the last party. The remaining troops at Helles were evacuated on 8 January 1916, meaning that the whole campaign utterly failed in terms of its original aims. It has been estimated that of 410,000 British and empire troops and 70,000 French who landed on the peninsula, more than half, 252,000 were dead, captured, taken away ill, or unaccounted for.[13] Yet, Attlee remained convinced of the soundness of the operation; what blame there was, if any, he laid at the door of the military authorities and field commanders: 'I have always held that the strategic conception was sound. The trouble was that it was not adequately supported. … Unfortunately, the military-authorities were Western-Front minded. Reinforcements were always sent too late. For an enterprise such as this the right leaders were not chosen.'[14] There is certainly a view that the military commanders 'bungled' the assault of 6 and 7 August 1915.[15] However, there is another view that the 'critical weakness was the failure to plan for an integrated naval and military option from the outset. Much of the blame for this lies with Churchill'.[16] The significant omission in Attlee's comments on Gallipoli is indeed the British politician most associated with it, Churchill. Whether he wanted to retain a dignified stance without resorting to an attack on Churchill is a moot point, but, written in 1954, it most likely shows Attlee's respect for Churchill – something he was to develop during their service together in government during the Second World War.

Attlee's next service post-Gallipoli was in Mesopotamia. He arrived at Basra on 4 March 1916 'in a terrific thunderstorm with torrents of rain which made us glad we were not on shore'. From there, he travelled on a paddle-boat up the River Tigris to Sheikh Saad. He was part of the attack on the Turks at El Hanna on 5 April 1916 and was in the centre of the line carrying a red artillery flag. He recalled that as he was planting the flag 'shrapnel got me from behind lifting me up like a big kick'. He was carried away – another timely exit from the field, missing two attacks in which his divison suffered significant losses. He was taken to Colata Hospital in Bombay and bore his wounds stoically, writing to Tom on 19 April 1916: 'It is surprising how little they hurt, especially at the time. My chief trouble was with my legs is they felt as if broken.'[17] The recovery was protracted: Attlee did not return to England until June and even then could only walk on his feet to a limited extent. After another month or two he moved to a training battalion in Shropshire, before in December 1916 joining a tank battalion in Dorset.

Twice Attlee went to France, the second time to Passchendaele, where he helped with the preparations for the famous attack on Poelcapelle, which took place on 9 October 1917. He was promoted to major, a title he used in political life for quite some time after the war, and returned to Dorset to begin a new battalion. However, a colonel took over who wanted officers of his own choosing, and these did not include Attlee, so he returned to the infantry. He went to a training camp in Biggar Bank, Barrow-in-Furness, before returning to France. There Attlee rode to and from the trenches on horseback, and he kept up his troops' morale with singing: 'I remember on one occasion marching up to the line with all the lads singing and getting a chit from a general congratu-lating me because it was seldom to hear men singing going back to the line.'[18] In August 1918, with the 5th territorial battalion of the South Lancashire Regiment, he was part of the offensive that led to the end of the war. In an attack on the front in the area of Lille, Attlee was asked to replace his com-manding officer who had been wounded. However, falling wood struck him on the back and he again left the battlefield injured and was soon back in hospital, this time in Wandsworth.

Attlee's wartime service had a profound impact on him. Of course, in many ways, he remained unchanged. He was still steeped in the Victorian class system, and considered the different social classes of the officers at the start and end of the conflict: 'In the 6th Battalion they were all from the Public Schools and many from Oxford or Cambridge. In the 5th there was far greater variety.' He added: 'I had a Lancashire miner who had been in Gallipoli with me and a lad who had been an errand boy, *but* they were very good material [my emphasis].'[19] He retained his prewar dislike of communism. Unsurprisingly, he disapproved of events in Russia, comparing the revolutionaries to the extreme left in Britain: 'The Russian debacle is rather appalling but quite explicable. ... Lenin and Trotsky appear to me to be of SPGB [Socialist Party of Great Britain] type or the wilder types of SDP [Social Democratic Party]. I can imagine the state of the country run by the Whitechapel Branch of the SDP.'[20] He maintained his socialist pro-war position, but still bore no ill will towards his brother in his choice not to serve his country: 'I don't know what chance there is of your release. ... I wish those damn fools in the govt would let you out.'[21] When the war ended, with Attlee in Wandsworth hospital, Tom was in nearby Wandsworth prison.

Attle did not feel he had altered a great deal, writing to Tom on 29 March 1918:

I do not find my outlook very much changed ... though ... I have attained slightly more catholicity ... there was a danger in ... [the Labour] ... movement in prewar days of taking too narrow a view ... what appeared the ideal life for us was the ideal life for everybody ... we were too Webby.[22]

Yet what this quotation also reveals is Attlee's growing realization of the necessity of practical measures to bring about widespread social change. He was no longer frequently writing poetry and caring for the poor *locally* in the East End while preaching socialist ideas; he had led troops on the front line in the worst of circumstances. Ideas had to be put into action at the political level to achieve change and Labour needed to broaden its appeal to progress as an influential political party. Attlee wholeheartedly approved of the Education Act of 1918, the work of Liberal politician Herbert Fisher, which, among other things, raised the school leaving age to 14 and provided additional services such as facilities for special needs children: 'Fisher's education bill seems a great step forward and appears to evoke opposition only in those ... who are probably not susceptible of education and those who like some of the mill owners look upon children mainly as profit-making machines.'[23] Fittingly, the war also forced Attlee to consider the hard choices that arise when beliefs are put into action. His view on the sanctity of life was that 'life is fallacious in that it is at times necessary to take life'.[24] This view was put to the test on the battlefield when a subaltern at Cailloux Keep disobeyed Attlee's order to move forward; he was weeping. Attlee went to him and told him he had to go and drew his revolver; the officer then went forward, though he later fainted. Could Attlee have shot him? 'Probably. So many men standing around – their lives at stake. Can't be sure, looking back. But my duty was clear.'[25] Attlee had a deep sense of social responsibility. He felt that, as individuals, people had to take responsibility for what the wider community did. In a neat inversion of Margaret Thatcher's famous dictum that individuals could not excuse crime by blaming society as a whole, he stated: 'I do not think we can obviate ourselves of responsibility for the sins of the community.'[26] It was to practical political action on behalf of the community that Attlee's mind now turned.

Chapter 4

THE POLITICAL APPRENTICESHIP, 1918–22

The most significant period of development in Attlee's political life was after the First World War. During this time, he gained experience of political realities – of political competition, political advancement, political achievement and, above all, political power. In his personal life, it was a tumultuous time, with the death of his mother in May 1920, the death of his sister Dorothy in the same year, marrying Violet Millar and becoming a father, his first child, Janet, being born in February 1923. In November 1922 he became an MP and, in almost exactly four years since the armistice, he had built himself a secure base from which to launch his lengthy political career.

On 16 January 1919, Attlee was discharged from the armed forces, and immediately returned to the East End. However, the Stepney Boys' Club had closed with no one to run it. He took a part-time job lecturing for the social welfare certificate. He was also able to live temporarily at Toynbee Hall before moving to his own flat in a building off Commercial Road in Limehouse. Local Conservatives had previously occupied the building, but it had fallen into disrepair. Attlee leased the property, took a flat on the first floor, let two other flats to party members and used part of it as a club for the local party. This was another example of Attlee's wealth allowing him to gain an advantage in politics. He also employed a servant: 'Just at this time a former batman of mine wrote to ask if he could come to me as a personal servant … he came and looked after me for some time, but then returned to Lancashire.' Attlee then secured the services of a lifelong friend: 'After an old club boy had looked after me for a month or two, I was fortunate to secure a local ex-Service lad, Charlie Griffiths, who has remained a close friend of my family and myself ever since.'[1]

With few concerns about money, Attlee could throw himself into politics. The three local parliamentary seats were Limehouse, Mile End and White-chapel. A chemist, Oscar Tobin, a Romanian Jew, had founded the Limehouse Labour Party. The Mile End Labour Party was founded by Matt Aylward, a Catholic trade unionist who was the leader of the local United Irish League. Tobin had also formed the Stepney borough Labour Party in 1918. He spoke to Attlee about standing in the London County Council elections. The choice was between Limehouse and Mile End: Attlee chose Limehouse. His fellow candidate for the two-seat ward was Con Bryan, a union official of the Waterman and Lighterman's Union. Bryan succeeded where Attlee failed, losing by 80 votes to 'an excellent man, a Liberal baker with a strong local following'.[2] Attlee blamed another candidate, a parson and ex-serviceman, for taking votes that would otherwise have gone to him.

Losing the election was not really a setback, as there were a number of other opportunities to progress. Attlee commented cryptically that, during the campaign, 'a demand had arisen'[3] for him to gain the nomination to fight the Limehouse parliamentary seat at the next general election. Why was Attlee so easily able to gain the nomination? Certainly his behaviour during the county council campaign has been put forward as one reason: 'Attlee's conduct during the campaign made a favourable impression on Aylward, who immediately proposed him as parliamentary candidate at the next general election.'[4] He already had money and was writing a book, *The Social Worker*. Attlee had clear strengths and weaknesses. His background enabled him to spend his time virtually as he wished without the pressure of having to support a family; yet, he himself was not of the working class. The reality is that parliamentary candidates often need strong local figures to help them on their way, and the founders of the Mile End and Limehouse parties supported Attlee. If he had one thing, it was an electoral appeal beyond Labour's working-class base, with his service in the war as stark evidence of his patriotism (he publicly continued to use the title 'Major') and his obviously middle-class origins. Attlee's selection as a parliamentary candidate meant that he did not seek election onto the Limehouse Board of Guardians to administer the Poor Law. However, he was co-opted at the board's first meeting and was also chairman of the children's home in Essex. Attlee had now moved from social worker to social administrator, and sought to put his principles into action: 'We changed the policy of the Limehouse Board, which had tended to be generally conducted on the principles of the Act of 1834. We did much to humanise the institutions, while seeking to preserve instead of breaking up the families that sought the assistance of the Poor Law.'[5]

In November 1919 came the elections to the borough council. Since all councillors retired every three years, there were 60 seats to contest in

Stepney. Two Liberals became Labour candidates, but otherwise the candidates were all new. Attlee penned the election address relying on the phrase 'Sack the Lot' to criticize the old council, and Labour swept the board in Limehouse with all 15 seats, and took 43 of the 60 seats on the Stepney borough council as a whole. Attlee was then the recipient of an incredible piece of political luck: he was co-opted as mayor of Stepney. At 36, he was the youngest person ever to hold the office and he had not even fought a seat. In fact, he had never won an election of any kind. It is unclear why the newly-elected councillors, all with the new legitimacy of a public mandate, decided to hand the mayoralty to the untested Attlee. It says more about the new councillors than about Attlee that he became mayor. It may be that the inexperienced councillors saw in him a safe pair of hands; it may be that, with the three very different Labour Party branches in Stepney, they trusted him more than they trusted each other.

Whatever the crucial reason, the Attlee of November 1919 had the credentials to become a future leading politician. He had a candidature for a winnable Labour seat and the opportunity to gain experience of local government. He greatly enjoyed the mayoral year, showing himself to be an able administrator, setting about a programme of social reform within the powers available to the borough council. Space was a problem in terms of building more houses, but Attlee sought to deal with the condition of the current stock. Over 40,000 legal notices were served on owners to repair property and these were enforced. Extra sanitary inspectors were appointed, and health visitors and antenatal clinics were introduced. Advice bureaux were created to assist tenants in knowing their rights under the rent restriction acts. It was also during Attlee's mayoral year that the five-yearly property valuation took place upon which the level of rates was based. Attlee was chairman of the valuation committee and employed professional valuation experts to add over £200,000 to the overall rateable value of the borough. Rates went up to over 20 shillings in the pound. Attlee also showed himself to be something of a patron of the arts: 'I suggested that, in cooperation with the Mayors of the London Boroughs, good plays at popular prices might be staged at the various Town Halls. This was with considerable success in some boroughs, though, unfortunately, in Stepney we had no suitable hall.'[6]

Like virtually every poor London borough, the major difficulty Stepney faced was the rising cost of unemployment benefit, with many people without work. Indeed, it was on this issue that Attlee was able to achieve wider prominence. Of the 26 London boroughs, 15 had Labour mayors and they formed an association of which Attlee became chairman. There was a standing joint committee and a number of 'Whitley' councils (formal consultative employer–employee meetings), and Attlee was Stepney's representative on them all. He was also vice-president of the Municipal Electricity Authorities. He called a conference on unemployment in Shoreditch town hall. The leading figure at the conference was George Lansbury, then mayor of Poplar, but Attlee was also at the forefront: 'I recall a meeting at the Mansion House where the Lord Mayor was proposing some mild measures. ... I made a forcible appeal for more vigorous measures and my fellow Mayors followed on the same lines, rather to the consternation of the City Fathers.'[7]

The government's inaction frustrated Attlee and the London mayors eventually decided on a deputation to the prime minister. The unemployed from each borough assembled at various locations behind their mayors and went to Downing Street to speak to Lloyd George. The mayors returned to the crowd of the unemployed and, with a riot in the offing, Attlee found the Stepney group and led it back to Stepney. A matter of weeks before the end of his mayoral year, Attlee was also chosen to become an alderman in place of a Mr Brennan, who had died. Aldermen were elected for five-year periods by all 60 borough councillors, so Attlee now had a durable political base for the future.

Attlee was also finding his voice in print. In 1920, *The Social Worker* was published, in which he asserted that there had been an alteration in 'the outlook of the social worker from the time when his principal object was benevolence down to the modern conception of social justice.'[8] In a sense, this reflected Attlee's own journey from a desire to help the poor to a wider conception of bringing about change in the political system. In a Fabian Society pamphlet published the same year, *Borough Councils: Their Constitution, Powers and Duties*, Attlee expressed the view that he thought there was a practical problem with some small boroughs:

> Generally it may be stated that the borough is a natural and useful governing body provided that it is big enough to have a separate life from the county, but there are very many small boroughs that are not nearly enough for economical and efficient administration and their position will have to be considered in any scheme for reform of areas.[9]

This pragmatic view was a significant factor in the formation of Attlee's position later in the decade when it came to structuring the electricity industry.

In the same pamphlet Attlee set out his preference for a mastery of detail in committee rather than for inspiring speeches: 'The hardest and most valuable work of the borough councillor is done in committee, and the man who thinks he can make a show by speeches in full meeting reported in the press without thoroughly mastering the work in committee will find himself disillusioned.'[10] Another student of the work of committees, C. Northcote Parkinson, put it slightly differently: 'we can assume that the people who will decide are members of the centre bloc. Delivery of speeches is therefore a waste of time. The one party will never agree and the other party has agreed already.'[11] Attlee maintained the view throughout his political career that quiet effectiveness was more productive than florid oratory. His priority was to understand issues in depth. Undoubtedly, the committee model also shaped his approach to leadership: he saw the committee structure, properly used, as a key vehicle for progress, not impeding it. The impartial chairman who was spokesman for the majority view was an example he took for his later leadership of the Labour Party.

As Attlee's political career progressed, tragedy struck in his personal life. His mother died on 19 May 1920 and his sister Dorothy died during the same year. This emphasized his loneliness: his single life had already intruded into his poetry pre-Gallipoli; for example, 'Love the Lamplighter':

> My lamp is burning but in vain, in vain
> Alone, alone I burn.[12]

He also saw the disadvantages of being single in practical terms:

> I was somewhat handicapped in my work as a Mayor by being unmarried. My sister, Margaret, was kind enough to act as Mayoress on several occasions, but living in Putney she could not get down to Stepney very often as she had to be with my mother a good deal.[13]

He was not to be single for much longer. In the summer of 1921 he met his future wife, Violet Millar. A friend of Tom, Edric Millar, invited him to come to Italy. Before leaving, Millar asked Attlee if his mother and youngest sister could come, and Attlee did not see this as a problem. Throughout the holiday, around Tuscany and Umbria, San Marino, Rimini and Cadenabbia, he became closer and closer to the sister. Born in 1896 as one of twins, Violet was then 24, and had worked as a nurse in a convalescent home during the First World War.[14]

Attlee was charming, as Lady Attlee confirmed: 'As a woman, I found that Clem Attlee had great charm and a delightful natural courtesy which made him very attractive. One felt better for his company. But allied to his gentle deference to the female sex was a full appreciation of one's abilities as a person.'[15] Lady Attlee further confirmed: 'Vi was not at all political. She left politics to Clem. She supported Clem.'[16] Attlee liked that: he did not want politics to intrude into his personal life unnecessarily. That said, Tony Benn recalled a meeting of the Labour Party's national executive committee in the 1950s when Violet thanked the party for all its kindness, particularly given that she was a

1. Mr and Mrs Attlee.

'lifelong Conservative'.[17] While there is no evidence that Violet later voted against her husband's party, it was unsurprising that Attlee worried about how she would view his political beliefs. He recalled: 'socialists were not so generally accepted in those days as they are now and I was just a street-corner agitator. I had thought it only fair that she [Violet] should see me orating from a platform on Hampstead Heath before proposing.'[18] Fortunately, she was not put off and they married in January 1922. Until then, Attlee had led a life remarkably free from responsibilities, able to throw himself into his social work with alacrity and to volunteer to serve in the First World War with no partner or children left to worry if he would ever return. He now had a wife and potential family to add to his political CV. All he had to do was wait for a general election and win Limehouse.

Chapter 5

A NEW MEMBER OF PARLIAMENT, 1922–24

On 19 October 1922, Conservative MPs famously met at the Carlton Club in London and voted to bring down the Lloyd George coalition government in which the party was the dominant partner. Andrew Bonar Law replaced Austen Chamberlain, who argued for the continuation of the coalition, as leader. A general election was subsequently called for Wednesday 15 November 1922, giving Attlee his big chance to enter parliament. His sole opponent in Limehouse was the Liberal Sir William Pearce, who had held the seat since the general election of 1906. Attlee ran what he himself described as a 'vigorous campaign', and declared that he had 'not much doubt' that he would win.[1] In the event, he had a majority of 1899, garnering 9688 votes to Pearce's 7789.

The Labour Party position across the country was promising. After a return of 63 seats in the 1918 general election from just under 2.4 million votes, it now had 142 MPs and a popular vote of 4.2 million. The Liberals were split between supporters of Asquith, whom Lloyd George had ousted from the premiership in December 1916, and those of Lloyd George. However, even in total, the Liberal MPs only numbered 116. The Conservatives swept to victory with 345 seats and an overall majority of 75, and Andrew Bonar Law became prime minister. In a precedent that was to have consequences for Attlee when he won the 1945 general election, when the new parliament met Ramsay MacDonald replaced J. R. Clynes, Labour's leader during the 1922 election campaign, and became the first Labour leader of the opposition. The parliamentary party, including Attlee, voted for the former leader who had returned to the House of Commons as MP for Aberavon. He had lost his seat in 1918 for having taken a pacifist stance in the First World War.

Attlee made his maiden speech on Thursday 23 November 1922. He was lucky to have got the chance to make his first speech so soon. His opportunity came about because the Speaker of the House of Commons wished to hear different arguments from those put by the left-wing 'Red' Clydesiders, the Labour MPs from the Glasgow urban areas on the banks of the River Clyde. The London whip Charlie Ammon invited Attlee to speak instead. The speech reads in *Hansard* like a classic left-wing call for state planning of the economy to deal with the interwar problem of unemployment, an issue about which he cared passionately:

Wealth flows through our borough up to London, but precious little stays there. We always have unemployment. The only time when unemployment was practically non-existent was the time of the War. …

We do want an economy campaign, but it must be a true economy campaign – economy in mankind, economy in flesh and blood, economy in the true wealth of the State and of the community, namely, its citizens. That can only be brought about by deliberately taking hold of the purchasing power of the nation, by directing the energies of the nation into the production of necessities for life, and not merely into the production of luxuries or necessities for profit.[2]

MacDonald appointed Attlee, together with Jack Lawson, another First World War service volunteer, as his parliamentary private secretaries (PPSs). Attlee formed a long-standing friendship with Lawson, who, on the face of it, had little in common with him. Lawson was a Durham miner and trade unionist who had won his parliamentary seat of Chester-le-Street in a by-election in 1919. But Attlee's parliamentary career was not to be one in which the old school tie dominated in his friendships and associations. In government after 1945, his closest friend and ally would be the distinctly working-class Ernest Bevin. He and Lawson had taken their first step towards ministerial office together. As a PPS, Attlee was not in a position to speak very often, as his role was to keep MacDonald informed of backbench opinion within the House of Commons.

Yet, reading Hansard, it is clear that Attlee did speak on a variety of topics. For example, in just 33 days from 15 February 1923, he brought up ten different issues, in oral and written form, on a range of subjects. Some were disparate: on 27 February he asked about oil steamers cleaning their tanks in the Bristol Channel[3] and on 20 March, he humanely put down a written question seeking the release of two child murderesses.[4] However, the issues that mattered to Attlee were crystallizing. He spoke several times on Britain's relationship with the wider world. On 15 February, he asked the chancellor, Stanley Baldwin, about agreement on interest payments to the USA on the country's debt.[5] On 28 February he rose to oppose strict control on immigration.[6] On 5 March, he asked if the French had been approached before the British government published its papers on inter-allied debts and reparations (and was told by Mr Ronald McNeill, under-secretary to Lord Curzon at the Foreign Office, that they had).[7] On 7 March, he asked about vessels on the Rhine being held up by the French at Duisburg-Ruhrort, and British importers having to pay charges to get their goods.[8] His loyalty to his local government background did not waver – on 14 March, together with George Lansbury, he put down questions on the lapse of certain provisions under the Local Authorities (Financial Provisions) Act (1921)[9] – and neither did his strong attachment to military service. On 15 March, he spoke on the army estimates. He noted that officers had been 'drawn from a fairly narrow class, a class that has some great virtues, but many serious deficiencies'.[10] He then declared rather sweepingly: 'Our Army was unfortunately very largely a stupid Army.'[11] He sought to help working people, querying hours at the Thatcham Board and Paper Mills Ltd on 7 March.[12] He did not lose sight of the fact that he was a London MP: on 6 March, he put down a written question regarding the removal of rails from Basingstoke and Alton railway under the Defence of the Realm Act.[13]

The reason for such a scattering of questions is the position in which Attlee found himself as a new MP who was PPS to the party leader. What the *specific* issues all have in common is that they were peripheral to the major concerns of the day. Even the issue of French occupation of the Ruhr is only referred to indirectly in terms of holding up British vessels on the Rhine. Unemployment itself stood at over 1.5 million in January 1923.[14] Yet, Attlee always ran the risk of saying something that could be interpreted as the party leader's thinking and the last thing he would have wanted to do was cause problems for MacDonald. As the second Labour prime minister was PPS to the first, it is often tempting to read too much into the historical symbolism of this appointment. In fact, it was simply a fairly natural step for a new, ambitious MP.

One consequence of Attlee's new role, however, was that it left far less time for extra-parliamentary activities. He had to leave his post at the London School of Economics and had new challenges at home. Violet took some time to get over the birth of their first child, Janet, in February 1923, but he did, however, find time to attend the annual party conference, which was held in June 1923 in London. Somewhat surprisingly, he advocated adopting a policy of voting against the service estimates each year. This issue was a frequent bone of contention for the Labour Party in the interwar period: the balance was between Labour's pacifist instincts and desire not to vote for arms at the disposal of a government it opposed on the one hand, and the desire for the party to be a respectable alternative government, willing to work in the national interest away from narrow party concerns, on the other. With his military experience and natural desire in parliament to work with the leadership, Attlee's behaviour seems out of character, but it may be that in these very early months his political views were still finding expression in what was a changing international situation. In any event, his speech reads almost pompously:

> He knew something about armies, and he knew that they could not demobilize all arms in one week. But there was all the difference in the world between making a temporary arrangement with regard to armaments, until they could do away with armaments, and in voting for armaments for Governments that were carrying out a policy to which the Party was opposed.[15]

Arthur Henderson cut him down to size: 'it was not often in the Conference discussion on an important resolution that a delegate, who ought to have moved it, but who, in this case, had spoken last, delivered himself over to the Philistines so completely as their friend Major Attlee had done.'[16]

Attlee's contributions in parliament in the summer of 1923 read overall as those of a man with underlying frustrations about the lack of government action on issues that mattered to him. But he was growing in confidence, putting his case more strongly. He cared passionately about families that had been bereaved during the First World War. On 2 July, in support of an amendment exempting from income tax pensions granted to widows whose husbands were killed in action Attlee was coruscating: 'you can see it written on boards in words in which they express what they mean when they say that the country needed them in 1914 but that in 1923 they can go hang.' The clause was, however, defeated.[17] Interestingly, India was also starting to feature in Attlee's priorities. On 17 July, during the committee stages of the East India Loans Bill, Attlee spoke against an amendment that would have kept 75 per cent of any money raised in Great Britain under the bill to be spent on domestic projects: 'It is about the most unstatesmanlike thing that could be done at this time ... you have enormous discontent in India ... the House is asked to tell India how she shall spend the money which she is borrowing, and on which she has to pay the interest.' The amendment was also negatived.[18] On 25 July he returned to the key issue of unemployment, harassing the minister of labour, Anderson Montague Barlow, pointing out that men in the area of the London dock dispute were being refused unemployment benefit despite being unemployed and receiving support *before* the dispute began; he demanded that labour exchanges be instructed to stop the men being deprived of what they were entitled to.[19]

If the source of Attlee's disquiet was the government's refusal to respond to the issues he raised, the only real answer was to change the government. Andrew Bonar Law resigned on grounds of ill-health because he was suffering from throat cancer and on 22 May 1923 Stanley Baldwin replaced him as prime minister. On 25 October, at the Conservative Party conference in Plymouth, Baldwin advocated a policy of protective tariffs for domestic industry – the issue that had brought about Attlee's sole foray into the debating society while at Oxford. He subsequently dissolved parliament, seeking a mandate for their introduction, and a general election was held on Thursday 6 December. Labour made further progress, returning 191 MPs with over 4.4 million votes. The newly-united Liberals returned 159 MPs and the Conservatives were reduced to 258 seats. Baldwin remained at the head of the largest party, but was 50 seats short of an overall majority. In Limehouse, Attlee, facing a Conservative opponent only, increased his majority to 6185, polling 11,473 votes to his opponent's 5288.

The first Labour government was now a distinct possibility. Attlee unquestionably had a vested interest: as one of the MPs elected in 1922 whom MacDonald knew personally and with his military and local government experience, he stood a strong chance of gaining ministerial office. However, Baldwin had every right to remain in office until he lost a vote of censure in the House of Commons, and did so. The question was what the Liberals would do. Tactically, their difficulty was the risk they ran of the Labour Party, the junior partner prior to 1914 that had now overtaken them in terms of both the popular vote and parliamentary seats, supplanting them on the left of British politics. Should they support the Conservatives and keep Labour out of office, try for a pro-free-trade but anti-Labour Asquith government with Conservative support, or vote down the government and allow the king to send for MacDonald? On 18 December the Liberals indicated that they would vote against the Conservatives. Asquith declared that if there was to be a Labour government, 'it could hardly be tried under safer conditions',[20] and on 21 January 1924 the government lost a vote of censure. On the following day, Baldwin resigned. MacDonald kissed hands and became the first British Labour prime minister.

At any time the Labour government could be voted out by a vote of no confidence, provided that both the Conservatives and Liberals backed this. So precarious was its position that some within the Labour Party doubted the wisdom of taking office at all in such circumstances. Retrospectively, Attlee was 'quite sure that they were wrong. The electors at that time needed to see a Labour Government … if they were to appreciate that Labour was now the alternative to a Conservative administration. Refusal ... might have given a new lease of life to the Liberal Party.'[21] On 23 January Attlee became under-secretary of state for war. The secretary of state was Stephen Walsh, and Attlee's fellow minister, the financial secretary, was Jack Lawson. Walsh had stood in the 1918 general election as Labour member of the Lloyd George coalition government, and had been opposed by an 'official' Labour Party candidate; but Attlee found him, despite his lack of military experience (he had been vice-president of the National Union of Mineworkers from 1922 to 1924) to be an excellent head liked by the army.

Attlee was ideally suited to this department. It was no surprise that he and Lawson 'got on excellently with all the soldiers'.[22] As a minister, Attlee was diligent and thorough, meticulous in his answers to questions in the House of Commons and able to give a broad strategic overview of the policy the depart-ments pursued. On 17 March, he spoke in the debates on the army estimates, and it is clear that underlying factors informed his decisions: 'Our Army is not at present intended as a great Continental Army going into a European war. We have to consider what is the particular purpose of our Army.'[23] He added:

> Whatever changes are made ... must be in relation to the position of international affairs and the policy of this country ... [which] ... is a policy of peace ... if we are not ... [contemplating] ... entering ... a European war on a large scale, we have to look upon ... preparations as part of a gradual scheme.[24]

Attlee's social conscience was also very much evident. On 13 March, during the same debate on the army estimates, he declared:

> the more we can continue education in the Army on the broadest possible lines, the better it will be for the Army and the country ... while in the Army a man may not only be trained as a soldier, but be trained as a citizen, and able to take his place in the work of the world when he comes out.[25]

While accepting the necessity of the death penalty, he was sparing as regards its use. On 2 April, he objected to an amendment changing the routes of appeal in courts martial regarding capital offences: 'this Clause ... will do precisely the opposite to what hon. Members intend. It will narrow down the appeal to points of law. ... I wish to see the utmost possible freedom of appeal on every possible grounds.'[26] The amendment was defeated. Attlee's humanist instincts had prevailed. On 8 July, he stressed that any enlistment of boys, while voluntary, required the consent of a parent or guardian.[27]

But however successful Attlee's tenure as a minister, the first Labour government was never going to last long. Whatever Attlee's merits, he was of no significance in terms of the party's leadership and direction. Labour was always going to have difficulties in foreign affairs in its relationship with the Soviet Union, the Bolshevik revolution having only happened just over six years before it took office: there was a risk that the party could be tainted by an association with it. It risked being seen as too pro-communist at the expense of Britain's national interest, and it was vital for Labour's long-term future as a realistic contender for government that it was not tarnished with the extremist left-wing brush. MacDonald therefore became prime minister *and* foreign secretary and tried to tread a very fine line. He gave the Soviet Union diplomatic recognition in February 1924 and began negotiations for two treaties providing for the Soviets to buy British goods, while, in return, in August 1924, he agreed to guarantee a loan to the Soviets. The agreement was never ratified, but it did not help Labour present itself as a respectable party of government. At a conference in London in July 1924, MacDonald managed to agree a compromise between France and Germany about reparations; in September 1924, he came to an agreement with France, the 'Geneva Protocol', over a system of collective security within the League of Nations framework. Attlee was disappointed that the Conservative government refused to ratify it. On the domestic front, John Wheatley, as housing minister, introduced a Housing Act that 'provided a £9 a year State subsidy for thirty years for every council house, compared with £6 a year for twenty years under Conservative legislation a year earlier.'[28]

The government eventually fell on the issue of the prosecution of J. R. Campbell, editor of the *Workers' Weekly*. Campbell was accused of sedition for an article calling on troops not to shoot at strikers; however, the attorney general dropped the prosecution. On 30 September 1924, in the Commons, MacDonald gave the misleading answer that he had not been consulted on the prosecution when he had, and had to give an apology in the debate on the matter back in the House of Commons on 8 October. It was, however, to no avail, for the government was defeated on a vote of censure and the next day MacDonald went to the King for a dissolution of parliament. A general election followed on 29 October, marred by the affair of the Zinoviev letter, published in the *Daily Mail* on 25 October. The letter, later proved a fake, was purportedly from the head of the Soviet Comintern, the body set up to foment revolution in the rest of the world, to the British Communist Party. The 'Red menace' hung over the electorate as they went to the polls to oust Labour from office.

Attlee was a direct beneficiary of Labour becoming the official opposition party in 1922 and taking power in 1924. Not only had he been PPS to the leader of the opposition but he had also had the chance to serve in government. He had set out the issues that mattered to him. He had not become a 'jack of all trades' but concentrated on those issues that interested him or in which he had direct experience – foreign affairs, local government, the fate of the poor and unemployed, and military matters. As a minister, his thoroughness and attention to detail had combined well with an ability to look beyond immediate administrative considerations to wider policy decisions. He had gained valuable experience for the future in only the first two years of his parliamentary career.

Chapter 6
OPPOSITION AND
INDIAN AFFAIRS, 1924–30

The 1924 general election produced the first 'modern' result, with a clear dividing line between the Conservatives and Labour as the viable parties of government, with the Liberals a distant third in terms of seats. The great victors were the Conservatives, gaining nearly 2.5 million votes and taking 419 seats. Labour increased its vote by over a million, but lost 40 seats, returning 151 MPs. The Liberals lost 1.3 million votes, and were reduced to just 40 MPs. Attlee's majority in Limehouse was 6021. He was now a full-time politician, having given up his job at the London School of Economics in 1922. Now in opposition, Attlee continued to take a strong interest in military matters, and the plight of the poor and unemployed, which he on occasions linked together. On 16 March 1925, for example, he related the performance of the army to the social conditions of the population: 'The real fact that emerges is that if we want to have a healthy lot of people for recruiting purposes we must have a higher standard of life in this country, and that the unemployment question affects every single sphere of life.'[1]

However, his energies were concentrated on two parliamentary bills. The first was health minister Neville Chamberlain's Rating and Valuation Bill, which transferred the raising of rates from Poor Law guardians to local councils. On 3 July 1925 Attlee criticized the way that provision for the poor inevitably fell on the poorer local authorities, the issue that George Lansbury and the Poplar councillors had been imprisoned for acting on: 'the burden is heaviest in poor districts such as West Ham, Poplar, and Stepney … it is precisely in those districts … that you are going to do the least good in relief of the local rates … you should not have your scheme fall too heavily on the poorer districts.'[2] On 23 November, during the report stage of the bill, he spoke against an amendment that would have set up a board of overseers in a local authority to set the rates rather than have the local authorities undertake this task themselves.[3] The autonomy of the local authorities was clearly vital to him; what he would have made of the modern-day trend of public sector auditing is a moot point. His central problem was, however, where the burden of the rates fell, and he continued the fight during the report stage. On 30 November 1925, he said, on an amendment regarding the level of rateable value and allowable concessions: 'It is about time that the Government gave something to the working classes in the towns.'[4] Chamberlain, however, backed by a large Conservative majority, had little difficulty in pursuing his desire to tidy up the provisions, with consistency of valuation across the board and without the concessions Attlee sought.

On the second issue, however, Attlee did exert more influence because of both his expertise on the subject and his experience of committees. In this period, Attlee developed his skills in the arena of the *parliamentary* committee. The issue was electricity provision, which he felt went to the heart of the division between rich and poor. The 1919 Electricity (Supply) Act was the basis of the existing system and had established an Electricity Commission together with a number of joint electricity authorities, including one for London and the Home Counties. The commission was set up as a regulator and electricity was provided by both private companies and local authority undertakings. Attlee was a member of the Stepney borough council electricity committee, and also for a time its chair. The battle was over the future of the industry: public versus private sector, local authority undertakings versus private companies, and Attlee wanted a national system for the generation and transmission of electricity in order that the smaller local authorities could work together on developing the industry in the public sector.

Electricity was at the time supplied in different places at a variety of voltages and frequencies. It fell woefully short of the supply to every household, rich or poor, that Attlee thought necessary. Baldwin's new Conservative government introduced a bill 'to coordinate main-line transmission and generation and to make possible joint action by smaller authorities. In fact, though not in strict terms, generation and main transmission were to be nationalized.'[5] Attlee was given a place on the parliamentary committee scrutinizing the bill. Throughout 1925 he kept up the pressure on the government with a series of well-informed speeches in parliament. His strategy was to push for greater national coordination within the government bill while at the same time trying to prevent private companies, through various private members' bills, taking over transmission and generation in certain regions. He favoured only measures that encouraged local authorities to work together.

On 25 February, he made a speech during the debate on the second reading of the London Electricity Supply Bill, and dealt with what he called 'one or two broad points about this thoroughly bad Bill', which

> put the whole area into the hands of a private company ... the way to develop Essex is for the people of Essex to have some control. ... It is purely a Private Bill in the interest of a single company. ... I hope that the House will reject it.[6]

On 2 March, he spoke during the debate on the second reading of the North Metropolitan Electric Bill, making the same point.[7] On 14 May, Attlee spoke in favour of an amendment to the London Electricity (No. 2) Bill, which would have reduced the allowed dividends to private enterprises after 1931 from 7 per cent to 5 per cent: 'Electricity supply may have been a risky business some time ago. ... To-day, when electricity is a well-established thing, is there any reason for paying a huge ransom to private enterprise. ...'[8] The amendment was, however, defeated.

Attlee's arguments found some favour with the government. When he spoke on 21 May, he sympathized with attempts to get local authorities working together, which was at the heart of the government's main bill. He referred to: 'taunts from ... the Member for Carnarvon Boroughs (Mr Lloyd George) and others about the ... parochialism of local authorities. Of course, that exists. There is also the petty selfishness of companies. ... For the last six years I have been endeavouring to keep the London authorities working together.'[9] In committee, there was deference to Attlee's views: 'In the course of time, the Ministers tended to wait for my approval or disapproval before accepting amendments. This was so marked that when we came to the Report Stage a Conservative objected to the undue deference shown to my views.'[10] The key here was Attlee's experience of committees – and his ability to impress others with his detailed knowledge. He did not lecture ministers or seek publicity with speeches outside parliament.

That did not mean that Attlee could let up in his fight to prevent private companies muscling in. On 22 February 1926 Attlee spoke on the London Power Company Bill: 'We are trying to concentrate the generation there in the hands of one big authority. This will be best for all suppliers of electricity. It will be best for all users of electricity. It will be best for large users and for small users.'[11] He had to fend off Tory cries of 'Municipal Socialism'; during the second reading of the Guildford Corporation Bill on 24 March he argued:

> I hope that every time a Bill of this kind comes before us we are not going to have an attempt to prejudice the fair consideration of the

question by a lot of talk about Municipal Socialism ... when [that] is done the other side have an extremely bad case.[12]

Yet, his speeches were also positive and he saw the great potential of electricity supply to improve the lot of working people; on 29 March, he felt that 'what we see in electrical development is the possibility of replanning both the life and the industries of this country to give better effect to industrial development, a better distribution of population and a better life for the people.'[13]

Attlee's final speeches on the electricity bill urged the government towards wholescale nationalization. On 12 November he moved that the house could not agree to the third reading of the electricity bill: 'To us electricity is primarily a great social question. We want the direction and the supply of electricity, the policy of the supply of electricity, to be determined on the broadest possible lines of social well-being.'[14] However, he would have to wait until he was prime minister to nationalize the industry formally in 1947. In the event, the Conservative government passed the Electricity (Supply) Act (1926), setting up a Central Electricity Board, which established a national grid with standardized supply. Under the act, a joint electricity authority for London and the Home Counties was created, and Attlee produced a scheme of representation whereby neighbouring authorities agreed a representative, which was taken up. He had also been able, much to his great pride, to scupper the two bills supported by private companies that would have taken areas away from the local authority undertakings. He had also been able to push a Municipal Electricity Bill through, assisting the local authorities, prompting *Punch* to depict him in the guise of a Greek hero fending off the private companies.

While Attlee worked to influence the construction of the nation's electricity system, and kept a watchful eye on the armed forces, the economy was sailing through very troubled waters. The coal industry was particularly badly affected, facing increased foreign competition with the recovering Germany again producing coal. Faced with a possible dispute between mine owners and mine workers over hours and pay, the Conservative government agreed to a temporary subsidy and a Royal Commission under the Liberal Herbert Samuel, a climb-down dubbed 'Red Friday', 31 July 1925. However, when the Samuel Commission reported in March 1926, miners still faced the prospect of longer hours and lower wages, and the TUC announced a general strike on 1 May 1926, which began on 3 May and lasted nine days.

Attlee blamed Churchill, by now chancellor, and his decision to return Britain to the gold standard at the prewar parity, which created unemployment. With hindsight, this judgement seems a valid one. The adoption of the gold standard meant that the pound could be converted to a fixed amount of gold.

While this on the face of it protects savings and arguably provides stability, the difficulty was that the highly valued pound affected exports and demanded high interest rates to support the exchange rate. Attlee's role in the general strike, though politically peripheral, was practically crucial. He served on the joint industrial council of the electricity industry, but, oddly, representing the employers. Inevitably, this role was one that was going to cause difficulties for a Labour politician ostensibly representing the interests of the workers. Faced with employers' calls to supply the factories and strikers' calls to cut them off during the general strike, Attlee found a middle way: only lighting and essential services were supplied. Finding a compromise view was to become a hallmark of the Attlee leadership style in later years.

Unfortunately for the Labour Party, however, under party pressure the government passed the Trade Disputes and Trade Union Act in 1927, which banned general and secondary strikes, and made the political levy paid by trade union members to the Labour Party subject to a 'contracting in' provision as opposed to the 'contract out' provision stipulated in the 1913 Trade Union Act, having an adverse effect on Labour Party funds. Attlee tried to protect the interests of the trade unions during the passage of the bill; on 31 May 1927, he spoke against a clause prohibiting compulsory membership of trade unions for employees of local authorities ('It is an out-of-date idea to think we can do without collective organization at the present day'),[15] but to no avail.

From this point until Attlee's appointment to ministerial office under the second Labour government of 1929–31, his interventions in the House of Commons became sporadic. On 12 December 1927 he was still drawn to protect local authorities from the heavy surcharges a district auditor imposed: 'All the council have to think about is how their decision will appeal to the district auditor. If they put on too much he comes round and allows a surcharge.'[16] But his attention was shifted from domestic politics to colonial affairs. The Government of India Act (1919) had provided for a statutory commission to consider its workings after a ten-year period of operation and further steps. In 1927, the secretary of state for India, Lord Birkenhead, announced the creation of the commission. Duly, in November 1927, Baldwin appointed seven MPs to a commission that became known as the Simon Commission after its chair, Sir John Simon. Attlee, together with South Wales miner Vernon Hartshorn, were the Labour representatives. Attlee's sound performance as a minister under MacDonald, together with the fact that he remained an unknown figure to the general public, were probably advantages since they kept MacDonald's options open: he would not have wanted his hand forced by a vociferous Labour member. Whatever the reason, however, history could not have provided a better training experience for the prime minister who was to grant independence to India.

After an initial visit in the autumn of 1927, on 3 February 1928 the commission arrived in Bombay to spend three months touring India before returning in the autumn of 1928; wives, including Violet Attlee, accompanied the members. The commission was to deal with the system implemented in 1919. The act had purportedly set up a 'dyarchy', in which both British and Indians governed the subcontinent. Some issues, including health and education, were transferred to the provinces, not under the control of the British viceroy while other 'reserved' issues, such as defence and foreign affairs, remained under viceregal control. The Imperial Council became a central legislature of two houses, including both political parties, notably including the Congress Party, which demanded independence, and representatives of the princely states (the areas of India governed by the princes). The Indian Congress Party of Gandhi, whose civil disobedience campaign to rid India of the British had begun in 1920, and Jawaharlal Nehru, boycotted the commission, but it continued its work regardless.

Attlee was not afraid to suggest new ideas for the governance of the subcontinent, to take the knowledge he had gathered and draw conclusions for the future. On the face of it, it was a great opportunity for a relatively young politician: it was rather like a well-equipped laboratory being provided to a budding scientist for him or her to gauge the evidence and set out arguments for consideration by peers. Attlee certainly grasped the opportunity. Documents available at the India Records Office contain no less than seven formal notes and memoranda written by Attlee, together with two draft sections for the final Simon Commission report. The material submitted provides a fascinating insight into how his mind worked. Attlee readily made suggestions, but they were generally *practical* solutions to *practical* problems. Broader democratic principles or ideas of political philosophy were clearly not part of his thinking on the issue. Perhaps as a consequence, Attlee's suggestions were sometimes faulty and open to criticism. At the same time, Attlee's work on the Simon Commission stands as evidence of a change in his thinking: in the two decades since his work in the East End he had matured into a pragmatic national politician.

After nine months in India, Attlee seemed deeply sceptical of finding a workable way forward for British India. Writing to Tom on 9 November 1928, he commented: 'The truth is that over here they have been trying to put an Anglo-Saxon facade on to a Mogul building + the two pieces of architecture are not structurally connected.'[17] Five days later, it was the communal difference that taxed him. 'The Hindu professes a belief in free + open competition because he is good at exams. The Muslim believes in adult suffrage because he is the poorer community.'[18] The problems of India seemed to magnify in his mind and, in New Delhi on 25 November 1928, Attlee set out pessimistically that political change of itself was not enough, that social and economic problems were deep rooted and would remain. 'The real trouble is that India's disabilities are social + economic – we have to deal with political change.'[19] Back in New Delhi on 7 December 1928, he was very glad of a break from dealing with the issue. 'It is rather a relief to be away from Hindu-Muslim squabbles and to discuss … the separation of India + Burma.'[20] He began to worry about misperception in Britain of the reality on the ground in India. Again, in New Delhi on 20 March 1929, he wrote: 'I fear it will be difficult to make people at home understand that we are not dealing with a *tabula rasa*, but a page that has been much scribbled over.'[21]

The papers Attlee provided to the commission were an exercise in trial and error. In a 'Note on the Indian States' dated April 1929, Attlee first turned his mind to the difficulty presented in setting the appropriate balance between the power of the central government and the Indian states:

> There are certain subjects, such as Defence, which cannot possibly be handed over [to] the Indian ministers, or to the Assembly, while on the other hand if subjects are not handed over we are exposed to the dangers and difficulties of Dyarchy. It is further to my mind unjust that certain subjects which properly belong to all-India should be handed over to Ministers who are responsible to persons elected from British India only. …
>
> I am inclined to think that the best line of approach towards Federation is by bringing the states into active partnership with British India on specific subjects.[22]

This was not a vague aspiration, but to be expressed – characteristically – in a series of *committees*: for example, a defence committee presided over by the commander-in-chief, with military members, members from the viceroy's cabinet, members from the Chamber of Princes (the body set up as a point of contact between those parts of India ruled by Indian princes and British India) and the assembly.

Attlee's further 'Note on the Central Government and the Problem of Federation' sensibly recognized that, while an ultimate aim of federation might be welcomed, a weakened assembly would not.[23] It also grappled with the problem of what the central government should do when a provincial government was failing in some respect. Attlee's position was that: 'The Governor General will be in touch with all India affairs and it will be for him by advice and admonition and, if necessary, by direct order to prevent the action or inaction of one province endangering the safety or interests of the Federation.'[24] So far so good: these contributions offered a way forward in a complex debate.

However, Attlee was unsure of his ground and, after discussions with one of the officials, W. T. Layton, he decided to vary some of the conclusions provided in an initial draft. 'The Commission has come to the provisional conclusion that intervention by the Central Government in the provincial sphere in cases of emergency must be by the Governor General acting through the Provincial Governors, and not by the Governor General in Council.'[25] He also mused: 'Apart, however, from intervention in emergencies, the questions arise as to what, if any, normative powers should be entrusted to the Central Government ... experience has shown the danger of leaving only ultimate emergency powers instead of also providing for a steady pressure directed to the maintenance of standards.'[26] Attlee was particularly concerned about law and order: 'We have already decided that the higher ranks of the police force should continue to be recruited on an all-India basis. We now propose that a certain proportion of the Police budget in every province should be provided from Central Revenues.'[27]

Having apparently decided on policy, in a further 'Memorandum on Central Government' dated 13 February 1930, Attlee set out his ideas on presentation:

To my mind the only logical line we can take up in refusing any extension at the Centre is to state: (a) that our aim is the federation of All India that the bulk of the subjects of Central Administration are such that All India is affected by them and that therefore until federation is complete they cannot be handed over...; (b) that the composition of India is such that precedents drawn from the Dominions do not apply and that we do not believe that the Central Legislature will develop into a Parliament with a majority Party in power through a Cabinet representative of it.[28]

He may have had in mind public opinion in Britain when setting this view: his opinion was that India should be presented as distinct within the British Empire and that the transfer of responsibilities away from British control at the centre should be slow ('until federation is complete'). The line, however, was open to the charge of underestimating the strength of feeling in India. On 26 January 1930, the Indian National Congress had issued a declaration of independence.

Unsurprisingly, Attlee's ideas received a sharp put-down, though its author is unclear: 'My main difficulty is with Major Attlee's proposal to base the conclusion about the Viceroy's Council upon the argument about Federation ... if say Federalism best goal, or most probable end, I feel sure the commission will be accused of having invented a new argument against political advance.'[29] Scathingly, the piece concludes: 'I do not think that Major

Attlee's scheme of Committees of the Assembly in charge of departments would commend itself to Indian opinion; the last thing they want is to be treated like another County Council.'[30]

Attlee's ideas elsewhere were as undeveloped as they had been on the powers of the central government. Aside from some sensible ideas about reducing the size of some provinces to prevent one or two, like the Bengal presidency, dominating smaller units in a future federation,[31] Attlee held fast to the idea of the North West Frontier province (one of modern-day Pakistan's four provinces bordering Afghanistan) being treated differently from others: 'The inherent right of a man to smoke a cigarette must necessarily be curtailed if he lives in a powder magazine.'[32] There was clearly no over-arching philosophy here, simply the practical problem posed by the troublesome North West Frontier Province. Not once did Attlee give any regard to principles of federalism, or even refer to other areas of the world where federalism had succeeded in producing long-term stable government. He clearly felt that there was little to learn from the United States, though admittedly the concept of 'dual federalism' employed there, with both states and the federal government as sovereign entities, was not something he ever envisaged for British India.

Attlee made a number of suggestions on the central social challenge of Hindu and Muslim communities coexisting in a single political entity. He did not appeal to any established principles of political science and again put forward different proposals, unafraid of changing his mind. He felt that the electoral systems used for provincial councils should seek to move away from communal politics and sought to design one that would facilitate this. He felt that direct elections with communal electorates ('water-tight compartments') reinforced the distance between Hindus and Muslims: 'the tendency will be for only extreme communal partisans to be returned.'[33] Attlee's answer was for each province to be carved up into 'primary constituencies', each choosing a 'secondary elector' 'who would then be assembled together with representatives, if any, of animists, depressed classes etc. if these could not actually elect'.[34] It was unclear how these other representatives would be chosen, but this 'electoral college' 'would then by the method of proportional representation as used in the election of Irish senates elect from their own number the members of the legislative council allotted to the electoral area.'[35] Attlee envisaged that 'the last one or the last two on the list would depend on votes other than those of their own community'.[36]

There were a number of obvious difficulties with this scheme. For a start, it is unclear how such a system of proportional representation would resemble that of the Irish senate if the electoral college elected 'from its own number'. The system adopted for the Irish senate (the Irish Upper House) in 1928 was an electorate of the outgoing members of the senate *plus* the Dail (the Lower

House) electing a third of the senate at each election. In Attlee's scheme, the electorate elects from among its own number only. While this is not unworkable *per se*, it does raise questions about how the system could be policed in terms of such a small number of electors in each area possibly making deals with each other in ensuring a favourable result. Attlee himself had identified the problem of bribery when considering the method, but felt that no system could entirely remove that threat.

Attlee retracted the scheme in another memorandum on 19 September 1929:

> I have come to the conclusion that the method proposed is undesirable, partly because it is doubtful whether it is possible to work election by the single transferable vote [whereby voters rank candidates who are then elected proportionately] under the system suggested and partly because, if the central legislature is to be indirectly elected from the provincial councils, those councils must be directly elected. I desire therefore to withdraw the suggestions then made.[37]

His new idea was for multi-member constituencies with seats designated for minorities. Minority groups would have to apply to the governor for a 'communal primary'; 'all persons of a particular community who desire to go before the general electorate for election to the council will be entitled to stand. The electors of that community will vote.'[38] All candidates receiving a set percentage of the vote would then be entitled to stand in the actual election.

Attlee set out the advantages and disadvantages of such a system, and knew that it, too, would be hard for the electorate to understand. To be fair to him, the problem with which he was grappling was almost intractable. An electoral scheme with a pull away from the communal divide was almost certainly likely to be more complex. And what India perhaps needed in the late 1920s was not a more nebulous system, but a clearer one, illustrating the Indian democratic contribution to British rule. Attlee was also operating within a very restricted framework. Radical change was not seen as a possibility. His view of India's position on the road to independence was clear: dominion status was not even a possibility, and his conception was of a reorganization within *British* government:

> Whilst Dominion status … is an impossibility, it seems to me possible to place India in a position of greater equality with the other Dominions … I … suggest … abolition of the India Office and the Indian Council, and the transfer of such functions as remain … [from] … the Home Government to the Dominions Office.[39]

The Simon Commission published its 17-volume report in June 1930. While it did advocate the establishment of representative government in the provinces in place of 'dyarchy', separate electorates were to be retained while communal tensions remained: Attlee's proposed electoral systems were not accepted. Even Attlee's view on dominion status was circumvented as the viceroy, Lord Irwin (the later Lord Halifax), 'conceived a plan so bold it would leapfrog the Commission'.[40] Irwin had declared that 'Dominion status' was the goal for India on 31 October 1929, and MacDonald supported him in the debate in the House of Commons just days later. Despite unpopularity within his party, Baldwin backed MacDonald, with Churchill resigning from the front bench in protest. Attlee would have to rethink his views. In the short term, Attlee's place on the Simon Commission proved unhelpful. He had not had a discernible impact on the commission's findings, and had received little, if any, credit among his political colleagues. At the 1931 Labour Party conference, when Lansbury proposed a motion on India, and declared that the Labour Party was 'going to stand for an imperial friendship ... upon the basis of free cooperation with the consent of the Indian people',[41] Attlee did not even receive a mention – perhaps unsurprisingly, given his views on dominion status. In the long term, of course, Attlee had gained invaluable knowledge. However, when he was in government between 1940 and 1951, there would be no possibility of pursuing policies and then retracting them later: his time for bouncing ideas around was at an end.

Chapter 7
IN GOVERNMENT, 1930–31

At the general election of 30 May 1929, Labour became the largest party in the House of Commons for the first time in its history. It received slightly fewer than 8.4 million votes, winning 288 seats, while the Conservatives, with more votes, over 8.6 million, won only 260 seats. The Liberals, with just over 5.3 million votes, won just 59 seats. Attlee increased his majority in Limehouse to 7288. MacDonald became prime minister for the second time. He gave the Foreign Office to Arthur Henderson; J. R. Clynes became home secretary and Philip Snowden returned to the Treasury. Attlee, with his local government experience, his mastery of detail on legislative proposals like the electricity bill and his having served in the 1924 administration with as much success as anyone, had excellent prospects of being appointed to a government post.

He was, however to be disappointed, later commenting in his autobiography: 'MacDonald had assured Hartshorn and myself that membership of the Indian Statutory Commission would not … militate against our inclusion in the next Labour Government. … However, neither of us was included, and it was characteristic … that he did not take the trouble to inform us.'[1] A feature of Attlee's account of his life is its lack of direct criticism of others. MacDonald was an exception. Attlee was never likely to be comfortable with MacDonald's personal style of leadership, but MacDonald had previously treated Attlee well, making him both his PPS and a minister in 1924. He has also given him the opportunity of serving on the Simon Commission. Attlee's comment that he '*lived to* regret'[2] (my emphasis) his vote for MacDonald in 1922 is revealing: he only came to dislike MacDonald during the period between 1929 and 1931. The failure to appoint him to ministerial office in 1929 was one thing; Attlee was to be appointed to office in 1930 in any event, but MacDonald's abandonment of the Labour Party in 1931 was something that he could not forgive.

In the short term, Attlee's time was in any event taken up by the preparation of the Simon Commission report. After the 1929 general election, he made only one significant contribution in the House of Commons during the rest of the year. Unable to resist intervening on defence, he offered light criticism to Lewes Conservative MP Rear Admiral Tufton Percy Hamilton Beamish, who had argued that Britain was unique in its pro-disarmament position. Attlee replied: 'I could not help thinking that he was falling into that pit into which popular novelists so often fall, in which they make their characters speak exactly with their own voices.'[3] While Attlee worked on drafting documents, the government found itself grappling with the problem of increasing unemployment. In June 1929, the jobless total stood at 1.164 million; this had increased to 1.52 million in January 1930.[4] Economic problems were spreading after the Wall Street Crash in the last week of October 1929. A crucial fault line in the government was how to deal with this problem. Recent analysis has suggested a number of options available.[5] First, there were large-scale public works schemes: the government could spend money to create jobs. Second, had the pound been allowed to float (downwards), it would have been possible to cut interest rates. Finally, the government could consider strong deflationary measures. For very understandable reasons, the government did not follow any of these courses. Oswald Mosley, the chancellor of the Duchy of Lancaster, wanted to introduce a retirement plan, raise the school leaving age to 15 and create a public works scheme. The rejection of Mosley's memorandum setting out these ideas brought about his resignation from the government and gave Attlee the opportunity to serve as a minister. On 23 May 1930, he became chancellor of the Duchy of Lancaster in Mosley's place.

The office was essentially a titular one only, with no specific departmental responsibilities, but it presented the opportunity to have an impact in a number of policy spheres. Attlee helped MacDonald at the 1930 Imperial Conference at which the Statute of Westminster, eventually passed in 1931, was agreed, formally giving the dominions legislative equality within the Commonwealth: the principle that Britain could no longer simply pass legislation applicable to other countries had already been agreed at a 1927 Imperial Conference. He was also on the prime minister's economic advisory council, which also included, among others, Philip Snowden, Ernest Bevin and John Maynard Keynes. He was asked to provide a view on the central issue of unemployment. On 16 July 1930, Attlee wrote excitedly to Tom from the House of Commons: 'I have the chance of getting my ideas tested by economic + [sic] business pundits.'[6] The enthusiasm was soon to dissipate. He produced a paper dated 29 July 1930 in which he set out his view on the economic difficulties: 'The general cause of the difficulties of British industry lies in its slowness of adjustment to economic changes affecting both home and world markets.' Britain had particularly suffered as a result of certain peculiar factors: not just the return to the gold standard, but also the 'conservatism of British industrialists', a 'loss of leeway' to, and protectionism in, other countries, debt and taxation, and, perhaps most surprisingly, the loss of labour market flexibility, with workers less mobile as a result of the 'growth of social services and trade union safeguards, in themselves highly desirable'.[7] The paper produced no discernible result, and was not even discussed by the cabinet. Attlee was disappointed with the government's failure to tackle unemployment. On 1 November 1930, he wrote to Tom: 'It needs a very strong push to overcome the timidity + conservatism of some ministers some departments of the Civil Service notably the Treasury + the Board of Trade.'[8] However, on 3 November 1930, Attlee stuck firmly to the government line during the debate on the king's speech: 'Our policy with regard to industry is perfectly clear. We do not believe in the capitalist system … we should like to see it ended, but the country has not yet said that we shall end it. We have no mandate for that.'[9] Clydeside MP James Maxton intervened, stating 'You have not got a mandate for anything else,' and Attlee responded strongly that he was 'asking us to shatter it to bits in the economic condition of the country at this time, and this is a thing you cannot do. What we have to do is to carry on the Government of the country in an exceedingly difficult position.'[10]

Attlee also provided assistance to Christopher Addison at the Board of Agriculture. Addison, who came from rural Lincolnshire, took over as minister from Noel Buxton on 5 June 1930. His under-secretary, Lord de la Warr, was in the Lords, so Attlee filled in on the duties of under-secretary in the Commons. Attlee was very impressed by Addison, who, in his view, had 'turned out to be about the best + most rigorous minister we've got. He knows how to make his department work + can work with others.'[11] It was very useful for Attlee to have had a sensible role model like Addison to follow. Prior to taking on the job, Attlee had applied his anti-private sector instincts to agriculture. On 21 February 1930, for example, he spoke during the second reading of the Rural Amenities Bill: 'There is a large part of our rural activities which ought to be removed from mere profiteering.'[12] His central view remained the same, but it certainly became more nuanced during the year. On 18 November 1930, he spoke in favour of the Agricultural Land (Utilization) Bill: 'We assert with regard to agriculture what we assert with regard to other industries, namely, that the assets of the community should be properly used.'[13] Addison's impression on Attlee was a lasting one, and he was leader of the House of Lords throughout Attlee's premiership.

On 2 March 1931, Sir Charles Trevelyan resigned from his post as minister at the Board of Education, and was replaced by Hastings Lees-Smith, who in turn left the post of postmaster-general vacant. Attlee was appointed to it and had four months in the role before returning to the opposition benches. It involved responsibility for the Post Office and other communications, including telegraphy. This was a job that could involve the mundane and trivial, but also more important questions of the development of communication systems and the neutrality of the BBC, as a selection of Attlee's parliamentary speeches illustrates. On 19 March 1931 he dealt with the key issue of broadcasting controversial matters: 'Some hon. Members say that there is too much of one thing, others that there is too much propaganda. ... In the matter of controversial broadcasts I think the ... [BBC] ... is steering a very careful course.'[14] Just over a month later, on 21 April, he was pressing for increasing the use of the telephone: 'if you want a cheap telephone service, a fully developed service, you cannot get it by discouraging people from using the telephone, but only by an increased user [sic].'[15] Yet, minor concerns were never too far away. On 31 July Attlee answered a question about whether he was aware that a new type of telephone 'cannot be taken to pieces for cleaning'; and asked if he would 'take such action as is possible ... to avoid the unhygienic conditions that might otherwise arise?' Attlee said that it 'is not necessary to take a telephone instrument to pieces in order to maintain it in a hygienic condition. Dismantling is very liable to damage the delicate parts of the instrument, and it is undesirable to facilitate such action.'[16]

Even with the question of the cleanliness of one's telephone, Attlee enjoyed the job enormously: he set about his work enthusiastically and turned his mind immediately to public relations. He set up a publicity committee and accepted its recommendation to create a public relations service. He took advice from the private sector. Businessmen whom he consulted included Sir F. W. Goodenough from the gas industry, and Sir William Crawford from advertising. He used the newspapers to advertise the Post Office and, again using the business expertise of the expert Harold Whitehead, sought to put into practice his desire to develop use of the telephone. Attlee also wished to decentralize the Post Office from the structure around Secretary Sir Evelyn Murray. His 'plan was the formulation of a functional council of officials under the Chairmanship of the Postmaster-General to deal with policy matters. It was adopted in substance by the Bridgeman Committee [Sir William Bridgeman later became chairman of the BBC] ... and provided a desirable reform.'[17]

It would be an overstatement to say that Attlee's tenure as postmaster-general bore any significance beyond a competent few months in charge of a large government enterprise during which he came up with some useful ideas. It would also be a mistake to try and impose comparisons from later Labour Party troubles over nationalization and privatization many years in the future. But, despite his earlier fight against private companies in electricity provision, there is no doubt that Attlee's tenure as postmaster-general had some distinctly 'New Labour' features – a concern with public relations, together with use of the media, a willingness to engage the private sector and adopt its ideas and a desire if necessary to reform the way the public sector was run.

Attlee's period in the second Labour government and his ability to enjoy himself while the government crumbled was another classic example of his ability to compartmentalize his life. It was not that he did not care about the fate of the government. Quite the opposite, in fact, but he was clearly able to deal with things within his own sphere of executive authority without constant worry about matters beyond his control. However, things were going from bad to worse for the government as a whole. Attlee wrote to Tom on 23 August 1931: 'I have been summoned to see the PM tomorrow, but whether on certain … [post office related] matters or on the general situation I know not.'[18] In fact, MacDonald told Attlee, and the rest of the government ministers outside the cabinet, of the fall of the Labour government and his decision to head a new coalition government.

MacDonald duly formed the national government, taking Chancellor Snowden, dominions secretary Jimmy Thomas and Lord Chancellor John Sankey with him. He was joined by four Conservatives, Stanley Baldwin, Neville Chamberlain, Sir Philip Cunliffe-Lister, and Sir Samuel Hoare and two Liberals, Sir Herbert Samuel and the Marquis of Reading. The Labour Party's governing national executive, the general council of the TUC and the parliamentary party's consultative committee met on 26 August and issued a joint manifesto, which declared that the new national government was 'determined to attack the standard of living of the workers in order to meet a situation caused by a policy pursued by private banking interests in the control of which the public has no part.'[19] The parliamentary party met on 28 August with members of the general council of the TUC also present. Arthur Henderson became leader in place of MacDonald. Attlee wrote to Tom on 2 September 1931: 'Things are pretty damnable – I fear we are in for a regime of fake economy and a general attack on the workers' standard of life.'[20] He directed his fire at MacDonald and Snowden: 'MacDonald had no constructive ideas, while at the Treasury Philip Snowden had fallen completely under the spell of orthodox finance and the influence of Montagu Norman, Governor of the Bank of England.'[21] The Labour Party's governing hierarchy seemed to share Attlee's disdain for MacDonald and expelled him and his followers from the party. They subsequently formed the 'National Labour Party'. Attlee, meanwhile, was back in opposition, where he was to stay for the rest of the decade.

Chapter 8
BACK IN OPPOSITION, 1931–35

On 10 September 1931, Snowden, as chancellor of the national government, introduced a budget cutting pay in the public sector and unemployment benefit by 10 per cent and, on 21 September, he abandoned the gold standard that the Labour government had sacrificed so much to preserve. Snowden's behaviour disgusted Attlee; on 2 October, in the Commons, he attacked him in unusually strong terms:

> The Chancellor has broken all Parliamentary records. He has not merely produced two Budgets in one Session; he has produced one on behalf of the Labour Party and the other on behalf of the united Capitalist parties. These two Budgets are based on entirely different social philosophies. The first one still retains, to some extent at all events, the social philosophy which the right hon. Gentleman has preached with such extreme success for the last 30 or 40 years; and the second one is based on a wholly different outlook. ... These two Budgets have, however, one thing in common: they are both quite inadequate to deal with the position of the national finances.[1]

The Labour Party was in crisis. The party conference at Scarborough began on 5 October with a sombre report from the national executive committee: 'It is with profound regret that the National Executive Committee have to record that after the greater portion of this Report had been prepared, political events occurred that necessitated the resignation of the second Labour Government.'[2] A melancholy conference heard on its final day, 8 October, that parliament was dissolved for a general election as the new government sought a 'doctor's mandate' to deal with the country's problems. The national government was divided between the protectionism of the Conservatives and the free trade principles of both Snowden and the 'National Liberal' faction led by Herbert Samuel. But it bridged this gap by allowing separate views within the campaign on this issue, and united itself around the position of standing as a bulwark against socialism; Snowden famously described the Labour Party's election platform as 'Bolshevism run mad'. MacDonald brandished banknotes to remind the public of German hyper-inflation of the mid-1920s. According to Attlee, Snowden also 'supported Walter Runciman and others in the lying story that the Labour Government had improperly used the money in the Post Office Savings Bank to maintain the unemployment fund.'[3]

In the event, the poll of Tuesday 27 October 1931 was quite simply a disaster for Labour. Reduced from 288 seats to just 52, it lost over 1.7 million votes, polling just over 6.6 million, 30.6 per cent of the votes cast. The national government took a commanding total of over 14.5 million votes – 67 per cent of the vote. Within this total, the Conservatives won 473 seats, the largest number of seats won by a single party at a general election in the whole of the twentieth century. MacDonald's National Labour Party won 13 seats, the National Liberals 35, and the remainder of the Liberals 33. This total number of Liberal seats was once again above that of Labour, the only saving grace being that the total Liberal share of the vote was only around 2.2 million, with another four independent Liberals sitting with Labour on the opposition benches. In Limehouse, Attlee's majority was cut to just 551. With such a small margin of victory, Attlee was undoubtedly lucky, but he could argue he deserved to hold on: he had a record in both social work and local politics, and was no mere carpetbagger.

Labour's parliamentary party was decimated. Of the old cabinet, aside from the four ministers who had joined the national government, only the former first commissioner of works, George Lansbury, remained. Of the government ministers, only the former solicitor-general Stafford Cripps and Attlee retained their seats. At the parliamentary party's first post-election meeting, Arthur Henderson sent Attlee a message that Lansbury would be proposed as leader with Attlee himself as deputy. This was unopposed, and Lansbury, Attlee and Cripps shared the leader of the opposition's room at the House of Commons: 'One ... was always present on the Front Bench throughout the sittings.'[4] Henderson remained leader of the party in name only until his resignation in October 1932. He did return to parliament, winning the Clay Cross by-election of 1 September 1933, but he was by then just days short of his seventieth birthday and was in any event chairing the World Disarmament Conference in Geneva. The new trio at the top of the parliamentary party were there to stay. In terms of representing the social classes in Britain, they were an ideal combination – working-class Lansbury, middle-class Attlee and distinctly aristocratic Cripps, son of Lord Parmoor – but they did not resonate with the British public. At the 1935 general election, the national government became the last government in the twentieth-century to be elected on a greater than 50 per cent share of the popular vote, which was hardly a resounding endorsement for their leadership.

The effect of the election for Attlee was to elevate him in the space of just three months from a competent, if nondescript, junior figure, to one of the party's three leading figures. Over the next four years, until the general election of 1935, he had an incredible opportunity to stamp his mark on the party. In the House of Commons, he had numerous opportunities to speak, and while he might not have produced sparkling invective, he did find himself able to land blows on the government and to set out the alternative vision in which he believed. Yet, Attlee has received his fair share of criticism for his parliamentary speeches during this period. The Labour historian Henry Pelling said that: 'Attlee and Cripps … inclined to … policies of extreme and barren militancy. Cripps … made speeches about the "sinister influence" of Buckingham Palace and … a temporary dictatorship by the party if Labour should win a general election. Attlee was more discreet … but his views were almost as extreme.'[5]

Considering the content of Attlee's speeches, this judgement is harsh. It is true that at one stage he did advocate the abolition of the House of Lords, but even then it was as something that was to happen at some point undefined in the future: 'One hopes to live long enough to see the House of Lords abolished and single Chamber Government established. … We do not think that it can be reformed. We think it ought to be abolished.'[6] However, most of Attlee's speeches centred on the major issues of the day – the government of India and wider issues with regard to the empire, including import tariffs; the country's spending on armaments; and, critically, of course, the economy and the basis upon which it should be run and organized. Jack Lawson recalled that 'Attlee, slight of figure, standing at the Despatch Box, must have felt submerged; but he showed no sign of it.'[7] If anything, Attlee's speeches during this period represent not a period of reckless extremism in rhetoric, but a manifesto of policies not in the political mainstream at the time but that he was to implement as prime minister in the years after 1945. After 1918, the Labour Party's two worst twentieth-century election defeats were in 1931 and 1983. Both were followed by landslide victories within 14 years. The difference between the first and second was that, in 1945, the voting public had moved towards Labour policy; in 1997, the Labour Party had had to adjust to the changing demands of the electorate.

When Attlee attacked the new national government on 11 November in the debate on the king's speech, he set out his priorities. It was now clear that unemployment was a lasting problem, and Attlee wanted positive state action to deal with it: 'in this Speech there is no suggestion whatever made about unemployment, not even "the passing tribute of a sigh".' Labour believed 'that the time has come when *laissez faire* is entirely out of date in world economic affairs ... [and] ... when you are dealing with the affairs of this country. We believe that what is needed for the world is coordinated economic planning.'[8] It was uplifting stuff and, despite the gloomy political outlook, Attlee was reasonably satisfied both with the tiny parliamentary party's efforts in responding to the national government and with his own personal achievements. On 16 November, he wrote to Tom: 'We put up a fair show on the address. ... We are a very happy family in the party and some of our fellows will now get their opportunity. ... We want to get the party away from immediate and on to basic socialism.'[9] He added: 'I gather that the PO [Post Office] regretted my departure which is satisfactory. It is a funny position being one of the seniors in the House now. I see that I've been put on the Cmtee [*sic*] of Privileges a very Elder statesman position.'[10] At this stage Attlee was a matter of months away from his forty-eighth birthday, certainly not by any means in the twilight of his political career. However, had he not been pushed to prominence by the demise of so many of his colleagues, he may well have just drifted into obscurity.

As it was, on 23 November, Attlee continued to set out the Labour vision of the future. This time the subject was free trade, which was to be a key issue in the early years of the national government. The party was not

for Protection or for Free Trade. We believe that industry has ... to be organized ... importation has got to be controlled. ... We are not satisfied unless the State gets full advantage to itself and to the people of this country in return for the advantages which it bestows.[11]

He also continued his interest in India. Leaving aside his previous views on the impossibility of dominion status, Attlee could now speak freely in opposition. Both main party leaders were committed to dominion status, and the situation had changed. On 25 November, he declared: 'we in this party stand for India's control of her own affairs ... our position is that India, as has been said, must be allowed to make her own mistakes.'[12] If Attlee's interest in India had been peripheral prior to the Simon Commission, it had now become central to his political aims. On 2 December, Attlee spoke in a debate on the government's policy on India after the second 'Round Table Conference', which Gandhi attended after agreeing to call off his campaign of civil disobedience in a deal with the viceroy, Lord Irwin. The prime minister opened the debate, with Attlee making the second speech on the problems of India: 'On their successful solution depends not only the future ... of ... people in India, not only the future of our own country, but ... the future of the world. I believe the solution of the questions between Europe and Asia will depend very largely on what is done.'[13]

When Attlee wrote to Tom on 18 December, he again showed his extra-ordinary ability to compartmentalize. After the Labour Party's great travails, and its relegation to a position that left it at least a generation away from political power, he was able to see the positive side: 'I had a very strenuous time during the session, having to speak on something or other every other day almost. GL [George Lansbury] makes an excellent leader. He has far more idea of teamwork than JRM [James Ramsay MacDonald] ever had.' It seemed that the party leadership was harmonious: 'We are quite a happy family.' As for the national government: 'I think a genuine Tory protectionist government would be better at this juncture than this crossbred animal. I fear JRM has completely gone. He revels in titled friends. He will have a rude awakening soon.'[14] Attlee no doubt had a more comfortable Christmas in 1931 that many others within the Labour Party.

It was probably just as well, since, after the Christmas recess, Attlee returned to his busiest year yet in parliament. As he put it modestly: 'In 1932 I filled more columns of Hansard than any other Member and, as I am generally con-sidered to be rather a laconic speaker, it can be judged that my interventions in Debate were numerous.'[15] One of the most significant political events of 1932 was the passing of the Import Duties Act, introduced into the House of Com-mons on 4 February 1932, which set a general 10 per cent tariff on imports. Attlee kept a distinctive line between those who believed in protection and the doctrinaire free traders: 'We … are not bigoted Free Traders or bigoted Protec-tionists. … We do not say that there is any awful sin in using it, but we do say that a tariff is a weapon that should be utilized only … in pursuit of some definite and clear policy.'[16] At the Imperial Economic Conference at Ottawa later in the year, Britain's dominions agreed on a system of imperial preference, which in effect placed the trade barriers around the empire. Whatever Attlee's view, the tariff barriers were cemented in place.

Unsurprisingly, the economic situation occupied most of his time in the house. On 20 April 1932, he opposed Neville Chamberlain's budget, which had been introduced the previous day. Despite a surplus, and having introduced protective tariffs, Chamberlain offered no tax reductions or increases in unem-ployment benefit. Attlee spoke in strong terms: 'It is clear that the nation, as interpreted by hon. and right hon. Gentlemen opposite, means the privileged classes, and not the workers. This Budget is going to put a heavier burden on the shoulders of those who can least afford to bear it.'[17] Given his lack of experience in economic matters, Attlee was quietly pleased with his perform-ance, writing to Tom on 25 April that the 'speech was, I think, considered a success. It was rather an ordeal. … I do not move easily amid the arcana of exchange, gold standards etc.'[18] Attlee was developing his economic rhetoric and, on 9 May, argued in colourful terms for direct government intervention to redistribute wealth:

> what is really needed in a healthy body is a free circulation of the blood to every part. If the blood – in this case currency – does not reach the extremities, you get cold feet and hands and the people who are in the chilliest part of the body politic today are the poorest people, because currency does not circulate freely to them. I suggest that there is another danger besides that of anaemia or apoplexy. There might be a clot in the brain or the heart. I suggest that the concentration of wealth in a small part of the nation affects both the brain and the heart of the nation.[19]

On 15 July, Attlee was still positive, both about the performance of the tiny parliamentary party and the future:

> I am somewhat relieved at the ending of the session as it has been pretty strenuous. I find that I have delivered 93 speeches in this house being second only to Cripps. It is generally admitted in the House that our fellows have done extraordinarily well … we hope to give a lead at the Leicester conference.[20]

The party conference opened on 3 October and Attlee, reflecting his new-found status, put one of the opening questions to Arthur Henderson, still the party leader in name (he resigned on 25 October), asking about a 'practical programme of international cooperation' with the Social Democratic Labour Party and Socialist International.[21] This was the conference dominated by the idea that the 'bankers' ramp' had brought down Labour in 1931, and the party accepted the proposal to nationalize the Bank of England. The conference also brought into the open the conflict between two important figures within the movement, who were both to be very significant in Attlee's career – Herbert Morrison and Ernest Bevin. Morrison, born in 1888, had been mayor of Hackney in 1920–21 and MP for South Hackney twice, in 1923–24 and in 1929–31, when he had served under MacDonald as minister for transport. Out of parliament, in 1933, he became leader of the Labour Group on the London County Council, and, when Labour won the county council election of 1934, its leader.

Under MacDonald, Morrison had sought to create a London Passenger Transport Board, a seven-member body responsible for public transport within the capital, and the national government had enacted his scheme in April 1933, with various tube lines, tramways and buses transferred to the new organization. Bevin, born in 1881, was a key figure in the formation of the

Transport and General Workers' Union in 1922, which became Britain's largest union. He served as its first general secretary, holding the post until 1945. The conflict between the two men was, on the face of it, fairly innocuous – whether trade unionists should as of right sit on boards set up to run nationalized industries. Naturally, Bevin favoured the idea. The issue itself was less important to Attlee than what it symbolized. These two men, both of his generation within the party, were to be in conflict over the next two decades – and mostly to Attlee's benefit.

Another of Attlee's potential rivals within the party, Cripps, also started to show a lack of judgement towards his immediate career prospects, which served not only to neutralize him as a potential threat for the future leadership but also to see him expelled from the party for a period. In August 1932 the left-wing ILP (Independent Labour Party), under the chairmanship of Fenner Brockway, had decided to disaffiliate. Formed in 1893, it had been one of the foundation stones of the Labour Representation Committee in 1900, and affiliated to the Labour Party, as it became known, in 1906. Attlee was not unduly concerned and told Tom on 8 August: 'I see that the ILP have determined to go their own way. I fancy that they will lose a very big proportion of their membership. The trouble is that they have no ideas on which to work.'[22] He was correct: membership did fall, and much of the status of the ILP was based on the personal standing of its central figures, notably James Maxton. Of greater significance was the formation of the Socialist League, an alternative movement formed by ILP members who remained in the party. Bevin, who had been the chair of the Society for Socialist Information and Propaganda, a group within the party that had been founded in 1931, was ousted, and Cripps, together with others such as the young Michael Foot, became leading lights within the Socialist League.

As for the national government, the major concern for delegates was the household means test. Introduced in 1931, it sought to reduce the cost of unemployment benefit by forcing claimants to exhaust the income of other members of their families before claiming a 'transitional benefit' (so labelled in Neville Chamberlain's 1927 Unemployment Insurance Act) that was available after the standard 15-week national insurance period. In practice, this meant that the whole family would be subjected to a humiliating investigation into its household finances and assets. The Amalgamated Engineering Union proposed a resolution of protest.

Meanwhile, Attlee kept up the pressure in the Commons on unemployment; on 7 November he lashed out at the government's arguments about a lack of money: 'let us remember that … is … what the bankers said in the Great War …: "You cannot go on with the War, because there is no more money" …[but] … we got on with it.'[23] He spoke on the fourth day of the debate on the king's speech on 25 November, and lamented the government's failure to intervene in the nation's economy. MacDonald was the central target of his attack: 'When the Prime Minister has a problem he is very pleased to face it. … He generally makes a declaration that he means to face them, and he then generally gets noisy and thumps the Box and the thing passes off in smoke and nothing happens.'[24] By 1 December, he was unable to contain his disdain for MacDonald in public, commenting that the 'Government took over one of our misfortunes – the Prime Minister.'[25]

It left Attlee reflective over the Christmas of 1932 and he wrote rather pessimistically to Tom on New Year's Day 1933. While Attlee's belief in world government was to become a central one for him, he accepted that solving domestic and international problems was going to be no more than a distant goal: 'I saw GL [George Lansbury] last Friday and found him very cheerful and going on well, but it will be a long job. … I am being forced to the conclusion that nothing short of a world state will be really effective in preventing war.'[26] Yet, aside from a burglary during the summer of 1932 – he wrote to Tom on 1 September 1932 that: 'Two blokes, obviously not professionals climbed in through the bathroom window which was left open. They ransacked the study being under the delusion that despatch cases must contain valuables. They also started on collecting silver articles' – Attlee had every reason to be positive. Politically, he was progressing quickly: he was performing well in the House of Commons and was the deputy to an ageing leader who was unlikely to be in the job much longer. While he was not to know it, his expertise in military matters was also about to become extremely useful. On 30 January 1933, Adolf Hitler was sworn in as chancellor of Germany and the issue of rearmament was to become a dominant theme of the 1930s.

In the short-term, he kept up the pressure on unemployment, declaring in the Commons on 16 February: 'The Government are afraid that if they put people into work somehow or other they will not be able to balance their budget.'[27] On 26 April, he spoke on the latest budget proposals and, three years before Keynes published his *General Theory*, he posited borrowing while in a deficit: 'Why is it so very wrong to borrow for the unemployed and so right to make no adequate provision for the unemployed, leave yourself with an unbalanced Budget and a heavy deficit, and then to borrow to meet that deficit?'[28] However, it was to foreign affairs that his attention turned. He opened the Easter adjournment debate on 13 April with a wide-ranging speech criticizing the 'Four Power Pact' that Mussolini proposed on 19 March, which in effect left the affairs of Europe in the hands of Britain, France, Germany and Italy at the expense of smaller nations, supported Germany's claim for the redress of grievance under the Versailles settlement, but wished to prevent the persecution of minorities.[29] Attlee's early view was that, while he abhorred the Nazi regime, the Versailles settlement was partly to blame for creating the monster, declaring in the Commons on 7 November: 'The party on this side … loathe the German regime probably more than anyone in this House, but we have to recognise that this Frankenstein has been made by the victorious Powers.' Notably, he did not want to ostracize Germany and continued to argue for world government:

> I do not believe that you will do very much by outlawing the Nazi regime … the whole failure since 1919 has been the failure to implement and develop what really was recognized at the time of the Peace Treaties, namely that you have got beyond the individual States and that you have to have some super-government of the world.[30]

Attlee's reasoning towards world government as the only true way to prevent conflict may yet still prove to be accurate, but in the 1930s it was totally impractical. Only a matter of days before the speech, Germany had withdrawn from the League of Nations, and the United States had never joined since Congress rejected President Woodrow Wilson's wishes in 1920.

Within the Labour Party, pacifism remained strong. At the 1933 party conference, in October, at Hastings, the official position was that war would only be supported if it was collective action through the League of Nations. Attlee's confidence had grown significantly and came out in a disagreement with, of all people, Ernest Bevin. Bevin had criticized the House of Lords for killing off a bill to raise the school leaving age. Attlee, however, defended his central belief in both constitutionalism and democracy: 'If you go to the Crown without a mandate to deal with the House of Lords, you will be sent back, and that is exactly where the danger of Fascism comes in. The danger of Fascism is for people to feel that democracy is not going to be effective.'[31] The Attlee of 1931 or 1932 was unlikely to have stood up to the dominant Bevin in this way. Such a growth in stature was well timed. In December 1933, Lansbury's illness gave Attlee the chance to act as leader for nine months. The significance of Henderson's message to the party for Lansbury to be elected leader and Attlee deputy after the general election defeat of 1931 was now clear. Cripps, while certainly part of the leadership team, did not have this formal title and had no claim to take over.

During this period, Attlee struck a careful balance between the pressing issues of foreign affairs and the party's major domestic concerns. In the Commons on 27 February he supported the hunger march, protesting against the Unemployment Insurance Bill, which provided for rates of assistance to be set nationally rather than locally,[32] and which would have led to lower rates in some areas. Eventually, while the government set up a centralized system of administration, the threatened lower rates did not materialize. On 17 April he lambasted the budget and told the chancellor, Neville Chamberlain:

> I should like to congratulate him … but I regret that I am entirely unable to do so. I think it is quite the meanest budget on record. … We regard it as an insult to the unemployed, from whom millions and millions have been taken, that they are being given, in exchange, a few paltry words of thanks, a few words of insolence and £3,500,000 and told that they must rest content.[33]

On 15 May, he intervened in a debate on the mining industry to assert that the introduction of health and safety measures should not be precluded by general economic circumstances. He declared: 'We should see that we do not buy our bread at the price of the lives of miners.'[34] On 6 June, reminiscing about his days in charge of the Post Office, he argued for better wages for low-paid postal workers.[35]

Attlee also called for strong action against fascists at home. On 14 June, in the Commons, he denounced Oswald Mosley and demanded an investigation into the British Union of Fascists after violence at the Olympia meeting of 7 June 1934.[36] Violence between fascists and anti-fascists was a feature of the mid-1930s, culminating with the Battle of Cable Street in the East End of London on 4 October 1936. The government's response in legislative terms was to ban the wearing of political uniforms and make police permission for marches a requirement under the Public Order Act of 1936. Yet, in 1934, Attlee remained convinced that the legal system was biased against the left, and was not afraid to express this view in strong terms. The subject of his ire was the Incitement to Disaffection Bill, which criminalized 'seducing' members of the armed forces from their duty. On 16 April 1934, in the Commons, Attlee said that Britain would become like Germany, where in Berlin people found in possession of John Stuart Mill's *On Liberty* had been arrested 'because of the danger that the book might overthrow the state'.[37] On 30 October, he attacked the very foundations of the judicial system. Juries, he declared, were inherently biased against the left. 'It is time that we debunked this idea of the impartiality of the law.'[38] Quite what Attlee would have made of modern-day anti-terror laws, with weeks of detention without charge allowed in exceptional cases is a moot point. In the short term, it is doubtful that this view of the legal system would have been expressed if he had seriously seen the Labour Party as a contender for government at the next general election, which had to be held by 1936 at the latest.

On foreign affairs, Attlee's line was one of strong support for the League of Nations and for enforcing its decisions. Yet, he was in a difficult position because the party still stood for disarmament and, when he spoke on 8 March, the confusion in Labour Party thinking was evident: 'We on this side are … for total disarmament, because we are realists and we recognize that war is no longer, if it ever was, "the sport of kings".' However, he added: 'In order to get peace it is necessary to have something more than mere reduction or even abolition of armaments. You must have a rule of law and the means to enforce that law.'[39] What was entirely unclear is what this 'means' was: if there were no armaments, how would any country acting in contravention of the League of Nations be brought back into line? How could any settlement ever be enforced? On 14 March, he prophesized complete destruction: 'It may be a few years off, but, unless the nations of the world … try to work out some way by which the world can settle those difficulties without war, we may find civilization crashing.'[40]

In his famous *History of the Labour Party*, the historian G. D. H. Cole characterized the strategic difficulty the party faced. Labour would leave the Conservatives to carry out rearmament and oppose it, not in principle but the 'Tory form' of it. 'For the Tories this attitude was a godsend. It enabled them to defend their own policy of half-hearted rearmament combined with "appeasement" on the ground that Labour opposition and its effects on public opinion did not allow them to do anything else.'[41] In other words, Labour's very opposition to rearmament was in fact giving the national government a further argument in support of doing that very thing; and to change policy would be extremely difficult due to Labour's deep pacifist roots, the greatest symbol of which was the leader himself, Lansbury. When Attlee criticized the lack of clarity in the government's foreign policy on 13 July – 'you either come out definitely for a collective system or you do not'[42] – it was his own party that he needed to deal with first.

The Labour Party's position against the necessity to spend on rearmament seemed to find some objective justification. On 18 June 1935, the Anglo-German naval agreement had limited the growth of the German navy to 35 per cent of that of the British, apparently reducing the need for naval rearmament.[43] In addition, that summer the Labour Party's support for the league seemed reflective of public opinion. The British League of Nations Union ran a private referendum containing five questions on the issue of Britain's membership of the League of Nations and the action to be taken in the event of one nation attacking another. The results on 27 June 1935 showed support for membership of the league at over 11 million votes, with only just over 350,000 against. Over 10 million people supported non-military action against an aggressor country, with only just over 600,000 against; a military response 'if necessary' was backed by over 6.8 million people with around 2.3 million against. The chair of the League of Nations Union was Lord Robert Cecil, who had been the senior barrister at Attlee's chambers of 4 Paper Buildings some 30 years before.

The issue initially came to a head at the 1934 party conference, held in October at Southport. Cripps, with the Socialist League, denounced the League of Nations as a capitalist club and came into conflict with Attlee. Attlee steered his way carefully, supporting the league and sanctions rather than military force as a method of enforcement, winning the debate by 1.519 million votes to 673,000. It was also a triumph for him personally, with election to the national executive committee on 2 October. In Division III: Constituency and Central Labour Parties and Federations of Constituency Labour Parties, Attlee came third, with 1.563 million votes, behind Hugh Dalton (1.893 million votes) and, at the top, Morrison (2.134 million votes).[44] Morrison's topping of the poll was, however, worrying for Attlee's future progression to the leadership. Despite an absence from parliament of three years, he had gained 25 per cent more votes than Attlee: evidently the London Labour Party victory in the 1934 county council elections was a more powerful factor than Attlee's valiant displays in the Commons. Dalton, a junior minister at the Foreign Office in the second Labour government, also absent from parliament, was ahead as well. Even the smallest of swings in Labour's favour would bring such figures back into parliament after the next general election, and the result showed that, while Attlee was now a substantial figure in his own right, he was going to face stiff competition from others to be leader of the party. However, the wider party membership and trade unions had no vote in any leadership contest (and did not do so until 1981, when the 'electoral college' system was introduced). So on the positive side Attlee would only need to persuade the MPs, but they would undoubtedly take their local party members' wishes into account.

The year 1935 also saw the culmination of the work on India started by the Simon Commission. MacDonald's attempts at three 'round table' conferences had failed. The Congress Party had failed to attend the first, from November 1930; in the second, from September 1931, Hindus and Muslims had been unable to reach agreement on safeguards within any political solution, and Gandhi opposed MacDonald's 'Communal Award' giving separate electorates to certain minorities. The final effort, from November 1932, saw Gandhi absent. On 27 March 1933 Attlee spoke in a Commons debate on constitutional reform for India:

> We reaffirm the right of the Indian peoples to full self-government and self-determination ... the policy of the British Government should be ... cooperation ... establishing India, at the earliest possible moment and by her consent, as an equal partner with the other members of the British Commonwealth of Nations.

With the failure of the 'round table' conferences, Attlee was an obvious choice to serve on the joint parliamentary committee chaired by Lord Linlithgow (soon to become Viceroy of India in 1936) set up to propose a solution. After its report in November 1934, the government introduced the Government of India Bill, which had found its way onto the statute book by August 1935. It introduced directly elected provincial assemblies, in which there would be increased Indian representation elected directly, and a central federation government (but with 'reserved subjects' like defence withheld – which in the event was not introduced). Burma was separated from India. The act was clearly a step towards democratization and Attlee could argue that it was essentially what the Simon Commission had envisaged.

However, for those in the Labour Party who were pro-Congress, it was a disappointment. The act generated so much controversy that Sir Samuel Hoare, the secretary of state for India, deliberately fudged the issue of the overall aim of the act to appease Tory die-hards who wished to hang onto British rule in India at all costs, and had not included any of the preamble that would usually set out the purpose of the legislation. The default position was still that set out by Irwin, of an ultimate goal of dominion status. The act therefore focused on the division of power between the British, Hindus, Muslims and Indian princes who, it was hoped, would join the federation, but, in the event, did not. The provincial legislatures retained a communal element, with both 'general' seats and seats reserved for certain communities. Attlee's complex systems were not adopted. Some legislatures were unicameral; some were bicameral and the electorate was fairly limited, using a property qualification to qualify to vote. The province governors retained powers of intervention as regards threats to law and order and protecting minority rights. Attlee's argument that the reforms were an advance when he broadcast in January 1935 was supported by Congress's takeover at the provincial level, which was a marked *de facto* change, but the offer of a central government was too restrictive to secure Congress's participation (at the centre the viceroy remained supremely powerful, with not just foreign affairs and defence within his remit, but priority given to spending on British commitments: 'dyarchy' remained); the attainment of dominion status still had no timescale.

Given the Labour Party vote against the act, the issue of India might, in other circumstances, have been a problem for Attlee at the 1935 party conference, held from 29 September at Brighton. As it was, Italian forces invaded Abyssinia on 3 October. This was the acid test for the League of Nations: a European nation was clearly an aggressor and the league would have to act to retain any credibility. Dalton moved a resolution supporting the use of 'all the necessary measures provided by the Covenant'.[45] Attlee defended the principle of collective security:

I would like everyone who objects to our policy to ask themselves this question. If, in January of this year, action had been taken firmly which had been effective in restraining Mussolini, would not they all have been going round on platforms and saying how much better the collective system was than the old war system? But mind you, that would only have been done successfully because there was the threat of force behind it.[46]

The main event, however, was to come later. Lansbury spoke to state strongly that he had 'never been more convinced that I am right, and that the Movement is making a terrible mistake, than I am to-day'.[47] Intriguingly, he singled out Attlee for praise:

I asked in Parliament – and Attlee has done it ably and consistently, and so have other of our members – this Government, during the last four years, to turn their minds away from war preparations, to turn their minds away from discussing the size of guns or the strength of poison gas, and to devote their energies to finding out how we would remove the causes of war.[48]

Bevin, who for some time had been moving towards a position in favour of rearmament, lambasted Lansbury and, in so doing, destroyed his leadership of the party and paved the way for Attlee's succession. There is no suggestion that Attlee and Bevin were in cohoots for Attlee to become leader: they were not close, either personally or politically, and in any event there was no guarantee that Attlee would be the successor. Bevin faced down Lansbury: 'If he finds that he ought to take a certain course, then his conscience should direct him as to the course he should take. It is placing the Executive and the Movement in an absolutely wrong position to be ... [directed by] ... your conscience.'[49] He was equally harsh on Cripps, labelling him 'cowardly'.[50] The difficulty of reconciling the pacifist wing of the party with support for the use of force by the League of Nations was now firmly expressed in a divide between Lansbury and the party conference. His position as leader was clearly untenable and he resigned when parliament returned on 8 October.

On 23 October Baldwin, who had replaced MacDonald as prime minister on 7 June, called a general election for 14 November. Attlee, as deputy, became caretaker leader during the campaign with a full leadership contest to be held after the poll. Indeed, the Labour leadership election of 26 November 1935 was one of the most significant in the party's history. It chose not only a leader who served for 20 years but also the first Labour prime minister of a majority government. At the time, only Labour MPs had a vote: there would be 'rounds' in which, if no candidate won a majority of the votes cast, the candidate receiving the lowest number of votes would drop out, until a candidate won a majority of votes cast. Of course, the MPs could not possibly have foreseen how important their choice was to prove to be because the general election had left Labour a long way away from power: the party would need at least another two parliamentary terms to have any hope of winning an overall majority. The government won the best part of 12 million votes, constituting 53.7 per cent of the votes cast, winning 432 seats. While the Liberal total had fallen to just over 1.4 million votes, 6.4 per cent, winning 20 seats, Labour, now with just over 8.3 million votes, 37.9 per cent, took 154 seats. The manifesto was a very short document clearly prepared by a party that felt it had no chance of taking power. Containing a mere 181 words in criticism of the national government for its 'four barren years'[51] it concluded in vague terms: 'Labour asks the Nation for a Parliamentary Majority to promote Socialism at home and Peace abroad.'[52]

Had the Labour MPs realized how significant the choice was, the result might of course have been very different. As it was, Attlee was nominated along with Arthur Greenwood and Herbert Morrison. He commented rather cryptically: 'I did not take any steps in the matter but found that I had been nominated.'[53] But Attlee was ambitious and never likely to miss an opportunity. The early 1930s had not been easy for his family life. He was now a father of four. After the birth of Janet in February 1923, Felicity had been born in August 1924, his only son, Martin, in August 1927, and Alison in April 1930. Violet had been ill several times. She had been ill after the birth of Janet in 1923 and had a number of problems with her health since Attlee's time as postmaster-general. In the summer of 1930 she suffered from 'sleeping sickness' and had a couple of spells in Westminster Hospital. In October 1931, the Attlees moved from Woodford Green to Stanmore in Middlesex, principally to be nearer Violet's family.[54]

It was not until December 1931 that Attlee was able to write confidently to Tom that she had been 'distinctly better lately and when we are through the winter I expect she will continue to make progress.'[55] However, she was ill again in the summer of 1932; Attlee reported to Tom that she was improving by 15 July: 'Vi has not been so well but is better.' In January 1933 she was recovering from a poisoned foot; in April she was feeling tired with a heavy cold.[56] In October 1934, she suffered from 'nasty … lumbago … caused … [in Attlee's view] … partly by the sudden change to cold weather and partly due to over exertion during a hiatus in the domestic staff.'[57] Attlee also remarked to Tom that she was feeling tired again in April 1935.[58] But Attlee did not neglect his family in the early 1930s in order to pursue his career. Even in his busiest parliamentary year, 1932, he made sure that he spent *quality* time with his family. On free days, he would not just stay at home, but would, for example, go out for a picnic.[59] He had even considered leaving politics at the end of 1933 due to the financial strain, but the wealthy Cripps provided assistance, with a donation of £500 to be used as a salary for Attlee while filling in for Lansbury.[60] In standing for the leadership, Attlee was not signalling his priority for his career over his family, but he was showing a very natural determination *both* to continue his political advancement and enjoy his family life, even with Violet's health difficulties. When he became party leader, his financial position was eased by the 1937 Ministers of the Crown Act, which gave the leader of the opposition an annual £2000 salary. At home, he tried to ensure that Violet was not lonely when he was at work: by October 1936, a Swedish girl was staying at the Attlee home both to learn English and to provide companionship to Violet.[61]

Attlee presented the result as follows: in the first ballot, Attlee took 58 votes, Morrison 44 and Greenwood 32. Greenwood then dropped out and the final result was Attlee 88, Morrison 44.[62] Why Attlee won this leadership election is one of the enduring mysteries of Labour Party history. Of course, as caretaker leader, he did have the advantage of being *in situ* and most of the small number of Labour MPs who had sat in the 1931–35 parliament supported him, but direct evidence about the contest is scant. The Greenwood papers contain no explanation.[63] There are the accounts of Morrison (a defeated candidate) and Dalton (his key supporter). Both cited, perhaps surprisingly, the Freemasons as an important factor. Morrison cited the support of the 1931–35 Labour MPs for Attlee, but argued that Greenwood, as a Mason, had the support of most fellow Masons. Some Masons kept Morrison informed of the situation and, as he 'had been warned to expect, all but four of Greenwood's supporters voted for Attlee'.[64] Dalton concurred with this analysis: 'Attlee's vote was very near that of the little Party in the last Parliament. They were herding together against the newcomers.'[65] He added: 'Greenwood was the Masons' candidate.'[66] As for the Greenwood supporters moving to Attlee, the Masons had apparently met on 22 November and Dalton, in something of an understatement, noted that the incident had 'some historical interest'.[67] Dalton also felt that there had been a 'prejudice, surprisingly strong and widespread, against Morrison. There was a feeling that, if he got the Leadership now, he would keep it, but that, if Attlee got it, there might be a change later. This feeling helped to explain the swing on the second vote.'[68] Kenneth Harris has expressed the view that Morrison's conception of nationalized industries run by a state board was a problem for union-sponsored MPs.[69] Plausible though all these explanations are, they remain supposition, but, if true, Attlee's performance in the Commons and his ability to avoid making enemies, particularly in this case Greenwood, were critical features.

Morrison declined nomination as deputy leader, preferring instead to concentrate on his leadership of the London County Council Labour Party. Greenwood therefore took the role. Attlee, in his acceptance speech, 'was diffident about the importance of the position, as it were, thrust on him. He stressed that it was just for a single session and then a change could come.'[70] By any standards this was an odd first speech. If Greenwood supporters had indeed voted for Attlee with the prospect of a future change in mind, there is an argument that he was simply living up to expectations. However, the Labour Party faced an uphill struggle in parliament for the next four to five years: given the arithmetic, there was little prospect of winning any votes or influencing government policy. While Attlee was rarely one for inspiring rhetoric, a steely determination might have been the order of the day. Dalton famously wrote in his diary: 'A wretched, disheartening result. And a little mouse shall lead them!'[71] Morrison, however, was sceptical about Attlee's motives: 'I am certain ... that in his own mind he intended, as indeed he succeeded in doing, to hold on to the reins put into his ostensibly unwilling hands. The grip never weakened dangerously in sixteen years.'[72] Events bore out this explanation: Attlee *wanted* to lead the party and, unsurprisingly, was determined to preserve the position once he had attained it.

Chapter 9
LABOUR LEADERSHIP, 1935–39

Whatever the machinations in the Labour Party, the Italian conquest of Abyssinia continued apace. On 7 October the League of Nations cited Italy as the aggressor and sought to impose sanctions, but Italy's stance was unaffected. To try to resolve the crisis, British foreign secretary Sir Samuel Hoare and French foreign minister Pierre Laval agreed a pact in which Abyssinia would be partitioned with substantial sections going to the Italians. The public outcry was such that both governments had to dissociate themselves from the agreement. If collective security of nations was to be upheld, it apparently made little sense to reward an aggressor with territory. On 22 December Anthony Eden replaced Hoare as British foreign secretary. Attlee amply demonstrated his penchant for lighter satirical poetry:

> Ten little Neville boys sitting in a line
> Hoare met with Laval and then there were nine.[1]

In his autobiography, Attlee characterized the early years of his leadership as 'Labour and Defence', and it was in the development of this crisis that he made his first significant speech in the Commons after winning the leadership, the first day after parliament had reassembled. He replied to Hoare: 'we have unremittingly urged the Government to make support of the League the whole basis of its policy.'[2] In addition, he set up a Labour defence committee, which discussed defence problems and sought briefings from serving officers to help MPs become better informed. So far so good, but the judgement on the early years of Attlee's leadership is mixed. Dalton was prominent as Labour's official spokesman on foreign affairs in the later 1930s and his biographer, Ben Pimlott, argues that 'Attlee was regarded as little more than a figurehead, whose

2. Supporters campaigning for Attlee.

departure was frequently predicted.'[3] The difficulty in deposing Attlee was not his depth of support, but the fact that 'only an earthquake could shift a Party Leader *in situ* whose sole offence was his inadequacy.'[4] Yet, Attlee does still have his defenders. He held together a party riddled with pacifism. The historian John Swift concluded that, while Attlee was seen as 'a leader that would not lead ... Dissent and disagreement either had to be accommodated within the party or driven from it. Attlee chose the former option, and paid the price that this entailed, in terms of criticism of his leadership, without complaint.'[5] Another historian, Matthew Worley, has argued that 'Ultimately ... Labour's critique of appeasement helped undermine the Chamberlain government and allowed for Labour's eventual return to office as part of a wartime coalition in 1940.'[6]

The problem was not so much what Attlee did but what he did not do. His overall strategy was fairly obvious; as the threat from the fascist powers materialized, the Labour Party moved steadily towards rearmament, which led to his opposition to Chamberlain's 'peace in our time' agreement negotiated at Munich in October 1938. He was to have difficulties grappling with certain issues, including the Spanish Civil War, and his pro-Establishment role in the abdication was unhelpful. Also, he did not carve out a distinctive identity for himself. He did not 'lead from the front', for example, by taking distinctive policy positions and arguing them through conference; and he did not create a 'Clement Attlee' persona the general public could recognize. Yet, any analysis of a failure of leadership has to be set in context. Attlee had no *intention* of creating a personal style of leadership. He saw himself as a spokesman for the settled policy of the party and his leadership style was a consensual one, seeking a common position to advocate. Secondly, MacDonald's type of personal leadership style was viewed with deep suspicion after his betrayal of 1931; such a style of leadership was not politically feasible for the Labour Party. In a wider sense, the late 1930s showed that Attlee's style of leadership was unsuitable in certain circumstances. However, the government had a commanding majority; the opposition was not politically significant. The policy of appeasement was centred on Neville Chamberlain, prime minister from 1937, and it is difficult to see how he would have lost a peacetime election to Attlee had one been held in 1939 or 1940. Gallup polls placed government support at 54 per cent in February 1939 and 51 per cent in February 1940.[7] A distinctive, well-known leader of the opposition would surely have made a greater impact.

Not every criticism of Attlee was well founded. In the short term, he sought to keep up the pressure on the government regarding measures towards Italy and, in a Commons debate on oil sanctions in February 1936, he reaffirmed the Labour Party position on rearmament, that arms should only be used through the League of Nations.

The international situation was worsening. On 7 March Hitler reoccupied the Rhineland, which the Treaty of Versailles had demilitarized in 1919 as part of the restrictions on the defeated Germany. Germany had accepted demilitarization in the 1925 treaties of Locarno and was now in clear breach of its international obligations, but the national government again took no action.

The Labour Party put down a vote of censure on 23 June, which was defeated by 384 votes to 170. The party published Attlee's speech as a pamphlet. He said: 'I understand perfectly the pacifist position. I respect those who hold it, but I do not hold it myself. … We were prepared to stand for collective security. … I say quite frankly … the League may go on as a debating society, but the Government have killed it.'[8] Morrison claimed that Attlee missed an historic opportunity, that if he had not 'inadvisedly questioned the honour of Baldwin and insinuated that many of his party would vote for the Labour motion of censure or at least abstain – thereby, in the view of Sir Austen Chamberlain, closing the Tory ranks – the course of history might have been different'.[9] It is difficult to see this as anything other than an over-statement by Morrison. Even in the famous Norway debate of 7–8 May 1940, Chamberlain still obtained a comfortable majority of over 80, and the idea that four years previously there would have been enough disquiet in the Tory ranks to oust Baldwin or change policy is not credible.

Meanwhile, the march of fascism in Europe continued. On 16 July, rebel Spanish army officers under General Franco revolted against the 'Popular Front' left-wing coalition government. The Spanish Civil War had begun, crystallizing the divisions between left and right on the continent of Europe, with fascist Italy and Germany supporting Franco, and Soviet Russia on the side of the government. Unsurprisingly, therefore, at the 1936 party conference in Edinburgh, rearmament was again the key issue. On 6 October, during the morning session, Dalton moved a resolution to distinguish between an arms race against other countries and 'maintaining such defence forces as are consistent with our country's responsibility as a Member of the League of Nations'. However, 'the armed strength of the countries loyal to the League of Nations must be conditioned by the armed strength of the potential aggressors.'[10] Dalton's argument was based on the quite simple truth that, since the Labour government had left office in 1931, 'the international sky had gone black'.[11] Henderson seconded the resolution: 'the former ideas we adopted for resisting imperialist wars are no longer relevant.'[12] Morrison also spoke strongly in support of it, pointing out that the maintenance of forces consistent with membership of the league reflected the party's promises at the 1935 general election. In the afternoon session, however, the debate became more complex.

Sydney Silverman, then MP for Nelson and Colne, laid down a challenge to party policy, declaring, along the same lines as Cripps had a year before, that the party's confidence in the League of Nations was a mistake since it was the instrument of the Great Powers, that there should be no cooperation with the government on rearmament, a 'movement of resistance' in the country and an effort to 're-establish international working-class unity in active resistance to capitalist and imperial war'.[13] Bevin spoke strongly against this: 'I would vote for armaments to defend democracy and our liberty, I would also say, strive with all our might to build the great moral authority behind international law.'[14] Cripps then added a further dimension by advocating the 'middle way' course of referring the resolution back to the national executive 'in order that they may produce one which will decisively say whether we are for or against rearmament in the hands of the British National Government'.[15] Attlee spoke last, and his clear aim was to find a united position: 'I think there is a far greater degree of unanimity than is often thought.'[16]

He trod a careful line between what he declared the 'extreme' views of pacifism on the one hand, and opposing any kind of armament in the hands of a capitalist government on the other. He gave a strong lead that rearmament was necessary: 'we reaffirm our policy to maintain such defence forces as are consistent with our country's responsibilities.' He also gave careful reassurance that the government would continue to oppose the national government: 'we are not prepared to support a Government that has betrayed the League.'[17] After a spat between Bevin and Morrison over whether the vote should be held that afternoon or the next morning, Silverman's amendment was defeated on a show of hands. Cripps's reference back was defeated by just over 1.438 million votes to 652,000; the executive's resolution was then passed by 1.738 million votes to 657,000.[18] This represented a further subtle change of policy: not just the use of arms through the league, but Britain now building up its own armaments *consistent with its responsibilities* – that is, to an extent that Attlee could leave open to definition.

On the specific question of the Spanish Civil War, it was not so simple. Attlee declared for non-intervention (Bevin took the same view), then condemned it within a matter of weeks. The left, including Bevan, argued for intervention against the fascists. The problem with intervention, aside from the practical one of entering a war between citizens of the *same* country, was the danger of escalating the conflict to a general European war against the fascist powers. To add to this, the French socialist prime minister, Leon Blum, advocated non-intervention in order to keep his 'Popular Front' government, which included the centre right, together. Attlee's problem with non-intervention was that Mussolini was clearly helping Franco: if other countries did nothing, only Franco would benefit. But he had no realistic alternative, and had to watch helplessly as German *Luftwaffe* volunteers, the Condor Legion, infamously bombed the Spanish city of Guernica on 26 April 1937. To appease the left, he could do little more than pay a visit to Spain in December 1937, when fascist aircraft chased his aeroplane. A further problem for Attlee was the speed with which events unfolded. He had to react quickly and he lacked sureness of foot. However, when Japan followed up the Anti-Comintern Pact with Germany on 25 November 1936 and invaded China in July 1937, the only advantage was that the situation was less complex and condemnation could be straightforward; in August 1937, the National Council of Labour (the Labour Party, the trade unions and the Cooperative Party) condemned Japan but felt war could still be averted.

Problems at home compounded the problems abroad. After the death of George V in January 1936, the crown had passed to his eldest son, Edward VIII. Society gossip that the new king was romantically involved with American divorcee Wallis Simpson proved correct and, in December 1936, the crisis broke. The king's determination to marry Mrs Simpson was a major obstacle to continuing on the throne. Aside from the social mores of the 1930s, the British monarch was Defender of the Faith and Supreme Governor of the Church of England and, after the Statute of Westminster, the common monarchy was the only constitutional link between Britain and the dominions.

There were three options – the king marry Mrs Simpson and she become queen consort; he marry her without her becoming queen (a 'morganatic marriage'); or he marry her and abdicate. Giving up Mrs Simpson was not an option. Attlee took a very traditional position, sought out Baldwin, and told him that 'while Labour people had no objection at all to an American becoming Queen, I was certain that they would not approve of Mrs Simpson for that position and would object to a morganatic marriage.'[19] In doing so he shored up Baldwin's position, for the abdication crisis presented an opportunity. The king had won some sympathy on the left with visits to poorer areas of the country, including South Wales and, with Baldwin holding to a choice for the king between Mrs Simpson and the throne, Attlee could have supported the king. This would have presented Baldwin with a dilemma, since the prime minister's ultimate weapon was the resignation of the government and, if the Labour Party *had* been willing to form an alternative administration, it was a weapon he might have been reluctant to use. The idea that the patriotic Attlee would ever have behaved other than in the way he did is not credible. He was a monarchist and wished to protect the reputation of the British crown. Politically, he felt that 'the Party – with the exception of a few of the intelligentsia who can be trusted to take the wrong view on any subject – were in agreement with the views I had expressed.' However, shoring up a Conservative prime minister and saving the monarchy were hardly likely to make him popular with his party.

Despite being leader of the opposition during such tumultuous years, Attlee found time to write. In 1937 he published *The Labour Party in Perspective*. It was his second major book on the Labour Party and the first that really moved beyond the summary of his parliamentary speeches that his 1935 book, *Labour Shows the Way: The Will and the Way to Socialism*, essentially was. He now argued that Labour would 'replace the chaotic triangle which has been created by the dictation of private interests into a coordinated system of control'.[20] The 'Labour Plan' included setting up import and export boards, 'socializing' industries, including the Bank of England, forming a national transport board, abolishing the means test and planning social services.[21] The international system should also be planned and the League of Nations was to be supported 'as the beginning of the World Federation'.[22] In *The Labour Party in Perspective*, he asserted, with typical modesty, 'Circumstances have called me to occupy a position of high responsibility within the movement.'[23] The book contained what were, by now, his 'standard' arguments – socialism in the form of common ownership at home, and support for collective security and the League of Nations abroad. Yet, in the book, he also expressed a frustration with his party: 'unnecessary suspicions and personal attacks play into the hands of our enemies.'[24] For a

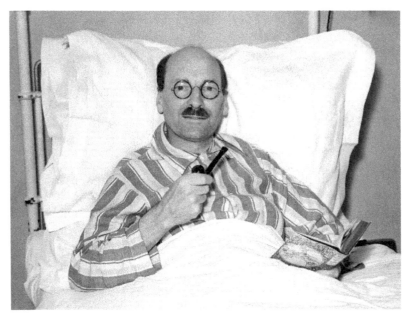

3. Clement Attlee after surgery.

man who was to become such a consensual prime minister, the final section of the book contains an oddly dictatorial conception of how an elected Labour government would behave: 'when it has received a mandate from the electors … the … programme must be carried out with the utmost vigour and resolution. … A Labour Government should make it quite plain that it will suffer nothing to hinder it in carrying out the popular will.'[25]

In other ways Attlee's views were moderating. His left-wing attacks on the legal system were very much in the past when, at the 1937 party conference at Bournemouth in October, he dealt firmly with complaints from delegates that the 1936 Public Order Act was being used against the working class and was an infringement on liberty: 'I believe the banning of uniforms has had a definitely good effect, and I have had evidence of that from those on the spot where most of the trouble takes place.'[26] Others within the party, however, were attempting to take more drastic action and becoming more extreme. In January 1937, the Communist Party combined with the Independent Labour Party and the Socialist League to launch a 'Unity Manifesto' with Cripps and Bevan among the signatories calling for class conflict rather than class collaboration. The national executive committee prohibited association with the Communist Party and the Socialist League dissolved two months later. Meanwhile, the party continued its move towards rearmament. In July, the parliamentary party changed its policy on voting against the service estimates and, at the party conference in the autumn, alongside Attlee's support for the Public Order Act, the policy document the National Council of Labour issued, *International Policy and Defence*, was approved, emphasizing defence of the nation in the current international climate alongside collective security. Cripps, once part of a leadership triumvirate at the head of the party, was drifting out of it. The national executive committee eventually expelled him from the party on 25 January 1939 after he advocated joining all other parties to bring down the Chamberlain government. He continued his campaign for a 'Popular Front' outside; Bevan, who soon joined him, was expelled from the party only weeks later. Attlee mused:

> The People's Flag is palest pink
> It's not red blood, but only ink.[27]

On 12 March 1938 Hitler annexed Austria to Germany in the *Anschluss* and subsequently demanded that the Sudetenland, the ethnically German region of Czechoslovakia, be ceded to Germany as well. Neville Chamberlain famously flew to Munich to meet Hitler and, on 30 September 1938, agreed to concede the Sudetenland to Germany before arriving back at Heston Aerodrome later that day to declare that he had secured 'peace for our time'. When he spoke in the Commons on 3 October, Attlee declared it a triumph for Hitler, but he was having little effect on the government's policy: the internal politics of the Conservative Party were much more important. Churchill's abstention in the vote on Munich was of greater significance than Attlee's opposition. Cripps tried to form an alliance between anti-appeasement MPs in the Conservative Party and Labour Party to remove Chamberlain, with Attlee allegedly in favour, but the Conservatives generally remained loyal.[28] Eden, who had resigned as foreign secretary on 20 February 1938, showed none of the disloyalty that would have reduced his chances of a return to government. On 15 March 1939, Germany invaded the rest of Czechoslovakia. By the end of the month, Britain and France had given a guarantee of independence to Poland.

Almost inevitably, Attlee's leadership came under threat. The Labour Party had changed its annual conference to Whitsun 1937; the national executive had decided not to hold a conference in 1938, so the next conference was held in Southport between 29 May and 2 June 1939, during which Attlee was taken ill. He had known that he would have to have a prostate operation at some stage, but the matter was forced. He entered a nursing home and had two operations, which kept him out of political action until late September. Arthur Greenwood moved the parliamentary report in Attlee's absence. Absence from a political meeting can often be as damaging as a direct challenge in one's presence, and when the national executive committee met just after the conference, with Greenwood in the chair, the issue of confidence in him was raised. In the event, the ill Attlee received a near-unanimous vote in support, with only Ellen Wilkinson, a supporter of Morrison, abstaining. But the marker had, however, been put down, and Attlee must have known that the issue was far from settled in his favour.

Chapter 10
FROM OPPOSITION TO GOVERNMENT, 1939–42

Just as he had loyally served his country on the battlefields in the First World War, Attlee served his country politically in the second. For five years from May 1940 he served continually in the war cabinet, and was the only person apart from Churchill who did so. Aside from the brief interlude of Churchill's caretaker government from 23 May to 26 July 1945, Attlee lived formally in Downing Street for eleven and a half years, at Number 11 (at Churchill's request) during the war, and at Number 10 after the landslide Labour victory in July 1945. Yet, in the first year of the war, even after he had accepted the sinecure office of Lord Privy Seal under Churchill, Attlee's reputation among his political colleagues and opponents did not improve. He was briefly challenged for the leadership of the Labour Party in November 1939, and his early months in government did not mark him out as a leading member of the coalition, let alone a potential peace-time prime minister. When he moved into Downing Street in 1940, not even his most ardent supporters would have argued that he was there to stay for the long term. However, after a difficult start, Attlee grew in confidence as a member of the wartime coalition and developed a constructive relationship with Churchill. While he did not become widely known to the general public, Attlee showed himself to be an able administrator at cabinet level during the Second World War, becoming from 1942 a capable deputy prime minister who often minded the shop at home while Churchill ran the military side of the conflict.

Hitler invaded Poland on Friday 1 September 1939, safe in the knowledge that the 'secret protocol' of the Nazi–Soviet Pact signed on 24 August 1939 had quietened any opposition from Soviet Russia. The agreement divided the East into 'spheres of influence' between the two ideological enemies and

Chamberlain's policy of appeasement, in so far as it aimed to prevent another European war, had failed. Even at this late stage, however, the prime minister paused before declaring war, despite the clear breach of the British guarantee of Poland. Attlee would have had the chance to put down his credentials for leadership in the debate in the House of Commons on the Saturday, but, in his absence, it was the deputizing Greenwood who followed the reticent Chamberlain, and to whom the Conservative MP Leo Amery famously shouted across the chamber – 'Speak for England!' In a statesmanlike speech, Greenwood asked for a definitive position from the government. He did not oppose a non-military solution, but emphasized the gravity of Nazi aggression. Attlee noted wryly that Greenwood 'rose finely to the occasion'.[1] On the Sunday, at 9 a.m., the British ambassador in Berlin, Neville Henderson, handed the German government an ultimatum that unless an indication was given by 11 a.m. that troops would be withdrawn from Poland, war would be declared. At 11.15 a.m., a sombre Chamberlain broadcast to the nation from Number 10 with the news that no such response had been received. Britain and France were at war with Germany.

The 'phoney war' had begun. Despite the declaration, a major military confrontation was still some months away. However, Chamberlain sought to broaden his government, with both Eden (as dominions secretary) and Churchill (as First Lord of the Admiralty) returning to government. The Labour Party declined to join Chamberlain's administration, and there was little controversy between Attlee, Greenwood or any other leading Labour figures about this. Attlee felt 'there was no confidence in Chamberlain and his immediate associates' and that there was 'much to be said for having an alternative administration available'.[2] Attlee did manage to attend the House of Commons and speak on a few occasions over the next few weeks, but he steered away from controversy; his first speech on 20 September concerned the machinery of government and how a small group of ministers without departmental responsibility could best direct the war effort. However, Attlee had to set out the Labour Party position in the context of the new international situation. He spoke to the Labour MPs and candidates on 8 November 1939, and the speech was another that was published as a pamphlet. He was keen to emphasize not just the challenge of the present, but the type of peace settlement required to secure the future: no enforced peace; countries able to decide their own futures (including India); war no longer to be used by countries that disagree; minority rights within countries enforced; an international body; and imperialism to end.[3] The theme of winning the war as a precondition to securing the type of peace the party believed in was to run through most of Attlee's wartime political speeches.

The speech did not, however, quell the threat to Attlee's leadership and, even before the meeting of the parliamentary party on 15 November, moves were made to decide when the leader for the next parliamentary session would be chosen. On 9 November, backbench MP Alfred Edwards[4] wrote to Dalton, Morrison and Greenwood to ask if they were willing to be nominated against Attlee. Morrison replied two days later that he did not feel it would be 'kindly or generous' to have a contest given Attlee's health problems.[5] However, all three were nominated, together with Attlee, and the stage was set for an open contest. Just as Bevin's loyalty to Attlee was to save him in 1945 and 1947, so it was Greenwood this time who stood by his side, speaking first (always a crucial speech in any political meeting) and refusing to accept nomination. Dalton sneered: 'He gave very poor reasons, his chief point being that it would encourage Hitler if we now had a contest for the leadership.'[6] More likely reasons for Greewood's behaviour are that he did not want to be leader in a difficult international situation and did not want to serve under anyone other than Attlee.[7] Morrison then stood and read out his letter to Edwards; Dalton, speaking last, also declined nomination, but in truth was stymied by the first two speakers: to have shown naked ambition at this stage would have been political suicide for any future leadership contests. Attlee was therefore elected unopposed. Whatever the views the candidates had of each other, it was unseating an *ill* leader that was so deeply troubling to many Labour MPs in 1939. Dalton called it a 'queer, desultory discussion, full of expressions of gentlemanly goodwill'.[8] The issue therefore became dormant, but was far from dead. One backbencher, Tom Smith, MP for Normanton, commented to Dalton: 'you all did the big thing this morning. But there will have to be a change one of these days.'[9]

Attlee, having survived, turned his mind to the Labour Party's political position in the context of the war. In January 1940 he broadcast to the nation and was proud of the text, which he quoted in full in his autobiography. It reads as an attempt to marry Labour's pacifist and 'collective security' instincts of the 1930s with its position of support for the war. Attlee relied on ethical principles. He was not afraid to criticize Britain, debunking imperialism and citing the Amritsar massacre of 1919 when British Indian troops under the control of Brigadier-General Reginald Dyer fired on a gathering of unarmed civilians, killing hundreds. Yet, he felt Britain was fighting *this* war on ethical principles and he declared that the Labour Party 'owes its inspiration not to some economic doctrine or to some theory of class domination. It has always based its propaganda on ethical principles.'[10] His peroration was not Church-illian, but it was effective in reminding Labour supporters up and down the country that the war was as much about the type of Britain that would emerge from the conflict as about simple military victory:

If we permit, as in the last war, inequality of sacrifice so that at the end
the gulf between rich and poor is greater than ever, we shall have failed
in our task. If we really wish to build a new world ... we must also build
a new Britain.[11]

In hindsight, the speech seems oddly unpatriotic. But, in context, this was
Attlee at his synthesizing best, cleverly reconciling support for the war with the
position of the 1930s Labour Party, which had so often found itself in bitter
conflict with the Conservative-dominated national government.

The position in the speech probably represented an essential stepping
stone between the party's opposition stance of the 1930s and its leading
members taking seats in government in May 1940. This was not how it would
have seemed at the time, however, and Attlee's stature either inside or
outside the party did not increase in the early months of 1940. In January, he
toured the military lines in France with the British Expeditionary Force
commander, Lord Gort, and in February went with Dalton to meet the
French government, but neither trip had any political effect. On 29 February
1940 he spoke at the London School of Economics about war aims. The 82-
year old Beatrice Webb, who was there to hear him, was scathing: 'To realize
that this little nonentity is the Parliamentary Leader of the Labour Party, the
representative of Her Majesty's Opposition at £2000 per year, and
presumably the future PM, is humiliating.'[12] Webb's diary entry is, however,
revealing because undoubtedly one of Attlee's key strengths, both then and
later, was the lack of a *widely acceptable* alternative: 'Alexander, who *has* a
personality but an unpleasant one, is not a socialist ... Clynes is decrepit.
Morrison is able and incisive but reactionary; Dalton an *arriviste* and
untrustworthy at that.'[13]

The issue of the leadership of Britain's second-largest political party was not,
however, a major concern for most British people. On 3 April 1940, Germany
invaded Norway, the port of Narvik being strategically important since
Swedish iron ore was shipped from there down to Germany. The British
responded using both armed landings and the navy. In mid-April, troops were
put ashore at the ports of Namsos in the north and Andalsnes to the south.
However, on 2 May, they had to be withdrawn. This military failure was the
beginning of a critical month for the future course of British history. The next
four weeks included a new prime minister, a change of government, the
acceptance of defeat in mainland Europe and the historic decision for Britain
to fight on the war alone. Attlee was hardly a central figure in these events, but
he was repeatedly present. He *did* have an influence, but it was not decisive.
The real significance for his career was that the service in wartime government
provided both a distraction from his own leadership and an opportunity to

prove himself. As leader of the former opposition, Attlee was entitled to a senior and meaningful position within a government of national unity.

On Tuesday 7 May the two-day debate on the Norway campaign began, ostensibly on the very minor issue of an adjournment motion. Chamberlain spoke first and tried to head off opposition with an announcement that Churchill would be given the authority to give orders to the Chiefs of Staff Committee. He was followed by Attlee who attacked the 'almost uninterrupted career of failure' of 'those mainly responsible'. Leo Amery famously spoke later in the day, quoting Oliver Crowell when he dismissed the Rump Parliament in 1653: 'You have sat too long here for any good you have been doing. Depart, I say, and let us have done with you. In the name of God, go.' Overnight, Attlee made a decisive personal contribution. Sensing that the mood of the House of Commons was changing, he considered matters:

> Accordingly, next day *I* [my italics] recommended to the Party that we should vote against the Motion for the Adjournment. *I* [my italics] told them that it must be clearly understood that this was a Vote of Censure and that if it brought the Government down we must be prepared to assume responsibility.

On Wednesday 8 May Morrison set out the party's new position. Lloyd George declared that Chamberlain should 'sacrifice the seals of office'. That evening, the huge government majority of over 200 fell to just 81, with 41 Conservative MPs voting against the government. Chamberlain had got the message and there was a clear force for a change of leadership.

On Thursday 9 May Dalton's diary records a bizarre conversation with Attlee, in which the possibility of Attlee becoming prime minister in place of Chamberlain was discussed:

> Lloyd George has seen Attlee and said that Chamberlain should resign and might then advise the King to send for Attlee. What should he do then? I told Attlee that I thought he could not possibly be PM in this situation. He quite agreed. The PM *must* be a Ministerialist. He agrees with my preference for Halifax over Churchill, but we both think that either would be tolerable.[14]

There is no way that Attlee could have become prime minister at this stage. The House of Commons consisted overwhelmingly of Conservative MPs. Whatever some of their views of Chamberlain, Attlee would have been totally unacceptable. This was not another 1931, with a Labour prime minister deemed as a useful front for harsh economic measures and cuts in unemployment benefit. Among the public, Attlee was still not well known. In a public opinion poll of 8 April 1940 on the preferred successor if Chamberlain should retire, 28 per cent opted for Eden, 25 per cent for Churchill, 7 per cent for Halifax, 6 per cent for Attlee and 5 per cent for Lloyd George.[15] At this stage Lloyd George was 77 years old, still tainted by the disgrace of the honours' scandal, and had been in the political wilderness for more than 17 years, yet Attlee was only 1 per cent ahead of him. Name recognition was, however, probably an important factor in the names given by members of the public, and Lloyd George, after all, was still 'the man who won the war' in 1918. That said, Attlee was hardly in a position to point to public acclaim as reason to be appointed to the highest political office in the land. The real mystery is why Lloyd George ever saw it as a possibility; Attlee, on the other hand, was able to give a reminder to Dalton that, despite the leadership troubles in the autumn of 1939, others still thought of him as a significant player.

On the same day, Chamberlain invited Attlee and Greenwood to Number 10. They spoke with him, Churchill and Lord Halifax. Attlee told Chamberlain that the Labour Party would not serve under him, but that he thought they would serve under a different prime minister. It was then agreed that Attlee would ask his party two questions. Would it enter a government under Chamberlain? And would it enter a government under someone else? On the morning of 10 May, Germany invaded the Netherlands, Belgium and Luxembourg. Attlee took a taxi with Dalton to Waterloo station and travelled to Bournemouth where the Labour Party conference was shortly to begin. In the afternoon the national executive unanimously voted to answer 'No' to the first question and 'Yes' to the second and, at 5 p.m., Attlee gave the answer to the prime minister's secretary. Attlee and Greenwood returned to London to find that Chamberlain had resigned.

The Labour Party decision not to serve under Chamberlain was a factor in the manoeuvrings taking place between the prime minister and his two potential successors, Churchill and Halifax. Halifax, then a peer, had long experience in government and administration. Known as the 'Holy Fox' as a consequence of his religion and fox-hunting he had served as Viceroy of India from 1926 to 1931 (under the title Lord Irwin) before returning to Britain and serving in the national government, eventually succeeding Anthony Eden as foreign secretary in 1938 after the latter's resignation. Halifax was the 'insider' candidate, the 'major force in steering the way from an appeasing to a resisting tack'.[16] He had put pressure on Chamberlain to change course on a number of issues, including giving a guarantee to Poland and introducing conscription. Churchill, by contrast, was the 'outsider', the critical voice from the wilderness of the 1930s, the anti-appeaser whose warnings about Nazi Germany had been vindicated.

But many Conservatives still viewed him with deep scepticism. He was impetuous and prone to bad judgement: even after the Gallipoli campaign in 1915, Churchill had proposed the invasion of Russia in 1919, and took a famously hard line in the general strike, apparently happy to send in armed forces against the strikers.

At 10 a.m. on 10 May, Kingsley Wood, then secretary of state for Air, told Churchill that Chamberlain had in fact canvassed whether that morning's news of the German onslaught on western Europe necessitated him remaining in place after all.[17] When Chamberlain, Churchill and Halifax met at 11 a.m. events were still unfolding rapidly on the continent. Chamberlain said that he could not form a national government: 'The response he had received from the Labour leaders left him in no doubt of this.'[18] The question, therefore, was the succession. Churchill felt that Chamberlain would have preferred Halifax: 'His biographer, Mr Feiling, states definitely that he preferred Lord Halifax.'[19] Halifax, however, ruled himself out, citing his position as a peer and without a seat in the House of Commons, as too difficult in terms of waging the war. He also felt unsuited to the job: 'he knew himself to be bored by and only semi-literate in matters of military strategy.'[20] Whatever the merits of the two men, Halifax had sacrificed himself. Churchill was to become prime minister and accepted the king's commission just after 6 p.m.

Later that evening, Attlee and Greenwood met Churchill and accepted his offer to serve under him. Churchill generously offered two seats in the war cabinet of five, and mentioned Ernest Bevin, A. V. Alexander, Herbert Morrison and Hugh Dalton for other places in the government. Alexander duly went to the Admiralty, Dalton took the Ministry of Economic Warfare and Bevin entered the Commons unopposed as MP for Wandsworth Central and became minister of labour. Morrison became minister of supply, coordinating materials to the armed forces. The critical balance, however, was within the five-member war cabinet. Alongside Churchill, Attlee, as Lord Privy Seal and Greenwood, as Minister Without Portfolio, Chamberlain accepted the post of Lord President of the Council, and Halifax entered the war cabinet in his current post of foreign secretary.

On 11 May 1940 the outlook in western Europe was bleak. German forces were advancing further through the Low Countries.[21] At home, Attlee had to deal with the 1940 party conference, which was taking place in Bournemouth. He moved an emergency resolution on the first day, Monday 13 May, to enter the government, and the historical nature of the moment was not lost on him: 'Friends, we are standing here today to take a decision not only on behalf of our own Movement, but on behalf of Labour all over the world.' He left the hall to three cheers, but a card vote to move to a final vote on the proposal was not initially carried.[22] The matter was debated and, at the end of the morning session of conference, there were 2.413 million votes in favour with only 170,000 against.[23] Dalton was scathing, calling it 'a ragged affair with a lot of freaks talking pathetic rubbish'.[24] But even Beatrice Webb, who heard the news of Labour's entry into government on the radio, was positive: 'I felt converted fighting Hitler to the bitter end. His mad aggression has become irredeemable.'[25] Shorn of its leader, the Parliamentary Labour Party elected H. B. Lees-Smith to act as leader of the opposition: an essential procedural step if parliament were still to run smoothly now that Attlee was a member of the government.

On 15 May, French Prime Minister Paul Reynaud told Churchill on the telephone that France had lost and, on 16–17 May, Churchill visited France, with Reynaud still asking for air support. Attlee agreed with Churchill that Britain could not commit all its air forces to defending France and consequently leave Britain defenceless. When Churchill visited again on 22 May, he met the newly-appointed French commander-in-chief, General Weygand, whose plan to halt the German advance was for the British Expeditionary Force and the French First Army to move south from the coast and for a new French force to be assembled and to move north from further along the front, thereby providing an attack on the Germans from both sides. The French counterattack never came to fruition, and the British commander, General Gort, thought evacuation the only option.

Between Sunday 26 and Tuesday 28 May there were nine meetings of the war cabinet, interspersed with a meeting between Churchill and all government ministers on the Tuesday afternoon, at which Dalton described Churchill as passionately setting out his 'fight to the end' view. 'It was idle to think that, if we tried to make peace now, we should get better terms from Germany than if we went on and fought it out.'[26] There was no dissent to Churchill's view. Roy Jenkins's view is that this was either a strategic move or simply luck – using the feelings of ministers generally to swing opinion within the war cabinet.[27] The historian Andrew Roberts argues that the war cabinet meetings featured 'a sharp disagreement between different perceptions of the present and future state of likely negotiating strengths' with Churchill wanting to wait a few months to see if further fighting, perhaps repelling a German invasion, could yield a better platform upon which to negotiate terms. Halifax wanted to negotiate with France, which was still in the war.[28] What was Attlee's position? Roy Jenkins, whose father Arthur was PPS to Attlee during this period, is dismissive of Attlee's contribution: 'In argument … Attlee followed rather than led. … Greenwood … next to Churchill made most of the intransigent running.'[29]

The official cabinet minutes certainly do not support any decisive contribution from Attlee. On 27 May, at the 4.30 p.m. meeting, 'considerable discussion' is recorded as having happened on the question of an approach to

Mussolini to seek peace and, since Reynaud's visit the previous day, it had become known that Roosevelt was making an approach to Mussolini, so: 'If France and Great Britain were now to make a direct approach to Signor Mussolini, this would only confuse the issue, might well be resented by President Roosevelt, and was likely to create an impression of weakness.'[30] At the 11.30 a.m. meeting the following day, Halifax cited a telegram from the ambassador in Washington indicating an 'entirely negative' response from Mussolini to Roosevelt's approach.[31] At the 4 p.m. meeting, the idea of the approach was dropped. Mussolini's attitude had undermined Halifax's case in any event. According to Roberts, 'Sinclair and Attlee, though silent during much of the earlier discussion, now sided with Churchill',[32] but this was at too late a stage to be significant.

Attlee visited Paris with Churchill on 31 May and later recalled the 'curious silence and almost deserted look of the city, which obviously had decided on surrender'.[33] Alongside the fall of France, the evacuation of Dunkirk from 27 May to 4 June, 'Operation Dynamo', was successful in that more than 300,000 troops were saved from death or capture at the hands of the Nazis in northern France and preserved for the defence of the mainland. Churchill, however, declared in the House of Commons on 4 June that 'Wars are not won by evacuations.' By 14 June the Germans were able to march in triumph down the Champs Elysée. On 18 June, Churchill addressed the House of Commons with perhaps his most famous speech of the whole war:

> What General Weygand called the Battle of France is over. I expect that the Battle of Britain is about to begin. … Let us therefore brace ourselves to our duties, and so bear ourselves that, if the British Empire and its Commonwealth last for a thousand years, men will still say, 'This was their finest hour'.[34]

On 22 June, in the same railway carriage in which the German surrender had been taken in 1918, France surrendered.

In July 1940 Attlee could have become the minister responsible for the Special Operations Executive, and it would have been an historical oddity if Attlee, with his unblemished, gentlemanly character had been in charge of subterfuge against the enemy. Dalton wrote to Attlee and Halifax simultaneously on 2 July, telling Attlee that 'I had you clearly in mind for the performance of this function'[35] and insisting to Halifax that 'the Minister who could best undertake this new and important task is the Lord Privy Seal, who is much interested in the whole question and, indeed, spoke to me about it some time ago.'[36] Dalton's motives here are unclear. He certainly viewed a role in the scheme for himself alongside Attlee: 'I am conscious, as you know of not being at present fully extended and I should be very glad to assist you in the work if you took it over.'[37] However, Attlee was unenthusiastic; Sir Campbell Stuart, whom the Foreign Office had originally appointed in such propaganda work in 1938, told Dalton on 16 August: 'He had lunch today with Attlee, who had been friendly but rather vague.'[38]

In the final couple of days of July 1940, Chamberlain's role in the government started to lose its significance because of his ill health: he had an operation for stomach cancer. On 2 August 1940, Max Beaverbrook, the proprietor of the *Daily Express*, joined the war cabinet. Since 14 May, he had been in the important position of minister of aircraft production. Indeed, over these months, the war in the air was the key to Britain's survival. There was no question that the British government's central aim in the summer and autumn of 1940 was Britain's survival as an independent, sovereign nation, in the face of the German control of western Europe. An invasion of Britain was expected and the government had to do all it could to ensure that it could be repulsed. Hitler's aim was simple: achieve air supremacy over Britain to facilitate a land invasion. In a recurring pattern, 13 August saw 45 German planes lost to only 13 British.[39] Churchill addressed the House of Commons on 20 August 1940: 'Never in the field of human conflict was so much owed by so many to so few.' The battle was not over, however, since, on 23 August, the Germans attacked in numbers again, concentrating on aircraft production centres and fuel storage facilities.[40] The early weeks of September saw Britain on invasion alert. Four spies had been caught on 4 September and they confirmed an imminent attack. However, K. R. Park, the air vice-marshal commanding number 11 group of the Royal Air Force, wrote to the headquarters of fighter command on 12 September 1940 that 'confidence is felt in our ability to hold the enemy by day and to prevent his obtaining superiority in the air over our territory, unless he greatly increases the scale or intensity of his attacks.'[41] The aim of German air ascendancy to neutralize British naval superiority and enable the ferrying over of the invasion force was not achieved. We now know that Hitler's mind was already moving towards an invasion of the Soviet Union, but that does not change the state of peril that Britain was in during August and September 1940. Not since 1066 had England been wholly conquered from outside and, had the air battle been lost, Britain's land defences would have faced the full might of the *Wehrmacht*. That Attlee was in the war cabinet during this period gives him a place in history in itself. But what exactly, if anything, was his contribution?

Attlee could not compete with Churchill's inspirational oratory and he did not try to. However, in a speech dated August or September 1940, Attlee tried to rally the nation, exclaiming that 'The workers refuse to be intimidated. ... I believe that the Battle of Britain is the turning point of the war.'[42] His reputation seemed to be growing. At the Trades Union Congress, speaking on 8

October, Attlee received loud cheers and was presented with the Gold Badge of Congress (given to a man of 'signal service' in the year): 'I am profoundly convinced that we are going to win. … I am profoundly convinced too that out of this victory we can build a new world.'[43] As Lord Privy Seal, with no specific departmental responsibility, he had exactly the type of role he had urged on the Chamberlain government in his speech of 20 September 1939. He was therefore free to serve on a number of cabinet committees. There was the defence committee, chaired by Churchill, with Attlee as deputy, and the lord president's committee, which oversaw domestic affairs, of which he was also a member under, first, Chamberlain, then John Anderson from 3 October 1940. Churchill was generous to the Labour Party in terms of its roles in government. As early as 25 July 1940, there was apparently 'resentment in high Civil Service circles about the amount of coordinating done by Attlee and Greenwood'.[44] There was, however, an element of Attlee being given jobs to do in an attempt to occupy his time. On 9 October the war cabinet asked him to look into why a November 1938 cabinet directive to increase the storage of gas from 500 to 2000 tons had not been met. Attlee's survey noted disagreements on whether, for example, gas containers should be reused or not, causing months of delay. When he reported on 18 November, he was scathing about the ineffective use of committees: 'The Committee, far from being a servant, becomes the master, and action is paralysed. There is no one person who insists upon a workable solution being quickly found and action driven forward to a conclusion.'[45] While he drew a sensible conclusion, a politician supposedly as senior as Attlee should not really have been asked to spend time working this out.

Indeed, Dalton records a less than favourable story in his diary on 31 October 1940:

> Morrison, when Minister of Supply … gave a tremendous wigging to a North of England firm, Green, Wood and Batley. They had not been doing their share in the arms drive. Having been duly ticked off … Macmillan said … 'I think you were rather hard on them. After all, they did very good work in peacetime, even though they may not have quite come up to scratch, so far, in time of war.' Morrison said, 'I don't care a damn what they did in time of peace; they're NBG in times of war.' Macmillan said, 'What did you say the name of the firm was? Was it Greenwood and Attlee?'[46]

Naturally, this story should be treated with caution. Morrison would clearly be happy to spread any gossip that damaged his long-time rival Attlee. Harold Macmillan was hardly a friend of the Labour leader, but it points to the truth about Attlee's reputation among his colleagues in the early months of the wartime coalition. Sir Alexander Cadogan, permanent under-secretary at the Foreign Office, records that only the issue of Spain drew any meaningful contribution from Attlee: 'otherwise a dormouse [on this issue he] becomes like a rabid rabbit'.[47] However, as a left-wing politician, there was a lot to be bothered about: Franco's regime sought revenge against anti-fascists, and many refugees from his regime in France now found themselves under the Nazi puppet regime of Marshal Pétain and were deported to concentration camps.

Yet, for all this criticism, Attlee was in a stronger position in late 1940 than he had been the previous year. His influence lay in Churchill's need to have a broad-based administration to fight the war and, so long as Churchill relied on him, his position was fairly secure. It also proved to be an advantage that Churchill did not see him as a threat: 'He knew Clem wouldn't do a coup or anything.'[48] There is some truth in Dalton's view that Attlee's health contributed to his poor performance in the early months of the war: 'as his own health returned and the war situation grew graver, he rose to the full height both of his duty and his opportunity.'[49] In addition, Attlee's role in the coalition represented a great personal and professional change. At Churchill's insistence, he moved into Number 11 Downing Street, where he worked and slept. He was separated from his family: Violet and the children continued to live at Stanmore. It was obviously not an easy time for a family to be separated: Violet found it hard; Attlee was pleased when she attended Felicity's confirmation in Somerset in March 1941: 'It will have done her good to have got away for a bit.'[50] Attlee remained close to his family: he made the most of weekends, taking Violet away when he could; when Alison fell off her bike in the summer of 1942, leaving her with blood pressing on her brain, Attlee got to hospital to be there while an operation took place.[51] Professionally, Attlee had never held cabinet office before and he was thrust straight into the five-member war cabinet during Britain's time of need. No wonder he was not the most vociferous member of the war cabinet. As the leader of a party with only just over 150 seats in the House of Commons, he simply had no mandate to be.

Once he was recovered, Attlee concentrated on doing his own job well and keeping the Labour Party united on the principle of serving in the coalition government. His confidence grew. Chamberlain resigned from the war cabinet on 1 October, dying only weeks later. Morrison was elevated to home secretary on 4 October, Bevin entered the war cabinet at the same time and Churchill sent Halifax to be ambassador to the United States in December. The two most senior Conservative figures of the original war cabinet had gone; Morrison's advance was balanced by that of his enemy Bevin. Attlee's New Year speech of 31 December 1940 ended with a flourish in Churchill-like fashion: 'The darkest hours have passed. Even if it be not day, this year will bring the first glimpse of a splendid dawn.'[52] The dawn did not, however, bring political relief for Attlee.

In the dark times of 1940, the all-consuming issue was the survival of Britain; as soon as the immediate danger had passed, the issue of planning for a postwar Britain emerged. Attlee's justification to his party for participation in the wartime coalition had always been twofold – not just winning the war, but also ensuring the emergence of a Britain that was more in tune with socialist ideals. If he argued for this within the war cabinet, he risked imperilling its unity: the Conservatives were never going to agree with the Labour vision of postwar Britain. In contrast, if he was not seen to be moving towards this goal, the Labour Party would put pressure on him to leave the coalition altogether. When Dalton talked about the 'freaks' talking 'pathetic rubbish' after Attlee's speech to the Labour Party conference to enter the coalition on 13 May 1940, he may well have been treating the delegates who opposed the move with contempt, but the phrasing also suggests that such people were outside the mainstream of the Labour Party. The leading dissenting figure within the parliamentary party was undoubtedly Aneurin Bevan, whom Churchill dubbed a 'squalid nuisance'. Bevan attacked Bevin and the measures he introduced to mobilize manpower at the Ministry of Labour, and later pushed hard for a second front to be opened in western Europe in order to take the pressure off the Soviet Union. These differences posed a challenge to Attlee in maintaining party unity. To his credit, it was a challenge to which he rose.

The means test and Trade Disputes and Trade Union Act of 1927 presented Attlee with two initial difficulties on the domestic front. In November 1940 the government set out plans to abolish the means test for pensioners, which was a significant sop to Labour Party opinion. When Labour spokesman Pethick-Lawrence argued in the House of Commons in favour of the proposal, which was a halfway house between retention and full abolition, Aneurin Bevan castigated him as 'hysterical'. Attlee knew that a measure of compromise was not enough in the long term. However, the position with the means test was better than that on the Trade Disputes and Trade Union Act. The trade unions, already concerned about the extent of government coercion introduced by emergency powers legislation, including requisition of private property, wanted the act repealed. Attlee's position with the trade unions depended very much on Ernest Bevin's position as minister of labour: having the general secretary of the largest union, the Transport and General Workers, in government, was critical. But, in 1941, the last time Attlee addressed the Trades Union Congress during the war, he was met with loud cheers as he declared at Edinburgh on 2 September:

the Trade Union Movement is something far greater than a necessary part of the economic machinery of our war effort. It stands, and has always stood, for an ideal. It asserts the dignity of the individual ... as against the conception of the worker as a mere instrument of production.[53]

Attlee was able to remain in the coalition with the Trade Disputes and Trade Union Act still in place: in fact, it was under his premiership in 1946 that the act was repealed.

On the more positive side, on 24 February 1941 it was confirmed that Churchill had approved precise terms of reference for a committee of the war cabinet on reconstruction problems. As early as 30 December 1940 he had minuted that 'Provision must now be made for the study of postwar problems.'[54] He had, however, sought to dampen expectations almost immediately in the House of Commons:

I must say a word about the functions of the Minister charged with the study of postwar problems. It is not his task to make a new world. ... It is not his duty to set up a new order or to create a new heart in the human breast.[55]

Attlee was a confirmed member with Greenwood as the chair: it appeared that the Labour Party had the driving seat in planning for the peace. The war cabinet's reconstruction problems committee met for the first time on 6 March 1941; Greenwood opened the meeting cautiously. While noting that 'the terms of reference of the Committee were wide and covered the whole field of reconstruction ... the Committee had not executive duties. The major decisions would be for the War Cabinet.'[56] Attlee made no more than occasional interjections; he noted that the organization of the medical profession had to be 'in conjunction' with hospital organization; and, with an eye on his previous experience of government as postmaster general in 1931, he mentioned that the machinery of government committee had paid particular attention to 'semi-commercial' aspects of government such as the Post Office.[57] However, despite its low-key start, the committee became more formalized as the year went on. Most significantly, in a memorandum dated 23 June 1941, Greenwood confirmed the setting up of the 'Interdepartmental Committee on Social Insurance and Allied Services' under the chairmanship of Sir William Beveridge.[58]

On the international scene the German advance continued. On 17 April 1941 Yugoslavia formally surrendered to Germany and, on 23 April, Greece capitulated. Operation Demon, a mini-Dunkirk in the Mediterranean, saw

4. The British war cabinet, 1941.

British and empire troops, together with some Polish, evacuated from Greece. Hitler moved forward relentlessly and had captured the British-held island of Crete by the end of May. Attlee carried a message of change for the future when he spoke on 3 June at the Labour Party conference at Westminster: 'I find in the speeches of statesmen on both sides of the Atlantic a realization that the foundation of Peace must be economic security, prosperity and social justice.' He also remained insistent on the preservation of Labour's distinctive identity: 'National unity does not mean the acceptance by one Party of the views and policy of another.'[59]

Attlee returned to his theme of conflicting values in a speech to the assembled representatives of the Allies on Friday 13 June 1941: this war is not a war fought between nations, but between ideologies – between democracy and freedom on the one hand, and dictatorship and tyranny on the other.[60] Indeed, the ultimate clash of ideologies was about to begin. On 22 June 1941 Operation Barbarossa, Hitler's invasion of the Soviet Union, began. Now Stalin was to enter the war on the Allied side. Churchill knew that help was also essential from the United States and, on 4 August 1941, he sailed from Scapa Flow on the battleship *Prince of Wales* to Placentia Bay, Newfoundland, to meet Roosevelt. The two met and issued the Atlantic

Charter, a compromise between the two nations on the principles to be adopted in the postwar world, dealing with issues such as self-determination, disarmament and nations agreeing not to make territorial gains. Attlee's contribution to the Atlantic Charter was to call a war cabinet after midnight and to reply to Churchill that a point should be added about social advancement, which became the fifth point of the charter. At home, he did things his own way. Writing to Tom on 9 August 1941, he noted: 'I had to take the place of the PM last week ... I eschewed embroidery. It is no use trying to stretch the bow of Ulysses.'[61] He was shortly to visit America himself. He left on 21 October by flying boat via Lisbon and Bermuda. He spoke at Columbia University, New York, before the International Labour Organization conference, again giving dual emphasis to being united in the struggle against Nazism and on creating a fairer, safer world after the war: 'They must not be content with destroying the Nazi system of tyranny and oppression. They must continue to work together so as to build up a world of freedom and security.'[62] This was a notable trip for Attlee personally. Not only did he join Roosevelt on a cruise down the Potomac, but he also had his first experience of what we would understand as a modern-day press conference, taking questions from journalists; he did not find it agreeable: 'they are one of the things of which I am naturally very frightened.'[63]

Attlee began to feel more comfortable within the coalition. At the same time international news became more positive. On 7 December 1941 Japanese aircraft attacked American ships and airbases at Pearl Harbor in Hawaii. America had at last been drawn into the war. Churchill immediately set off for Washington on the battleship *Duke of York* on 12 December. His increased travel abroad during the following years was to leave Attlee in a more influential position at home. News was also more positive in the east: as autumn turned into winter on the Russian front, the weather famously came to the rescue of the Red Army. At Christmas 1941 Moscow remained in Russian hands. By the turn of the year, Attlee felt able to speak out strongly on party political lines for common ownership of land after the war: 'That [efficient rebuilding of bombed areas] will only be possible by public ownership.'[64] However, political problems were never far away. With Churchill away, Dalton took the opportunity to state his case to Attlee about the expansion of his responsibilities; on 30 December 1941, he sent a note to Attlee complaining that the merger of the Special Operations Executive with the section of the BBC broadcasting to enemy territory (the 'Political Warfare Executive') under Dalton, the foreign secretary and the minister of information had 'not worked very well'.[65] He added: 'Since you are handling the whole matter in the PM's absence it is your discretion to take it up with the PM after his return.'[66] He pushed his ambitions strongly: 'I should hate to be an under-worked Minister. ... Let me ... have charge of all propaganda directed towards enemy and enemy-occupied territories.'[67] But the matter was about more than just Dalton's ambition. Brendan Bracken, the 40-year old minister of information, was a devotee of Churchill and an arch anti-socialist with whom Dalton found it difficult to work. As it happened, the problem solved itself: events on the international scene forced a reshuffle in government at home.

Chapter 11
DEPUTY PRIME MINISTER AND DOMINIONS SECRETARY, 1942–43

The opening months of 1942 brought several pieces of bad news for Britain. In North Africa, Rommel was carving out his reputation as the 'Desert Fox' with a new offensive driving the British back towards Egypt. Japan had invaded Burma and its aircraft had sunk the battleship *Prince of Wales*. On 15 February the crucial naval base of Singapore fell. Churchill restructured his government, with Attlee officially given the title of deputy prime minister, alongside the departmental responsibility of dominions secretary. Greenwood resigned from the government, and replaced Lees-Smith as leader of the opposition; however, his departure was balanced by the appointment of Stafford Cripps as Lord Privy Seal and leader of the house. Cripps, still outside the Labour Party, had been appointed by Churchill as ambassador in Moscow in 1940, but, after the invasion by Nazi Germany, his presence was no longer necessary. Meanwhile, Bevin won a stand-off with Beaverbrook: Bevin had threatened to resign if Beaverbrook as minister of production controlled the country's manpower, while Beaverbrook had threatened to resign if not given the post. Churchill gave in to Bevin and Beaverbrook left the government.

At the age of 59, Attlee was deputizing for the highest political office in the land. For the first time, he was also a departmental cabinet minister. Yet the position of dominions secretary was by no means a straightforward one. Attlee's predecessor (and in fact successor) was Lord Cranborne, descendant of the Cecil family whose famous political names included the two-time prime minister the Marquis of Salisbury. Cranborne had set out the problems he faced in a note to Churchill on 18 November 1941:

The main purpose of my job, as I understand it, is to act as a Liaison between His Majesty's Government here and the Dominion Governments. This is done partly by exchange of telegrams and partly by personal contact with the Dominion High Commissioners here with whom ... I have daily meetings.

The central difficulty was that 'I do not know myself what is going on ... if they [the high commissioners] want secret information, they tend more and more to go, not to me, but to other sources which apparently talk more freely.'[1]

A successful dominions secretary therefore had to be the principal source of information for the high commissioners: any dominions secretary who was not would be wholly ineffective in the role. However, Attlee was a natural. There was his innate patriotism, which could manifest itself in his dealings in the department. On 16 June, in sympathy with the views of the high commissioners, he confided to Churchill his annoyance at the American habit of speaking of the British Empire's decline: 'It would be well for the Americans ... to be aware that the British Colonial Empire is not a kind of private possession of the Old Country, but is part of a larger whole in which the other Dominions are also interested.'[2] He also got on well with officials. Lord Harlech (formerly Ormsby-Gore), the high commissioner in South Africa, told him by letter dated 15 March 1943: 'The Prussian military tradition ever since Frederick the Great's ghastly father has been the arch enemy of peace and progress in Europe ... Germany east of the Elbe has been the cancer of Europe for over two hundred years.'[3] Attlee replied, dryly, that he was 'much interested to have your views on the need for the destruction of Prussianism'.[4]

Attlee was an enthusiastic advocate for the cause of the dominions within cabinet. On 2 July 1942, when the British position in North Africa was dire, he directed Churchill towards their interests:

I suggest that it would be helpful if you could find time ... to send a personal message to the Dominion Prime Ministers. Such a message should be a stiffening one, and could give them such inner information about the Egyptian position ... as you might feel able to let them have.[5]

In 1943, with the outlook more positive, Attlee put pressure on Churchill for a meeting of the prime ministers of Canada (Mackenzie King), Australia (Curtin), New Zealand (Fraser) and South Africa (Smuts) to discuss the postwar situation.[6] In September he told Churchill that the dominions should be individually represented at the postwar peace conference (as they had been in

Paris in 1919) if they wished.[7] Attlee's concern was such that he even requested that Churchill amend a telegram to the US commander in the Far East, General MacArthur, in February 1943, to include favourable reference to Australia – 'my most cordial congratulations upon the capture of Burma by American and Australian forces.'[8] He also kept an eye on Eire, which had taken a further step away from association with Britain and adopted its own constitution in 1937. Attlee was fully aware of the threat of a German invasion through southern Ireland. On 9 June 1942 he reminded Churchill that 'if things should go wrong in Russia we might have the Germans upon us here very quickly.'[9] He wished to maintain good relations on the ground if possible: 'there is the question of the relations between our soldiers and the Southern Irish military forces. ... Relations can be kept on this footing by an occasional "sweetener" in the form of supply of a minimum material. The time for such a sweetener has, I am sure, now come.'[10]

Above all, Attlee enjoyed the job from the start. He wrote to Lord Harlech on 10 April 1942: 'I find this office enormously interesting and far from being the "without portfolio" kind that people imagine. With my other functions I find that there is not much unoccupied time between after breakfast and midnight.'[11] One of these functions was to chair the cabinet's India committee, which was formed in February 1942. Despite Attlee's principal responsibility for Australia, Canada, New Zealand and South Africa, and the presence of Leo Amery as secretary of state for India, Attlee and Cripps were in prominent roles over policy towards the raj during 1942.

On his appointment as dominions secretary, Attlee immediately sought a concentration of British military resources in the Far East. On 25 February 1942 he minuted to Churchill: 'I should like consideration to be given to the question of using our heavy bombers from Indian and Ceylon bases. I think the Air Ministry are inclined to be too rigidly devoted to ... bombing Germany.'[12] Buoyed by a telegram from the chiefs of staff to Field Marshal Wavell, commander-in-chief in India ('Serious position of India and Ceylon is fully apparent to us and we are well aware from your previous telegrams the critical need for air striking force and long range reconnaissance'),[13] Attlee approached Churchill again on 16 April: 'I think that there is a strong case for giving priority during the next few months to giving all possible support to our land and sea forces in the Indian area even at the expense of a less intensive attack on Germany.'[14] Churchill was not so convinced: 'These views are certainly very fashionable. ... However it is not possible to make any decisive change. ... We have built up a great plant here for bombing Germany which is which is the only way in our power of helping Russia.'[15]

Instead, it was the 'Cripps Mission' to India of March 1942 that perhaps most shaped the postwar independence settlement that Attlee implemented. When Britain had declared war in 1939, the Viceroy of India, Lord Linlithgow, had simply declared India at war as well, without any consultation with Indian leaders. Congress withdrew from the provincial legislatures set up in 1935 in protest, but Jinnah, on behalf of the Muslim League, sensed an opportunity to influence policy and so in March 1940 made his 'Lahore declaration' for a Muslim state, Pakistan. A few months later, Linlithgow made what came to be known as the 'August offer' of a constitution drafted by Indians with a legislative assembly. This was rejected by Gandhi who intensified his civil disobedience campaign. As Japanese forces moved closer to India, there was a greater urgency for a compromise to be found. In addition, there was the anti-imperialist President Roosevelt, who had to be kept on side at all costs. Roosevelt saw parallels between the British position in India and the American war of independence.[17] Should the mission fail, it was clearly crucial that the blame should not be laid at Britian's door.

Cripps hit the ground running. On his appointment in February 1942, he immediately disagreed with Amery on the composition of a 'Defence of India Council'. Cripps preferred that 'the whole body should be elected by the Provincial Legislatures voting as a single constituency', citing the simplicity of his scheme as an advantage over Amery's tripartite method of election from provincial legislatures, the central legislature and a list nominated by the viceroy.[18] On 7 March 1942 Attlee, on behalf of the cabinet committee for India, submitted a revised draft declaration for the war cabinet's consideration. The draft included a promise that 'immediately upon the cessation of hostilities', an elected body would be set up to frame a new constitution for India. Cripps's suggestion was partially adopted in that the lower houses would elect representatives to the constitution-making body, with the Indian states invited to appoint representatives in proportion to their populations. Meantime, Britain would take responsibility for India's defence. It was on this basis that Cripps went to India to try to engineer a solution. He was ideally qualified to do so, well-known for his expertise in Indian affairs and known to have close contacts with many members of Congress. Attlee, back at home, was left in the background.

On 28 March Cripps sent a telegram to Churchill indicating that the key issue regarding defence responsibility would be dealt with the next day: 'I have made it clear that under no circumstances can we give up any responsibility for defence.'[19] The only compromise Cripps was in a position to offer on this issue was the form of words in the declaration. Cripps, in consultation with Churchill, amended it to include that the 'organising to the full the military moral and material resources of India must be the responsibility of the Government of India with the cooperation of the peoples of India.'[20] It was not enough and a disappointed Cripps reported to Churchill on 1 April 1942: 'From all appearances it seems certain that Congress will turn down the proposals. There are a multitude of currents and cross currents but they are selecting the question of defence as the main platform of their opposition.'[21] Churchill replied to Cripps on 2 April 1942 that the cabinet was unwilling to alter the words of the declaration any further, and felt that the Indians were using the issue of defence to avoid a settlement.[22] The game was over and any chance of a negotiated solution between Britain and India was seemingly ruled out for the duration of the war. Britain had, however, demonstrated to Roosevelt that it had at least sought a negotiated solution.

The goverment now turned to an approach of suppression. In August 1942, Gandhi launched his 'Quit India' movement and, on 9 August, it was Attlee who ordered the arrests of Gandhi and Nehru. It was unquestionably an illiberal act, prima facie out of character, but one he felt was essential. He defended his decision stoutly 19 years later in the following discussion with Francis Williams. Attlee did not feel that the civilian population of India was turned against the British as a result: 'I think at the bottom of their minds they knew perfectly well that the Japanese were not really going to fight for the liberation of India. ... We had to make the arrests to stop a dangerous drift.'[23] It was an act that drew criticism from Labour MPs. On 2 October 1942 Bevan attacked Attlee strongly in *Tribune*: 'Mr Attlee is no longer the spokesman of the movement which carried him from obscurity to the second position in the land. ... Now in the name of Labour and Socialism he has underwritten one of the blackest documents which imperialist bigotry ever devised – Mr Churchill's India effusion.'[24]

It was not the only problem Attlee had with his party during 1942, but most dissension was kept within limits. The 1942 party conference took place from 25 to 28 May in Westminster. The conference report mildly rebuked the government: 'Regret was expressed (August 5, 1941) at the failure to release political prisoners in India.'[25] Attlee commented wistfully on 25 May that 'Every person according to his own inclination draws up his own balance sheet,' but later added:

when ... history ... comes to be written it will be recorded that the British Labour Movement ... played a very great part in defeating the forces of barbarism ... it will also be said that in the period after the war the British Labour Movement … took a leading part in establishing a new world.[26]

A resolution on having no compromise with the means test was put and defeated, Jim Griffiths arguing for 'improvement immediately'.[27] However, the parliamentary party was putting down markers on the amount of room for compromise available to Attlee. A coalition White Paper on 3 June advocated requisitioning the coal mines, but fudged the question of common ownership; only an immediate wage increase saw off a confrontation. A month later, 63 MPs voted against a low pension increase of 2s 6d a week, the parliamentary party putting down an amendment against the government.

Attlee's early months as deputy prime minister were uncomfortable. Failures were far more common than successes on the military front. By March 1942 Attlee was disappointed in Auchinleck, the British commander-in-chief in North Africa who, in his view gave an impression of 'infinite stale mate [sic] at best',[28] drawing Churchill to swipe at the field marshal: 'Armies are expected to fight, not stand about month after month waiting for a certainty which never occurs. … The reputation of the British army now lies unhappily very low.'[29] It was about to get lower as, on 21 June 1942, the Libyan port of Tobruk surrendered to Rommel.

On the eastern side of Libya, close to the Egyptian border, Britain's historic control of the Suez Canal was at risk, together with the prospect of German control of the whole Mediterranean. British links to India would have to be via the Cape of Good Hope, putting major pressure on its shipping resources. With Churchill away, Attlee made the Commons statement on the defeat. On 30 June, the parliamentary party demanded an inquiry into the loss of Tobruk, but Churchill survived the Commons vote by 475 to 25 votes. With the government securing temporary respite, Attlee spent part of the parliamentary recess in Newfoundland, a self-governing dominion that had had its governing constitution suspended because of monetary problems. On his return to Britain there were more positive developments in the war situation. On 23 October 1942 Montgomery, now commanding the Eighth Army in North Africa, attacked the German and Italian forces at El Alamein in Egypt. Rommel eventually withdrew on 4 November. On 8 November 1942 Allied troops launched 'Operation Torch', landing in French North Africa (Morocco and Algeria) hitherto controlled by Vichy France. By 13 November the British and Commonwealth troops had again reached Tobruk. On 15 November, bells rang out over Britain to celebrate.

While it might not have been immediately discernible, the tide of social reform was also moving in the direction of the Labour Party. In November 1942 Sir William Beveridge published his report on *Social Insurance and Allied*

Services. The government set out its plans on 1 December. When one considers the report today, its striking feature is its striving to give the impression that what it offered was a national *minimum* that did not stifle the incentive of individual self-improvement. Beveridge did declare the moment revolutionary, but noted that the report was a contribution to a broader social policy.[30]

Following the success in the North African campaign in November 1942, attention turned to the position of Italy, dubbed the Axis' 'soft underbelly' by Churchill. Attlee was concerned about the possibility of a postwar fascist regime in Italy; on 8 December 1942 he reported to Churchill his worry that: 'if some Fascist overthrew Mussolini, USA and Britain would accept peace overtures which would leave the Fascist regime intact.'[31] However, when Churchill was at the Casablanca conference with Roosevelt in January 1943, at Attlee's insistence he agreed that Italy's surrender would have to be an unconditional one. In the event, the Allies invaded Sicily on 9 July 1943 and, on the 25th, King Victor Emmanuel III dismissed and arrested Mussolini on leaving the royal palace. The Allies invaded mainland Italy on 3 September 1943 and the new Italian government negotiated a peace, then declared war on Germany on 13 October. The position on the Eastern front was also improving. For most of late 1942 the German army had been fighting the Red Army street-by-street in Stalingrad. On 31 January 1943 Field Marshal Friedrich Paulus, commander of the German Sixth Army in the city, surrendered.

By the start of 1943, Attlee had been in the government for nearly three years. His reputation among his coalition colleagues as a sound administrator (if not a political heavyweight) was such that, in April 1943, he was a serious candidate to become Viceroy of India. As early as August 1941 Lord Linlithgow had made it clear that he would be leaving the viceroyalty in April 1943; indeed, he was only staying a further year at Churchill's behest.[32] On 16 April 1943 Amery wrote to Churchill setting out his views on the appointment, which he felt was critical:

> Almost everything will depend on the personality of the next Viceroy and his successor. The job is the biggest one in the whole Empire and intrinsically more important than any in the Government here. Next to winning the war, keeping India in the Empire should be the supreme goal of British policy.[33]

As regards the individual, he placed Eden at the top of the list, Sam Hoare and John Anderson next, with Attlee fourth:

> I would … suggest serious consideration of Attlee. He knows the Indian problem and has no illusions about Congress. If he lacks personality he

has at any rate ability and shrewd judgement and would, I think, handle his Council effectively. The appointment would be well received here and in America. It would leave you with a fight in the Labour Party for the succession; but whether you got Morrison or Bevin as successor, the fight would not be very long and things would settle down. I cannot imagine any permanent danger to the stability of the Coalition being involved.[34]

On 19 April 1943 Lascelles recorded: 'Attlee's name is being put forward, and the PM, rather surprisingly, favours the idea; so is Eden's, but it would surely be madness to send him to India now. I believe they will ultimately fall back on Sam Hoare.'[35]

However, when Churchill wrote to the king on 24 April, his choice was Eden: 'No one had the qualities and reputation of Mr Eden.'[36] The king was, however, opposed to this since he felt Eden was Churchill's 'Second-in-command in many respects'.[37] No successor had been found by the end of April and Linlithgow was left *in situ*. The search became increasingly desperate and, on 8 June 1943, Amery, while still pressing the claims of Eden, worried about the inexperience of Oliver Lyttelton, but again suggested Sam Hoare and, as a final option, himself. The next day Churchill sent a telegram to Linlithgow: 'I have never in my life had to solve a more puzzling appointment.' Eden, Lyttelton and Anderson were ruled out: 'I am loth to disturb the smooth running of the War Cabinet.' Hoare's links to Munich and the Hoare–Laval pact of 1935 precluded him, leaving Sir Miles Lampson (Lord Killearn) and Lord Wavell. Churchill prejudged Linlithgow's preference: 'It seems to me after reading your various messages that Wavell would be far the better man.'[38] Linlithgow agreed, and Churchill duly appointed Wavell, with Auchinleck as commander-in chief. Altogether, 17 names had been considered in a tortuous process; Lord Wavell replaced Lord Linlithgow on 1 October 1943. This decision was to have far-reaching consequences for Attlee as prime minister. Had he himself been chosen as viceroy, it is difficult to gauge what his response would have been, but one imagines that his patriotism might have led to him offering his service, though he would no doubt have had reservations about the impact on his family. As it was, the appointment was not *political* in the sense of putting a 'big player' such as Eden in position, and it left a military man, Wavell, to deal with the complex politics of independence.

By the summer of 1943 Attlee was clearly conscious of the movement of the political tide into the mainstream of Labour ideas about universal welfare. The national executive committee welcomed the Beveridge Report, but noted that 'its general framework conformed to the terms of the resolution approved at the last Annual Conference of the Party' – comprehensive social security provision, cash payments 'whatever the contingency', family allowances and also a National Health Service.[39] In addition, the National Council of Labour, which consisted of representatives of the TUC, the Labour Party (including Attlee and Greenwood, but noticeably not Morrison) and the Cooperative Union, approved Beveridge on 17 December 1942. When Attlee spoke at the 1943 party conference on 14 June, he was confident that victory in the battle of ideas had been secured: 'I doubt if we recognise sufficiently the progress our ideas have made. The British never know when they are beaten, and British Socialists seldom know when they have won.'[40] Attlee's analysis was prescient. The executive's resolution to approve Beveridge was put, with an amendment from Sydney Silverman MP, wishing to record the 'profound distrust' of the government's commitment to the Beveridge principles, and called on the parliamentary party to 'continue its efforts to secure immediate legislation'; the amendment was defeated only by 1,715,000 to 955,000 and the executive resolution was carried.[41]

It was not this principle that was the major problem, however, but the question of why Attlee was unwilling to take Labour out of the wartime coalition and capitalize on the popularity of its ideas. Attlee argued back: 'I do not believe that we have reached the stage in this war at which we are so free from danger that we can afford to throw away the unity that has carried us so far.'[42] Fortunately, Bevan, probably the coalition's most vocal opponent, made a sensible speech that day. After noting the problem of not knowing how long the war would last, he declared: 'The suggestion that we should carry the resolution today withdrawing from the Government would give a false impression right throughout the whole of the armed forces of Great Britain.'[43] Attlee knew that he had some breathing space on the issue, and was ready to settle further into his role within the coalition.

Chapter 12
DEPUTY PRIME MINISTER AND LORD PRESIDENT OF THE COUNCIL, 1943–45

In September 1943 the chancellor, Kingsley Wood, died and John Anderson, the lord president of the council, replaced him. Attlee took Anderson's place, returning the Dominions Office back to Cranborne. His new role gave him a greater coordinating role in government, the Lord President's Committee (which he now chaired) being the principal forum for considering legislation on the domestic front. He also chaired the cabinet frequently in Churchill's absence: his travels abroad included the great conferences with Roosevelt and Stalin at Tehran in December 1943, and Yalta in February 1945. Attlee – always well-organized during his life – was also sensible and thorough in government. In November 1943, he led in the debate on the king's speech, preparing his text meticulously. He ended with a firm commitment to planning for the postwar peace:

> as we draw nearer to victory ... men and women ... ask what our position will be when peace comes. ... It is the duty of this Government and this House to remove the fears and to satisfy the reasonable hopes of all our fellow citizens who in the days when extremist peril threatened all we hold dear, added to our history one of its most glorious pages.[1]

Emboldened, Attlee made it clear that he wished to broadcast the New Year's message in place of Churchill, a note being sent to that effect to the Ministry of Information on 18 December. It was an exercise in putting the case for postwar reconstruction and was undoubtedly useful in giving him arguments to use within the Labour Party for continuing within the coalition. He put the demise of the Nazis ('Cold and dark is the outlook of Hitler and the Nazis for the New Year. The passing year has been for their forces one of continual retreat and of failure by land, sea and air') alongside the need to prepare for the peace:

> we are preparing for the problems which will confront us in the difficult period which will follow victory ... between the cessation of hostilities and the establishment of settled conditions – and this may last some time – whatever Government may be in power ... will have to work on plans made well ahead.[2]

The broadcast was very well received. Some wrote letters of congratulation to Attlee on the day of the broadcast. Edna Lloyd George (it is unclear if she was a relation of David Lloyd George) wrote from Pembrokeshire on the same day that the broadcast 'was really the best one I have ever heard'.[3] Some 16 further letters were received in the early days of January. Even Morrison's ally Ellen Wilkinson wrote to congratulate him.[4] Within the coalition, he gained further in confidence, but, conscious of retaining unity, stuck to non-controversial issues. He became the chair of the armistice terms and civil administration committee, which considered the treatment of a defeated Germany. At the end of 1943 it recommended that Germany be divided into zones of occupation under the British, American and Soviet forces. Attlee took a strong line on defeated Germany, positing an enforced settlement, finally to tame the beast of German militarism. In April 1944 the committee's remit was extended and it became known as the armistice and postwar committee. Attlee disagreed with the powerful Eden on his zonal plan, Eden being unhappy with *enforcing* the settlement on Germany. But taking a more extreme view than a coalition Conservative on Germany was hardly being out on a limb. Indeed, the warm relationship between the two men in correspondence did not suffer. When Attlee consulted Eden on replying to Pietro Nenni, the socialist leader in the occupied part of Italy who had sent a message to the Labour Party, Eden raised no objection: 'I thank you for your greetings and have communicated them to the Labour Party. I trust that all Italian socialists will do their utmost to secure a united effort to defeat Nazism, the essential condition for the victory of democracy, liberty and socialism.'[5] There was a mutual respect between Attlee and Eden.[6] Attlee showed what an effective committee chairman he was: brisk and efficient. In the Lord President's Committee, he recalled:

> We decided differences between Ministers and acted on a whole range of matters that needed a serious decision but weren't big enough to come to the Cabinet. It made for rapid business. We kept it small. ...

Below … we set up functional committees to deal with particular aspects of business or for special jobs. It all worked very smoothly.[7]

The more the end of war drew nearer, the greater came the demand from within the Labour Party to leave the coalition. On 16 December 1943 James Maxton interrupted an Attlee Commons speech on Newfoundland, in which he bemoaned the fact that adults up to the age of 30 had not cast a vote in the territory: 'May I remind the right hon. Gentleman that there are people up to 28 years of age in this country who have not cast a vote in a General Election?'[8] Yet, Attlee stuck rigidly to defending Labour's involvement in the coalition. In a speech at a Ministry of Information meeting at Sunderland on 30 January 1944, he triumphantly declared that 'Education has been lifted out of the sphere of party controversy.'[9] Of course it had not and this attitude was one that led Attlee's government to relative inaction on the issue, but, at the time, what became Butler's Education Act of 1944 looked a major step forward. It raised the school leaving age to 15, and cemented the division of state schools into grammars and secondary moderns.[10] Whatever the iniquities of the '11-plus', which Tony Crosland castigated in the 1950s and 1960s, it looked as if working-class children had a route to advancement through the grammar schools, which could realistically compete with the surviving public schools. When Attlee attended the opening of Thornton Grammar School in Bradford on 22 July, he called it 'the greatest Education Bill that this country has seen. … Possibly such a great advance could only have been made under an all-party Government in time of war when sectional interests are subdued to the needs of the nation.'[11] Yet, when he spoke at the speech day of Leeds Modern School on 24 February 1945, he also put his heart-felt view that private *and* state schools should be retained:

> I am myself very strongly in favour of an educational system which will break down class barriers and will preserve the unity of the nation, but I am also in favour of variety and entirely opposed to the abolition of old traditions and the levelling of everything to a dull uniformity.[12]

Indeed, writing to Tom some years before, on 9 August 1941, Attlee had declared that public schools, 'like most of our institutions … should not be killed but adapted'.[13] The Education Act of 1944 may be credited to Butler, but it was also an accurate picture of how Attlee ideally saw the education system in Britain.

Attlee combined his advocacy of the achievements on the domestic front with those in the war effort. On leaving Sunderland on 30 January, he spoke at a party meeting in Hartlepool:

I was proud to be a member of our Party in those days when most of us were voices crying in the wilderness. I am more proud today to belong to a movement which both on its political and industrial sides has made such a mighty contribution to saving the world.[14]

Despite such public pronouncements, Attlee was too wise a politician not to think carefully about the electoral truce. There is a fascinating handwritten note in his papers, which is unsigned, but looks as if he had written it. It sets out a number of reasons for the poor performance of government candidates in by-elections, and identifies the particular difficulties of Labour voters who found it hard to feel that the coalition was their government, and who knew of the leftward swing on dealing with postwar problems.[15] The document discusses the pros and cons of again allowing party competition in by-elections. Attlee had recently been sent a newspaper article on the adopted Labour candidate for Taunton who, despite the electoral truce, was clearly running the partisan campaign – 'Win Taunton for Labour'.[16] The document reaffirms, however, that the Labour Party was still 'strongly convinced of the need for the present Government at least until the defeat of Germany'. In support of this position, the Labour Party press department produced a 'Record of Things Done' in March 1944.[17] Attlee sought information from departments about the increases in social services and was given figures to prove increases in unemployment insurance, unemployment assistance, health insurance, workmen's compensation, disability service pensions and supplementary old-age pensions. Some 8.5 million employees had secured a 'guaranteed week' under the essential works order of 16 February 1944 and there were large increases in canteens (more than sixfold) and school meals (nearly threefold).[18]

However, it was clear that Attlee's approach changed in early 1944. His public pronouncements no longer tried to force the pace within the coalition (he found it 'more and more difficult to get postwar projects before the Cabinet'[19]) but sought to dampen expectations within the Labour Party. Speaking at Exeter on 12 March, he declared: 'I have many plans for the post-war period sent to me which are very neat and complete as one might get an architect's plan for a new house, but I cannot tell when the site will be vacant, what shape it will be or what materials will be available.'[20] Attlee's central political problem of Labour winning the battle of ideas but not having the chance to reap the electoral dividends remained. Speaking on 29 March 1944 at the county councils' association meeting, Attlee declared: 'We are living in days when the conception of planning has been accepted by most thoughtful people,'[21] but at the Yorkshire regional council of Labour on 1 April 1944, he was forced to concede: 'I know that some of you are impatient at the continuance of the electoral truce.'[22] Meanwhile, tensions between Bevin and Bevan came to a head in the Commons in April 1944, when Bevin, after a winter coal strike over a minimum wage for miners, sought to increase the government's powers through the defence regulations to deal with strikes in key services. After Bevan castigated Bevin in the Commons, Attlee actually recommended the expulsion of Bevan from the parliamentary party, but Bevan escaped with a slap on the wrist from the national executive committee, being asked only that he would promise to abide by the parliamentary party's standing orders (the parliamentary party's formal written rules, including measures of discipline).

Attlee's problems with party management were not going to go away. On 15 April he received a letter stating that the Society of Labour Candidates' executive committee had been organizing regional meetings. Attlee was asked to speak out: 'Candidates, as you know, are in a somewhat uncertain frame of mind and some guidance and encouragement would be deeply appreciated.'[23] Attlee was once more on the defensive, and on 13 May 1944 he addressed the Midland regional council of the Labour Party, and vigorously defended the decision to join the coalition. 'Did the Party gain or lose by that action? I say it gained immeasurably. It gained in stature and in credit with the whole nation. I do not want what we gained then to be thrown away by displays of irresponsibility now.'[24] Indeed, in May 1944, Attlee was assisted by the government White Paper on employment policy, which declared: 'The Government accepts as one of their primary aims and responsibilities the maintenance of a high and stable level of employment after the war' and proposed 'an extension of State control over the volume of employment' with an extended system of social insurance.[25] What he was not helped by was the coalition government's continued failure to implement any of these emerging social reform ideas.

The focus of the nation was, however, still turned to the war effort, as British and Allied forces returned to France on D-Day, 6 June 1944. A bridgehead was quickly established and, by August, Attlee was able to tour the various front lines around Europe. Attlee flew first to Gibraltar then on to Algiers to meet the anti-Vichy French before moving on to Italy, when he met Pietro Nenni to whom he had sent a warm message some months before. Attlee, typically, was not impressed by his agreement with communists. He then moved on to Normandy and was impressed by the artificial 'Mulberry' harbour, thence to the Netherlands and Belgium, meeting Montgomery in a caravan in the woods. It was clear that, while the Germans were being driven back on all fronts, the problems of dealing with the newly-free countries – not least in the immediate terms of ensuring that their populations did not starve – had only just begun.

At home, with Hitler's latest weapon of unmanned flying bombs falling upon London, the housing situation was acute. On 30 August 1944, Morrison produced a memorandum on the housing situation in London alone:

> The number of houses destroyed or damaged beyond repair ... is at present over 100,000; the number seriously damaged was 150,000 before flying bomb attacks began and may well be approaching 250,000 ...; the number ... capable of first-aid repair ... [with] ... further attention ... is over a million.[26]

On 8 September 1944, at the reconstruction committee of which Attlee, Morrison and Bevin were all members, as was Jowitt (the other members were Butler and Woolton), Woolton, as minister of reconstruction, declared housing the most present reconstruction problem and appointed a housing subcommittee chaired by himself, with Bevin, but not Attlee, among the members.[27]

On the weekend of 6–8 October 1944 Attlee travelled north to Whitehaven where he attended the conference of the Cumberland Federation of Labour Parties at Workington, as well as two public meetings.[28] His speech to the party struck the same cautious note he had adopted throughout 1944. The government proposals on social insurance had been published the previous week: 'It is worth considering also how many are the changes and chances of this mortal life for which provision had to be made. It is one thing to form a general plan. It is quite another matter to work out its detailed application.'[29] He did, however, allow himself one sentimental glance back over his career:

> I recall and took part in the campaign for the abolition of the Poor Law initiated by the Webbs and George Lansbury. I recall the bitter fights with the advocates of the old Poor Law principles. I have lived long enough to see the principles of that great Minority Report adopted.[30]

There was an unmistakable sense that Attlee was coming to the end of his career in government. When he attended the twenty-fifth birthday dinner of the Electrical Development Association on 30 November, it was as if he was a man whose great personal battles had been in the past.

The daily work of being deputy prime minister in the coalition did, however, continue apace. Britain was heavily dependent on American aid and Attlee did his bit to ensure that relations between the two Allies remained cordial. On 8 November 1944 he spoke at a lunch at Claridge's for the promotion of Anglo-American relations: 'World trade depends on interdependency. Economic isolation is as dangerous to the peace of the world as political isolation.'[31] On 4 December he maintained the theme in a broadcast to America from the Office of War Information at the American embassy: 'I look forward to an era of expanding world trade wherein Britain and the United States will be engaged not in cut throat competition, but in rivalry in the service of humanity.'[32]

The issue of remaining in the coalition was at a critical point when the 1944 party conference took place from 11 to 15 December. Greenwood spoke in favour of the national executive committee's resolution on 11 December: 'It announces quite boldly that we are in this war to the end.'[33] Bevan criticized it on the basis that it left political flexibility in the hands of the Conservative Party.[34] However, the two 'references back' (the procedural method of sending resolutions back to the executive to reconsider them) were defeated, and the report carried 'by a large majority'.[35] Attlee, in a more comfortable position, took the opportunity to speak on one of the issues close to his heart, world government, saying on 12 December: 'The chief of the principles is that there must be an authority armed with power that transcends the will of the individual State.'[36]

When Attlee received a Christmas message in 1944 sending him good wishes for 'the coming victorious year'[37] he must have felt jubilation, not just at the prospect of an imminent conclusion to war, but also that the question of the continuation of the wartime coalition would soon be settled one way or the other. The year began with a private attack on Churchill's conduct of government business, which served as evidence both of the development of the relationship between the two men and of Attlee's firm view of how government business should be conducted.

The day after a war cabinet meeting on 18 January Attlee sent a letter to Churchill in which he cited his failure to read the conclusions of cabinet committees prior to war cabinet meetings. 'Instead of assuming that agreement having been reached, there is a prima facie case for the proposal, it is assumed that it is due to the malevolent intrigues of socialist Ministers who have beguiled their weak Conservative colleagues.' In Attlee's view, this created delays and he abhorred the deference shown to the views of the Lord Privy Seal, Lord Beaverbrook, and the minister of information, Brendan Bracken, neither of whom were in the war cabinet (and both of whom were virulently anti-socialist).[38] Churchill's initial anger, referring to 'Atler or Hitlee', was calmed, with Attlee's arguments finding support from the most unlikely people, including Clementine Churchill and Lord Beaverbrook, and he merely sent a brief acknowledgment in response.[39]

Attlee may have been simply expressing his frustration with the inefficiency of government business: and given the way he was to conduct government as prime minister, this is credible. Jenkins is dismissive of the extent of the change resulting from the letter: 'a little, but not much',[40] but Attlee was also sending a political message to Churchill that, despite the left-leaning nature of social reconstruction considered in cabinet committees, the Labour ministers remained loyal to the coalition and he resented any suggestion to the contrary. The Attlee of 1940 would not have dreamed of sending such a message. But now he felt he could, without damaging their relationship. Churchill and Attlee were never very close friends, but there was a mutual respect between them: Attlee admired Churchill's conduct of the war – 'no one could have done the job he did'[41] – and Churchill appreciated Attlee's abilities and loyal service. Later, he famously remarked that Attlee was a modest man with much to be modest about. This respect was reflected in the behaviour of their wives; back in May 1943, Clementine Churchill had attended a thanksgiving service at St Paul's Cathedral with Attlee and Violet.[42] Indeed, in postwar elections, the two women often shopped together during campaigns while their husbands battled for votes.[43] But all this is not to say that Attlee did not see Churchill's faults. His remark that a monologue was not a decision showed that, while he admired Churchill's oratory, he also felt that Churchill could let his mouth run away with him – to the detriment of efficiency in government: 'Winston was sometimes an awful nuisance because he started all sorts of hares, but he always accepted the verdict of the Chiefs of Staff when it came to it.'[44]

Victory in the war was now inevitable. On 7 February 1945, Attlee spoke at the World Trade Union conference at County Hall: 'Victory … is certain, and while we must maintain to the utmost our war effort it is natural that our minds should turn to peace and its problems.'[45] Attlee returned to his theme of pressing for social reform, announcing at the Nurses Speech Day at Harrow Hospital on 3 February: 'I am hoping that before long we may get into legislative form the Government proposals for a National Health Service.'[46] When he spoke to the Woolwich Labour Party on 11 February, he was moving into election mode: the Labour Party would 'fight the election responsibly … face the problems of the peace with the conviction that they can only be met by the application of Labour's principles.'[47]

At a war cabinet meeting on 22 February, a concerned Churchill sought to retain control over domestic policy: 'He thought it essential that no bill dealing with a controversial subject should be introduced unless the policy had been considered and approved by the War Cabinet.'[48] However, the obvious forum for disagreement, the reconstruction committee, was still able to find common ground on a number of issues. On 8 January 1945, ministers discussed family allowances, and disagreements were on practicalities, not on the central principles of the bill; even when Morrsion expressed his view, which was not universally held, that the wife should have the right to the payments, a way forward was found:

> The general opinion was … that the bill should provide … the allowance 'belonged' to the husband. … It was not thought right that

this … be left to a free vote in Parliament. If … the debate disclosed a majority view in favour of conferring the legal right on the mother, the Minister could promise to reconsider.[49]

On 22 January, with Morrison absent, there was

general agreement with the view that it would be undesirable at present time to take any avoidable step which might provoke political pressure for an increase in the basic rate of pensions. It was, in general, inexpedient that any rates of benefit should be increased in anticipation of the new comprehensive scheme of national insurance.[50]

On 12 March the issue of the sale of medical practices was raised, yet an agreed conclusion was forthcoming on consultation 'regarding the steps which the Government should take in order to deal with the problem of the disposal of medical practices without endangering progress towards the establishment of a National Health Service'.[51] Similarly, on 7 May, in the final meeting of the wartime coalition reconstruction committee, with Attlee absent, Jowitt, the minister of national insurance, was able to announce that he 'believed that his new proposals would facilitate acceptance of the Industrial Injuries Insurance Bill by the Trades Union Congress and the Labour Party'.[52] These proposals included the application to workers temporarily in the country and accidents suffered on the way to, and leaving, work.[53]

The divisions in the reconstruction committee were, however, becoming more frequent. On 9 April 1945, the committee decided 'that it would not be practicable to secure agreement at the present time on any scheme for the reorganization of the electricity supply industry', despite Morrison's assertion that 'Electricity supply was essentially a public utility and two-thirds of the industry was already in the hands of public authorities.' Attlee 'regretted that it had not been possible to come to a decision at an earlier date since it was now more difficult to reach agreement'.[54] On 30 April 1945, with Attlee absent, Morrison and Butler clashed in the reconstruction committee on the subject of iron and steel nationalization, which Butler vehemently opposed.[55]

Against this background, Attlee continued to work assiduously as deputy prime minister. On 6 March, he left at the behest of the war cabinet for a six-day visit of France, Belgium and the Netherlands in order to assess the urgent situation regarding the distribution of food and supplies. He drew the fairly obvious conclusion that it was 'necessary to make a great effort to get the authorities in America to appreciate that the successful rehabilitation of the West European democracies is an essential part of our war aims'.[56] Duff Cooper reported from the British embassy to Eden that 'the visit [to France] was in every way successful' and that Attlee had met de Gaulle; the French in Cooper's view had been given evidence of British interest in their supply issues; they were grateful for the opportunity to ask again for immediate assistance and further help would be accepted.[57] It was the kind of wartime task in which Attlee excelled – fairly uncontentious politically, requiring a sensible, safe pair of hands to make the right noises to those he met and coming back with a firm administrative conclusion based upon observation.

On his final foreign trip as part of the wartime coalition, in May Attlee set off to San Francisco as part of the British team headed by Eden to discuss the forming of the United Nations. He had laid the groundwork on 6 April when, in a broadcast to America, he expressed concern that the San Francisco conference should result in 'something more than a mere spasmodic concert or alliance'. On 2 May he confidently told the Commonwealth Club of San Francisco: 'Our conception of a world organization is an integral part of Labour's creed.'[58] He managed to combine a united front for the British team with an election broadcast while there: 'In a short time from now, maybe in a matter of weeks, there will be a General election. If, as a result of this, the people of Britain return a Labour government, we shall take the first steps along the road to a Socialist Britain.'[59]

Attlee had continued to advance the idea that Labour had won the battle of ideas. He spoke to the Bradford Labour Party on 25 February: 'I want to remind you that the Labour Party has for years taken its stand on collective security … let us rejoice that others now accept the principles to which we are attached.'[60] Addressing the Nottingham Labour Party on 25 March, he added: 'I know men who in peace time worked for private profit but have found in war time the satisfaction of working for the people.' But, he cautioned: 'I know that conditions immediately after the war are going to be very difficult for this country.'[61] When he broadcast triumphantly on 18 May that 'National planning was vindicated',[62] it was the culmination of the arguments he had been putting in various guises since being propelled to the forefront of the parliamentary party in 1931.

On 30 April 1945 Hitler committed suicide in his bunker in Berlin. Britain had won the Second World War. Churchill had taken the premiership in the nation's darkest hour and led the country to victory. For all Attlee's wartime work – and he had served with great distinction – he lacked the status in the public eye of either Morrison as home secretary or Bevin as minister of labour. Too much of his work had been behind the scenes. Morrison had been very visible to the public, often visiting bomb sites, and the 'Bevin Boys' doing essential service in the native industries like coal had become part of national folklore. Had there not been a war it is very doubtful whether Attlee's leadership would have lasted for the ten years between 1935 and 1945. That he stood less than two months away from the Labour Party's first – and perhaps greatest – landslide election victory would have been inconceivable. As Churchill rightly took the plaudits for his wartime service, Attlee remained in the background, his position by no means certain. His career rested on not just the election result but also on the position of his main political rivals, Morrison and Bevin. Fortunately for him they disliked each other intensely.

Chapter 13
THE 1945 GENERAL ELECTION

During the twentieth century there were three great election victories for progressives. Midway between the Liberal landslide of 1906 and the New Labour victory of 1997 lies the Labour victory of 1945. It was the first time the party had ever won an overall majority in the House of Commons and it marked an incredible transformation for the party that had been reduced to a mere 52 seats in 1931. The election was held on 5 July 1945, but due to the difficulties of having to collect and count votes from servicemen still stationed all over the world, the results were not declared until 26 July. Although, on 5 July, *The Times* declared Churchill to be in 'supremely confident mood',[1] the Labour Party took nearly 12 million votes, 47.8 per cent, winning 393 seats. The Conservatives won 213 seats on just under 10 million votes, 39.8 per cent, and the Liberals fell to only 12 seats on less than 2.3 million votes, just 9 per cent. With a majority of 146 seats, *The Times* hailed 'A Sweeping Labour Victory', with a list of the defeated Tory MPs including Leo Amery, Brendan Bracken, secretary of state for war James Grigg, future prime minister Harold Macmillan and the caretaker home secretary Sir Donald Somervell.

It had not been clear that the Labour Party was going to fight a July election at all. At the end of the war in Europe, Churchill had written to Attlee indicating that he wanted the coalition to remain until the defeat of Japan, rather than the autumn, which was his impression of Labour's preferred position. On 21 May, the first day of the 1945 Labour Party conference in Blackpool, at 2 p.m., in private session, Churchill's letter was considered. Only two hands were raised in support of continuing until the autumn. Delegates approved Attlee's reply, which reiterated that participation *could* continue until the autumn and that a July election would 'cause bitter resentment among the men of the fighting Services'.[2] This was a clever way of avoiding the real issue, which was that of continuing in the coalition into peacetime, as Churchill undoubtedly would have welcomed. It left Churchill trapped in the position of having to call an election in July, with the statesmanlike Attlee advocating the needs of the troops (even though it was not entirely clear why an autumn election, during an intense ongoing conflict with Japan, would not also have caused resentment among the troops).

The timing of the election was not, however, controversial and why the political earthquake occurred as it did has taxed commentators ever since. Just as Lloyd George's coalition had won triumphantly in 1918, Churchill was expected to win in 1945. His personal reputation was, understandably, at its zenith. The evidence of a left-wing swing was, however, real. The difficulty in interpreting wartime by-elections was the electoral truce: there would simply be a government candidate, rather than a Labour versus Conservative contest. However, the Common Wealth Party, founded on 26 June 1942, and Independent Labour candidates did well in by-elections in the final two years of the war. The Common Wealth Party was a *type* of progressive party. 'The professional ethic and the ideal of service, rather than class interest, were the basis of its appeal ... managers and workers were to own factories and cooperate in running them.'[3] It won at Eddisbury in April 1943, Skipton in January 1944 and Chelmsford in April 1945. Addison concluded:

> failure to sense Labour's growing majority was a measure of the lack of communication between the world of Westminster ... and the mood of the public ... polls conducted by the British Institute of Public Opinion predicted a Labour victory on six occasions after June 1943. But ... study of voting behaviour ... was only ... beginning ... pundits ... ignored its conclusions.[4]

There were, of course those who thought that Labour would win. Lascelles noted wryly in his diary that 'though I hadn't anticipated as big a swing as this, it doesn't surprise me.'[5]

The factors explaining this left-wing swing have been well-documented by historians: much of the Labour electoral machine was still at home in the UK, working in industries such as coal mining, so had not been called up to fight, whereas Tory agents and canvassers remained overseas. Longer-term factors included the 'retrospective judgement on the 1930s' – namely that the election was a rejection of the supposedly free market policies at home and appeasement policies abroad of the Conservative-dominated national government of the 1930s. Certainly, Labour's general election manifesto, *Let Us Face the Future*, reminded the public that the economic dislocation of the interwar years was no accident, but the product of power concentrated in the hands of a few men.

5. Clement Attlee broadcasting.

Historians have also considered the 'Forces Vote' – that the votes of those serving went to Labour in the hope of a better life once they returned home. The war was the ultimate expression of working together, of collectivism, and Labour seemed most likely to proceed with the Beveridge reforms. This said, the Labour historian Kenneth O. Morgan has argued that it was not mainly the effect of the services vote due to low turnout among the forces, organizational factors (since many Labour agents were drafted in at such a late stage and were inexperienced in any event), the election campaign (due to lack of evidence of influence on how people voted) and that there is no evidence of a 'swing of the pendulum' theory to suggest anything other than a Chamberlain victory in 1940. For him, 'Labour was uniquely identified with a sweeping change of mood during the war years.'[6] Another esteemed Labour historian, Henry Pelling, emphasizes the longer-term factors, including, in fact, the 'swing of the pendulum' effect with memories of the 1930s still in voters' minds, a fear of a return to unemployment, the performance of the Red Army, Labour's association with attempts to solve housing difficulties, the first Labour government having passed Wheatley's Housing Act in 1924, and a perception among some voters that voting against the Conservatives did not mean voting out Churchill.[7]

The key factor here, as far as Attlee was concerned, is that on *none* of these arguments is the victory attributed even in part to him. Addison's seminal book

The Road to 1945 has a chapter entitled 'Attlee's Consensus', but it is not suggested that a personal vote for Attlee was a key to the 1945 victory.[8] The weight of the evidence, therefore, points to Attlee as a passive beneficiary rather than a creative force. However, if the election campaign had had an impact on voting, Attlee's contribution *would* have been significant. On 4 June 1945, Churchill made what has been widely regarded as an ill-judged party political broadcast on the BBC, in which he famously declared: 'No Socialist Government conducting the entire life and industry of the country could afford to allow free, sharp, or violently worded expressions of public discontent. They would have to fall back on some kind of Gestapo, no doubt very humanely directed in the first instance.'[9] The next day, Attlee responded calmly: 'He wanted electors to understand how great was the difference between Winston Churchill the great leader in war of a United Nation, and Mr Churchill the Party leader of the Conservatives.' He added: 'the voice we heard last night was that of Mr Churchill, but the mind was that of Lord Beaverbrook.'[10] He still viewed the arch anti-socialist Beaverbrook with deep suspicion. Evidence of the direct impact of this broadcast is scant: for example, there are no opinion polls on the days before and after Churchill and Attlee spoke. But, given the size of the Labour victory, Attlee's impact could not have been very negative.

Attlee's greatest problem during the campaign came from within. The chair of the Labour Party in 1945 was Harold Laski, professor at the London School of Economics. His first missive was an undated, handwritten letter sent to Attlee when the coalition government ended on 28 May: 'in all sincerity ... it would be widely and profoundly felt that a change from your leadership now would add greatly to our chance of victory.'[11]

Attlee simply sent a one-line response saying his thoughts had been 'noted', but Laski was not finished yet. Behind the scenes, Churchill had written to Attlee on 31 May 1945, offering him and Bevin, 'in strict personal secrecy', the 'facilities to see papers on the main developments in foreign affairs and strategy'. He felt Attlee should be present at the Three Power Conference starting on 15 July with no election result until ten days later. Attlee finally accepted the offer on 8 June, though notably on behalf of himself alone and not including Bevin. Colville noted on 15 June that 'Mr Bevin was not to be included in any arrangement'.[12] Whether this was because he wanted to take advantage of the fact that he was still the leader of his party (and did not wish to give the impression of any perceived threat from anyone else), or because he simply felt that Bevin had no greater right to access than any other senior member of the party, is unclear. Laski, however, wrote a further handwritten note on 14 June: 'I assume that you will take steps to make it clear that neither you nor the Party can be regarded as bound by any decisions taken at the meeting, and that you can be present for information and consultation only.'[13]

The impression of Attlee attending but with his hands tied by his party was not a favourable one and Churchill tried to press home the advantage with a letter to Attlee demanding clarification on the position of the Labour prime minister in relation to his party. Attlee responded by drawing a distinction between the *parliamentary party* and the party organization as a whole. However, the strict constitutional position suggested that Laski was correct; the party conference decided party policy. As stated in Clause V Part 1 of the Labour Party Constitution: 'The Party Conference shall decide from time to time what specific proposals of legislative, financial or administrative reform shall be included in the Party Programme.' Yet, it appears that Attlee avoided another 'Zinoviev letter', as in 1924, even after the matter appeared on the front page of Beaverbrook's *Daily Express* on 17 June. The ghost of MacDonald waving banknotes in 1931, misrepresenting Labour policy, must have been visible at the feast when, on 20 June, Laski issued writs for libel in respect of allegations in the *Nottingham Guardian* that Labour would 'use violence' if required to achieve its ends.[14]

The most significant letter to Attlee arrived on 26 July from Churchill. With the majority of results counted, he indicated that he was tendering his resignation at 7 p.m., giving Attlee his best wishes in the 'heavy burden you are about to assume'.[15] Laski, still in unhelpful vein, gloated: 'At long last we have made possible full friendship with the Soviet Union', and then added just for good measure, 'as the temporary head of the Socialist *Gestapo*, say that not all of us have been treated with generosity in this election'.[16] Attlee was more circumspect: 'The country has put its confidence in Labour. It will not put that confidence in vain.'[17] That there ever was a question of who should be prime minister, with Attlee having led his party to this kind of victory, shows that some of his Labour colleagues failed to notice how effectively he conducted government business in wartime. Henry Pelling suggests that 'Attlee's achievements were largely behind the scenes and perhaps not many people knew of his skill as a chairman of Cabinet committees.'[18] When the second Sea Lord, A. C. Willis, wrote to Attlee on 27 July, 'Heartiest congratulations on your great victory, especially the personal aspect thereof,'[19] he could not have known of the political machinations that had occurred over the past 48 hours.

The immediate threat to Attlee's position came from his old rival, Morrison, who made a direct bid for the party leadership. Dalton records that Morrison gave notice of his intentions with a letter to Attlee that he should not go to the palace to kiss hands as prime minister, but wait 48 hours until the Parliamentary Labour Party had met to choose a leader; Morrison would be a candidate.[20] In fact, Morrison's letter preceded the declaration of the election results:

This envelope contains a personal and private letter from Mr Morrison to Mr Attlee dated July 24, 1945 and is to be sealed and kept in a safe place. It should only be opened by Mr Attlee personally or destroyed on his instructions. On his leaving office the sealed envelope should be given to him unopened.

The letter was clear in its intentions:

A number of our colleagues have approached me, provisionally, asking that I should accept nomination for the leadership of the Parliamentary Party …

Whatever the result of the election may be, the new Parliamentary Party is bound to include many new members. They should, I think, have an opportunity of deciding as to the type of leadership they want.

In these circumstances, I have decided that, if I am elected to the new Parliament, I should accept nomination to the leadership of the Party.

That I am animated solely by considerations of the interest of the party … I need hardly assure you.

A copy of this letter is being forwarded to the secretary of the Parliamentary Party for his information.[21]

There should be no doubt about Morrison's intentions. In his autobiography, he unconvincingly tried to defend his position:

Some misunderstanding has since arisen because I am alleged to have attempted to obtain the premiership for myself. This is untrue. What happened is I was pressed by members of the Parliamentary Labour Party to see that the democratic principles of the Party were observed as regards choice of our leader and therefore the nation's prime minister.[22]

Even in this most defensive paragraph he concedes the crucial point about the delay in Attlee kissing hands: 'It would, of course, leave the door open for anybody to stand, including myself. I myself had no doubt that the party would confirm Attlee's position as leader.'[23]

On the afternoon of 26 July, in Labour Party headquarters at Transport House, party secretary Morgan Phillips, Bevin and Morrison met Attlee. At one stage Cripps telephoned Morrison, ironically, it appears, to support Morrison's view about waiting 48 hours, and Morrison left the room.

While Morrison was out of the room taking the telephone call from Cripps,

6. Batting it out on the cricket pitch, 27 July 1945.

Bevin asked Morgan Phillips: 'If I stood against Clem, should I win?' Morgan Phillips replied: 'On a split vote, I think you would.' Then Bevin turned to Attlee and said: 'Clem, you go to the Palace straightaway.'[24]

Why did Bevin take this stance? Of course, he disliked Morrison. Dalton learnt 'later from another source that, when Attlee told Bevin of Morrison's letter, Bevin had said: "I won't have it. You leave him to me." He had then rung Morrison up and said: "If you go on mucking about like this, you won't be in the bloody Government at all."' It was, however, deeper than that for Bevin. There was his central trade union value of loyalty, and his view on the kind of leader he felt the party needed. Dalton records:

> Arthur Deakin [Bevin's successor as general secretary of the Transport and General Workers' Union], he said, had been incited by Laski to come and ask Bevin himself to be Leader, with Morrison as his Deputy. He had said to Deakin: 'How dare you come and talk to me like this?' He had also said to several people: 'You should read history', and had referred to Campbell-Bannerman and his gift of holding a team of clever men together. ... But we didn't want, he said, any more personal leadership like MacDonald's or Churchill's.[25]

Bevin's loyalty to Attlee was crucial at this stage, and was to be crucial again in the currency crisis of 1947. Attlee's later remark that if you had a good dog

7. Ernest Bevin and Clement Attlee.

like Ernest Bevin, there was no point barking yourself was aptly demonstrated.

It is difficult to believe that Attlee's position on 26 July 1945 was anything but uncertain. In stark contrast to Tony Blair's triumphant entrance to Downing Street on 2 May 1997 on the back of the twentieth-century's second Labour landslide, Attlee was in a precarious position. He went to the palace on Bevin's instruction and, on arrival, Lascelles records:

> Attlee came 7.30, obviously in a state of some bewilderment – the poor little man had only heard a couple of hours before that he was to be called upon immediately to fill Winston's place; it struck me that he may not be sure whether his followers are prepared to follow him, or may prefer another leader – he has had no chance of consulting them. Anyway, he kissed hands all right, so he is now committed to forming a Government – or trying to.[26]

Chapter 14
ATTLEE AS PRIME MINISTER

The composition of the original 1945 cabinet was a testament to Bevin's faith in Attlee's ability to unite the different strands of the Labour Party. All the major streams of thought had a champion at the cabinet table, and Attlee's offers were not turned down by any significant figure. No one was unhappy in their posts, or felt they had not received an office worthy of their standing within the party, save perhaps for Morrison, though satisfying his ambition would undoubtedly have meant the end of Attlee's leadership. The key appointments at the top were Dalton and Bevin: the famous 'switch' between Dalton as foreign secretary and Bevin at the Treasury, to the other way around.

That Bevin was such a great success as foreign secretary has made the decision, in retrospect, seem an inspired one, but Bevin's *absence* from the Treasury was equally as significant. With Attlee 'tone deaf'[1] on economics, the chancellor was always likely to be a very powerful figure in the government, and it was economic crises that were to rock the government in both 1947 and 1949. Bevin would probably have made a good chancellor as well: his steadying hand on the tiller would have been reassuring within the government during both these periods. Bevin was to shore up Attlee's leadership in 1947 in any event, but, had he been chancellor, directly *responsible* for economic policy, it is difficult to see how a move to press him into replacing Attlee would have got off the ground on the basis that his leadership was needed in difficult economic times.

Attlee made the appointments he did principally because he wanted to keep Bevin and Morrison apart – Morrison dealing with domestic affairs, Bevin with foreign affairs. Both Dalton and Bevin would have been happy with the positions originally intended. Bevin wanted to be chancellor, while Dalton had carved out a significant reputation for himself as Labour's foreign affairs spokesman in the late 1930s. Lascelles records the king pleading with Attlee on the evening of 26 July: 'He [Attlee] told the King that he was thinking of making Dalton Foreign Secretary; HM begged him to substitute Bevin.'[2] Attlee may well have shown some deference to the king's wishes – indeed, it was not to be the last time he did this, but on 27 July Attlee saw Dalton prior to lunch and indicated his preference for him, which was unchanged – 'almost certainly the Foreign Office'.[3] When he saw him again just after 4 p.m. on the same day, he told him he was to become chancellor of the exchequer, giving keeping Bevin and Morrison apart as one reason.[4] This would suggest that Attlee changed his mind that afternoon rather than on seeing the king. Indeed, Morrison records a meeting that afternoon between himself, Attlee and the chief whip, the Durham miner William Whiteley: 'I advised ... the two proposed appointments would be better the other way around. ... Whiteley agreed; then Attlee agreed; and so the appointments were made. ... Of the two men, Bevin was undoubtedly the wiser choice for diplomatic work.'[5] Attlee knew of the threat Morrison posed, but did not argue with either Morrison or his chief whip.

Attlee made four further appointments to form his initial submission to the king. Morrison would of course need to be given a very senior position and was duly appointed Lord President of the Council and leader of the House of Commons. In effect, this made Morrison the dominant figure, after Attlee, in directing the government's domestic policy, and his deputy prime minister. Arthur Greenwood was another with a claim to high office and was leader of the opposition at the end of the war. He took the sinecure office of Lord Privy Seal, in effect a minister without portfolio. The last 'big player' to place was Cripps. In 1945 he rejoined the Labour Party and Attlee appointed him president of the Board of Trade, second only to the chancellor in the economic portfolios. Finally, William Jowitt, Attlee's old schoolmate at Northaw Place, was appointed Lord Chancellor. Jowitt had been a barrister and had had something of a chequered political career. Having served as attorney-general in the second Labour government, he followed MacDonald into the national government in 1931, and was expelled from the Labour Party before being allowed to rejoin in 1936. In 1939 he won the Ashton-under-Lyme by-election, before serving in various positions in the wartime coalition – first as solicitor-general before assuming responsibility for postwar reconstruction, being paymaster general, minister without portfolio and, from 1944, minister of national insurance. In short, with his experience, legal background and personal link to Attlee, he was an ideal choice for the role.

Attlee constructed his government in pencil on scraps of paper. He tried to place all the new MPs into categories – 'Women', 'Lawyers' (including, appropriately, a barrister/solicitor distinction), 'Teachers', 'Dockers', 'Young Men'.

8. Britain's postwar Labour cabinet.

He then wrote out an initial list in which Ellen Wilkinson was clearly considered as minister of health before Bevan.[6] Attlee then wrote out his choices on a large 'Table of Political Offices' mounted on cardboard.[7]

Some choices had been crossed through and changes made. James Chuter Ede was once placed at the ministry of labour, but was replaced by George Isaacs, who was originally placed at fuel and power before the office went to the Clydesider Emmanuel Shinwell. The home secretary was the one post for which the Attlee jigsaw piece changed the most – William Whiteley, who became chief whip, then Alfred Barnes, back to Whiteley again, before, finally, Chuter Ede, a former teacher and parliamentary secretary to the Board of Education during the wartime coalition. Isaacs, a union man who had been general secretary of the National Society of Operative Printers and Assistants, followed in the giant footsteps of Ernest Bevin at the Ministry of Labour; the minister of works was originally Barnes, then Fred Marshall, then, finally, George Tomlinson; Barnes went on to become minister of war transport. Ellen Wilkinson, as key Morrison ally who had served with him at the Home Office during the war, became the second female cabinet minister, in education. Attlee showed great magnanimity by appointing the wartime rebel Bevan as minister of health, a tremendous example not only of managing a potential malcontent but of getting the creative best out of a fellow politician. A. V. Alexander began a third stint as First Lord of the Admiralty, having held the post in 1929–31 and in the wartime coalition, and Viscount Stansgate, father of Tony Benn, took Air. Pethick-Lawrence, an upper-class rebel like Dalton (an Eton-educated barrister, who did nine months in 1912 for his involvement in Christabel Pankhurst's direct action in smashing windows for the Women's Social and Political Union), was created a peer and, at the age of 73, became Secretary of State for India, with the even older Viscount Addison appointed Secretary of State for Dominion Affairs at the age of 76. Like Churchill, Attlee became his own minister of defence, before appointing Alexander to the office in December 1946.

The cabinet has often been seen as a group of elderly men, mostly born in the late Victorian area and shaped by a conservative outlook. Bevan, at 48, was the youngest member and, while Hugh Gaitskell entered it in October 1947 as minister of fuel and power at 41, with Harold Wilson joining at the same time as president of the Board of Trade at just 31, the overwhelming age profile was of men in their sixties and seventies. Attlee was 62. Yet, compared with his twentieth-century predecessors, this was not a particularly old age to hold the office for the first time. Indeed, of the nine previous men to have become prime minister in the twentieth-century, five had been younger than Attlee on taking office for the first time and four older, including his two immediate predecessors Chamberlain (68) and Churchill (66).[8] Indeed, the economist Evan Durbin argued that Attlee was physically very suited to the premiership:

> He must be the lightest man who has ever been Prime Minister. Yet he is extraordinarily strong and wiry. He plays golf well, and he … can keep his end up on the tennis court. Apparently completely tireless and enjoying astonishing powers of recovery, he can work to all hours throughout the week almost without sleep.[9]

As prime minister, Attlee kept to the routine of a daily walk after breakfast in St James's Park.[10]

Attlee was well-prepared for the highest political office in the land. He was well-travelled. Free from the responsibilities of government office in the 1930s, he had visited continental Europe every year. Aside from his trip to wartorn Spain in 1937, Attle had been at the international conference of the League of Nations at Montreux in Switzerland in 1933 and, in 1934, he met Beneš, the Czechoslovakian president at the time of the Munich agreement. As regards the Soviet Union, Attlee retained his healthy scepticism. Unlike Sidney and Beatrice Webb, who travelled to the Soviet Union in 1932 and accepted the official statistics and accounts given to them before publishing *Soviet Communism: A New Civilization?* in 1935, Attlee was fully aware that when he and his party (his private secretary John Dugdale and his mother) visited Leningrad and Moscow some months later that they 'saw only that which it was intended we should see'.[11] In the summer of 1938 he holidayed in Copenhagen and saw Denmark prior to the German occupation of April 1940.

His wartime service had included both a specific departmental responsibility at the Dominions Office and a wider coordinating role. As Lord President of the Council and leader of the House of Commons he was an experienced parliamentarian. He had been an MP for 22 years and had led his party for a decade. He had also reflected on how to structure government. Aside from a unified Ministry of Defence, which he had argued for during the 1930s, Attlee had considered having a small cabinet with few departmental responsibilities, enabling a clear distinction between administration and overall policy, with which such a cabinet would be better equipped to deal. Attlee was the ultimate 'committee' prime minister: the historian Peter Hennessy has argued that under him the idea was 'taken to extremes'.[12] During his premiership there were 148 standing committees (of both ministers and officials) and 313 *ad hoc* ones.[13] Attlee's initial 'General Plan of working of Govt' consisted of three small pieces of paper on which he constructed his main cabinet committees. The defence committee would deal principally with the war against Japan and Attlee himself would chair it. There were then a number of other committees set up: Greenwood would chair the social services committee; Morrison the economic committee (according to one piece of paper and Cripps according to another); Morrison the legislation committee; Bevin the external affairs committee; and Morrison the Lord President's committee.[14] The key figure at this stage was Morrison, who had the major responsibilities as an overseer on the domestic front, including economic policy direction and, in his Lord President's committee, the nationalizations.

Virtually all the major events of Attlee's premiership spawned a committee of some kind. A small group was set up to deal with the negotiation of the American loan in 1945 and, four years later, a small working party was set up to deal with devaluation in 1949. Even when the Attlee government took the secret decision to start developing an independent nuclear deterrent, it was still done by committee. One committee he did not create was a small group of senior cabinet ministers free from departmental responsibility: he had propounded this in the early 1930s and Sir John Anderson, as chair of the cabinet machinery of government committee at the end of Churchill's wartime administration, had also put forward the idea in 1945. However, Morrison was nominally in charge on the domestic front with Bevin doing the same in foreign affairs. On a personal basis – certainly in terms of maintaining his leadership – Attlee relied far more on Bevin.

Attlee did not surround himself with special advisers at Number 10. His first principal private secretary, from 1945 to 1947, Leslie Rowan, he inherited from Churchill. His successor from 1947 to 1950, Laurence Helsby, was in the same civil service mould. His first cabinet secretary, Edward Bridges, combined the post with permanent secretary to the Treasury until 1946; Norman Brook, in this period additional secretary to the cabinet, succeeded Bridges as cabinet secretary in 1946, from which time Bridges concentrated on his Treasury job. The closest he came to a political appointee was probably Douglas Jay, an economic assistant at Number 10 until leaving to become MP for North Battersea on 25 July 1946. Jay was part of a group of Oxford-educated Keynesian economists who advocated economic planning; another, Evan Durbin, had been an assistant to Attlee as deputy prime minister during the Second World War, but died tragically by drowning while saving his daughter in September 1948. His press secretary, Francis Williams, was not a political appointment. *Presenting* policy to the press did not concern Attlee: Williams had to persuade him to have Press Association tapes updating him with news in Number 10 at all.

Attlee himself – modest, understated and laconic – did not change on becoming prime minister. The general public knew so little about him that, on 28 July 1945, *The Times* ran a feature to explain who he was:

> Mr Attlee is a man of simple tastes and his great modesty and dislike of ostentation and publicity have made him a less well-known public figure than many of his political colleagues. His shyness and reticence have sometimes made him seem aloof to those of his colleagues who are little in contact with him. His qualities have not in the past made him an outstanding personality in Parliament, but in the face of possible rivals his disinterested service to his party and his high conception of public duty have established him firmly in the affections of the Labour Party as its undisputed leader.[15]

Attlee's long-term leadership of the party was still by no means secure, but in every other way this was an accurate portrayal. His later PPS, Arthur Moyle, described him as: 'completely natural in all situations, without affectation of any kind and there was about him an unassuming integrity. He did not wear power on his sleeve, but kept it in reserve only to be used when necessary.' Attlee 'did everything with military precision. ... He was a master of simple English and often expressed his deepest thoughts in monosyllables. He detested verbosity and tedious repetition.' He would never waste time:

> In all he did he personified economy. He would bath, shave, dress and present himself for breakfast in 20 minutes. For a busy Prime Minister every minute is vital. Interviews had to be brief. ... He would place his pipe on the table blotting-pad, lift himself out of his chair, take a deep breath ... and grunt. This mannerism was deadly. It rarely failed to

speed the visitor on his way. Sometimes he varied the technique. Once he looked up at a colleague who had let loose a veritable Niagara of words. Quietly, the Prime Minister asked, 'How is your aunt?' It had the desired effect.[16]

Moyle's summary was: 'For me the epitaph most fitting to him would be "No Prime Minister in our Parliamentary history discharged his responsiblities with less fuss."'[17] He could also be ruthless when he needed to be:

One of his Ministers was called to see him. The Prime Minister sniffed, looked up at him and said, 'Don't you think you ought to resign?' 'Why?' he was asked, 'what's wrong?' 'Nothing, lad, except that you don't measure up to the job.'[18]

He did not overburden newly-appointed ministers with advice, and expected them to get on with the jobs with which they were tasked. He told James Callaghan, on being appointed parliamentary secretary of the Ministry of Transport: 'Remember you are playing for the first eleven now, not the second eleven. And if you are going to negotiate with someone tomorrow, don't insult him today.' Attlee then 'nodded and said goodbye'.[19] Interestingly, it was also as prime minister that Attlee doodled more frequently during meetings. Moyle could read into the shape of his doodles: 'I could tell from the design of the doodles what kind of meeting there had been. If circular and with a regular pattern – harmony, if circular with a simple design – boredom, but if it were one of his best, a central pattern surrounded by geometrical points – conflict.'[20] Yet his doodling was not an indication of a lazy politician who was not listening. Evan Durbin described him as having:

a voracious appetite for papers and telegrams. He consumes them like a boa-constrictor and it one of the chief jobs of his Private Secretaries to see that he never runs short of official reading matter from 8 o'clock in the morning to 1 o'clock the next morning. In this way he covers an immense amount of ground.[21]

Attlee's personal life still provided great stability. His lifelong love of cricket remained – he kept up to date with the Middlesex scores throughout his time at Number 10. His family meant a great deal to him; on his first full day as prime minister he found time to send a telegram to Martin, then a midshipman on the SS *Menelaus* in Nova Scotia: 'Everything going very well. Family send love. Daddy 27th July.'[22] Attlee continued to spend 'quality time' with his family – when he was with them on weekends, he closed his mind to work.

The family did not generally discuss politics and he was good at DIY, carrying out minor repairs when necessary.[23] Money was less of a problem. In 1948 the Attlees sold Stanmore and bought another house, Cherry Cottage at Great Missenden in Buckinghamshire, which was rented out. Violet guarded their personal freedom jealously. Attlee often read books aloud to her and, in January 1947, they celebrated their silver wedding anniversary at Number 10. Violet still took little interest in politics: her greatest practical contribution to Attlee's daily political responsiblities was to drive him around in the car during election campaigns. She was also sometimes ill; Attlee reported to Tom on 23 February 1948: 'Vi is a lot better but still has to take things easy.'[24] At times, she was 'jealous of the office which she felt took her husband away too much from her. She could be miserable and difficult, and needed reassurance.'[25] Others, notably Morrison, were jealous of the fact that Attlee held the office at all. Yet hold onto it he did, despite three economic crises, one major plot against his leadership and a clash between Bevan and Gaitskell in March 1951, which laid bare the underlying personality tensions at the top of the Labour Party that Attlee had managed so well for so long. In doing so he provided a great example of the successes of a particular style of leadership – and also of its limitations.

Chapter 15

THE SCALE OF THE CHALLENGE, JULY–NOVEMBER 1945

Between 26 July 1945, when Attlee was appointed prime minister, and 28 November, when the government concluded its negotiations with the United States on the terms of Britain's 50-year loan, the essential strands of postwar British policy both at home and abroad were put into place. On 28 July, *The Times* laid out the challenge Attlee faced: 'The time is due for practical projects in concrete terms to rebuild what has been shattered and to guard against a return of the conditions of economic disharmony in which the seeds of war as well as poverty are sown.'[1] The economy was a major concern. After the First World War there had been a postwar boom, but then the country had struggled to adapt to peace-time conditions and unemployment soared to over two million in the early 1920s. When Attlee broadcast on 3 September that 'We have won a great victory' he added that the government would 'release the maximum number of men and women from the Forces at the earliest moment'.[2] He gave an average figure of 45,000 per week for the rest of the year. These men would expect jobs on their return home and the Attlee government was expected to create the favourable economic conditions necessary. This would be difficult. On 11 March 1941, the United States Congress had passed the Lend-Lease Act, giving aid to Allied countries, including Britain in return for military bases, but at the end of the war, on 21 August 1945, this abruptly ended, leaving Britain in 1945 facing what Keynes famously called a 'financial Dunkirk'.

Attlee's premiership also faced the initial challenge of the conference at Potsdam. *The Times* declared: 'The most immediate issue of policy confronting the Labour Government and the FOREIGN SECRETARY is, however, naturally that of the resettlement of Europe, and, in particular, of the future of

Germany.'[3] Attlee and Bevin left for Potsdam from Northolt at 13.45 on 28 July, arriving at Gatow at 18.40 local time. Bevin was so unprepared for foreign travel that a doctor was provided to give him a typhus inoculation on arrival if needed.[4] Much of the shape of the postwar settlement had already been worked out. President Roosevelt, addressing a joint session of Congress on 1 March 1945, had set out the agreement reached at Yalta, summarizing the progress thus far: Germany would be occupied in four zones by the USA, Russia, Britain and France; Nazi war criminals would be punished; there would be no *financial* reparations for Germany as in 1919, but Germany would be prevented from maintaining 'any ability to wage aggressive war'[5] and an international organization for world peace would be established.[6]

Attlee had been in San Francisco hammering out the details of the United Nations: with his history of support for the league and world government, he strongly welcomed it. On 22 August, he spoke in the Commons in favour of ratifying the charter, welcoming the International Court of Justice and, with a touch of old Victorian imperialism, the doctrine of trusteeship in respect of certain colonial territories. Aside from the empire, the government also had to ensure that the British-controlled areas of Germany and Austria did not starve, and surplus army rations together with such foods that could either be spared in the UK (including tea), or were outside the ambit of UK law (including excessively sulphurated dried fruits)[7] were provided.

In one area Attlee and Bevin failed to progress – Greece. The Nazis had withdrawn in October 1944 and a civil war had broken out between the communists and royalists in December. Britain had managed to contain the civil war to the extent that the communist forces agreed to a general election. A major concern was the Soviet Union dominating Greece, but the chiefs of staff restricted Attlee and Bevin's freedom of manoeuvre, telling them on 29 July: 'In our view the defence of the Greek frontier must be left to Greek forces and later guaranteed by world security organization. ... In [the] absence of American troops in Greece we cannot entertain the idea of unilateral British military action in [the] Balkans.'[8] On 31 July, the Foreign Office sent a rueful telegram to Washington: 'British Delegation at Terminal now state that there is little possibility of further progress being made with this subject at Potsdam. Soviet Government will clearly not agree to participate in supervision.'[9] It took the Truman doctrine of March 1947 – namely that the United States would support governments against communism – and American aid to Greece to prevent a communist takeover: this was an early example of Britain's new reliance on the United States for influence around the world. There was no danger that Attlee was going to follow Laski's enthusiasm and embrace the Soviet Union. He must have sympathized with the cable he received on 13 September from a William A. Taylor in Canada who felt that Laski's 'loose language [was] provoking devastating comment perfect … for Britains [*sic*] baiters and haters'.[10] Not even diplomats in Moscow felt that Stalin took the Laski idea very seriously. 'Continuance of close Anglo-Soviet relations is taken for granted but there seems to be a general assumption that Britain will now be so preoccupied with domestic questions that she will devote less attention to foreign affairs.'[11]

As prime minister, Attlee's attention could never, however, be entirely on the task in hand. On 30 July Morrison cabled about the 'go slow' protest on wages at the Surrey Commercial. Docks:

> Reports today … indicate go slow on two newly arrived food ships but normal piece working on third newly arrived food ship. Government announced 23rd July that no avoidable delay would be permitted … wish to know if you concur in use of military labour if reports tomorrow confirm go-slow. … Very urgent.[12]

Attlee did concur and, within days of the Labour government taking office, military labour was sent in to break a strike. It was not to be the last time Attlee used strong-arm tactics to deal with strikes. When the dockers went on strike in June 1948, he also utilized troops and declared a state of national emergency. With the dockers out again between May and July 1949, while Attlee stopped short of declaring a national emergency he also used troops and ended the strike quickly. Though dockers' wages had certainly risen far less than those of workers in other industries, Attlee felt that improved conditions and a guaranteed minimum wage were major steps forward. In 1947 the government also introduced the National Dock Labour Board to curtail the old casual employment regime; in a number of ports, there was then control of the hiring of labour, with workers and employees represented on the board. Attlee was therefore out of sympathy with the strikers.

In general, his relationship with the trade unions was very positive. On 28 July a letter arrived from the TUC general secretary Walter Citrine, which set the tone. Citrine asked for a 'general chat' as he was 'particularly concerned that there should be the closest cooperation between the Trades Union Congress and your Government, as both in 1924 and 1929 the lack of this led to misunderstanding and trouble'.[13] On the pretext of Attlee being busy, he also wrote to Morrison by letter dated 30 July, no doubt hedging his bets in case Morrison ever became prime minister. He asked about repeal of the 1927 Trade Disputes and Trade Unions Act and reduction in hours of work. Morrison replied that he was sympathetic, but 'obviously' not in a position to commit the government, and the correspondence was passed to Attlee on 3 August. On 8 August Citrine personally congratulated Attlee on becoming prime minister and invited him to address the TUC at Blackpool before they met on 9 August.[14] Attlee addressed the delegates for the first time since 1941 on 12 September. He was cautious: 'I need not stress to you the difficulties of our own situation. ... Now that the war is at an end, Lend-Lease and mutual aid also end and we have to face a new situation.'[15] But the response of the president, Eddy Edwards, was probably the best that any incoming Labour government could hope for: 'we are giving no promises in advance that we will not criticize the Labour Government. What we will not allow, however, is outsiders, who are not part of our movement, stabbing either the individual members of the Government or the Government as a whole.'[16]

Edwards need not have been unduly concerned about the government's attitude to working people. Within a matter of days the government started to construct the welfare state. On 18 September 1945 the National Insurance (Industrial Injuries) Bill was published, building on the Workmen's Compensation Act of 1897, which provided compensation for personal injury. The bill set out a scheme of payments for workers becoming disabled due to accidents at work. Ten days later, Jim Griffiths, minister of national insurance, produced a memorandum to the cabinet social services committee, which dealt with concerns the TUC and miners raised about the benefits for partial disability being less than under the Workmen's Compensation Act, and concern about injuries suffered by the armed forces and industrial injuries being different. The government had produced a table of the extent of disability arising from various injuries, including 40 per cent for the loss of an eye and 100 per cent for absolute deafness. This early memorandum showed the Attlee government's determination to create a welfare state and to consult fully the trade union movement throughout.

Attlee was deeply conscious of the difficulties of the second Labour government, and the perception that it had drifted away from its own MPs before striking the reef of seeking to cut unemployment benefits in the face of strong TUC opposition. To correct this, links between backbenchers and the government were institutionalized. A liaison committee was established, with the secretary, the leader of the House of Commons and the chief whip serving on it. Various subject groups within the parliamentary party were also set up and, in contrast to 1929–31, ministers were to meet groups of MPs for discussion.[17] On 14 August, at Seymour Place, a reception was held for party members to meet members of the government; the next day, the national executive committee held a joint meeting with the Parliamentary Party on the day of the king's speech opening the new parliament. Attlee set the tone for a consultative approach, putting his speech together painstakingly, carefully making enquiries of other departments, including the Foreign Office, Bevin himself, Morrison, and Bridges and the Lord Chancellor read it over on constitutional matters.[18] The various drafts take up the majority of a whole box of Attlee papers – some 248 pages. The ghost of MacDonald undoubtedly stalked the corridors of the Palace of Westminster in the summer of 1945.

Money was essential for virtually every Attlee government policy and without it there could be few British commitments abroad, let alone nationalizations, a welfare state and National Health Service at home.[19] On 24 August Attlee had made a statement to the House of Commons confirming Truman's cancellation of lend-lease, but confirming that Lord Halifax, Keynes and Brand, the Treasury representative in Washington, and other officials were to return to Washington for talks about the way forward. The task was not an easy one. Many Americans viewed the Attlee government's socialism with suspicion. In February 1944 the American Economic Council Review of Books observed: 'Sir William Beveridge may be contemplating a totalitarian regime in Britain, and so too the British people.'[20] Attlee pressed on and set up a committee called Gen. 89, 'Financial Negotiations and Commercial Policy', which met for the first time on 14 September 1945. Of the senior cabinet ministers, it included Bevin, Dalton, Cripps, Pethick-Lawrence, Shinwell and the minister for agriculture and fisheries, Tom Williams. The debate centred on the curiously named 'Nabob 372', a cypher on 21 November 1945 that set out the American position in draft form. Dalton was horrified:

> The Americans have rejected … a credit of $2½ billion, including Lend-Lease at $½ billion, at 2 per cent, together with a right to draw a further $2 billion, free of interest, for the purpose of clearing up the Sterling Area. We must be prepared to accept 2 per cent on the whole of any credit we take up, for whatever purpose. …
>
> In my judgement, the proposals are unacceptable, both in form and spirit.[21]

Dalton sent a strong telegram to Keynes on 24 November: 'The fact is that we could not stomach much of Nabob 372 any more than I suspect you can. That is not the kind of agreement you went out to obtain or would like to bring back with you.'[22] Any expectations that the Americans might be inclined to provide money as a gift had long since dissipated. Attlee was calmer, cabling Halifax on 26 November that 'the clock is ticking against the Americans at least as much as against us.'[23] Dalton's dissatisfaction proved well-founded. The United States government made a line of credit available of $3.75 billion until 31 December 1951 when, in 50 annual instalments, the money would be repaid with 2 per cent interest added each year. Clause 7 of the loan agreement was the famous 'convertibility clause' that pledged that, 'not later than the date

9. US loans to Britain, 5 February 1946.

of one year after the end of this agreement', sterling would be 'freely available for current transactions in any currency without discrimination'.[24] The loan was in fact only paid off in the final months of Tony Blair's premiership. The Attlee government now had the money to get its policies off the ground, but on harsher terms than it expected. The 'convertibility clause' was to prove a major problem when it came into effect in July 1947, producing a drain on sterling that precipitated an economic crisis and a threat to Attlee's leadership. But Britain was not in a position to argue.

Indeed, fortunately for Attlee, it appeared that the American government could compartmentalize in the way he could because, throughout the period that the loan was negotiated, Truman and Attlee were embroiled in an acrimonious disagreement about allowing 100,000 Jews into Palestine. The issue of Palestine awaited Attlee on his entry to Number 10. To understand it as it presented itself to him, it is necessary to understand the history of Britain's involvement. This was crystallized by the Balfour Declaration of 1917: Arthur Balfour, then foreign secretary, declared British support for a national Jewish home in Palestine. In 1922 the League of Nations approved the British mandate of Palestine, which took effect from 23 September 1923, with Britain having to facilitate Jewish immigration while protecting the rights of the Arab inhabitants. However, increased immigration from the Nazi regime in Germany, together with the Arab uprising against Jewish immigration from 1936 to 1939, precipitated a White Paper from the then colonial secretary,

Malcolm MacDonald, on 17 May 1939. It confirmed that Britain had overseen the best part of half a million Jews moving into Palestine and that, for the next four years, 75,000 Jews would be admitted; thereafter the Arabs would have to sanction further admissions. A letter from Truman to Churchill dated 24 July 1945 urged the 'lifting on these cruel restrictions which deny to Jews, who have been so cruelly uprooted by ruthless Nazi persecutions, entrance into the land which represents for so many of them their only hope of survival'.[25] Attlee sent a reply asking for time to consider the matter.

However, Truman was insistent and, on 31 August, sent a famous further letter to Attlee on the issue. He urged Attlee to provide the 100,000 immigration certificates: 'no other single matter is so important for those who have known the horror of concentration camps for over a decade as is the future of immigration possibilities into Palestine.'[26] Attlee responded by telegram on 16 September that the Jews were 'not now using the … certificates available and … have not taken up the 1500 available for this month … they are insisting upon the complete repudiation of the White Paper … quite regardless of the effect on the situation in the Middle East.'[27] Truman was not satisfied. On 29 September, Halifax telegraphed from Washington to the Foreign Office that the American president had publicly 'appealed to … Attlee to open up Palestine for the emigration of the remaining estimated 100,000 Jews in Germany and Austria.'[28] On 1 October Attlee was forced into a press release:

> Statements have been made in Washington that the Prime Minister has not sent any reply to President Truman's letter to him of August 31st on the subject of Jewish immigration into Palestine. In fact the Prime Minister sent a reply on September 16th and he understood that no further action would be taken until after Mr Byrnes [the US Secretary of State] had returned to Washington.[29]

The problem for Attlee on Palestine had crystallized. Truman, with his personal commitment to a Jewish homeland, and undoubtedly with an eye on Jewish votes in the United States, was going to push for the fastest immigration of Jews into Palestine. Britain was left with trying to balance this against the interests of the Arabs. It was a problem the Attlee government was to prove unable to solve and the issue was handed over to the United Nations in 1947. There was a wave of sympathy for the Jews in world opinion as the full horrors of the Nazi Holocaust emerged. Attlee could not have been anything but aware of this. In the Attlee papers is a memorandum on the position of the Jewish population: 'With few exceptions those Jews are intensely desirous of immigrating to some place where they can forget what they have been through.

They turn to Palestine.'[30] The issue left a stain on the reputation of the Attlee government; whether that was justified will be discussed in a later chapter.

The initial direction of policy on India, towards some sort of self-determination, was also set in the early weeks of the Attlee premiership. On 19 September, Attlee broadcast to India with an apparently simple message:

India has shared to the full with the rest of the United Nations the task of saving freedom and democracy. Victory came through unity and through the readiness of all to sink their differences in order to attain the supreme object.

I would ask all Indians to follow this great example and to join together in a united effort to make a constitution which majority and minority communities will accept as just and fair, a constitution in which both States and Provinces can find their place. The British Government will do their utmost to give every assistance in their power and India can be assured of the sympathy of the British people.[31]

Wavell, still viceroy, telegraphed that he was unhappy and that the penultimate sentence above should be substituted with: 'I would ask all Indians to follow this great example and to join in a settlement which majority and minority communities will accept as just and fair and in which both States and Provinces can find their place.' Since he was concerned that, as originally formulated, it would be read as ruling out partition and right of succession, which he thought unwise at this stage, Attlee altered it to: 'I would ask all Indians to follow this *just* example and to join together in a united effort to *work out* a constitution which majority and minority communities will accept as just and fair, a constitution in which both States and Provinces can find their place.'

The viceroy was authorized, on an interim basis, to take steps after the election to form an executive council,[32] but the very early signs of disagreement with Attlee had materialized. There is no suggestion that Attlee envisaged a change of viceroy at this early stage, but, ominously for Wavell, on 8 August, his successor, Mountbatten had contacted Attlee directly to ask to 'come and pay his respects … one day this week'.[33]

Yet, within Britain's final victory in the war in the Far East during this period, an even greater challenge presented itself – the very survival of human civilization in the nuclear age. On 6 and 9 August, atomic bombs had been dropped on first Hiroshima and then Nagasaki, forcing the Japanese surrender on 2 September taken by General MacArthur on board the US battleship *Missouri* in Tokyo Bay. On 28 August Attlee had produced a memorandum of his own on the atomic bomb for his 'Gen 75' cabinet committee on atomic energy. The document has an urgent tone, 'The most we have is a few years start,' and a real sense that the atomic weapon had changed world warfare completely. At this stage it was unclear what could be done. Attlee felt that that the only way the danger of proliferation could be dealt with was by America, Britain and the Soviet Union taking action together.[34] The nature of such action was entirely unclear and reflected the problem the Attlee government had in second-guessing the approach of either Truman or Stalin. In the months and years to come, Attlee took the decision to develop an independent nuclear deterrent. It was a decision he shrouded in the utmost secrecy, not just from parliament but also from many cabinet colleagues. That this most consultative of prime ministers took such a grave decision in this way was perhaps the greatest paradox of Attlee's career in government.

Chapter 16

FULFILLING THE PARTY'S AMBITIONS: NATIONAL INSURANCE, NATIONAL HEALTH AND NATIONALIZATION, 1945–48

When the tiny Parliamentary Labour Party fought the means test in the 1930s, Attlee could scarcely have believed that he would one day lead a Labour government with a three-figure Commons majority and a mandate to introduce full-scale welfare provision. The government had signalled its intent with the publication of the National Insurance (Industrial Injuries) Bill and followed this up on 1 December 1945 when Greenwood drafted a report to cabinet from the social services committee. It contained the framework of the welfare state. It went further than the White Paper on employment in 1944, and returned to the Beveridge model of sickness and unemployment benefit without a limited period during which these benefits could be claimed. Pensions were made available to all on retirement and widows' pensions were introduced.[1]

Dalton was unhappy with some of the proposals and in his own memorandum dated 5 December 1945 he objected to three aspects of the report – the failure to limit the period for claiming unemployment, paying a single pensioner more than half the weekly amount for a couple, and paying a pension even where the person had not retired.[2] The cabinet met on 6 December and agreed that a pension should be conditional on retirement but otherwise concluded indecisively, Attlee commenting rather flatly that 'he hoped it would be possible for the Cabinet to resume their consideration of these matters during the following week.'[3] Greenwood produced a further memorandum on 11 December, in which he noted that the difference between payment for a single pensioner and that of a couple had been resolved. Dalton had agreed to pay a single pensioner more than half that of a couple (namely 26 as opposed to 21 shillings a week). The remaining outstanding matter was that of a time limit for claiming unemployment benefit, with Jim Griffiths still against such a limit. At cabinet, Attlee intervened in what was to become typical style, seeking unity: 'the preponderant view in the Cabinet was ... a time-limit on the duration of unemployment benefit. At the same time, however, the Social Services Committee should examine further the question of the conditions on which claimants would be entitled to assistance after the exhaustion of their right to benefit.'[4] A 30-week limit was agreed, 'but with extensions for contributors with good employment records'.[5] Griffiths tried to reopen the question when he produced a further memorandum to cabinet on 15 January 1946, by suggesting an 'emergency' two-year period due to the particular conditions of postwar Britain, in which there could be an extended period of 26 weeks during which the benefit could be claimed.[6] There was also the further problem that Dalton had raised to Attlee on 14 January, suggesting, on the basis of a meeting of ministers, that the chancellor have the power to vary the levels of insurance contribution by order.[7] Attlee replied to Dalton on 16 January that such a power was 'rejected by the coalition Government on the ground of the danger or suspicion that it might be manipulated for political purposes. It should, therefore, come before the Cabinet as a principle is involved.'[8] When the cabinet met on 17 January Bevin suggested the final compromise on the issue of the limit for unemployment benefit payments: for five years, the Court of Referees would consider the circumstances of a particular case and make a recommendation to the minister for continuation of benefits. On varying the contribution rates, Attlee asked if it was 'not dangerous to take a wide power of this kind which would be exercised without reference to any objective standard?' He suggested the unemployment level or world trade, but Dalton stuck to his guns, citing the lack of data for such a test, and Morrison thought the inclusion of such matters of reference was 'impossible' – hence the compromise position that the bill 'would not preclude the making of an order providing for automatic variation by reference to some objective test'.[9]

This may read as a defeat for the prime minister, but the fact was that this was a good example of the Attlee cabinet – and the Attlee leadership style – working well. When compromises were needed, they had been found. An enormously significant piece of legislation had been agreed upon by a cabinet working together constructively, with a prime minister guiding the discussion towards firm conclusions. When Attlee spoke in the House of Commons on the National Insurance Bill on 7 February 1946, he was able to look back fondly at his own experiences:

The first breach in that fortress of 1834 was the Old Age Pensions Act, but the battle was really joined, as I remember very well, over the representations of the Majority Commission on the Poor Law. I myself took a small part with Mr and Mrs Sidney Webb and George Lansbury in that propaganda fight.[10]

Alongside the National Insurance Act of 1946, the National Insurance (Industrial Injuries) Act reached the statute book in the same year; these were then complemented by the National Assistance Act of 1948, which obliged local authorities to provide services, including, if necessary, residential accommodation, for the disabled. It also provided 'National Assistance' payments to those who had exhausted their national insurance entitlement or had not built up sufficient national insurance contributions in the first place. Attlee's journey from the poverty of the East End was complete.

Attlee's major contribution to government policy in 1948 was in relation to the creation of the National Health Service. Perhaps typically, it was his *refusal* to do something that was so critical. In early 1948 Attlee manoeuvred Bevan in his negotiations with the doctors so as to restrict his health minister's freedom of movement, and *structured* his negotiations with the health professionals. The original National Health Service Act had reached the statute book in 1946, but passing the act was only the start of the battle to create the service. Throughout 1947 and the first half of 1948, Bevan was engaged in negotiations with the British Medical Association. Those negotiations and Bevan's strategy of resolve and then compromise brought the service into existence on 5 July 1948. Bevan and the secretary of state for Scotland, Woodburn, met the BMA's negotiating committee for a gruelling two-day session on Tuesday 2 and Wednesday 3 December 1947.[11]

Bevan was concerned about the tone and content of the negotiating committee's case document, completed on 7 November 1947. It made a scathing attack on the National Health Service Act (1946): 'to bring it into force as it stands will create chaotic conditions.'[12] He therefore opened the meeting very aggressively: 'Was it ... a Negotiating Committee? The Committee's statement to the profession, in substance, declared the *whole* Act [my emphasis] to be unacceptable.'[13] Dr H. Guy Dain, chairman of the council of the BMA, replied tartly that the purpose of the meeting was 'to discover from the Minister ... whether he was prepared to secure the necessary amendments to the Act'.[14] The four major issues for Bevan to deal with were GPs' ownership of the goodwill of their practices; GPs' freedom to practice without being directed as to where; a right of appeal to the regular courts against dismissal; and fixed remuneration (a key issue in terms of whether GPs felt they could retain their independence or whether they felt they would become akin to full-time paid civil servants).[15] Bevan's default line was the proposition that since the National Health Service was the will of parliament, it should be done.[16]

By early 1948 problems for Bevan were mounting. At a special representative meeting of the BMA on 8 January 1948, a complete lack of confidence was expressed in Bevan.[17] Without the cooperation of a substantial number of medical professionals, the National Health Service could not possibly work. Both carrot and stick were available to Bevan: the stick was most certainly what he termed the 'constitutional point' – namely that the BMA, as an interest group, could not prevent a piece of legislation passed by an elected Parliament from being implemented. The BMA could not be, and would not *want* to be, the sole reason why the people could not have their health service. The carrot was the concessions that Bevan could or should make, and that was the question to which his mind now turned. The only positive point was that the special representative meeting of the BMA on 8 January set the level of GP opposition in the forthcoming February plebiscite at only 13,000 out of 20,500, in order to justify non-cooperation with the service.[18] Bevan would not need to convince a majority of GPs to accept the service.

On 16 January 1948, an increasingly concerned Attlee asked Bevan to report to cabinet on developments 'in view of the publicity given to the difficulties which appear to have arisen in your discussions with the BMA'.[19] Bevan produced a memorandum for cabinet consideration.[20] In it, he attacked the BMA Secretary, Dr Charles Hill, for his negativity and his desire to 'sabotage' the act. Hill was certainly not a political soulmate, later serving as a Conservative cabinet minister.[21] Bevan then concentrated on three areas of dispute – the position of partnerships, for which he now proposed a concession to appoint a legal committee to consider the options; the right of appeal to the ordinary courts from a tribunal decision on dismissal; and the issue of the fixed salary, no compromise being proposed on the last two points.

> Nothing, I believe, could prevent the doctors – as an organization – from voting against the Act this month. That does not mean that they will not, as individuals, take part in it. If we keep firmly to our 'appointed day' those who do not take part will (a) lose their present panel income, (b) lose their right to share in the £66,000,000 compensation for capital values when they later come in, (c) lose all right to have any private patient in any pay-bed in any hospital.[22]

Norman Brook, summarizing the document for Attlee, agreed with Bevan's position on partnerships and the appeal to the courts, but felt that if Bevan's only argument against changing fixed fees was an administrative one, that was a possible area for compromise, which could be announced before the plebiscite along with the concession on partnership agreements.[23]

On 22 January 1948, at a cabinet meeting, Bevan said that: 'The Negotiating Committee had … been dominated by a reactionary and vocal group who, partly for political reasons, were seeking to prevent the Act from coming into operation.' The cabinet agreed to bring the service into operation on the intended date of 5 July. Bevan's strategy was to separate the BMA's position from that of the individual doctor. Anticipating a significant vote against the service in the BMA plebiscite, on 29 January 1948 Bevan sought, and received, permission from Attlee to give an oral answer in the House of Commons on how the ballot was conducted.[24] He attacked the BMA's failure to hold a secret ballot: 'It was because open votes of this sort were removed from our constitutional practice that the secret ballot was established.'[25] The risk for Bevan was that the BMA would refuse to work with him as an individual and appeal over his head to Attlee.

On 2 February 1948, the cabinet set the date of the debate in the House of Commons for 9 February. At this, the motion was agreed, welcoming the service into force on 5 July and declaring 'that the conditions under which all the professions concerned are invited to participate are generous and fully in accord with their traditional freedoms and dignity'.[26] Bevan again set out a strong position:

> The Minister of Health said that he did not in fact contemplate making any further concessions to the doctors; but it was the view of the Cabinet that the passage of a motion in these terms would not preclude the Government from making changes in the scheme, if they thought fit, before 5th July.[27]

Bevan asked for Attlee's support: 'He would, however, be glad if the Prime Minister would also speak in the debate. The Prime Minister said that he would hold himself in readiness to speak and would decide, according to the course of the debate, whether it was desirable that he should intervene.'

This was the critical moment for Attlee to shape the negotiations. On 6 February 1948, the Ministry of Health wrote to Helsby, Attlee's private secretary, enclosing a suggested note for the prime minister's intervention. There were essentially two points to make: on the one hand, the assurance that the cabinet was behind Bevan and that he was not isolated on the issue; second, from a constitutional perspective, to reject the notion that 'Governments can be forced to do other than they and Parliament intend by a campaign of deliberately organized sabotage.'[28] Bevan clearly needed Attlee to intervene if he was to pursue a tough line in the coming months. Attlee's intervention would have shown the stiffness of the government's resolve that the service should come into operation and that the BMA should not be able to block it. It would also have protected Bevan from being isolated from his colleagues and take away the possibility of the BMA seeking to negotiate directly with Attlee in which case Bevan himself might become a potential casualty.

Attlee declined, with a short note on the day of the debate indicating that he had decided 'after all not to speak in the National Health Service debate'.[29] Bevan could not have felt anything but frustration at this. It locked him and the BMA into a contest in which Bevan's hands had been partially tied, save in one respect. The cabinet had agreed not to delay the implementation date of the service. Bevan's strategy therefore had to be one of compromise as opposed to belligerence; but he knew that the extent of the compromise need not be critical to the fundamental principles upon which the National Health Service was based. Attlee had framed the terms of the negotiation for Bevan. It was undoubtedly a calculated gamble, made in the knowledge of the set date for bringing the service into effect, but also in the full knowledge of the kind of politician Bevan was – unquestionably creative and determined, but prone to lashing out in temper. Indeed, in the Commons debate on 9 February 1948, Bevan shot in anger at the BMA as 'politically poisoned people'. But this did not detract from his overall approach. He wanted to show that he *was* willing to compromise with individual doctors: the problem was the BMA. Bevan emphasized the concession made on allowing specialists to accept privately-paying patients. In anticipation of the plebiscite results, Helsby was contacted by the permanent secretary at the Ministry of Health, Sir William Douglas. Bevan clearly still trusted his belief in what individual doctors would do, but he remained concerned about a direct appeal to Attlee over his head. Helsby noted to Attlee that: 'the only real issue still outstanding is that concerned with the basic salary'; and that Sir William Douglas was 'merely bringing me up to date on the background, especially since this might be useful if, as seemed likely, we received letters at No. 10 urging that the Prime Minister should intervene in the dispute in some way'.[30] Attlee still took no positive steps, neither backing Bevan nor intervening over his head.

The 21 February plebiscite results brought the results Bevan had expected: 17,037 GP voted against the service, well in excess of the 13,000 threshold set,[31] though Bevan only had to change the views of around 4000 doctors to meet the BMA criterion. At a special representative meeting of the BMA on 17 March 1948, an approach to Attlee to reopen negotiations was rejected.[32] Lord Moran of the Royal College of Physicians, wrote to Bevan on 24 March 1948 'conveying the view of the Physicians that the cooperation of the general practitioners could be won if the Minister made it crystal clear that no whole-time salaried medical service would be brought in ever, either by legislation or by departmental regulation'.[33] On 6 April 1948, *The Times* ran the story of the Royal College of Physicians' move to ask Bevan to introduce an 'amending Bill to make impossible the introduction of a whole-time salaried service by regulation'. The view expressed in *The Times* was that this appeared to 'offer a real prospect of a peaceful solution to the controversy'.[34] Bevan was already alive to this and, in a note dated 5 April 1948, asked for a meeting with Attlee and Addison.[35]

The stage was now set for Bevan and he made a statement in the House of Commons on 7 April 1948. Moran's request was one with which he could easily deal, primarily because it was an illusory compromise: Bevan had never said anything different. He confirmed that full-time salaried service would require further legislation and made two further concessions: there would be the Amending Act and some changes on the capitation fee, something Brook had previously identified to Attlee as a possible area for compromise. With the BMA holding a further plebiscite in May 1948, Bevan thought that there would be sufficient support among doctors to bring the National Health Service into operation on 5 July, even though that plebiscite was likely to be lost.[36]

The strategy of limited compromise forced upon him by Attlee succeeded: of the original 20,500 GPs who could vote, fewer than half had opposed the service. The BMA council was able to take the view that 'on some fundamental issues the profession has gained a substantial victory'.[37] Bevan remained concerned that Attlee had not been sufficiently partisan on the issue, and he wrote to him on 2 July 1948: 'Our people all over the country will be making speeches this week-end claiming credit for the Labour Party for these great Acts. They will be made to look foolish if their leader attributes their parentage to all-Party inspiration.'[38] On the same day, Bevan made the speech he had wanted to make for so long at a party rally in Manchester: 'We now have the moral leadership of the world and before many years we shall have people coming here as to a modern Mecca.'[39]

Bevan's own view on persuading the professionals to accept the NHS was summed up in his famous phrase, 'I stuffed their mouths with gold.' Bevan's natural attitude was undoubtedly the one that he displayed at the start of the meeting with the negotiating committee in December 1947. He wanted to be aggressive; he wanted to make it clear that the doctors could not frustrate the will of parliament. Attlee's failure to intervene in the National Health Service debate in February 1948 took away that option. This not so much cast Bevan adrift as reined in some of his more aggressive attitude towards the BMA. Bevan and the BMA were locked into a strategic game with an end date of 5 July. Bevan feared that he would lose his authority if the BMA went over his head and that the service would fail at the outset if the doctors failed to cooperate; the BMA feared public opposition if it stood in the way of the service and the prospect of losing its authority if individual doctors decided to cooperate.

From his speech of 9 February 1948 in the House of Commons, Bevan sought to isolate the BMA from the doctors it represented and was able to implement the National Health Service Act on a basis of limited compromise with its principles essentially intact. Attlee's decision not to intervene was crucial. It tempered the freedom with which Bevan could express his views towards doctors, and reined in some of his more aggressive pronouncements. What the result would have been had Bevan adopted a stronger line from February 1948 is unknown. It was not so much that the doctors had their mouths stuffed with gold, though undoubtedly finance was part of the bargain. The reality was that they were slowly manoeuvred into position by a determined navigator working under the watchful eye of his cautious captain.

Unfortunately, Bevan's anger was famously vented at the party rally in Manchester on 4 July, when he cast aside any image of conciliation with his remark that the Conservative Party was 'lower than vermin'. In context, the remark reads less harshly than it was later portrayed. Talking about his upbringing in Ebbw Vale, Bevan declared that no 'attempts at ethical or social seduction, can eradicate from my heart a deep burning hatred for the Tory Party that inflicted those bitter experiences on me. So far as I am concerned they are lower than vermin. They condemned millions of first-class people to semi-starvation'. However, it gave the Conservatives inspiration, with members creating 'vermin clubs' in opposition to Bevan. As Morrison noted, the speech 'did much more to make the Tories work and vote an election than the Conservative Central Office could have done'.[40]

There were some other historical scores to settle. Fittingly, after the financial crisis of 1931, the first Attlee government nationalization was of the Bank of England. Like nationalizations to follow, this took place under the auspices of Morrison's Lord President's Committee and was uncontroversial. Bank stock was substituted by government stock, with proceeds going to the Treasury rather than dividends being paid out to private investors. The government was now to appoint the court of directors, including the governor. No other banks were made subject to any form of public control and Churchill did not even oppose the measure.

Attention was also paid to the coal industry, often perceived as the soul of the twentieth-century Labour movement. There had been early problems in the industry at the end of the war. On 21 September 1945, Shinwell produced a report on coal production in August 1945 for the Lord President's Committee, and noted that 'output was exceptionally low'; absenteeism was

10. Bevan all tied up by Attlee, c.1948.

at 18 per cent and 'output per manshift overall ... only 0.92 tons'.[41] Shinwell proposed to nationalize the coal industry on the basis of 'brevity and simplicity' with a nine-member National Coal Board appointed by the minister of fuel and power to 'carry on coalmining, and such ancillary activities as are transferred to it by the Bill'.[42]

On 2 October the Lord President's Committee considered the proposals, and Morrison expressed the view that 'the Committee were agreed that the coal problem threatened to provide, after housing, the most serious source of social distress this winter, and it must be tackled with the utmost vigour and determination.'[43] Attlee's response was simply to write in blue pencil on the minutes that (Douglas) Jay should have an input.[44] When Shinwell submitted the draft bill on 21 November 1945, together with a memorandum, Attlee's response was again to order input from Jay.[45] The Lord President's Committee considered Shinwell's scheme, the issues of board formation and remuneration, together with compensation for the private undertakings. On 11 December 1945 Attlee agreed that salaries for the members of the National Coal Board should have a parity with the civil service[46] and, on 13 December, the cabinet approved the draft bill.[47] Parliament subsequently passed the Coal Industry (Nationalization) Act of 1946. Attlee had again shown how the 'chairmanship' model of leadership could work: his colleagues, unencumbered by unnecessary prime ministerial interference, had reached a satisfactory conclusion quickly and efficiently. Equally efficient were the other two major nationalization measures in 1946. Cable and Wireless Ltd was fully bought by the government, and civil aviation nationalization brought together smaller private aviation companies into three corporations. That this was uncontroversial is unsurprising, given that it had been under Neville Chamberlain in 1940 that one of the corporations, the British Overseas Airways Corporation, had been formed: this was the forerunner of the modern-day private company British Airways.

Attlee's reputation was high throughout 1946. On 11 June, at the party conference in Bournemouth, MacDonald was firmly wiped from the pages of Labour history, as Noel-Baker, chairing the conference, introduced Attlee: 'This Report will be introduced by the first Socialist Prime Minister of Great Britain.'[48] The significance of the moment was not lost on Attlee, even if he was a little more circumspect. 'For the first time we have a Report of the work of a Labour Government in power, a Labour Government supported by a great majority in the House of Commons, a Labour Government carrying out the policies of the Socialist Movement.'[49] Attlee praised his team of 'good and loyal comrades' and specifically mentioned Morrison, Greenwood, Dalton, Bevin, Addison and the Chancellor of the Duchy of Lancaster, John Hynd, for his work on the occupation of Germany.[50] He declared:

No one realizes more clearly that I do that we have a long way to go yet to reach the Britain of our dreams and the world of our desires. ... We have, I believe, made a good beginning. We shall not falter. With faith in the justice of our cause and our ability to serve the nation we confidently face the future.[51]

Similarly, at the TUC conference held at Brighton in October, Attlee was received by standing delegates, loud applause and singing 'For he's a jolly good fellow'.

The 1947 nationalizations had more of a mixed impact, both within and outside the government. Attlee felt a deep sense of pride with the nationalization of electricity, a cause for which he had fought during the mid-1920s. Much of the cabinet discussion related to issues of practicality: how the nationalized boards should be organized and the amount of compensation to be paid to private undertakings. Principle was not at stake and, with the Electricity Act of 1947 Vesting Day was quickly confirmed as 1 April 1948. Walter Citrine would chair a Central Electricity Authority with control over more than 14 area boards. The measure meant a great deal to Attlee and brought out in him an episode of bad temper against Hugh Gaitskell, then minister of fuel and power, in July 1948. On 25 August 1947, Gaitskell had mooted an increase in the cost of electricity and gas.[52] The Clow Committee, established in February 1947 had looked at the problems of peak demand. It recommended further tariffs, higher in winter and lower in other months; Gaitskell suggested that the higher tariff would be needed as it was the only quick way to reduce winter demand. He did not think that, bearing in mind a lower summer tariff, people would end up paying the same: 'This is of course not practicable in the case of individual consumer who are bound to be different in different ways.'[53] Attlee, clearly unhappy, uncharacteristically snapped back on 28 July 1948: 'I do not like the last sentence and do not know what it means. Presumably it means that the seasonal demands of individual consumers are different.'[54] No peak pricing was subsequently introduced and Attlee's dream of nationalized electricity remained untarnished.

The greatest controversy surrounded the nationalization of transport in 1947. Rail nationalization, from 1 January 1948, was straightforward. There were only four major private rail companies to take into public ownership – Great Western; Southern; London and North-Eastern; and London, Midland and Scottish Railway – and the network was heavily war damaged. The 'road haulage' part of the Transport Act of 1947 was far more difficult. A distinction was drawn between A, B and C licensees. The holder of an A licence was permitted to carry goods for hire or reward; B licence holders could carry their own goods and, subject to certain requirements, the goods of others; whereas C license holders could only carry their own goods. The proposal was that A and B licences would be purchased, and C licensees would be restricted to a radius of 40 miles.[55] *The Times* reported on 8 April 1946: 'Opposition to the Government's proposals to nationalize road transport has been emphatically expressed, the British Road Federation states, at recent meetings of about 250 industrial and commercial organizations.'[56] Morrison intervened and produced his own memorandum of 1 July 1946, which set out the problem of not restricting C licences: there is a 'tendency for private enterprise to counter the public monopoly by buying vehicles and taking out C licences. It would be unfortunate if the result were to accentuate that drift or if the national undertaking were forced to quote unduly low rates in order to arrest it'.[57] Cabinet then agreed the suggested restriction of 40 miles on 4 July.[58] On 1 November 1946, Alfred Barnes, then minister for war transport, provided a draft transport bill to cabinet; a 25-mile radius was to be imposed on short-distance vehicles owned by independent hauliers, and the 40-mile radius on C licensees as agreed, with exemptions to be adjudicated upon by a licensing authority.[59]

Attlee had to intervene. By 23 December he had received 'a considerable number of communications ... about the Transport Bill'. Some were from road hauliers, 'but the majority came from local Chambers of Trade and Commerce, who all ask for a public enquiry before irrevocable steps are taken'.[60] For public ownership to work, the government needed to prevent those holding A and B licences from simply changing to C licences to avoid nationalization; yet, in restricting C licences, the government was in the absurd position of telling traders they could only carry their *own* goods a certain distance. Unsurprisingly, on 13 March, the cabinet dropped its restrictions on C licence vehicles.[61] On 19 April, a rattled Attlee minuted to Barnes and Lewis Silkin, the minister of town and country planning, that where any amendments in the House of Lords 'may be likely to cause trouble, you should seek authority from me before accepting them'.[62] The longer-term impact was, however, significant. The first rumblings against state restriction on freedom under nationalization had been heard; no longer was it simply seen as practical necessity. When George Orwell published his famous book *1984* in 1949 his warnings against an encroachment by the state on individual freedom could be related to Attlee's government. Practically, C licences did increase, as feared, from around 350,000 in 1946 to 766,578 in June 1951.[63] The Churchill government, which was returned to power in 1951, denationalized much of the road haulage industry in 1953, selling off vehicles bought under nationalization and freeing up the licensing system. Practically and politically, the measure did not work. It also showed at an early stage the potential weaknesses in Attlee's leadership style. It had been to him directly that letters of protest had been directed in late 1946, yet he did not intervene in the debate at an early stage. The difficulty was that when consensus emerged, it was unworkable: agreement in itself between ministers was no guarantee of success, and Attlee was not providing an 'overseeing' mechanism for when this occurred.

The two remaining major nationalizations could not have been more different. On 17 April 1947 Attlee told the cabinet that a decision needed to be made about whether to include the nationalization of gas (uncontroversial) or of iron and steel (very controversial) in the 1947–48 session. The cabinet, with no dissent from Attlee, took gas first, and it lived up to expectations.[64] It was announced in the king's speech on 21 October 1947 and was based on the same principles as the Electricity Act: there would be 12 area boards under a central gas council, which would 'in effect, act as a central financing body for the industry'.[65] The only real concern expressed in cabinet on 13 January 1948 was about the degree of independence given to the gas boards, which were allowed to 'promote and oppose' bills in parliament. It was considered unlikely that an electricity area board would oppose a bill put forward by a gas area board.[66] The government was not averse to providing additional compensation to the private sector either and, on 16 November 1949, the cabinet's economic policy committee agreed to amend the Gas Act 'with a view to compensating stockholders for losses incurred on account of the recent fall in the value of gilt-edged securities'.[67] The iron and steel bill, in contrast, proved to be anything but straightforward, and the Gas Act proved to be the last of the Attlee government's straightforward measures of nationalization.

These substantial achievements between 1945 and 1948: the creation of the welfare state, together with public ownership of vast swathes of the economy, showed the Attlee government – and his style of leadership – at its constructive best. With the exception of the nationalization of road haulage, all these measures, which the labour movement had wanted for so long and yet implemented so quickly, stood the test of time. The National Health Service remains today, with its central principle of healthcare free at the point of delivery, almost entirely intact. More than 60 years later, no political party would dare suggest privatization at a general election. The welfare state has been substantially reformed, but the basic entitlements to sickness and unemployment benefit have remained on the statute book. The Attlee government's model of public ownership remained the accepted economic approach for a generation, swept away only by Margaret Thatcher more than 30 years later. Leadership is about results – and during this three-year period on the domestic front, Attlee's leadership delivered. Whatever one's political perspective, there can be little but praise to him for that.

Chapter 17
INDIA

Two of the twentieth-century's greatest novels form the book ends of Attlee's contribution to the history of India. E. M. Forster's *A Passage to India*, published in 1924, just 23 years before independence, sets out the uncomfortable feelings of the colonizer in the later years of the raj, and Salman Rushdie's 1981 novel *Midnight's Children* sets out the fate of the Indian peoples after independence. It was an independence that was given to India from midnight on 15 August 1947, when the first prime minister, Jawaharlal Nehru, declared the redemption of India's 'tryst with destiny'. Pakistan, the two Muslim-majority areas in the northeastern and northwestern corners of India, became independent separately. The central figure behind the independence of India and the partition into India and Pakistan was Attlee. The people of the subcontinent may not have been Attlee's people, but it was certainly Attlee's midnight from which they took their own path of freedom. Attlee did not merely preside over Indian independence; he intervened and shaped policy. Within the government, only Cripps had any significant say in policy on India besides Attlee. Peter Clarke, Cripps's biographer, has said that it was 'Attlee and Cripps … who really determined the Government's stance on India'.[1] The veteran secretary of state for India, Pethick-Lawrence, was put in the Lords, and was no political heavyweight. The praise for finding a workable solution – or blame for the difficulties of the agreed settlement – lies with Attlee.

With partition, Attlee found the only viable solution, but implemented it too quickly. His navigation of the difficult channel towards an agreed form of independence still deserves great credit. His replacement of Wavell as viceroy with Mountbatten made a settlement possible. The issue remains that, while a set deadline probably *was* necessary to force agreement, the short period left – merely weeks – to decide the destiny of the millions of people was simply not long enough. Coupled with the 'hands off' approach after the quick withdrawal, it led to a great human tragedy. While the barrister Sir Cyril Radcliffe – like Attlee an old Haileyburian – pored over maps and charts to delineate the borders between the new states, violence continued on a daily basis, with majority populations trying to kill or force out minorities to ensure that they fell on their preferred side of the so-called 'Radcliffe lines'. Thousands were displaced from their homes. 'Pug' Ismay, then Mountbatten's chief of staff, reported on 5 October 1947: 'The road movement of refugees from East to West Punjab and vice versa is an indescribable sight – miles and miles of humanity – some organized and with their poor possessions, others straggling and utterly destitute.'[2] The haste also contributed to problems over the princely states – the 565[3] self-governing states under native Indian princes that had submitted to the paramoutcy of the raj. While there was only trouble over a tiny number of such states, in one case Kashmir, the difficulties had major long-term consequences for the relationship between India and Pakistan.

By the time Labour came in it had come to be accepted that British rule should cease, but there was agreement neither on the number or nature of the successor states nor on how India should be governed during the transition. When Attlee initially turned his mind to India, there was no agreement on the immediate future, let alone the long-term goal. Just weeks before he became prime minister, Wavell's conference at Simla – the summer capital of British India – broke down. Wavell had proposed setting up an executive council that would contain members nominated by the various political parties. However, Jinnah argued that his Muslim League represented *all* Muslims and therefore should put forward all the Muslim members. This was unacceptable to Congress, which, with many Muslim members, claimed to represent all communities within India, and wished to nominate Muslim representatives as well. Attlee's and Wavell's broadcasts of 16 September had not helped the situation, with both Congress and the Muslim League still refusing to participate in any constitution-making body. In general and provincial elections over the winter of 1946, Congress swept the board in non-Muslim areas and the Muslim League did likewise in strong Muslim areas. Even with the limited franchise under the Government of India Act (1935), it was obvious that the two organizations represented their respective communities, and they both had to be accommodated in any settlement.

Attlee fell back on the idea of a 'Cabinet Mission', so sent Cripps, Pethick-Lawrence and his trusted friend Alexander to India in March 1946. On 1 April, Cripps gave a press conference in Delhi at which he confirmed: 'The decision on independence having been made, the mission's duty was to help the Indians arrive at agreement for a new constitutional structure.'[4] On 10 May Pethick-Lawrence reported: 'Our progress barometer goes up [and] down rapidly.'[5] On

16 May, the Cabinet Mission set out its proposals. There would be a central 'Union of India' comprising both British India and the princely states. This would have an executive and legislature dealing with foreign affairs, defence and communications, with all other powers left to the 11 provinces. An intermediate level of government was also permitted, with three groups of provinces (it was not specified which at this stage) that could combine on certain policy areas if they so wished. Finally, there would be an interim government, all-Indian save for the viceroy and British military commander-in-chief. Just over a week later, Congress accepted the plan but not the interim government. On 1 June, Pethick-Lawrence wrote to Attlee that the difficulty was that of ensuring a position of parity between Congress and the Muslim League in the interim government. He added a postscript stating that he wished to know where Attlee was likely to be during what he thought would be a critical phase between 8 and 15 June.[6] In fact, the Muslim League initially accepted both the plan and the interim government; however, when Nehru announced in July that Congress would cooperate but wished to make changes in the Cabinet Mission plan, Jinnah refused to cooperate with the interim government. Stalemate had been reached once again.

Attlee was conscious of Wavell's weaknesses and wrote to him on 22 July 1946: 'In the difficult months ahead it seems to me that your hand would be strengthened if you had with you someone well versed in these things who could act as an intermediary for you with the politicians.'[7] Wavell wrote to Attlee on 1 August 1946: 'the prospects of the Constituent Assembly are not bright at the moment, it cannot get very far without the Muslims.'[8] He offered Attlee a way of changing viceroy: 'you and HMG may feel that you would rather have a politician than a soldier at the head of India at present. ... I shall of course accept your decision.' However, he was clearly daring Attlee to back him or sack him: 'I must be allowed to exercise my own judgement. ... I do not believe it has been so very far wrong up to date.' It was not a good time to throw down the gauntlet. The Muslim League had deemed 16 August 'Direct Action Day' in support of an independent Muslim state. It was envisaged merely as a general strike, but predictably it sparked off riots in Calcutta and revenge attacks by Congress supporters. Thousands died, many more were made homeless and there were further riots in the surrounding provinces. Attlee replied rather weakly on 20 August: 'I am still hopeful that your efforts will be crowned with success.'[9] Wavell replied tartly on 28 August: 'From your silence on the matter, I assume that you wish me to remain in my present post.'[10]

Had Wavell had more political instinct he would have realized how untenable his position was. He said he would be submitting a policy he regarded as 'the only possible one in the present conditions'. He also complained to Attlee about

Cripps and Pethick-Lawrence dealing with Congress behind his back.[11] A telegram on the very same day from Sudhir Ghosh sealed his fate: 'Gandhi says Viceroy unnerved owing Bengal tragedy. ... Please tell friends he should be assisted by abler and legal mind otherwise repetition of tragedy certainty.'[12] Ghosh spoke by telephone to Number 10: 'The relationship between Nehru and the Viceroy could only work if the personalities were sympathetic. He believed that the most important step was to replace ... Wavell.' The civil servant taking the call added: 'I was not very favourably impressed by Mr Ghosh. He seemed excitable, confused.'[13] Attlee did not need any lectures about Ghosh. He had already met him. On 3 August 1946, the civil servant Adamson at the India Office felt that it was 'clearly out of the question' for Attlee to meet Ghosh 'in the near future'[14] but the letter requesting this was passed to Attlee, who took a completely different view and met Ghosh within days. He then sent a very friendly letter to Gandhi: 'Thank you for introducing your friend Mr Ghosh. I much enjoyed talking with him. I trust that a complete settlement between our two countries may be attained.' He added: 'I think that the last time we met was in the House of Commons with Mr George Lansbury.'[15]

Wavell pressed on unabashed. On 7 September, he produced his 'Breakdown Plan' and wrote to Attlee on 30 October: 'I am wondering whether you received my letter of August 28, since I have had no reply to or an acknowledgment of it.'[16] Attlee disliked the plan. This set out a timetable for British withdrawal by 31 March 1948 in the absence of a Hindu–Muslim agreement on the way forward. Britain would transfer control to Congress in the Congress-dominated provinces, but retain it in the two Muslim-majority areas on the frontiers of the raj. Wavell's biographer, Adrian Fort, has argued that to 'the military mind, it was a sound insurance policy',[17] but it was a plan that accepted defeat in trying to find a settlement, and Attlee and Bevin were already worried about the effect on British public opinion if the colonial jewel was seen to be abandoned without honour. Bevin took a strong line in the Commons on 22 October 1946 against critics of British imperialism:

> The House will be conversant with our difficulties from the large amount of propaganda which is put out against the British Empire and Commonwealth, and the temptation there always is to reply, which often makes things worse. But I have taken the view that our contribution to these two world wars, the price we have paid in blood and money, our moral claim as well as the sacrifices which we have already given, do not call for a justification of our existence every five minutes.[18]

Attlee spoke the next day and, having specifically mentioned India (Bevin did

11. Negotiating Indian independence, 14 May 1946.

not), declared that Britain would not 'seek to thrust' its 'views upon other nations' and was, rather, 'seeking to set an example of how individual freedom and the interests of the community can be harmonised'.[19]

On 14 October, Wavell invited the Muslim League back into the interim government, and Jinnah accepted. There appeared to be a glimmer of hope and, on 3 December, the Indian leaders came to London to meet the British government. Jinnah was accompanied by Liaquat Ali Khan and Nehru by Sardar Baldev Singh; they met, variously, Attlee, Cripps Alexander, and Pethick-Lawrence. In preparation, the 'notes for discussion' set out four different options for Attlee. First, there was the re-establishment of British authority in India, 'already ruled out as politically impossible'. Second, was a new settlement, which would be partition, but thought impractical on the basis of Congress' non-acceptance and the resultant need for Britain to stay in India to set it up. Third, Congress could be given power, with Britain trying to use its remaining influence to help the minorities ('I do not think this is an honourable or wise policy'). Fourth, there was the 'Breakdown Plan', which envisaged an announcement that, with no settlement, Britain would withdraw in its own time and any interference with that process would be treated as an act of war. While there, Britain would continue to seek agreement and hand over to established governmental bodies; the plan was 'intended for use not merely when widespread disorder has broken out, but for use in the event of a political breakdown and *before* disorder has broken out'.[20] The 'notes' recommended that the Cabinet Mission plan be restored, failing which a policy choice would have to be made between the various alternatives.

The talks with the Indians produced no agreement and Attlee was running out of options. At a cabinet meeting on 10 December Attlee, adopting the Churchillian analogy of 'scuttle', declared that 'world opinion' would regard the 'breakdown plan' as 'a policy of scuttle unworthy of a great power'.[21] Before Attlee moved into this final phase of negotiation, he firmly decided to recall Wavell. For his replacement, Attlee favoured Mountbatten for a variety of reasons. As supreme allied commander in Southeast Asia, Mountbatten's judgement on the independence of Burma had proved justified. Aung San, a communist revolutionary who had sought independence for Burma from Britain, had been war minister under the Japanese in the war before organizing an uprising against them. He was unacceptable to the previous governor of Burma, Sir Reginald Dorman-Smith, but Mountbatten saw his leadership as the only realistic way forward for Burma. Although Aung San was assassinated in July 1947, Attlee remained convinced that he would have led Burma effectively. 'The so-called experts had been wrong about Aung Sang, and Dickie [Mountbatten] had been right.'[22] Attlee knew Mountbatten well. As early as 25 November 1945 Mountbatten had told Attlee that his wife Edwina was of 'the greatest value' to him and, no sooner had he done so than, on 30 November 1945, Violet promptly invited her to lunch.[23] Attlee also supported Mountbatten in what Lascelles termed his 'somewhat film-starish attitude towards his proposed barony – saying that SEAC [Southeast Asia Command] will not understand his accepting it while they are still fighting the Indonesians'.[24] The king sent Lascelles to Attlee on 17 December, but to no avail: 'Attlee was adamant, basing his view, I am certain, on the view of the Services.'[25] Attlee made his offer to Mountbatten in December 1946 and, on 20 December, Mountbatten replied: 'In the circumstances, I feel I could only be of use to you if I were to go out at the open invitation of the Indian parties, in a capacity which they would themselves define.'[26] The situation in India was becoming desperate. In October, in Noakhili, part of the Muslim-dominated northeastern corner of India, Hindus were ejected or killed, as part of a cycle of ongoing retribution between the two communities. Attlee wrote to the Conservative Lord Salisbury on 21 December 1946: 'I agree with you that the situation in India is grave.' The problem was the 'failure of Indians to agree amongst themselves'.[27] On Christmas Eve, Wavell wrote entirely unhelpfully to Attlee that 'it is impossible to say what the next move by the Congress or the Muslim League will be.'[28] On New Year's Day 1947, less than a fortnight later, Attlee called Mountbatten to Downing Street. The Indian parties would clearly not *invite* Mountbatten to India, but Attlee's suggestion that Cripps indicate to them that Mountbatten wanted their support was accepted.[29] Attlee's strategy was now simple – set a firm withdrawal date and *force* the parties to reach an agreement between themselves. 'Indians must be faced with the fact that within a short space of time they would have responsibility thrust upon them.'[30]

Attlee's approach to India was a gamble. Mountbatten sought maximum flexibility of action – 'virtually plenipotentiary powers. He felt that he had to be allowed to act on his own initiative without having to refer everything back to Whitehall'.[31] Attlee gave him this flexibility. In doing so, he put his own reputation in the hands of Mountbatten: he could rightly share in Moutbatten's successes, but would find it difficult to avoid blame for his failures. In addition, his senior colleagues were not united behind him. After an inconclusive cabinet meeting on New Year's Eve, Bevin took up his pen in anger and sent Attlee a strong six-page letter on New Year's Day: 'I must express my strong views with regard to India, as I mentioned to you this morning.'[32] Bevin's language was harsh: 'I cannot help feeling that the defeatist attitude adopted both by the Cabinet and by … Wavell is just completely letting us down. … I would strongly recommend that he be recalled and that you find somebody with courage.'[33] Bevin lashed out at Cripps as too pro-Congress and the minister of defence, Alexander, as too pro-Muslim. He then declared his position unequivocally: 'I am against fixing a date. I am willing to support a declaration, as we have done, that we are ready to hand India over as a going concern to established governments.'[34] But, 'I cannot get it out of my head that there must be millions of Indians who, as a result of the murder incidents in the last few months, would welcome a strong and courageous lead so as to preserve their safety.'[35]

For Bevin, a key factor was not just the remaining British troops in India, but also that he did not accept that men could not be found to administer the country: 'if we were able to move into Germany and other occupied countries and find administrators among the young men from the services, as we had to, why can't we find them from the Forces in India and at home?'[36] Bevin wanted Attlee to issue a declaration to 'hand it over as a going concern and to place the responsibility squarely on their shoulders of failure in that respect'.[37] He pleaded with Attlee:

> within the British Empire, we knuckle under at the first blow and yet we are expected to preserve the position. It cannot be done and I beg of you in all sincerity, even if it does involve a certain risk, to take it, and I believe the world will respect us.[38]

He also felt the United States could bring pressure to bear on the Indian politicians.

Attlee was equally strong in a five-page response the next day. On Wavell: 'I agree with you that Wavell has a defeatist mind and I am contemplating replacing him.'[39] On his own position, 'I am not defeatist but realist.' In the event of communal strife, he felt the Indian army would split. He also felt that Britain had governed India with Indians. 'Without the tens of thousands of lesser functionaries we could not carry on. ... It would be quite impossible even if you could find the men for a few hundred British to administer against the active opposition of ... the politically minded of the population.'[40] Attlee was sarcastic about Bevin's suggestion of recruiting administrators from the army: 'How could Army officers with only a slight knowledge of the language and no knowledge of administration deal with such a matter as the collection of land revenue, the backbone of Indian Finance, if they had not even got Indian clerical assistance?'[41] He went on: 'You suggest that we are knuckling under at the first blow, but this entirely ignores the history of the past twenty-five years.' To stay, and put in more troops would be 'to go back on the pledges that have been given by Governments of every political colour'.[42] Attlee defended his policy vigorously. He was seeking to leave

> with dignity and to avoid an ignominious scuttle. But a scuttle it will be if things are allowed to drift. ... The declaration that we are determined to hand over as a going concern is precisely what we are making clear to the Indians and we are placing responsibility on their shoulders.[43]

Attlee felt that the Indians had 'very little inclination' to take advice from America, and added a final paragraph: 'If you disagree with what is proposed, you must offer a practical alternative. I fail to find one in your letter.'[44]

Attlee's letter had finessed the issues Bevin was really putting to him. The letters are not so much staying in India versus getting out. Bevin's letter was putting a *different* route out: rather than setting a date of departure, laying down the 'going concern' criterion so that India would be given an incentive to stability; once stable, independence could be granted and, if such independence was not forthcoming soon, the Indians would take the blame. This reads as a politically attractive argument, yet it is clear from the tone of Attlee's letter that he felt it was wholly unrealistic. All negotiations under Attlee had been based on the assumption that Britain could not retain control of India even if it wanted to. In this he was probably correct. Realistically, of the four courses set out in the notes for the December 1946 leader's meeting, only partition or the 'breakdown plan' were achievable. Britain was spending heavily at home, creating a welfare state and National Health Service with the help of the American loan. Even if the United States had been in favour of a continuation of British rule in India, Britain was not in a position to fund it. Yet, what was not answered firmly is *how long* Britain could have remained in India. The key question is formulated by the historian Lawrence James, 'Was it [Britain's departure] too quick?'[45]

The idea of handing over to Congress with Britain intervening on behalf of the Muslim minority was vague and unrealistic. How could India be truly sovereign with a foreign power having some sort of ill-defined power to protect a minority? And how, practically, could this ever be done? Would Britain retain some sort of military presence on foreign soil? If it did, what would its remit be, and under whose orders, the Indian government, or the British, would it act? With the political cost of the 'breakdown plan' deemed too high, the only way out was some sort of all-India settlement agreed between the parties, with either the Muslim League conceding its goal of an independent Pakistan, or Congress accepting defeat in its goal of *all*-Indian independence. With both Attlee and Wavell's plans involving setting a date for departure, all Jinnah effectively had to do was retain control over the Muslim areas to secure partition, by now the only realistic solution. To achieve any sort of solution, Attlee disposed of Wavell ruthlessly in the early months of 1947. He wrote to him on 8 January 1947 that, while he could see the argument for a firm withdrawal date, he was not in favour of simply withdrawing along the lines of the 'breakdown plan'. 'While there was agreement that in the event of the Moslem League failing to enter the Constituent Assembly it would be desirable to announce a time limit for the continuance of British rule in India, it was considered that it would not be advisable to fix a day.' He added:

> The Cabinet did not approve of the approach to the problem on the basis of a military evacuation. It was considered that a different approach was required – viz. that of close cooperation with the Indian Governments at the Centre and in the Provinces in order to work out with them plans for handing over the Government in India, as a going concern.[46]

Attlee asked Wavell to return to London. Wavell had lost his temper by 17

January when he wrote to Attlee: 'I must, however, put it on record that in my opinion the Cabinet's decision, or lack of decision, increases the risk to our nationals in India, and is likely to diminish the chances of a settlement between the two parties.'[47] Wavell lamented: 'All I can do at present is to draw up plans against the possibility of an emergency withdrawal'; he refused to come back to London: 'My return would cause much speculation.'[48] The inevitable reply came from Attlee on 31 January: 'I think that you may agree that the time has come to make a change in the Vice-royalty.'[49] Wavell lashed back on 5 February:

> You are causing me to be removed because of what you term a wide divergence of policy. The divergence, as I see it, is between my wanting a definite policy for the Interim period and HMG refusing to give me one. I will not at this time enter into further argument on this.[50]

Wavell was also hurt by the notice period being a few weeks rather than the normal six months, though he accepted an earldom. The subsequent announcement was delayed until the afternoon of 20 February due to Attlee's daughter Janet's wedding that day.

Attlee then also ensured that the withdrawal date was announced formally in the Commons: Britain would leave by the end of June 1948. With the end game set, Mountbatten replaced Wavell as viceroy with a swearing-in on 24 March 1947. His tenure, so historically significant, lasted a mere 113 days. Over the early weeks, the new viceroy worked furiously against a background of ongoing communal violence. Throughout April, there were riots in the North-West Frontier province and the Punjab, with thousands killed. Mountbatten spoke to all the major Indian leaders, and invited the provincial governors to a conference on 15 April. Within a matter of weeks, he had become convinced that only partition could provide a way out. An initial plan, known as the 'Balkanization' of India, was produced in late April, but Mountbatten quickly changed it after Nehru objected. It would have allowed each province to determine its own future, but this was clearly a recipe for fragmentation, and it was altered to what became known as the 'Mountbatten Plan', still with a vote in each province but only posing a choice of joining India or Pakistan.

The princely states would legally become independent when the British left, and were left to make their own arrangements with the two new nations. Nehru and Jinnah accepted the plan and cabinet approved it on 27 May. In early June Mountbatten tried one last-ditch attempt to find agreement on the all-India independence proposed by the 1946 Cabinet Mission in early June, but, having failed, he gave a press conference on the new plan on 4 June, and remarked that he felt independence would be possible by 15 August 1947. In putting forward this date, he secured India's place in the Commonwealth.

Congress had wanted a transfer of power to an Indian constituent assembly that would establish a republic outside the Commonwealth. What it got was a 1947 transfer but to a dominion with Moutbatten remaining as governor-general of India (Jinnah insisted on being governor-general of Pakistan). For Attlee, India's place in the Commonwealth was highly important. In 1948, he secured alteration of the understanding that all Commonwealth countries were bound by common loyalty to the crown, so that India could remain in the Commonwealth as a republic. There was a dual purpose to this – a counter-weight to the effects of partition, and joint action with the rest of the Commonwealth.[51] Attlee praised Mountbatten highly in a letter to Tom dated 3 June 1947: 'He has done a wonderful work and so has Edwina in getting on personal terms with Indians of every point of view including people who had never had contact with Government being regarded as wild extremists.'[52] Attlee was appreciative of Edwina's work. While Mountbatten negotiated the terms for independence during the day, 'Edwina would spend the day bringing the Indian wives along to the same point.' He once remarked that one of Wavell's problems was that 'the men agreed over the day's work and in the evening the [Indian] wives undid them.' The tone of the letter suggests that Attlee was ignorant of Edwina's *alleged* affair with Nehru. He wrote to Mountbatten on 17 July: 'I am very conscious that I put you in to bat on a very sticky wicket to pull the game out of the first. Few people would have taken it on and few, if any, could have pulled the game around as you have.'[53]

Attlee's speech on second reading of the Indian Independence Bill on 10 July captured the significance of the moment:

> I am afraid I shall have to ask the indulgence of the House for taking up more of its time than is my custom, but the theme is a great one. … There have been many instances in history when States at the point of the sword have been forced to surrender government over another people. It is very rare for a people that have long enjoyed power over another nation to surrender it voluntarily. My mind recalls as the nearest parallel the action of the Liberal Government of Sir Henry Campbell-Bannerman, in 1906, when he gave back to the Dutch in South Africa the freedom to manage their own affairs which they had lost in the South African war.[54]

Harold Macmillan, replying in place of the absent Churchill, complimented Attlee: 'I should like to congratulate the Prime Minister on the lucidity, moderation and dignity with which he has performed his formidable task.'[55]

The act confirmed Mountbatten's withdrawal date of 15 August 1947. On that day, *The Times* noted 'a general air of apathy on the part of the people' in Karachi, but in Delhi 'several thousand people' gathered at 'the main entrance to the Council House'.[56] Both Attlee and Mountbatten left India with their personal reputations high. In March 1947, J. T. Hughes at the UK publicity office in New Delhi confirmed: 'the Prime Minister has a very high personal reputation.'[57] When Mountbatten handed over his role as governor-general to his Indian successor, Chakravarti Rajagopalachari, the latter wrote warmly to Attlee on 23 June 1948: 'Mountbatten has wound up Indo-British history in a manner which has secured for Britain a re-conquest of heart as historic and as valuable as any imperial acquisition of which Britain may be proud.'[58] Mountbatten had scrupulously carried out his role as governor-general, and told Attlee that he should only communicate with him on government business through official channels, not private and personal letters any more.[59] Attlee's two major contributions – setting a withdrawal date and appointing Mountbatten to find agreement between the parties – created an agreed solution where none was forthcoming before. When viewed against Wavell's 'Breakdown Plan' the scale of Attlee's achievement is even greater. Wavell felt that the subcontinent could only be held for a matter of months and had the government been forced to withdraw militarily with no agreed solution in place – as happened in Palestine – Attlee's reputation both at the time and in history would be very different. Attlee had steered independence through with nothing like the fuss the more limited Government of India Act (1935) had generated, and Britain had extricated itself from India with a measure of Indian goodwill, in stark contrast to examples such as the messy exits of the Netherlands from Indonesia or of France from Indochina.

Yet, it is not difficult to set out a case in criticism of Attlee's actions. The obvious question partition posed was precisely where the two boundaries with the new Pakistan were drawn. West Pakistan encompassed only part of the Punjab; East Pakistan contained only part of Bengal. In early June, Radcliffe had been appointed to chair two boundary commissions to set each of the borders. Two Muslim judges and two Hindu judges sat alongside him, but Radcliffe obviously held the casting vote. He arrived in India on 13 July, with just weeks to complete the work. He had never visited India before and had no links to any of the parties, which gave him the appearance of objectivity but an obvious lack of knowledge. Violence continued in early August while he drew the borders: thousands of Hindus surrounded the Muslim Meo[60] village of Silgaon in northwestern India and massacred many inhabitants.[61] When the 'Radcliffe lines' were eventually announced on 17 August, the raj had already ended. There were some minor anomalies – for example the Chittagong Hill Tracts were almost entirely non-Muslim but went to East Pakistan. There was also the fateful late change to give India a border with Kashmir. Yet, the broader picture was even worse. India and Pakistan were left to police their own new borders, meaning that British troops could only protect refugees indirectly if their line of march or overnight encampment overlapped. A Punjab boundary force of 55,000 men, set up in July under Major-General T. W. Rees, was quite inadequate to cover such a large area. *The Times* reported on 5 September 1947: 'More than 1,000,000 and possibly as many as 2,000,000 people – Muslims trekking west and Sikhs and Hindus trekking east – are on the move in the Punjab as a consequence of the communal massacres.'[62] A series of melancholy telegrams between the UK high commissioner in India and the Commonwealth Relations Office set out the course of the violence. In early October, respite came only from flooding: 'Nature's violence has caused a lull in human violence was the summary given by a military spokesman of events in this area [northern part of East Punjab including Punjab Sikh districts] during the last week.'[63] Drowning, lack of food, sickness, exposure and exhaustion became rife: 1500 had died in one refugee convoy alone.[64] Gandhi went to the Punjab to try and calm matters, but within a matter of months, in January 1948, he was assassinated by a Hindu extremist.

Attlee maintained a 'hands off' approach, but more could have been done to prevent the bloodshed either by giving more time for preparation by setting a later withdrawal date, by slightly delaying the date of independence once the problems of meeting it became clear, or by taking more active steps whether before or after the withdrawal itself. Moutbatten's daughter, Pamela, defended the need to hand over power on 15 August vigorously: 'This would be ten months earlier than the original deadline but it was necessary if there was any hope of avoiding civil war.'[65] However, the trouble afterwards was entirely foreseeable. In July 1947 Ismay had predicted that panic and fear would cause great strife; while the scale of the violence took him by surprise, the problems themselves did not surprise him.[66] Attlee had no intention of intervening on one side or the other. When Jinnah wrote to him on 1 October that the Sikhs had to be dealt with 'immediately with an iron hand' he did not receive a reply.[67] However, Addison visited India and Pakistan between 18 and 21 October, reporting: 'the Indian atmosphere is one of terror and hatred ... the transfer of power does not relieve this country of moral responsibility to do anything within its power to reduce the suffering in the period after the hand-over.'[68] Addison envisaged some sort of diplomatic presence beyond the usual high commissioner, which could have been a sensible option. Bevin, however, raised practical difficulties with this: 'Whoever we sent would surely only be a target for Indian resentment'[69] and on 20 November Attlee declared the matter 'closed'.[70] By early November, attacks seemed to have eased only to a limited extent: refugees were interchanging and kidnapped women on either side were being found: 1300 women and children were recovered from the East Punjab alone.[71]

Partition also had longer-term consequences for world history. In fact, a major territorial dispute still remains unsolved in the Kashmir. The state was one of four princely states that caused difficulty, the others being Hyderabad, Junagadh and Tripura. As viceroy, Mountbatten pressed the princely states to opt for India or Pakistan and this was largely successful. However, Hyderabad (a Muslim-ruled Hindu state) tried to remain apart from the newly-independent India before being militarily conquered in September 1948. Junagadh (also a Muslim-ruled Hindu state) sought to join Pakistan. A plebiscite was suggested by India, but rejected by Pakistan. An exile government was formed, but in the confusion India was asked to restore order and the state duly acceded to India. Tripura remained independent before joining India in 1949. Kashmir (Hindu-ruled with a Muslim majority) was far more troublesome.

First, it was obvious how important Kashmir was to Nehru. The Nehru family belonged to the Kashmiri Saraswat Brahmin caste of Hindus. Nehru's close friend, Sheikh Abdullar, leader of the Kashmiri popular front, was in prison and he wanted to visit the state. When he was dissuaded (because the senior available Congress party figure Vallabhbhai Patel feared that he too would be imprisoned), Nehru wept, declaring Kashmir his most important issue at that time.[72] Mountbatten visited the maharajah in June, but failed to persuade him to accede to India or Pakistan, so 15 August passed with the maharajah trying to delay matters in an attempt to retain control over the state. In October 1947, Pakistani tribesmen invaded. The maharajah asked India (directly bordering Kashmir as a result of Radcliffe's border) to assist, but Mountbatten would only offer military aid if the maharajah first acceded to India.[73] India's position remains that the maharaja *did* then sign an accession document in October 1947 giving it a legitimate right to the province (Pakistan disputes this document). Nehru told Attlee that Pakistani 'raiders' were looting buildings and maiming women, pulling out their earrings. The Indian forces were acting as police to keep law and order; only when the Pakistanis had left would India proceed to a referendum.[74] When the cabinet received a summary of events for December 1947, it was confirmed that stalemate had been reached at Lahore on 8 December: Pakistan would not ask the tribesmen to withdraw *until* a neutral administration was set up to ensure the safety of Muslims; India reserved its legal right, from accession, to restore and keep order before a plebiscite.[75] Attlee told Nehru on 29 December that he felt it was only through the United Nations that a settlement could be achieved.[76]

The problem with this approach was that it put Mountbatten in a very difficult position. In carrying out Attlee's wishes, Mountbatten pushed hard for India to place the matter in the hands of the UN, and wrote a worried letter to Attlee on 14 February 1948. Given that he was 'largely responsible' for persuading Nehru to make the reference, he was worried about his own position becoming untenable if the Indian government suffered as a result of his advice. His fear was that if the Security Council provided a solution in favour of

Pakistan, the Nehru government would fall. He reiterated that Kashmir's accession to India was 'perfectly legal'. The Pakistani government had to stop helping the raiders. Mountbatten summed up his own weakness: 'I myself am deeply involved.'[77] Attlee was more circumspect in his response: 'I am sure you will realize that the Indian claim has never been brushed aside or put behind the Pakistan claim for a fair plebiscite.' He felt that direct negotiation still might provide the answer, but was concerned about appearing to undermine the authority of the Security Council.[78] In the event, Resolution 47 of 21 April 1948 provided for the Pakistani army to withdraw and for a referendum, but such a vote was never held. Nehru, with his Kashmiri origins, was particularly sympathetic to the Hindus in the province, and never carried out his promise of a plebiscite.[79] Back in London in July 1948, having ended his period as governor-general, Mountbatten laid the blame for the problem at the maharajah's door. He said that, prior to partition, he had spent four days with the maharajah, and told him to ascertain the wishes of his people and accede by 14 August. Mountbatten's view was that had he acceded to Pakistan, the Indian government had assured him that there would not have been a problem.[80]

In Kashmir, fighting during the monsoon season was minimal. It was a window of opportunity, and Britain called for a simple cease-fire, hoping to reduce tension. On 27 July Churchill wrote to Attlee that Kashmir should settle its future by plebiscite (he argued the same in respect of Hyderabad) and appealed to Attlee to push the agenda forward: 'Without this much blood will flow and our promises be broken.'[81] Attlee was having a quiet day away from papers on doctor's orders on 26 August 1948, so Listowel (the minister of state for colonial affairs) dealt with the matter by calling for the ceasefire and pointing out that the Security Council was in recess until 15 September and a reference back by the commission would serve no useful purpose.[82] However, within days, the Indian airforce bombed Gilgit, killing civilians and destroying non-military property. The United Nations Commission for India and Pakistan had been set up to resolve outstanding differences and passed further resolutions of 13 August 1948 and 5 January 1949, which secured a cease-fire. Attlee immediately drew praise from the Indian politician, S. C. Guha, who wrote to the Commonwealth Relations Office on the same day: 'convey my hearty thanks to … Attlee … for his highminded good action for the cessation of fight and bloodshed in Kashmir State … presumed … due to his free discussion in the Common Wealth Relation Meetings held in London.'[83] Attlee's general attitude remained one of frustration towards Pakistan. On 31 January 1949, he told Philip Noel-Baker, by now secretary of state for commonwealth relations: 'It appears to me, and I know that Addison and Cripps share my view, that all the concessions are being asked from India, while Pakistan concedes little or nothing.'[84]

No long-term settlement was forthcoming and when Attlee later tried to press the parties it was too late. He set up a meeting with the Commonwealth prime ministers on 9 January 1951. He met Nehru and Liaquat Ali Khan in the Australian Prime Minister Menzies's room at the Savoy Hotel, with Louis St Laurent (Canada), Sir Sidney Holland (New Zealand) and D. S. Senanayake (Ceylon). Attlee opened the discussion on the basis that all sides were agreed on a plebiscite to settle the dispute and that the key difference was over the conditions under which such a vote would occur. However, Ali Khan sought a decision on the basis that Kashmir was a Muslim state; Nehru felt this would cause trouble in India. Attlee argued that it was more dangerous for the current uncertainty to continue. The following Sunday, 14 January, Attlee and Menzies saw Nehru and Khan at Chequers. Nehru still raised objections about the administration of the plebiscite; a mixed Pakistan–Indian force was ruled out as Pakistan should not be in Kashmir in the first place, and he also rejected a force from both Hindu and Muslim Kashmiris. Attlee felt that Nehru was raising less and less pertinent objections, and concluded that he did not want to resolve the matter.[85] In that judgement he was probably correct.

Attlee's policy on India poses three major questions. Was partition the best solution? Even if it was, could it have been implemented with less bloodshed? And what, if anything, could have been done about Kashmir? After independence, Attlee remained deeply uncomfortable with partition and was particularly sceptical of Jinnah. He was concerned about the treatment of minorities and the viability of Pakistan: 'any such partition would necessarily leave minorities in both States. We doubted also whether Pakistan, with an important unit geographically separate from the Centre of the new State, was viable.'[86] Attlee's preferred option was unquestionably along the lines proposed by the Cabinet Mission of 1946: all India as one independent state. Yet the only agreement that could have been forthcoming before the deadline Attlee set for withdrawal deadline was with an independent Pakistan. Attlee might have been able to persevere for a longer period in trying to find an 'all India' solution, but it is difficult to avoid the conclusion that that was simply not feasible. While Jinnah had originally agreed the 1946 Cabinet Mission's proposals, it was during the period when the game of chess between the British government, the League and Congress was still ongoing, and it is unclear whether it was a real acceptance or an attempt to win favour with the British in the face of the initial obduracy of Congress.

Mountbatten's judgement in the early weeks of his viceroyalty that some sort of partition was inevitable was correct. The Muslim League's support was based on its advocacy of an independent Pakistan and to concede it was a far greater sacrifice than Congress ceding the Muslim-dominated areas of the sub-continent. However, on *timing* Attlee can be criticized. Partition could arguably have been implemented with less bloodshed. The Indian Independence Act of July 1947 left only four weeks to leave; four weeks during which Radcliffe drew a map that shaped the lives – and deaths – of literally millions of people. Announcing the lines *after* partition – in effect leaving any resulting communal problems in the hands of the newly independent states – contributed to the endemic violence and refugee crisis that followed. Radcliffe did have an unenviable job. Wherever he had drawn the line, he would have been subjected to criticism, and communal violence was already ongoing long before he arrived in Delhi. Unfortunately, however, the historical evidence to defend the work of the commission is not available, as the boundary commission's papers no longer exist. The four-week period, coupled with the 'hands off' approach afterwards, contributed to a human tragedy that Britain – including Attlee – could have done more to alleviate.

As regards Kashmir, the policy of allowing Moutbatten to press the princely states into accession was successful in that, of the hundreds of princely states, only four proved difficult. However, the fact is that one of these four proved disastrous in the long-term. Most of the blame for subsequent Indo–Pakistani disputes must lie with those countries' leaders,[87] but Attlee could have *reduced* tension between the two had he anticipated and resolved the Kashmir issue. One option was to have allowed Kashmir to remain independent, but, with its population of only around 14 million, it was thought to be of doubtful viability. This was not the most persuasive argument: many states are much smaller; more importantly, had a precedent been set with allowing Kashmir independence, this might have led other princely states to demand independence as well. Another option was to press the maharaja into joining Pakistan; with no agreement of accession, the dispute would not have arisen. But Attlee maintained his 'hands off' approach until the dispute had already crystallized; Mountbatten may have spent four days trying to persuade the maharajah to accede, but, once he had failed, there was scope for Attlee to intervene. Of course, Attlee might not have been successful in any event, but without any effort having been made, that will remain an unanswered question.

Chapter 18
BRITAIN AND AMERICA, 1945–51

Churchill popularized the term 'special relationship' in his famous 'Iron Curtain' speech at Fulton, Missouri, on 5 March 1946. By then, Britain's financial dependence on the United States was already obvious. In July 1944, at Mount Hotel, Bretton Woods, New Hampshire, Keynes negotiated the agreement that became known simply as 'Bretton Woods': International Monetary Fund subscriptions/quotas were set in US dollars, which was the only major convertible currency, backed by a large US balance of payments surplus. The dollar was convertible into gold at the rate of $35 per ounce and, *de facto*, the value of other currencies was set in terms of the US dollar. Dollars would therefore dominate the world financial system. Britain's direct financial relationship with the United States was cemented into place from the moment that the American loan was agreed in November 1945. From 1947, when Bevin accepted the offer of aid from the new United States secretary of state, George Marshall, Britain received more direct aid from the United States than any other aid recipient. In the successive currency crises of 1947 and 1949, it was to Washington that Britain had to turn for assistance. Against this financial background, there was little real chance of Britain achieving a friendship with the Soviet Union. Instead, the Attlee government is credited with having laid the foundations of the close postwar relationship between Britain and the United States, signing the North Atlantic Treaty in 1949 guaranteeing United States action in the event of a Soviet attack on Western Europe.

Attlee applied his non-personalized leadership style in the sphere of foreign policy. Attlee and Truman were not personally close in the way that were, say, Thatcher and Reagan. Remarkably, Attlee only met Truman twice after Potsdam. He flew to Washington on two occasions, arriving for the first time on 10 November 1945, just prior to agreeing the American loan, and did not visit again for a further five years; on 5 December 1950, during the Korean War, with Bevin ill, Truman gave a dinner for Attlee on board the USS *Williamsburg*. Academic study of British foreign policy between 1945 and 1951 has focused on Ernest Bevin; Alan Bullock's three-volume life of Bevin completed in 1983 stood as the leading survey of immediate postwar British foreign policy. But any study of the 'special relationship' must start by considering the personalities at the top. In the absence of a number of face-to-face meetings, it is the correspondence between the two men that is revealing.

On one issue in particular their relationship was strained and the Attlee government's reputation severely damaged – Palestine. Attlee's initial response in the summer and autumn of 1945 was to refuse Truman's request to allow 100,000 Jews into Palestine. He took no interest in domestic American politics. The State Department disagreed with Truman's pro-Jewish policy and the then secretary of state George Marshall opposed his recognition of the state of Israel just minutes after it was proclaimed on 14 May 1948. In March 1948, when Truman had assured the head of the Jewish Agency, Chaim Weizmann, of his commitment to a United Nations solution for Palestine, Senator Warren Austin, the United States representative on the Security Council, put forward a tripartite trusteeship of the United States, Britain and France. Truman remarked that there were 'people on the 3rd and 4th levels of the State Dept. who have always wanted to cut my throat'.[1] Arab states in the Middle East sat on significant oil reserves and there was an impact on the whole Middle East of inserting a large group of new people into it. Yet, Attlee gave scant recognition to Truman's position: the American president knew the political impact of the significant Jewish vote at home, and pursued his policy vigorously, even with such strong State Department opposition. Attlee did not even take the time to visit Truman to discuss the matter or discover what his underlying motivations might have been.

In November 1945, the British government proposed to the United States that an Anglo-American Committee of Inquiry be set up to deal with the issue. The proposal was, however, uncompromising on the situation in the short term: 'In regard to the immediate future, His Majesty's Government have decided that the only practicable course is to maintain the present arrangement for immigration'[2] – that is 1500 people per month. The committee, made up of six American and six British participants, reported in April 1946 and, aside from recommending that Palestine should be neither a Jewish nor an Arab state, with neither dominating, concluded that 100,000 Jews should be admitted into Palestine immediately. On 10 May 1946 Attlee wrote to Truman to ask that 'every effort should be made to convene a conference and which Arab and Jewish representatives would meet with representatives of our two Governments',[3] but Truman publicly approved the proposal to admit 100,000 Jews immediately. On 24 June, Attlee cabled to Truman that 'Tension is mounting in Palestine and we are satisfied that precipitate action on the immigration question alone would provoke widespread violence.'[4] On 29 June, he wrote in strong terms:

> In view of the continuance of terrorist activity in Palestine culminating in the recent kidnapping of six British officers, His Majesty's Government have come to the conclusion that drastic action can no longer be postponed. …
>
> … It is proposed to raid the Jewish Agency and to occupy it for a period necessary to search for incriminating documents. At the same time members of the Agency considered implicated directly or indirectly in Haganah [a Jewish paramilitary organization] outrages will be arrested. Similar action will be taken in the case of headquarters of the illegal organisations.[5]

To find an agreed position between Britain and the United States, 'experts' met from both sides: cabinet secretary Norman Brook chaired for the British, and the diplomat Henry F. Grady chaired for the United States. However, violence continued and, on 22 July 1946, the militant Zionist group *Irgun* bombed the King David Hotel in Jerusalem, with the loss of 91 lives. The 'experts' put forward proposals for a government to have overall control of Jerusalem and Bethlehem with an Arab and a Jewish state within a federal structure; admission of the further 100,000 Jews should be on the basis of Arab consent. This was known as the Morrison–Grady Plan; Morrison at this stage was chairing the cabinet's Palestine committee. Given his earlier commitments to Jewish immigration, Truman was never likely to approve this and duly declined to do so. On 18 August 1946 Attlee wrote to Truman that it was 'a great disappointment to us that you should feel yourself unable to give support to the plan recommended by the Anglo-American Expert delegations.'[6] However, he pressed on with the idea of bringing the sides together to discuss the proposals: 'it is, as I have said, our intention to place the outlines of the provincial autonomy plan before the conference.'[7] Attlee was, however, overly optimistic – the Jewish Agency simply refused to attend the September conference, the Palestinian Arabs did not attend either and the remaining Arab states would not contemplate a Jewish state in Palestine.

Truman did not give up easily on this issue and sent a telegram to Attlee in no uncertain terms in the early hours of 4 October 1946 containing a draft statement for issue the next day:

> I deeply regret that it has been found necessary to postpone further

meetings of the Palestine Conference in London until December 16th and I sincerely hope that it will be found possible in the interim to begin moving on a large scale the 100,000 displaced Jews in Europe who are awaiting admission to Palestine.[8]

Attlee requested a postponement with Bevin in Paris talking to Zionist leaders there, but was refused it. The following morning he replied bad-temperedly that the statement's effects might well:

include the frustration of the patient efforts to achieve a settlement and the loss of still more lives in Palestine.

I am astonished that you did not wait to acquaint yourself with the reasons for the suspension of the Conference with the Arabs. ...

I shall await with interest to learn what were the imperative reasons which compelled this precipitancy.[9]

Truman replied by telegram on 10 October setting out the deep-seated American feeling on the issue:

My feeling was that the announcement of the adjournment until December 16 of the discussions with the Arabs had brought such depression to the Jewish displaced persons in Europe and to millions of American citizens concerned with the fact of these unfortunate people that I could not even for a single day postpone making clear the continued interest of this government in their welfare.[10]

World moral opinion was against Attlee on the issue. As the full horrors of the six million Jews systematically murdered by the Nazis emerged, the call for a Jewish homeland was louder than ever. When on 2 January 1947 *The Times* reviewed the year 1946, it declared: 'the year closed with a fresh outbreak of terrorist activity in Palestine and with little hope of an accommodation between Jews and Arabs.' It added:

The suggestion that 100,000 Jewish refugees should be admitted to Palestine as soon as practicable caught the imagination of humanitarian circles both in Britain and the United States, and Zionist opinion in the United States as well as in Palestine was greatly encouraged, and shows signs of even more dangerous impatience at British endeavours to prevent all Jewish immigration not sanctioned by the small minority quota.[11]

Emboldened by Truman's support, in January 1947 the Jewish Agency demanded all of Palestine as a Jewish state – 'acting apparently on the principle that it is necessary to ask for a yard to get a foot', noted *The Times*.[12] Bevin remained opposed to changing the British policy of minimal immigration and there was anti-Semitism in this view. On 19 April 1948, just one month before the proclamation of the state of Israel, Bevin wrote to Lord Inverchapel, Halifax's successor as British ambassador to the United States:

> As I saw it, the fundamental difficulty over Palestine was that the Jews refused to admit that the Arabs were their equals. If they could be brought to see that the principle of one man one vote applied in Palestine to Jews and Arabs alike as much as anywhere else our diffi-culties might be solved, and in such an atmosphere even the introduction of 100,000 Jewish immigrants might be possible.[13]

In the early months of 1947, Britain, facing a fuel crisis at home, was scaling back its overseas commitments. In late 1946 it committed itself to pulling out of Egypt. Under the Anglo-Egyptian Treaty of 1936, it was allowed to station troops in Egypt for the purposes of defending the Suez Canal. In October 1946, Bevin renegotiated the treaty. Britain was to withdraw from Alexandria, Cairo and the Nile Delta by 31 March 1947, and then completely by 1 September 1949. In February 1947, Britain announced that it would end financial assistance to Greece and indicated a gradual withdrawal of troops. At the same time, Attlee was setting a final date for British withdrawal from India. Cabinet discussions throughout February considered the various Palestine options: Arthur Creech Jones, the colonial secretary, argued for partition; Bevin asked for a five-year period of trusteeship to prepare for a Jew-Arab state; and Bevan argued the case for acting in favour of the Jews.[14] Bevan was in a minority and it was accepted that a solution could not be provided by Britain alone. On 2 April, the government referred the matter to the United Nations, for the issue of Palestine to go before the General Assembly. If the UN failed to reach an agreement, it would strengthen Britain's hand.

On 28 April, the day that a special session of the United Nations opened, Rowan sent a note to Attlee: 'I do not like any of this. … The only result that I can see is that this country will be put in the dock quite unjustifiably.'[15] He was prescient, for, over the summer, there was unexpected Soviet support for partition into Jewish and Arab states, and concern regarding an anti-Semitic backlash. On 31 August 1947 it emerged that two British sergeants who had been kidnapped had been hanged. 'Such is the latest savagery committed by terrorist Palestine,' commented *The Times*.[16] Attlee created an official com-mittee on 30 October to coordinate withdrawal and, on 25 November, a memorandum by the committee on Palestine set out a timetable, starting with military withdrawal from the Gaza civil district by 29 February 1948 with the whole military withdrawal complete by 31 July 1948.[17] On 29 November 1947, the General Assembly passed United Nations Resolution 181 to end Britain's mandate by 1 August 1948 and introduce a 'two-state' solution. Britain announced that it would withdraw by 15 May 1948. This was followed by the Jerusalem riots, with Arabs attacking Jewish neighbourhoods, and *Haganah* responded, with its related organization, the *Irgun* running a bombing campaign against Arab civilians.

On 4 December 1947 the Cabinet endorsed Creech Jones's melancholy recommendations that the government 'should do nothing to obstruct the carrying out of the United Nations decision in favour of the partition of Palestine, but that British troops and the British administration should in no circumstances become involved in enforcing that decision, or in maintaining law and order while the United Nations Commission enforced it.'[18] The civil war in Palestine continued. The *Irgun* continued to bomb public areas and, in retaliation in February 1948, the Arabs placed a bomb outside the Jewish Agency headquarters. From April *Haganah* stepped up its efforts and took a number of cities, including the port of Jaffa in early May. On 14 May 1948, the day preceding the expiry of the British Mandate, the State of Israel was declared. The next day, Egypt, Syria, Jordan, Lebanon and Iraq all invaded Palestine, triggering the Arab-Israeli war of 1948–49. By the time of the armistice agreements of 1949, the new state of Israel had claimed nearly four-fifths of the old British mandate territory. The Palestinian Arabs had been restricted to two major areas: the West Bank, controlled at this stage by Jordan, and the Gaza Strip, controlled by Egypt. Hundreds of thousands of Palestinians were made refugees, their right of return remaining a major bone of contention in Middle East peace settlements today.

Bevin tried to avoid the impression that Britain had simply abandoned Palestine to civil war. On 2 June 1948 he reported to the House of Commons that the government had been 'concentrating all their efforts on an endeavour to bring about a cease-fire and to create conditions in which the two parties would be brought together with a view to achieving a final solution of this problem'.[19] Viscount Elibank remarked wistfully in the Lords on 9 June 1948 that he could 'only say' that he hoped that Britain's 'taking up this Mandate reluctantly … and the degree to which people have lost their lives and suffered, will be borne in mind in future when this question is being discussed in other parts of the world'.[20] On 26 August 1948 Bevin said in cabinet that he was 'convinced that any attempt to make further progress through direct discussions [British] between the Arabs and Jews themselves would fail, and that the only hope lay in the imposition of a settlement by the

United Nations'.[21] The perception was that Britain had entirely washed its hands of the affair.

With so many historical problems, the question is what the alternative could have been. With Palestine, the alternative was clear: accede to Truman's request for 100,000 immigration certificates for the Jews. On the other hand, Attlee and Bevin hoped to maintain Britain's influence in the Middle East and that meant accommodating the wishes of the Arab states. Britain *did* maintain an element of goodwill in the Arab world; a memorandum by the official committee on Palestine dated 5 November 1947 noted: 'Various Arab Governments have threatened to use their Armed Forces in Palestine in certain eventualities, though they have all said that they have no intention of becoming involved in action against British Forces or the British Administration.'[22] In the short term, Britain's influence in Egypt was maintained by a joint defence board making recommendations to both governments.[23] This meant a new relationship of equality. Attlee minuted to Bevin on 10 August 1947 that Britain could not simply *demand* a military base in Egypt.[24] Britain's apparent Arab bias remained after the 1948–49 Arab-Israeli war. During the war, Britian adhered to the UN arms embargo on arms supplies to theatre to the detriment of the Arabs (Israel remained able to buy Soviet-bloc arms). But afterwards, on 29 August 1949, Peter Fraser, the prime minister of New Zealand, wrote to Attlee to express his concern about the British government supplying arms to Arab states (despite the embargo of 29 May 1948 having been lifted). Attlee indicated that the 'Arab states have urgent need of this material for their internal security and defence'; and with the embargo lifted there was no justification for not fulfilling contractual obligations. Attlee emphasized that, in the case of Egypt, the Egyptian armed forces' cooperation was considered essential to protect the British position in the Middle East.[25] By this of course he meant the Suez Canal; even with Indian independence, an historic trading route. In 1950, the USA, Britain and France issued the 'Tri-partite Declaration' pledging action to maintain the 1949 armistice borders, and the control of arms sales to the region to prevent either Israel or the Arabs gaining a preponderance of weapons. But Britain was always going to have historical difficulties with Arab states. It had, after all, issued the Balfour Declaration of 1917 to establish a Jewish homeland. Egyptian cooperation was abandoned when Nasser nationalized the Suez Canal in July 1956.

Practically, the British policy proved futile and difficult to justify on a moral basis. Gerald Kaufman accused Attlee of 'ingrained anti-Semitism' and said that he 'betrayed the Jews without appeasing the Arabs'.[26] Britain interned thousands of Jews seeking illegal entry to Palestine in camps on Cyprus. Palestine remained in a state of civil war, with atrocities taking place on an almost weekly basis. Truman was unable to engage constructively in any plan for a solution without the demand for 100,000 immigration certificates being granted. In ending the mandate, British policy had not prevented war and chaos; it had not prevented the establishment of Israel and it had not prevented the displacement of hundreds of thousands of Palestinians from their own homes. Attlee must bear much of the blame for this. He never sought any real detail from Truman about the request for the immigration certificates. Neither he nor Bevin – nor, it has to be said, the Foreign Office – had sufficient engagement with American politics to appreciate the crucial role of the Jewish vote. Attlee totally misunderstood the Jewish desire for their own state. When Bevin did visit the United States, Attlee's second-hand understanding of the problem was contained in what he told Tom on 29 December 1946:

> Bevin came over on Friday and gave a full account of his American experiences. It appears that Zionism has become a profitable racket over there. A Zionist is defined as a Jew who collects money from another Jew to send another Jew to Palestine. The collector, I gather takes a good percentage of his collections.[27]

This was hardly a soaring exposition of the desire for Jewish nationhood. Had Attlee realized the importance of that desire, and granted Truman his wish, the United States would have been in a position to press the Jewish Agency into finding some kind of solution. Whether such a solution would have been forthcoming – and how the Arab states would have responded to Britain – can only be a matter of speculation. Granting the certificates in themselves in the summer of 1945, with the Holocaust exposed, could have been done on the basis of a strong moral argument. The opportunity was missed and Britain's historical reputation has suffered as a result.

It was not just over Palestine that British–American relations were less than cooperative. Joint work between Britain and the United States on nuclear weapons also ended after the Manhattan Project had reached its conclusion with the bombings of Hiroshima and Nagasaki in August 1945. On 19 August 1943 Churchill and Roosevelt had signed the Quebec Agreement, sharing atomic research and agreeing that each nation required the consent of the other to launch an atomic attack. Had such collaboration continued, the question of an independent nuclear deterrent for Britain would not have arisen. As it was, Truman signed the McMahon Act on 1 August 1946, placing control of nuclear weapons development under the United States Atomic Energy Commission, and preventing the sharing of information with other countries. This left Attlee with the question of developing Britain's own deterrent. On 25 October 1946, in a 'Gen 75' cabinet committee meeting Bevin made the famous comment that the bomb had to have a 'bloody Union Jack' on top of it, defeating Dalton and Cripps, both of whom were concerned about cost.[28] When the final decision that 'research and development work on atomic weapons should be undertaken' was made on 8 January 1947, it was with a new cabinet committee, 'Gen 163' that Attlee took the decision. Aside from Attlee, only Morrison, Bevin, Addison, Alexander and Wilmot, the minister of supply, were present.[29] It was a remarkable breach of collective cabinet decision-making, with the rest of the cabinet not informed, and an undermining of the role of parliament. When Churchill returned as prime minister in 1951, he demanded to know 'How was it that the £100 millions for atomic research and manufacture was provided without Parliament being informed?'[30] Nonetheless, Churchill pressed on, and the first British nuclear test took place on 3 October 1952.

Alexander had tentatively told the Commons on 12 May 1948 that there was atomic research in progress, but had given no further details on grounds of public interest. At the 1948 party conference, Attlee obliquely referred to nuclear weapons: 'It has been said that one of the greatest dangers of civilization today is that man's conquests in the realms of science have outstripped his moral progress.'[31] But this was as far as it went. It remains a key paradox: probably Britain's most consensual postwar prime minister took the greatest security decision of postwar British history in the utmost secrecy. But the paradox can be unpicked. Attlee felt that the only way to respond to a nuclear attack was with a nuclear attack; he also knew that belligerents would almost always use the most extreme weapon available – just as gas had been used in the trenches during the First World War.[32] The way Attlee saw it, *any* breach of security in these early stages might have threatened Britain's ability to develop a nuclear weapon. Just as the McMahon Act kept American research a secret, and Stalin kept Soviet research a secret, Britain had to do the same to maintain any comparative advantage it gained in the field of research. In Attlee's view, this matter was so critical that even members of his government could not be trusted. Not even the whole cabinet, let alone the wider public, ever debated whether it was right that Britain should develop its own nuclear deterrent. There was a flip side to Attlee's secrecy: other cabinet colleagues probably 'preferred not to know': to be officially in the dark and not to have to express a view, not least Cripps (who, as chancellor, would have been very remiss not to notice the money being allocated). Whether Attlee was right depends on whether one feels the possession of a nuclear deterrent was crucial to British postwar status and foreign policy. If it was, the Attlee government was highly effective in bringing it about with the minimum of controversy; if it was not, Attlee as prime minister carries the blame for taking Britain into the nuclear age in dictatorial style.

For all the apparent difficulties between Britain and the United States, Attlee placed Britain firmly on the side of America in the cold war. He and Bevin sought mutual defence pacts among the Western European states in the event of a Soviet attack, and sought to tie in the United States. On 4 March 1947 Britain and France signed the Dunkirk Treaty of mutual assistance; on 17 March 1948 the Brussels Treaty was signed, which included not just Britain and France but Belgium, the Netherlands and Luxembourg as well. In July 1948, the United States was encouraged to station nuclear-capable B-29 bombers in Britain, starting to cement its military commitment to Western Europe. Ominously, on 12 June 1948 the Soviets declared the Autobahn into Berlin closed and followed, within a few days, by closing other transport routes. Berlin was in an unusual position. Within the Soviet zone of occupation, a mere 44 miles from the border with Poland, it had itself been subdivided between the allies; as a consequence West Berlin was a small pocket of French–British–American territory within the Soviet zone of Germany.

The Soviets had allowed road and rail access to West Berlin, together with airspace. Now it challenged the Western allies to find a way of supplying Berlin. Trying to do so by land risked open conflict with the Soviet Union, so an airlift began on 25 June. The Soviets tried to disrupt it, with balloons released into the air and a fake radio beacon being among the measures used, but the airlift proved a great success; when in August the Soviets offered food to anyone coming across to East Berlin, the offer failed to make any significant impact. The airlift continued through the winter, with the French assisting the British and Americans, and gained strength in the spring of 1949; the Soviets accepted its success and the blockade ended on 11 May 1949. Just a month before, the North Atlantic Treaty Organization (NATO) was created on 4 April 1949 in Washington. The United States was now committed to the defence of Western Europe. In a third world war, there would be no need to wait patiently for America's entry.

Just over a year later, the United States entered its first major armed conflict since 1945. The Korean War was significant as it was the first proxy conflict of the cold war with the Soviet Union, but it also showed what British diplomacy could still achieve with the United States. The conflict began on 5 June 1950. Using Soviet military equipment, North Korean troops crossed the 38th parallel (the line of latitude forming the border between North and South Korea). They were remarkably successful. An American task force, which intervened at Osan, just south of Seoul, was brushed aside on 5 July and, by September, only Pusan, on the southern part of the Korean peninsula remained out of the hands of the north. Acting under United Nations authority (Resolution 85 of 31 July 1950 had given the United States command of the military operation to repel North Korea), the Americans and South Korean forces held Pusan, with the first British troops arriving on 28 August. The combined forces then struck back. On 7 October, a British resolution carried by the UN General Assembly called on UN forces to cross the 38th parallel, restore 'stability throughout Korea' and hold elections. On 19 October, the US Eighth Army captured the North Korean capital, Pyongyang. This all prompted Mao Zedong, chairman of the ruling Chinese Communist Party, to enter the conflict, with some Soviet air support, and the American troops, having stormed so far north, were rapidly driven back.

Attlee's final meeting with Truman was in December 1950. He crossed the Atlantic because Bevin was ill and he had a number of issues to raise notably because, aside from British troops, there were also Australian, Canadian, New Zealand and South African troops in the theatre. Also, Attlee's government had recognized the new Chinese republic established by the communist revolution of 1949, while Truman still supported the old regime of Chiang Kai-Shek and wished to protect his forces in Formosa. Attlee was also concerned that the US president might once again use an atomic bomb in the Far East and spread the conflict across Southeast Asia. Attlee did not particularly impress Truman: 'The position of the British on Asia is, to say the least, fantastic. We cannot agree to their suggestions. Yet they say they will support us whatever we do!'[33] No agreement was forthcoming on Formosa.[34] However, Attlee *did* gain an assurance that the USA would not use its nuclear weapons without consulting the UK and Canada.[35] While such an assurance from Truman would not bind subsequent US presidents, back in the Commons Churchill considered the visit a success. The impression grew that Attlee had stopped Truman using nuclear weapons over Korea – incorrect, but a powerful myth that was effective in the 1951 general election campaign.[36] Meanwhile, on the ground, by January 1951 the Chinese had taken the South Korean capital, Seoul. While an American counterattack recaptured Seoul in March 1951, the offensive this time stopped just north of the 38th parallel. There were no further major territorial changes, though the war continued until the armistice on 27 July 1953.

By then Attlee had been out of power for the best part of two years. He had made his contribution to Anglo-American relations. His government's great achievement was to tie the United States into defending Western Europe in the event of any future attack. During the Korean War, he had personally shown that American presidents would listen to British concerns if argued appropriately. Britain was no mere financial dependent but an essential ally in the cold war. Yet, Attlee's failure to meet Truman for over five years unquestionably contributed to his failure of policy in Palestine. And while it was America who slammed the door in Britain's face over nuclear weapons, Attlee had not made any special effort even to speak to Truman on the matter either before or after the McMahon Act. In the major financial trips to Washington – for the loan in 1945, on the convertibility clause in 1947 and over devaluation in 1949 – Attlee preferred to send other people. Britain's special relationship with the United States was largely based on finance (if it came to the worst it was better to hope for salvation from America than make terms with Moscow) rather than the enthusiasm for America – and its society – Churchill showed both in his relationship with Roosevelt and his speeches after 1945. Churchill, with his American mother, was always a more natural pro-American than Attlee. Attlee was more comfortable dealing with issues of empire – it was unquestionably India on which he spent most prime ministerial time prior to independence. Given Attlee's apparent ability to deal positively – at least in some way – with Truman in Washington in December 1950, he might have achieved a great deal more had he met him personally more often.

Chapter 19

COAL AND CURRENCY: ATTLEE'S LEADERSHIP CRISIS OF 1947

One of the most potent slogans the Conservatives used against the Attlee government was 'Shiver with Shinwell' – the fuel shortage over the harsh winter of 1946–47 that directly affected millions of British people. The weather *was* unpredictably bad, with snow falling somewhere in the UK every day from 22 January to 17 March 1947. With prolonged cold weather, snow accumulated, with some drifts as high as five metres.[1] However, the toxic combination of a perceived policy failure together with a tangible effect on the lives of so many gave the Conservatives an electoral present. While, understandably, the minister of fuel and power, Shinwell, was the government minister associated with the crisis, Attlee was also fully aware of the potential difficulties of that winter. Had he intervened earlier and more decisively in the development of events, the impact of the weather could have been mitigated.

Attlee's mode of leadership relied on his cabinet ministers performing well. Shinwell made errors in the summer and autumn of 1946: 'I have no intention whatever of denying that I made optimistic speeches about the coal situation.'[2] He put this down to his faith in the mining industry; his mitigation was that he could not have foreseen how bad that winter's 'big freeze' was to be: 'I believed that in spite of fewer men the coal would be produced. I may have erred in not finding expert advice to forecast the phenomenal rise in industrial consumption of coal and and power but I could not prophesy the weather.'[3] While that may be so, there was no shortage of warnings about taking stringent measures to limit coal consumption *in the event* of worse weather than expected. Shinwell honestly recorded: 'The risks of such a crisis had been occupying our attention at the Ministry of Fuel and Power for at least seven months.'[4]

On 18 October 1946 Attlee wrote to both Dalton and Shinwell that he was 'disturbed by the coal prospects for the coming winter', doubted whether domestic consumers could manage with less coal than at present and asked whether, if cuts on industrial consumers were being contemplated, they could be done immediately?[5] On 22 October, in response, Shinwell tried to buy time: he thought selective cuts were possible (by delivering less coal) but wanted more detail.[6] A minute from Norman Brook to Attlee on 13 November crystallized the issues. Officials from the Board of Trade and Ministry of Power had worked out a scheme of compulsory rationing, which the FBI and TUC would have accepted; however, on 8 November at the Lord President's Committee, Shinwell felt there was some improvement in production and proposed a voluntary scheme. Brook felt there were 'strong arguments in favour of a compulsory scheme'.[7] A disagreement between Shinwell and the permanent civil service was born. But Shinwell did not understate the situation or mislead Attlee in any way: 'We are … faced with the likelihood that total supplies this winter will fall short of total requirements by something like 2 and 5 million tons.' To Shinwell, the question was not whether measures should be taken, but which.[8] When the critical decision about preparatory measures was taken at cabinet on 19 November, Attlee was in full possession of the facts.[9] On the face of it, Shinwell's proposals were ingenious. To avoid a public announcement about cuts in allocations of coal, cuts in actual deliveries against allocation should be made; for gas and electricity, a directive would be issued. Average weekly consumption for that month would be set as a maximum for use each week over the winter. Deliveries of coal to hotels, clubs and 'places of amusement' should be cut by 10 per cent, and the gas and electricity directive would apply to them. On 25 November, Attlee 'said that further reference to the Cabinet would not be necessary if the Ministers directly concerned were content with the scheme it was now proposed to introduce'.[10] Attlee had made his choice and dismissed the obvious alternative of a *compulsory* scheme at this stage. He missed his opportunity to intervene at an early stage.

When he did intervene, it was too late. In a panicky memorandum dated 3 January 1947, Shinwell sombrely concluded:

> I feel it my duty to warn the Cabinet that for some considerable time there will not be sufficient fuel and power to meet the requirements put forward by Departments in view of the rising trend of consumption …
> if we are to avoid dislocation in every industry there must be some allocation of raw materials.[11]

On 6 January, Morrison intervened and circulated his own memorandum in which he was concerned about the political effect of moving from what had been agreed with industry the previous month, but felt a reduction in electricity consumption was the way forward.[12] On 7 January the cabinet agreed on a new system of allocations.[13] However, the next day the *Daily Telegraph* ran the story that further large cuts in coal had been decided at cabinet. A bad-tempered Attlee sent a harsh note to Cripps and Shinwell regarding the failure to give guidance to those responsible for public relations in each department. Cripps pointed out that the problem was that he and Shinwell were left to work out the reduced allocations, so immediate guidance was not possible.[14] By 5 February Shinwell had told Attlee that, due to the weather, coal movement was such that there was a 'grave risk' of power stations having to close down.[15] At cabinet on 11 February Attlee could do no more than ask for Shinwell to circulate daily reports.[16] The next day, for the first time, Attlee chaired a cabinet committee established by him to deal with policy issues presented by the crisis and measures to prevent a repeat in 1948.[17] But by then great political damage was unavoidable. On 19 February Attlee was embarrassed in the House of Commons:

> Mr Attlee, with one elbow on the dispatch box, did not linger over the reading of his statement. He began in a low and rapid monotone, and was soon greeted with requests to speak up. His repetition, in a sharply emphatic voice, of his opening sentence, that the position had improved, was greeted with loud Ministerial cheers.[18]

The scale of the crisis was such that the priority of movement given on the railways to coal a year previously could not be withdrawn until 26 February 1948.[19] It was an early indication of the limitations of Attlee's leadership style. He relied on his ministers to carry out their tasks competently; when they did not, or, as in this case, they flagrantly ignored official advice, the strategy could fail. The government had unquestionably taken a knock as a result. There is of course no guarantee that a compulsory scheme could have worked during that harsh winter of 1947, but the immediate availability of more coal would have had a mitigating effect. Of course, had Attlee backed a compulsory scheme against Shinwell's wishes, there was a danger of Shinwell's resignation. Yet, the fact is that during the key cabinet meeting on 19 November 1946, Attlee did not even put the case for the compulsory scheme. There is no evidence that he saw Shinwell privately, either. In these circumstances, the country may well have shivered with Shinwell, but they shivered with Attlee as well.

The event was merely a precursor for the later crisis of 1947. The effect of 1947 on Attlee was said to have been profound enough for Kenneth O. Morgan to conclude that 'Attlee's position thereafter was more withdrawn. The pipe-smoking, silent, remote figure whom Sir Harold Wilson and others beheld at the head of the Cabinet table was reborn.'[20] When a supremely confident

Attlee declared at the 1947 party conference on 27 May that: 'today there is no coherent alternative policy to Labour's in this country'[21] he was probably correct, but without money Labour policies could not continue. The crisis centred on the balance of payments: put simply, the difficulty was that Britain was importing far more than it was exporting. *The Times*, in a January 1947 'survey of export industries', declared that 'the increase of productive efficiency here must be used to bring about a growth of exports which is appreciably in excess of any increase in imports.'[22] Provided the American loan was in place, this gap could be bridged, as it was in 1946, when the balance of payments stood at £380 million.[23] On 25 April 1947 the Treasury produced a memorandum: 'Balance of Payments Working Party: Import Programme for 1947–48', which started grimly: 'We now face a crisis in our external financial position which affects our ability to import our food and also raw materials for employment. ... By June 1947 nearly half of the North American credits will have been exhausted; we shall have left £650 millions.'[24] This had a number of causes: a rise in world prices, the fuel shortage affecting exports, 'losses suffered by United Kingdom agriculture', slow recovery from the ravages of war in Europe and the East, meaning that importation from there was difficult, the price of restructuring Germany, and a dollar shortage. A £200 million cut in imports was suggested. It is added that 'What concerns us is our obligation to convert current sterling earnings as from 15th July and our obligation to release some of the accumulated wartime balances for current transactions anywhere [many sterling area countries had not been directly paid for goods and services provided during the war].'[25] The difficulty was that, with organizations being able to demand payment in dollars rather than pounds, those dollars could then be spent outside Britain. Britain would be spending far more dollars than it was earning.

The political elephant in the room was of course the impact of reductions in imports (principally food and clothing), which would adversely affect living standards, with the twin political impacts of apparent economic incompetence and a directly negative impact on the lives of ordinary people. Unsurprisingly, when Attlee, Bevin, Morrison, Dalton and Cripps met on 5 May, they sought 'revised proposals for reducing existing departmental programmes for imports in the year 1947/48 by £150 millions, instead of the figure of £200 millions proposed'.[26] The government's options were, however, very limited. The Treasury had considered a number of choices – reducing further Britain's overseas commitments ('an alteration in the financial burden of Germany is the only significant possibility'); blocking sterling balances ('no one will sell any more to us for blocked sterling'); requiring payments for exports in convertible currencies and putting pressure on the USA to fund its own exports ('there are not enough dollars in those parts of the world which need dollars most');

increasing supplies from other non-dollar areas ('the creation of new sources of supply inevitable takes time'); using the reserves ('only if it was plain that this was a very temporary drain'); and going to the International Monetary Fund ('we could not count on securing the agreement of International Monetary Fund to drawings of £80 millions in 1947–48 to meet a continuing disequilibrium').[27] At a further meeting of the same six ministers on 19 May, Attlee recounted a recent conversation between the minister of food and the US ambassador to the UK, who had apparently said that further credit should be made available by the USA to the UK:

> If the British people were subjected to further strain at this moment, he thought they might react politically by moving away from the Centre and towards the Left and Right wings, thus producing an anti-Labour administration faced by a militant and uncooperative industrial Labour movement which would be more or less under Communist leadership.[28]

Attlee commented that 'he did not endorse all that the United States Ambassador had said to the Minister of Food', but 'was seriously concerned at the proposed reduction in the programme of food imports'.[29] The reduction was agreed, save for the restoration of canned meat and fish at a cost of £19 million.[30] Food was not the only issue though and other major items included petrol and clothing. Dalton's memorandum to cabinet of 28 May 1947 suggested a 10 per cent reduction in the imports of petroleum[31] and Cripps prepared a memorandum to cabinet dated 2 June that sought to export more cloth, cutting the clothing ration to '4 coupons a month during most of next year'.[32]

The looming deadline was 15 July, and Dalton rather unwisely commented in the House of Commons on 8 July that 'the additional burden of assuming these new obligations under the Anglo-American Loan Agreement will be noticeably less than many people may suppose.'[33] By 25 July, he was alarmed: 'The prospects in front of us are rapidly growing worse and worse.'[34] At cabinet on 29 July, Attlee opened:

> A difficult situation had arisen owing to the rapid exhaustion of the United States credit. It was essential that the government should meet this situation by positive action designed to preserve the standard of life of the people and to maintain the position of the United Kingdom. He proposed that the Cabinet should have a general discussion in the first instance and that at a later meeting, on 1st August, they should consider specific proposals.[35]

It was hardly an urgent response and, the next day, Isaacs, the minister of labour and national service, proposed a 'National Crisis Scheme': 'The only course, as after Dunkirk, is to secure as a crisis measure an immediate increase of output by an immediate lengthening of hours of work.'[36] If Attlee was in any doubt at all about how difficult the situation was, Dalton's memorandum of the same day would have rammed the point home. The facts, he said were 'very simple and very unpleasant'. He stated:

> I warned the Cabinet on 5th June last that 'if the present rate of drawing on the United States Credit continued, this Credit would be exhausted as early as the end of 1947'. It is now quite clear that, at the present rate of drawing, the Credit will not last beyond November and will probably be exhausted in October, or even possibly in September.[37]

Both memoranda came before cabinet on 1 August and, remarkably, Attlee was not present at the meeting. Bevin had suggested an approach to the US government[38] and a telegram was sent on 2 August. Marshall replied by telegram on 4 August 1947 that he was 'prepared to accept the suggestion of His Majesty's Government that a discussion should take place forthwith between us on a high official level concerning your position and its immediate implications.'[39] Attlee did, however, speak during the first day of a two-day Commons debate on 6 August 1947, defending the government against the accusation that it had wasted the American loan: 'We should have liked, we all know, a larger amount. We doubted then whether this loan would buy sufficient time.'[40] He added: 'We are compelled to buy largely from the Western Hemisphere in dollars at high prices. The rest of the world is suffering from the same difficulties.'[41]

On 16 August, British officials led by joint Second Treasury Secretary Sir Wilfred Eady left for Washington. The next day Number 10 announced that 'When Parliament adjourned on 13th August the Prime Minister asked a small group of Ministers to remain in London to keep continuously under review the development of the economic situation.'[42] When cabinet met later on the same day, Dalton proposed the suspension of convertibility: 'it was the only way of checking the present drain of dollars.'[43] He felt that Eady should explain this in his first discussions with the US government on 18 August. There is no mention of Attlee in the confidential annex in the cabinet records containing these decisions. Indeed, on 18 August 1947, he sent a personal minute to Dalton considering a point made by Morrison about the danger of taking a different approach to non-sterling, as opposed to sterling, countries: 'The sense of the meeting was, in my view, that this distinction should not be made. May I take it that this was also your impression and that action will be taken accordingly?'[44] He sent a further minute to Strachey wanting 'specific announcements as soon as possible' on food.[45]

On 19 August *The Times* reported the 'American Delegation's Divided Views', Snyder at the Treasury advocating a strict interpretation of the loan agreement, and the State Department wishing to avoid problems in the UK.[46] It was added: 'The PM was at Downing Street all day, but it is not expected that his return to [his family on holiday in] North Wales will be long delayed. During the day he saw several members of Cabinet individually, but he held no meeting with any group of ministers.'[47] Morrison, Bevin, Dalton and Bevan had also all interrupted their holidays: 'of these, Mr Morrison only is expected to remain in London for the time being.'[48] However, the suspension was agreed; when the cabinet met at 12 p.m. on the same day, it was deferred for 24 hours, to assuage the Americans, but no more.[49] On 20 August, *The Times* reported: 'Mr Attlee presided over a meeting of ministers yesterday and afterwards returned to Wales to continue his interrupted holiday,' adding:

> The Prime Minister's return to Wales suggests that the sudden and unheralded Cabinet activity has temporarily spent itself but the second interruption of Sir Stafford Cripps' holiday emphasizes the difficulty the Government are meeting in carrying out their plan to tackle the economic crisis while so many questions affecting it are still under discussion in Washington and elsewhere.[50]

Attlee's political reputation was under threat. Throughout the crisis he had stuck rigidly to his preferred method of managing the cabinet, namely allowing consensus to emerge and offering no firm policy direction. In such circumstances, his model of leadership was clearly inadequate. There was some truth in the judgement of the diplomat Harold Nicolson, who, on lunching with Attlee nine years previously, had concluded that he was a 'delightful man … but not a pilot in a hurricane'.[51] In such circumstances, the pilot must take a firm grip of the controls and inspire confidence in his passengers that they will come through the difficult weather; Attlee's position as a speaker for a majority view was untenable. His quick return to North Wales only added to his difficulties, as, the next day, it was Morrison who fielded questions from the press. *The Times* reported on 21 August: 'Asked if Mr Attlee intended to retire, Mr Morrison said writers who reported that possibility did not seem to know what they were talking about.'[52] Attlee was clearly discomfited. In a document entitled 'Notes on the Present Situation' dated 19 August, addressed to Morrison, the full political impact was considered:

> Tomorrow's announcement about convertibility will seem far less

serious to the general public than it really is. They will assume that the Government has again lost control of the situation. They do not yet know the effect of this financial crisis on their lives. ...

With each delay in specific announcements there will be more resistance to the cuts which we know are necessary. ...

Not only is it politically necessary to bring home the situation to the people but it is also vital that we should do all we can to save imports. ...

We cannot be fair and equitable. Therefore it is well that as many people as possible should be to some extent affected.[53]

Suggestions included reducing the meat ration from one pound to half a pound, sugar to half a pound, and bread by 10 per cent. The source of the document on the accompanying note appears to be the Central Economic Planning Staff, and it is signed by its acting head, 'Hugh Weeks', on Morrison's 'express instructions' the document was brought to Attlee that night.[54] Attlee replied strongly:

I do not know what individuals are responsible for this document, but they appear to be giving advice to the Government on psychological and political grounds. The proposals are designed to impress our own people and the foreigners. There is no clear economic basis and no plan. The concrete proposals are not directly related to the dollar crisis. They are supported by no figures. Insofar as they are aimed at setting free labour from less essential works, this may be desirable, but there is no plan for absorbing the workers or the materials. I do not know whether Departments have been consulted. Obviously Ministers will have to consider them very closely before adopting them.

... to put out these ill-considered and undigested proposals this week would be to create panic and unemployment, and give the impression that the Government had lost its nerve. The right announcement will be that a series of actions are being taken to implement the Government's decisions, which will be announced in the course of the next few weeks – beginning with the agricultural programme, the food cuts, etc.[55]

As with the fuel crisis, Attlee's intervention was too late. He seemed to be losing his grip. On the same day, Eady sent a telegram to the Foreign Office indicating that an exchange of letters had been agreed with the US government: 'We are sure you will agree that the letters were designed with friendly intent and we said so.'[56] When cabinet met at 12.15 p.m. on 20 August, it was Morrison presiding in the absence of Attlee, who agreed the letters.[57] It was

Dalton who then wrote to US Treasury Secretary John W. Snyder: 'the system of transferable accounts will be modified at the close of business to-day, 20th August, so as to make it possible effectively to control dollar outpayments.' He added: 'This action is of an emergency and temporary nature.'[58] On 20 August at 5 p.m., Morrison chaired a meeting in the absence of Attlee. Bevin, Dalton, Cripps, Alexander, Shinwell and Williams made up a septet. No final agreement was reached, though putting a stop to foreign travel and preventing 'the export of maturing capital investments' (and looking at reinvestment here) found general acceptance, with Bevin asking for further time to consider the travel ban; the meeting was to resume on 25 August.[59]

There is an argument that, by remaining on holiday, Attlee was trying to quell the sense of crisis. But it is difficult to see how it could have been any worse. While Strachey sought to assuage Attlee's concerns with a note on 21 August, assuring him that 'We have got the situation under close review from day to day – indeed from hour to hour – in the closest consultation with the Treasury',[60] Attlee should have had the situation under close review. At cabinet on 25 August, Attlee could do no more than state the obvious:

> in all recent public statements the Government had emphasized the fact that our financial difficulties must be met partly by increasing exports, partly by reducing imports and partly by the increased production of food and other products which would otherwise have to be imported from hard-currency areas. It was necessary to maintain a proper balance between these aspects of the Government's policy.[61]

On 25 August, *The Times* warned of 'coming reductions in food rations',[62] but the next day noted that Bevin and Attlee were 'cheered as they arrived and left' Downing Street.[63] Agreement on ration reductions was finally reached and the announcement from Number 10 took place on 27 August. It was a thoroughly unpleasant announcement for any government to have to make, and brings home the effect of austerity on the lives of those who lived in the Britain of 1947. The meat ration was to fall from 7 September to one shilling; the tea ration was frozen; from 14 September, guests could no longer stay in hotels for four days without giving up their ration books, but only two; restaurant allowances would fall by 15–18 per cent from 14 September; the import of luxury foods was curtailed; an intended curtailment in allowances for foreign travel was brought forward with immediate effect and, from 1 October, foreign currency for pleasure trips abroad would not be allowed at all. *The Times* reported on 28 August: 'Food cuts; Basic Petrol to be stopped; Rigorous Limits on Travel Abroad; Prospect of further economies.'[64]

The political attacks from the Conservatives began. On Saturday 30 August

Eden, speaking at Carnoustie in Scotland before a crowd of almost 20,000, criticized the government's 'internal differences as well as foolish complacency'.[65] The TUC was equally critical on 2 September: 'Speeches criticizing the Government's proposals for overcoming the economic crisis were applauded enthusiastically at the Trades Union Congress.'[66] Attlee was in deep political trouble. Eight years later, at the height of the controversy to expel Bevan from the party, Attlee acknowledged that in 1947 there were moves to get rid of him, but they all came to nothing 'owing to Bevin's loyalty'.[67] This was an accurate summary. Behind the move to replace Attlee was Cripps, who approached Dalton at 9.45 a.m. on 5 September: 'He said we *must* now shift Attlee and replace him by Bevin. Otherwise the Government, the Party and the country were all sunk. There was no leadership, no grip, no decision.'[68] As early as 17 August, Cripps and Dalton had been to the Foreign Office to see Bevin to canvass the idea with him, but he had not agreed to it. Attlee's major advantage was the relationship between Bevin and Morrison. Cripps's idea that he, Dalton and Morrison should go together to ask Attlee to resign in favour of Bevin was naïve: Morrison would never have agreed to topple Attlee in favour of anyone but himself. Morrison had been ill, having suffered a thrombosis in the leg and pneumonia, but his ambition was undimmed. He later said, tongue in cheek, 'I have never felt up to indulging in high conspiracy and I refused to participate.'[69] Dalton's account has more of a ring of truth: 'Morrison fully agreed about Attlee, but not about Bevin. He thought that *he* should be Prime Minister. ... He wouldn't serve under Bevin.'[70] When Cripps did visit Attlee on 9 September, it was alone. He suggested that Bevin become prime minister and minister of production, Attlee chancellor and Dalton foreign secretary. Attlee replied, somewhat undermining himself, that he 'had no head for these financial questions' but added, tellingly, that Bevin would not wish to leave the Foreign Office, the party would not accept his leadership and he could not get on with Morrison in any event.[71] Attlee rang Bevin and asked if he wanted to change jobs; Bevin confirmed that he did not.[72] Attlee then offered Cripps the job of being the minister in charge of economic affairs. A defeated Cripps accepted, but the real loser of the whole piece was Morrison, whose influence over domestic policy was curtailed as a result.

Over the next few weeks Attlee reshuffled the government. The first obvious change was the chancellor, Dalton, who could quite conceivably take the blame for the fiasco given his control of economic policy, but Attlee knew that he did not have the political authority to demote Dalton. The second was much easier: Shinwell was demoted to the War Office and stripped of cabinet rank. Attlee injected new blood by replacing Cripps at the Board of Trade with 31-year old Harold Wilson and making 41-year old Hugh Gaitskell minister of fuel and power in place of Shinwell. He also pushed out the heavy drinker

Arthur Greenwood, by then minister without portfolio, giving his roles as chair of the legislation committee and of the social services committee to Morrison to compensate him for the loss of control of domestic economic affairs: a new economic policy committee was created with Attlee as chair. This left an uneasy situation with Cripps ostensibly in control of 'economic affairs' and overall strategy, but with Dalton still at the Treasury. There was no clear distinction between the roles and it might have developed into an unfortunate turf war between the two ministers. Luck was, however, on Attlee's side as the situation resolved itself. Dalton arrived at the House of Commons to deliver his budget on 12 November 1947, just before 3 p.m., and gave John Carvel, a lobby correspondent for the *Star*, some details: he told him 'in a single sentence what the principal points would be – no more on tobacco; a penny on beer; something on dogs and pools but not on horses; increase in Purchase Tax, but only on articles now taxable; Profits Tax doubled'.[73] These proposals were published at 3.45 p.m. in a newspaper scoop. Dalton apologized to the House of Commons the next day and took the blame for the leak. It was not enough and, on 17 November, Attlee told the cabinet of the resignation of Dalton, and the Cabinet agreed to accept the opposition's request, if made, for a selection committee to look into the matter;[74] Churchill duly put forward the matter and Attlee agreed in the Commons that afternoon. Dalton pleaded that Carvel was a man he knew, a man of discretion, but Brook, in a damning note to Attlee on 18 November (in which he noted Morrison's agreement with his views), felt that any argument that Dalton stated his comments were 'off the record' possibly strengthened the case against him, since it implied he knew he should not have done it. The select committee report on 11 December concluded: 'Mr Dalton made a premature and unpremeditated disclosure to Mr Carvel of the contents of his Budget, which disclosure he had no right to make.'[75] For Attlee – whose personal life was untarnished with scandal – it was hard to deal with. Harold Wilson recalled that it was 'the only time I ever saw Attlee rattled'.[76] Yet the affair provided the opportunity to change his chancellor and Cripps, after only six weeks as minister for economic affairs, took the post. It also neutered Dalton as a major political force: when he did return to government on 31 May 1948, it was as chancellor of the Duchy of Lancaster, a far more junior office.

By the close of 1947 there was also some good news on the economic front. US Secretary of State George Marshall had concluded, in April 1947, after the failure of the foreign ministers council meeting in Moscow, that Stalin was counting on the economic collapse of western Europe. In June Marshall made a speech offering to assist 'the revival of a working economy … so as to permit the emergence of political and social conditions in which free institutions can exist'. On 12 July a conference on European construction began in Paris. The

Soviet Union was invited, but Molotov attended and then walked out. On 16 July *The Times* reported Marshall as telling the annual conference of state governors in Salt Lake City that either the USA 'must finish the task of assisting those countries to adjust themselves to the changed demands of the new age or it must reconcile itself to seeing them move in directions which are consistent neither with their own traditions nor with those of this country'.[77] The door was open for Britain to receive substantial aid, and Bevin moved to accept. Britain received around three billion dollars between April 1948 and December 1951, more than any other recipient. The assistance was timely and staved off another acute economic crisis until 1949, when the issue of currency – in the form of devaluation – came back to haunt Attlee.

Chapter 20
MISSED OPPORTUNITIES? 1948–49

At the 1948 Labour Party conference at Scarborough, Attlee had every reason to feel a political and personal sense of achievement. He had survived the leadership crisis of 1947 and was secure for the immediate future. From being 12.5 per cent behind in the polls in November 1947, the party had closed the gap to just 4 per cent.[1] No by-elections had been lost. Bevan was a matter of weeks away from introducing the National Health Service. Attlee spoke on 19 May: 'I am not given much to complacency, but I am proud of the Party and of the Government.'[2] Yet a number of decisions taken in 1948 and 1949 had both long and short-term significance for the Attlee government and the agenda of the left. Criticism of the Attlee government has often centred on what it failed to do. In education, it failed to take the opportunity to abolish private schools, and cemented into place the division in state education between grammar and secondary modern schools. It allowed a wholly hereditary House of Lords to remain in existence. Capital and corporal punishment (at least in prisons) were retained. The government's actions during this period also created difficulty. It built houses, but not enough to satisfy demand, and proceeded with the deeply controversial and unpopular nationalization of the iron and steel industry; it also legislated to change the electoral boundaries in 1948 in a way that cost the party a number of seats before any votes were even cast in 1950 and 1951. These are all distinct issues and each needs to be considered in turn to establish whether the criticism is justified, and, if so, to what extent Attlee carries any blame.

If there was a failure in education, it was of policy direction, not implementation. Attlee believed in the education system over which his government presided. He never wanted to abolish private schools. He believed in the Butler Education Act of 1944. When Michael Stewart issued Circular 10/65 in 1965 starting the substantial move to comprehensive education, taken up so enthusiastically by Tony Crosland, it was not because the Attlee government had lacked the political will to do the same thing; Attlee had simply taken a different view on education. Correspondence during the Attlee government with the Ministry of Education shows a tolerance towards diversity of educational provision, which was a key feature of the system. In a letter dated 24 September 1946, the civil servant Sir William Cleary at the Ministry of Education wrote to Canon E. F. Hall of the National Society (the General Council of the Church of England for Religious Education), confirming the interpretation of the 1944 Education Act as providing for 'special agreement' (in modern-day parlance, a faith school) primary as well as secondary schools. Concerns about local authority grants restricting such schools were unfounded. The only minor policy controversy came on the issue of whether boarding facilities should be provided to enable children to attend a particular faith school. Cleary felt that: 'provision of boarding facilities for pupils purely for the purpose of enabling them to attend a school of a particular denomination, irrespective of whether they were pupils for whom education under boarding conditions is desirable is a very different matter.'[3] However, he took no action to prevent this, and the overall picture of educational diversity was certainly not a default position that the government simply accepted. Attlee still felt that the Butler Education Act had taken education out of the field of party controversy and the only major political event at the department was the tragic death of Ellen Wilkinson in February 1947 from a drug overdose: George Tomlinson replaced her. Whether the Attlee government missed an opportunity in education policy depends on one's perspective. The debate on the existence of private schools remains a fierce one – a balance between the right of children's parents to spend their money on education and the concept of buying advantage in life. In state schools, the effectiveness of the grammar schools versus comprehensives is an open question. When John Major promised a grammar school in every town in the 1997 Conservative manifesto it was a throwback to the 1940s system, and an indication that the debate is by no means settled one way or the other.

It is difficult to put the same argument in respect of the failure to democratize the House of Lords. The House of Lords had long been the obvious target for reform of progressive forces in British politics. That legislators should sit in the British parliament by accident of birth had long been an affront to many in the Labour Party. Yet, the hereditary principle in the House of Lords managed to survive not only the 1945 Labour landslide but also the large victories in the elections of 1966, 1997 and 2001. Today's House of Lords contains 92 hereditary peers, a product of the deal brokered between the Blair government and Lord Cranborne, a descendant of the Cecil family, and the then leader of the Conservative Party in the Upper House. Derry Irvine, Blair's former pupil-master from his days as a barrister, and then lord chancellor, was forced to concede from 10 per cent of the hereditary peers (around 75) to 90, and then made to add the Lord Great Chamberlain and the Earl Marshall, making 92. Should the Blair government have had to have dealt with this problem? Was the time to change the House of Lords in the wake of the Second World War? The Attlee government's 1949 Parliament Act amended the 1911 Parliament Act passed by the Liberal government of 1905–15. The 1911 act took away the absolute veto of the House of Lords over passing legislation and replaced it with a suspensory veto. Any bill the House of Commons passed in three sessions within two years would become law, even if the Lords rejected it. The 1949 act reduced this to two sessions and one year and unquestionably represented a curtailment in power.

Arguably, this was a realistic and practical change. In going further, the government could have created an imbalance in the parliamentary system so severe that legislating might have become unduly onerous. The abolition of the House of Lords was fraught with difficulty, not least in foisting onto the House of Commons detailed, but essential, work of scrutiny for which it might lack the time, and perhaps even expertise, to cope. Electing the Upper House might create a rival chamber to the House of Commons: with both elected on the popular vote, the House of Lords might interfere so much as to cause gridlock. Appointing the House of Lords has always raised the question of who does the appointing, with the risk that royal patronage is simply replaced by prime ministerial patronage; in 1968, when the Wilson government proposed to replace the Lords with an essentially appointed second chamber, Michael Foot from the left and Enoch Powell from the right combined forces to defeat the bill. The Attlee government reform, cautious though it was, was fraught with controversy.

The lord chancellor, Jowitt, produced a paper on possible reform on 11 October 1946: he suggested curtailing the powers of the Lords to delay legislation down to two sessions (one year) as this could be effected simply by inserting words into the 1911 Parliament Act.[4] Attlee was not particularly interested in pursuing the matter at all, but noted on 13 October 1946 that he wanted only to 'discuss the procedure on this with the Lord President'.[5] On 24 October, the cabinet duly put the matter on hold with Attlee agreeing to arrange for proposals to be put together, bearing in mind that, under the terms of the 1911 act, any legislation would have to be introduced in the 1947–48 session in order for it to come into effect.[6] On 20 November, in response to a question on whether he had any instructions on reform, Attlee discussed the matter with Jowitt and the leader of the Lords, and tersely answered: 'No'.[7] The matter came back before cabinet on 14 October 1947, and it is clear that on the recorded discussion, major steps such as abolition or the total removal of the hereditary principle were not even remotely considered. 'The Cabinet first discussed whether it was expedient that such legislation should be introduced at the present time.' The precise words used in the 1945 manifesto were analysed: 'We give clear notice that we will not tolerate obstruction of the people's will by the House of Lords.'[8] Since the House of Lords had not been obstructive, did the government have the mandate to introduce reform? In the end, three arguments were put forward in favour of it – increasing the chances of nationalizing iron and steel during the present parliament, which would inevitably be blocked by the Lords; legislating while the government was still undefeated in by-elections; and dealing with the issue *before* a problem between the two houses arose.[9] The cabinet did not reach an agreed position on the form the legislation should take, referring it to the machinery of government committee, but a number of views were aired, both asserting the utility of the second chamber and objecting to affirming the existence of a bicameral legislature. Others felt that a bill setting out a limited delaying power could legitimize the interference of the Lords and 'might even strengthen their position'; another position was that the delaying period could be reduced further than Jowitt had originally suggested, to six months or the end of a current session, 'whichever was the longer period'.[10]

Attlee's position is not directly recorded in the cabinet discussion. However, he took the initiative the next day, telegraphing the Lord Privy Seal Addison, who was in Colombo, that: 'It was decided to introduce Bill to reduce period of delaying action of Lords provided under Parliament Act on general lines proposed last year by Lord Chancellor.'[11] The record of the cabinet discussion does not support the idea that this was a consensus opinion, which would suggest that Attlee was pushing his own view. Morrison adopted a similar position in his memorandum of 18 October summing up the views of the previous day's meeting of the machinery of government committee; he took the 'broad alternatives' from the cabinet discussion as a power of delay for one session only; or for two sessions within a minimum of one year, favouring the latter on the basis that 'there is some time for reflection in both Houses; and we think that a certain measure of delay is valuable for that purpose.'[12] At cabinet on 20 October, Morrison proposed this course of action and stressed that, even if rejected by the Lords, the bill would become law in the later part of 1949 under the 1911 act. The agreed cabinet line was to justify the measure in practical terms regarding the passage of legislation: 'Nothing should be said to imply that it reflected the views of the Labour Party on the broader question of House of Lords reform, or that the party favoured the retention of a reformed House of Lords.'[13] Remarkably, the government's position on Lords reform had been set within the space of only six days. The draft bill, dated 28

October 1947, lived up to the simplicity promised, covering barely one-and-a-half sides of paper.[14] The question of the hereditary right to vote did, however, rear its head again at cabinet on 30 October, when the returning Addison, indicated that he would have preferred the bill to be proposed together with a constitutional change such as the abolition of the hereditary right to vote. The general cabinet view was, however, summarized in the minutes as: 'This … was not a suitable moment for reforming the constitution of the House of Lords.'[15]

From this moment, the terms of the debate were framed and the government was locked into a debate on the technicalities of the bill and the period of delay. When a 'Conference of Party Leaders'[16] took place between February and April 1948 Attlee's aim was clearly to secure a position as close as he could to the period of delay proposed. On 9 March 1948 Attlee produced his own memorandum – a rarity in itself – indicating a disposition towards a compromise position of '*either* twelve months from Second Reading *or* nine months from Third Reading, whichever is the longer', as opposed to the Conservative position of 'not less than twelve months from the first occasion on which it received its Third Reading in the Commons'.[17] Attlee was unable to find a compromise and at a meeting of party leaders on 11 March the Conservative leader in the Lords, Salisbury, said he felt the Attlee suggestion did not constitute a compromise, though he and the Conservative Party could perhaps have accepted 18 months, exactly halfway between the time proposed in the 1911 Parliament Act and that of the proposed bill.[18] There was also the even tighter Conservative proposal of 12 months from third reading, but even this was away from the government position. No agreement was therefore reached and the government pushed forward with the position of two sessions or one year. In an intriguing postscript, Attlee set himself firmly against hereditary peeresses taking seats in the Lords. On 29 July he told Jowitt firmly: 'I do not like tampering with the basis of the House of Lords unaccompanied by a clear definition of powers. To introduce such a Bill would open the door to a proposal for Life Peers or, indeed, to Conservative Reform proposals. I should prefer to leave it alone.'[19] That final sentence was an indication of his overall attitude. Attlee was interested to the extent that any problem posed by the Lords in respect of other reforms should be dealt with, but he had no intention of embarking on wholesale change. As prime minister, Attlee sought constructive change to society; his view on the Lords was wholly pragmatic. Provided his government could advance its policy agenda, he saw radical constitutional reform as unnecessary.

If some within the party could stomach the compromise position on the Lords on grounds of practicality, the retention of capital and corporal punishment sits oddly with the Attlee government's progressive, humanitarian policies in welfare reform. Under the minority second Labour government, a 1930 select committee had considered abolishing the death penalty and the 1930 Army Act had abolished the death penalty for cowardice and desertion within the armed forces. With the Attlee government's landslide, abolition of the death penalty – and birching – on a free vote would seem likely. Attlee, while no passionate advocate of the death penalty, thought it necessary; while, throughout the lengthy cabinet discussions and memoranda on the issue, he – typically – allowed the debate to reach its natural conclusion with little intervention, he voted in the Commons for retention. On 19 June 1947 the cabinet discussed Ede's memorandum on a Criminal Justice Bill for the 1947–48 session of parliament.[20] The lord chancellor was unhappy about the abolition of corporal punishment, but (since the bill introduced in 1938 had gone that far), he saw the political difficulties in retention now. While there was 'general agreement' that the courts should no longer have the power to pass sentences of corporal punishment, 'some ministers' wanted it retained for breaches of prison discipline. The odd logic behind this decision was that if someone was already in prison, there needed to be some greater punishment beyond a deprivation of liberty for any further offences committed while incarcerated. The concept of adding days to the sentence was not aired. Attlee's direct view was not made explicit, but this was the compromise position the cabinet reached.

On the death penalty, the same minutes state innocuously: 'On the question whether on merits it would be desirable to abolish capital punishment Ministers were divided.' When cabinet met on 15 July 1947, Jowitt reported that judges were 'unanimously opposed' to abolition, feeling that it was 'the only effective deterrent in certain cases'.[21] The cabinet concluded in a spirit of compromise, looking at first whether it was possible to draft a bill precluding an amendment on capital punishment; whether Morrison could see if it was possible to persuade those in favour of abolition within the parliamentary party to refrain from pursuing it in the interests of the passage of the bill; and considering Jowitt's suggestion to look at distinguishing between certain types of murder (though Ede subsequently declared this impractical).[22] The issue was raised again after a parliamentary party meeting in the autumn, and Morrison indicated that he would be raising the matter orally at cabinet on 3 November 1947. Cabinet agreed a free Commons vote at the report stage, but sought further information from Ede to decide if the government should take a position.[23] Ede's further memorandum of 13 November 1947 dealt with a new point about 'present-day circumstances': 'Many people may be, and probably are, inclined to think that war experiences, and especially the experiences of young men trained in the Commandos, have weakened the sense of the sanctity of human life.'[24]

This was the key point and, on 18 November, the cabinet majority decided not to abolish capital punishment.[25] On 25 November, Attlee approved Ede's draft statement in which he indicated the government's view that the moment was 'inopportune'; on an amendment being moved, which it was hoped would be left to the report stage, the government would 'more fully review' its reasoning.[26] On 4 April 1948 the cabinet agreed that members of the government should abstain on the issue.[27] The parliamentary party met on 14 April at 10.30 a.m., before the debate began at 3.34 p.m., with the final speech beginning at 9.59 p.m. The famous campaigner for abolition, Sydney Silverman, moved an amendment to suspend the death penalty for five years. The motion to read it for a second time was won by 245 to 222, with both Attlee and Ede voting against. The cabinet the next day agreed that the death penalty would be commuted to life imprisonment while the bill was continuing its passage through parliament.[28] Ede announced this in the Commons on 16 April, but was forced to retract on 10 June, on the basis that the exercise of the royal prerogative of mercy could only be on a case-by-case basis. Ede produced yet another memorandum on 2 July 1948 that the death penalty would only be retained for certain classes of murder – murder in connection with other crimes such as robbery or sexual offences; murder of constables or prison officers; murders involving 'systematic administration' of poison; and murders by people who had already committed murder.[29] Cabinet approved it on 5 July.[30] On 13 July Attlee received a letter from four MPs, including Silverman, saying that if the government indicated that the compromise was as far as it would go and that the Parliament Act would be invoked in the event of rejection by the Lords, they would support it.[31] But on 15 July the cabinet agreed that this was 'a mistake in tactics'.[32] The clause passed through the Commons by 307 votes to 209. On 20 July the Lords rejected the clause by 99 votes to 19. On 22 July the cabinet in effect ended the debate by deciding to accept the Lords' amendment, with the bill becoming law shorn of the change in the application of capital punishment. Ede was, however, authorized to consider measures to limit the use of the death penalty.[33] In the Commons that afternoon he moved the acceptance of the Lords amendment. On 3 November Ede produced another memorandum indicating that, with the government committed to further investigation after the debate of 22 July, the question was what form that investigation should take; a royal commission was proposed.[34] On 6 November Brook advised Attlee that a royal commission could be 'a waste of time and effort' as the home secretary could in any event take into account the summer's debates in his discretion as regards which cases should attract the death penalty.[35] Cabinet felt that such an enquiry was unavoidable, but, on 15 November, limited its terms of reference to limiting or modifying the existing laws on the death penalty, rather than total abolition.[36]

It is easy to criticize the Attlee government on its apparently inhumane criminal justice policy. Yet, the overriding sense of the minutes is of a cabinet wanting to do the right thing but anxious to avoid undue emotion on the subject. Ede's numerous memoranda were all about pros and cons, and the critical part of the debate was the issue of *timing*. After six years of killing in the war, the value of human life had to be re-established before abolition of the death penalty was appropriate. For opponents of the death penalty, most notably Sydney Silverman who eventually introduced the landmark private member's bill for suspension in 1965, the government had simply not gone far enough. In July 1948 even Silverman conceded to a position in which the death penalty was retained for certain classes of murder; abolition was clearly not a debate the Attlee government could have won easily, even if it had wished to. Prison birching was finally abolished in 1967. In the twenty-first century it is too easy to judge the Attlee government by modern standards. Many people today may consider such punishments barbaric, but the Attlee government was dealing with a very different type of society. Divorce remained a scandal; and abortion and homosexuality were still the best part of two decades away from legalization. Even in the permissive 1960s capital punishment was only suspended in 1965, before being abolished in 1969 save for a very small number of offences such as treason. In any event, Attlee had no majority in cabinet for either the total abolition of corporal punishment or the abolition of the death penalty. If that was inhumane, he shared his inhumanity with a significant number of leading Labour politicians.

Education, House of Lords reform and criminal justice policy are all probably of greater interest to historians than they were to the general public in the late 1940s. None featured as major electoral issues in 1950 or 1951. In contrast, housing was a major electoral issue. Harold Macmillan, the housing minister under Churchill from 1951, established a reputation by achieving a target of building 300,000 houses a year on the Conservatives' return to power. However, the challenge facing Labour in 1945 was formidable. On 30 July 1945 *The Times* published what is claimed was 'the first aerial view of London which it has been permitted to take since the war began' showing the scale of the devastation with which the government had to deal: property was heavily damaged across the picture. On 6 May 1946 Bevan reported to cabinet on progress up to 31 March. Local authorities had provided 741 new permanent houses; 2570 new houses had been built and 791 rebuilt under licence; 19,482 temporary houses and 3200 temporary huts had been installed; 12,573 existing premises had been adapted; 78,224 unoccupied war-damaged houses had been repaired and 18,370 had been requisitioned for residential use.[37] While a lack of building labour was always going to be an issue in the very early postwar period, with men leaving the forces and finding and settling down into new jobs across the economy, a critical problem was a lack of timber. On 8 November 1946 Bevan sought to bring this to the cabinet's attention.[38] Attlee, however, was curt in his reply: 'There is no need to bring this to Cabinet. The principle of getting as much timber as possible is agreed. You should now get in touch with your colleagues on particular problems as they arise.'[39] Nonetheless, when Bevan proposed a target of 240,000 houses for 1947 in his cabinet memorandum of 10 December 1946, he commented: 'The most serious difficulty is with regard to timber.'[40]

Between 22 and 24 April 1947 *The Times* published a series of three articles on the government's housing programme. The first, headed 'Many Houses Begun But Few Completed' cited 'Scarcity of Building Materials' as the problem, noting that, 'to the end of 1946 some 170,000 families were found accommodation by the repair or refashioning of existing dwellings, as against 150,000 families rehoused by the construction of new dwellings.'[41] The next day, *The Times* led with the bald fact: 'Held up by Lack of Timber' adding that:

Even without the 60,000 temporary dwellings also to be provided, the total programme presupposes a rate of house-building attained only in the ninth and tenth years after the 1914–18 war (1927 and 1928) and not thereafter maintained or surpassed until the sixteenth year, 1934. This high target represents, however, no more than the nation would be entitled to expect from 300,000 operatives working with normal efficiency and supported by a normal supply of materials.[42]

The Times finished with a flourish on 24 April, setting out three tasks for the government: 'to reduce the official programme to realistic dimensions; to use the system of building controls to maintain a balance between building projects and materials available; and to secure from operatives a substantially quicker rate of output.' Blame was laid at the door of the government's wage policy; *output* should be rewarded, rather than maximum wage rates being set by unions and employers fearing competition: 'The least they can do now is to revoke the ban on output bonuses and restore to employers and their clients, the local authorities, some degree of freedom to manage their own affairs.'

By a number of standards, the Attlee government's rate of house-building was impressive. When the Central Statistical Office researched the matter at the behest of Cripps on 27 April 1948, it was calculated that between April 1945 and March 1948, 396,000 houses had been built – 227,000 new, 23,000 rebuilt and 146,000 temporary. The annual rate was therefore 132,000 houses; the post-First World War average from January 1919 to September 1922 was 56,000.[43] Unfortunately, the cuts in public spending from 1948 to 1949 led to a reduction in the number of houses built – the 217,000 completed in 1948 fell to 205,000 in 1949, the same number is 1950 and 202,000 in 1951. In 1954 the

Conservatives managed 354,000.[44] The difficulties remained even when Bevan reluctantly compromised on his design to ensure that every new home had a bathroom. The real problem was that the government needed to turn its domestic labour to producing more material for exports, *not* housing in Britain.[45] Whatever the difficulties – whether shortage of materials, the need to increase exports or the impressive rate of house-building judged against a number of yardsticks – the Attlee government had not completed enough houses for the voters, which in the short-term was the only test that mattered.

A further direct impact against the interest of the Labour Party in the 1950 and 1951 elections was made by the 1948 Representation of the People Act, which changed the electoral boundaries for Westminster, creating a number of new constituencies favourable to the Conservatives. Attlee's failure to manip-ulate the situation to his party's advantage was an example of his personal integrity, but perhaps a touch naïve. The report of the committee on electoral registration was published at the start of 1947,[46] and on 28 February Ede and the then secretary of state for Scotland, Joseph Westwood, produced a memo-randum to cabinet recommending that a cabinet committee be set up to get the legislation through parliament during the 1947–48 session in time for the next election.[47] There were a number of key procedural issues, including having an up-to-date register of voters, the logistics of organizing the voting of those serving in the armed forces, hours of polling and so on. However, the politically crucial issue was the redistribution of seats. When the cabinet com-mittee was set up on 6 March 1947, Attlee was not interested in serving on it and Ede took the chair.[48] On 3 July 1947 the committee produced a set of recommendations including the abolition of the university franchise ('We do not consider that there is any justification in modern conditions for the award of the privilege of a second vote based on the possession of an academic distinction') and the business premises vote.[49] An odd quirk of the electoral system was the City of London, which had been given special treatment in the 1931 Representation of the People Act, but this too was to be abolished, with only 4585 voters left after the abolition of the business premises qualification. On 12 December 1947 the committee produced a further set of recommen-dations, based on the initial reports of the boundary commissioners, in which it was proposed that eight boroughs – Battersea, Blackburn, East Ham, Gateshead, Hammersmith, Norwich, Paddington and Reading, with electorates of 80,000–88,000 – should only have one MP rather than two.

The obvious difficulty in departing from the boundary commissioners' recommendations was that, once some changes were made, other areas would make further demands and the whole scheme might be threatened.[50] The recommendation was therefore to accept the boundary commissioners' proposals, including the reduction in London seats from 60 to 40. However, in the cabinet discussion on 18 December 1947, it was agreed that Ede should consider giving the eight boroughs two members.[51] He duly produced a memorandum on 3 January 1948 stating that such a change would 'disturb the balance of representation between urban and rural constituencies to the disadvantage of the latter', and cited a number of other constituencies with electorates of over 70,000 that would also have demands for two seats.[52] On 17 January Brook noted to Attlee that 'the balance of advantage probably lies on the side of adopting the Boundary Commission's recommendations without alteration.'[53] On 19 January, the cabinet decided on this course, though Morrison expressed the view that it would be better to include amended proposals for 'where the Commission's proposals seemed to be indefensible'.[54]

Morrison's fears proved accurate and Ede had to produce another set of proposals on 4 March, after MPs raised complaints during the second reading of the bill. Noting that 'in England urban areas are under-represented in comparison with rural areas', Ede suggested that the eight boroughs originally identified be given a further seat, together with extra seats for Birmingham, Bradford, Bristol, Leeds, Leicester, Liverpool, Manchester, Nottingham and Sheffield; Ede ruled out Plymouth on the basis that an extra seat there would give an average electorate of 47,000 (Leicester was the lowest of the additional list, at 51,827).[55] This was agreed by cabinet on 8 March,[56] and Ede confirmed to the House of Commons on 7 April 1948 that the boundary commissioners would consider the proposal for 17 further seats.[57] Eventually, the number of seats in the Commons was reduced from 640 to 625.

This remarkable discussion took place without any mention of the party political effects. One would not expect to find these discussed in official cabinet minutes, but there was never any suggestion of delaying the coming into force of the act until after the next election. Even when MPs raised the issue of the over-representation of rural areas (generally Conservative) compared with towns and cities (generally Labour), there was no attempt to make further changes beyond the proposal for just 17 more seats. It was a sound piece of administration: the government managed to achieve consensus for its proposals and a number of welcome changes – such as the abolition of the university and business franchises – were made. Yet the favouring of rural areas in the act was of great benefit to the Conservatives.

What were certainly not naïve were the government's attempts to nationalize the iron and steel industry. Deeply controversial, it was one of the nationalizations (along with road haulage) that the Churchill government reversed. The Attlee government's nationalized Iron and Steel Corporation, established in 1951, lasted only two years: in 1953 the Iron and Steel Board was re-established with regulatory powers including some over pricing, and companies started to return to the private sector. While other Attlee government nationalizations could easily be justified in practical terms, this one could not. The iron and steel industry was highly fragmented, with many supporting and ancillary industries; it was not organized into a small number of private companies already, as, say, rail had been. The relationship between management and unions was not strained. Even at the 1934 Labour Party conference, a Socialist League amendment regarding state ownership and control of iron and steel had been rejected.[58]

The cabinet discussions on the issue reveal a keen recognition of how controversial the issue was, but a concern about letting backbench MPs down if the measure were not taken. Little thought was given to finding some sort of compromise that the Conservatives would accept when they returned to power. Even when the government sought some sort of agreement with the iron and steel industry in the summer of 1947, Attlee delegated the task to Morrison and did not give the efforts prime ministerial weight. He believed in nationalization: unlike Lords reform, this was an ideological agenda he felt had a direct benefit to wider society, for there were a number of options apart from nationalization. As early as 7 November 1945 John Wilmot, as minister of supply and aircraft production, produced a memorandum for the Lord President's Committee on iron and steel.[59] In it, three options were considered – regulation as before 1939, with the government controlling prices to influence development and control imports; a reconstruction plan under an appointed public body; and nationalization. Being concerned about the division of responsibility in the second option, and the leadership in the industry coupled with the lack of government power to respond to pressure in the first, Wilmot recommended nationalization, but carefully set out the significant difficulties. The problem was the sheer breadth of the industry: 'from ore and coal mining to the production of many important semi-manufactured and finished goods, including chemicals, fertilisers, plant and machinery and steel furniture; and the industry branches into ship building and structural engineering'. As Wilmot put it: 'Any line of demarcation raises difficult problems as to the assets to be taken over or to remain in private ownership.'[60] In December 1945 the British Iron and Steel Federation produced a report to Wilmot that the Churchill caretaker government had requested on 31 May. The report proposed 'modernization' at a cost of £168 million, including the building of 24 blast furnaces together with rolling mill plant.[61] On 15 March 1946 Morrison, chairing the cabinet committee on the socialization of industries, made a firm statement that 'the balance of advantage lay in socialising the industry'.[62] The big guns were lining up in favour. Bridges wrote a note to Attlee dated 28 March 1946 in which he advised strongly against nationalization, questioning whether the good feeling on both sides of industry in the quest for production would remain should the decision be announced, and pointing out that already the Bank of England, coal, cable and wireless, gas, electricity, the railways, hospitals and medical services were included in the nationalization programme: 'I suppose it is a common place to say that most Governments are judged, not so much by the quantity of legislation passed in the lifetime of a Parliament, but by the success with which difficult situations are overcome and the country kept on an even keel.'[63] However, he also wrote to Rowan at 10 Downing Street: 'My position in this matter is delicate, as the Chancellor is in favour of an immediate decision to nationalize iron and steel.'[64]

At cabinet on 4 April 1946, Attlee put the problem of timing. With the 1946–47 parliamentary session already too crowded, it was agreed that a central control board would direct the industry until legislation to nationalize was introduced in the 1947–48 session.[65] On 17 April, Wilmot announced in the Commons that the government had 'reached the conclusion that the position of the industry and its importance in the national economy necessitate a large measure of public ownership'.[66] In a bad-tempered debate, Attlee refused to give an assurance to Churchill that he was 'not going to take any important, decisive administrative step' prior to debate, and the Conservative Sir Waldron Smithers MP called him 'Hitler'.[67] On 1 August Wilmot reported that the Iron and Steel Federation 'would not associate themselves with a Board whose duties included giving guidance and advice on technical matters arising in regard to nationalization', but cabinet agreed to take control through government purchase of controlling shares in the equity of the private companies.[68] Wilmot produced a memorandum for the committee on the socialization of industries, proposing a scheme whereby a central authority would direct the companies, which would retain their own identity. There would be no area boards as in, for example, electricity and gas nationalization.[69] The government proposed to take over production of home iron ore, importation of iron ore, ore-handling at ports, pig-iron production, steel making, heavy rolling, re-rolling, sheet-making, plate production and tin-plate production. In doing so, the government would acquire other interests automatically, including perhaps 'even in the production of such finished articles as umbrella frames, steel tennis rackets, and moth balls'.[70] Excluded were wrought iron, iron and steel castings, forgings, tube production, 'fringe sections of the steel industry', raw materials and merchants. As Wilmot put it in his subsequent memorandum to cabinet dated 14 April 1947:

> The primary objective would be to bring under public ownership the central core of the iron and steel industry – i.e. the production of iron ore, pig iron and steel, together with certain closely-allied processes in the re-rolling sections of the industry, including the production of plates, sheet steel and tinplate.[71]

On 6 May 1947, at cabinet, Attlee, bearing in mind press coverage, 'thought it desirable that Cabinet should satisfy themselves at this stage as to the strength of the case'; the cabinet reaffirmed its decision to include a bill in the 1947–48 session.[72] On 21 May 1947 Attlee, together with Morrison and Wilmot, met Sir Andrew Duncan and Mr Ellis Hunter on behalf of the Iron and Steel Federation. Attlee was firm on the government's position: 'the solid core of the industry should be brought into public ownership, and ... the things not directly in the solid core should be hived off.'[73] Sir Andrew Duncan said that 'you will achieve far more, in my judgement, by a gradual evolution in the industry on the basis of cooperation.' When Morrison later withdrew from the meeting, Sir Andrew Duncan put the point forcefully to Attlee and Wilmot: 'you are not any longer, under these proposals, dealing with the thing you set out to deal with, nor are you achieving the objective that you set out to achieve, viz. the efficient organization of the industry as a whole.'[74] On 22 May, when Attlee was given the verbatim report of the meeting, he was reminded that he had agreed to consider what had been said, but he confirmed that he was leaving the matter with Morrison and Wilmot.[75]

Enough had been done, however, in the meeting of 21 May, for Wilmot to report to the committee on the socialization of industries on 18 June that:

The Federation representatives had stated that the industry fully accepted the need for complete and effective Government policy control and, where necessary, a measure of government financial participation and even of full ownership. This attitude suggested, what had hitherto seemed impossible, that it might be possible to attain the Government's objectives in agreement with the Iron and Steel Federation.[76]

Even Dalton, who professed himself still in favour of full nationalization, declared that he 'would not himself rule out the possibility of proceeding in a more leisurely way if this was necessary to minimise opposition and upset to the national economy'.[77] On 26 June 1947 cabinet agreed with the committee on the socialization of industries' recommendations on the preparation of legislation for nationalization that there should be 'confidential discussions with representatives of the Federation in order to give the latter an opportunity of developing their ideas as to the possible alternative scheme'.[78] On 28 June 1947 Attlee appointed Morrison and Wilmot to do this.[79] While Attlee had a multitude of other matters to deal with in the summer of 1947 – not least the currency crisis and independence for India – this was an indication that he was not deliberately seeking compromise. Morrison and Wilmot duly met Duncan and Hunter on 10 July 1947; Morrison asked Duncan to explain what he had meant by saying that the federation would agree 'power to take specific undertakings under public ownership if the Minister, after consultation with the Iron and Steel Board, decided that this was necessary in the public interest'. Duncan responded that this would be either in the event of war or if private companies were unwilling to carry out a required development.[80] Morrison and Wilmot produced a memorandum dated 21 July 1947 that indicated that the federation would agree 'a power of acquisition of iron and steel undertakings only on the tacit understanding that the Government did not propose to proceed forthwith ... to bring the industry under public ownership'; the government would only buy undertakings 'when the Iron and Steel Board reported that it was necessary to acquire a particular undertaking ... they fully recognized that the Government of the day must be free to reconsider the position at a later date – e.g. in the next Parliament.'[81]

However, Morrison and Wilmot further indicated that their favoured solution in the current economic climate was to 'secure next Session, by agreement with the industry, the immediate transfer to the Government of all the mechanism of regulation and control which has been the mainspring of the Iron and Steel Federation'[82] as a step towards nationalization at a later time. To the cabinet on 24 July Attlee said that 'in the present economic situation it would be inexpedient to proceed with legislation bringing the iron and steel industry under public ownership in the 1947/48 session.'[83] On 31 July the cabinet split became very clear: Morrison argued that there was a 'strong case' for his compromise proposals; Bevan and Dalton were opposed, pointing out the disappointment that would be caused to government supporters. Cripps supported Dalton.[84] The final and critical contribution, however, was from Bevin, who declared that the Morrison compromise 'would be regarded by Government supporters as amounting to an abandonment of the full socialization plan in deference to the resistance of the Iron and Steel Federation'. However, he added that the unions should be consulted. Attlee gladly accepted the way out. Declaring that 'he could not accept that the postponement of legislation to give effect to the scheme approved by Cabinet would amount to a betrayal of the Government's political principles', he agreed with Bevin that the 'next step should be to consult the trade unions concerned'.[85]

H. Douglas, the assistant general secretary of the Iron and Steel Trades Confederation, wrote to Attlee on 23 August 1947 that the executive council demanded 'full and immediate nationalization'.[86] On 21 October Attlee confirmed in the Commons that the government intended 'in the present Parliament to nationalize the relevant portions of the iron and steel industry'.[87] Morrison was deeply disappointed. In his memoirs, he recalled that he had 'got the Federation to the point that there should be an Iron and Steel Board with extensive powers, including the power, subject to parliament, to take over unsatisfactory undertakings'. Attlee had 'with unaccustomed geniality' agreed to 'support something on those lines'. But in cabinet he had not done so, simply summarizing the views of colleagues opposing the compromise proposals. Privately, Morrison accused him of letting him down and, he said, supposedly received no substantial response: an 'example of the way Attlee could completely disguise his real feelings and intentions'.[88] Attlee, in short, had never wanted to compromise with the industry.

To borrow an Attlee metaphor, the government was left on a sticky wicket. On 20 May 1948 the new minister of supply, Strauss, produced a memorandum, which stated revealingly that 'There is no question in this industry of inefficiency, or of disinclination or inability to carry through essential modernization. The main argument must be that a basic industry cannot remain in private hands.'[89] Brook noted to Attlee on 29 May that the 'scheme will be ... criticized on the ground that it removes all incentive to efficiency in management. It will be said that it removes the profit motive and puts nothing in its place'.[90] The entire structure of parliamentary business was being dictated by trying to get the Iron and Steel Bill onto the statute book within the scope of the new Parliament Bill. The Lords rejected the Parliament Bill and, on 11 June 1948, Morrison set out a future timetable where there would be a short September–October 1948 session of parliament in which the Parliament Bill could pass its committee and report stages and go to the Lords for second reading; a long 1948–49 session for the Parliament Bill to be sent to the Lords a third and last time together with the Iron and Steel Bill for the first time; and a short session from January 1950 to send the Iron and Steel Bill to the Lords for the second and last time.[91] Churchill duly savaged Morrison in the Commons on 24 June: 'Is this not a piece of manipulation against the spirit of the Constitution and of the Parliament Act? Is it not designed to bring in some fake Session for some little paltry manoeuvre which is far below the dignity of Parliament?'[92]

The cabinet was struggling to justify the Iron and Steel Bill on any objective grounds. Morrison produced a note dated 15 July entitled 'Iron and Steel Bill: Review of Arguments', in which he argued that iron and steel would be at the heart of European economic integration.[93] Bevin responded by letter to Morrison on 17 July that he was not 'on very sound ground here' pointing out that in France and Belgium, for example, iron and steel were not nationalized.[94] Attlee was forced to issue a note to ministers on 22 July that they should 'avoid being drawn into public controversy on this subject or putting forward detailed arguments in support of the Bill at this stage'.[95] Finally, on 1 October 1948, Strauss, now minister of supply, produced a draft bill, which was published on 29 October, thereby excluding it from the debate on the king's speech.[96] This was, however, only delaying the inevitable attack. On second reading, 16

November 1948, Churchill lashed into the government: 'Today the Socialists boast that they are the opponents of Communism. … Indeed, as this Bill shows, they are the handmaids and heralds of Communism.'[97]

Each criticism of the Attlee government is about a discrete, self-contained issue. His education policy, to implement the 1944 Education Act, and his position on capital punishment, were based on his personal beliefs. While his position on corporal punishment was not made explicit, he never expressed any dissent from the government line of retention in prisons. On the House of Lords Attlee was conservative. He did not want to upset the balance of the British constitution without good reason. Change in society was more important to him than the abolition of the hereditary principle. One can disagree with any of these positions – but they all have one thing in common, which is that they are not failures of government policy but rather the product of a government implementing what its prime minister – and many leading cabinet ministers – believed in. The same logic could apply to iron and steel: Attlee believed in nationalization, and, while he sought compromise with the iron and steel industry in 1947, it was behind Bevin's suggestion that the unions be consulted and the matter then proceed that he positioned himself. Given the events of 1949–51, however, it was a shame for his government that he allowed it to dominate the government's later years. In 1947, in the midst of the economic crisis, there was sufficient political cover to argue for a compromise. Attlee never did. On the other hand, all that he was doing was taking forward the consensus position, both with his own parliamentary party, and within cabinet. Perhaps the real lesson of the iron and steel nationalization is not that it was a political error, but a further consequence of Attlee's leadership style.

Chapter 21
POLITICAL TROUBLES, 1949–51

The last two years of the Attlee premiership were tumultuous. In September 1949, beset by yet another economic crisis, the government was forced to devalue the pound against the dollar. Stafford Cripps became ill and Hugh Gaitskell replaced him as chancellor. Ernest Bevin died, and five weeks before his death his longstanding enemy Herbert Morrison replaced him as foreign secretary. Bevan, Harold Wilson and John Freeman all resigned in March 1951 over Gaitskell's imposition of charges in the NHS, brought about ostensibly by the cost of rearmament in the light of the Korean War. Two elections were fought, on 23 February 1950 and 26 October 1951. The first yielded a Labour majority of just five seats, the second a Conservative one of 17. The significance of this period went beyond the political theatre of the short term. For decades the Labour Party had argued from the wilderness about nationalization and state planning. In 1945 history had given the party the chance to put its thoughts into practical action, and there is little doubt that its achievements were considerable. Yet, this two-year period was an historical hinge, which determined the party's future path. Once the Labour government had secured the finance for the welfare state and nationalization, it was clear that what was to happen *after* the party had constructed its New Jerusalem was as important to the party's future as the achievements themselves.

In June 1949, the Labour Party conference took place in Blackpool. The party remained in good heart, in blissful ignorance of the crises that were about to erupt. Sam Watson, chairing, gave a great welcome to Attlee, referring back to the 1945 campaign, and Attlee's reply to Churchill's 'Gestapo' broadcast – 'the quiet, dignified, constructive statesmanship and leadership that won the hearts of the nation in 1945 and has kept them ever since'.[1] Attlee was proud of what the government had achieved: 'The 1945 Conference was a historic

Conference: it marked the beginning of a new era. This 1949 Conference will also be historic. It will go down in history as the Conference in which the broad lines of Labour's second programme were laid down.'[2] There was a two-day debate on the policy document *Labour Believes in Britain*. Morrison crisply set out the problem: Labour's 1945 plans 'lifted into the programme items of policy with which we were familiar and behind it all there was 40 years of thought and propaganda'; the new programme 'is not quite so simple as the task was in 1945'.[3] Morrison set out two aims – to 'improve, modify and develop work done in the present Parliament'; and to develop policies for 'new advances, new reforms economic and social'. 'Above all, we have to make this programme of such a character that it will ring a bell in the mind of the average intelligent British citizen.'[4] Even Bevan declared that 'It is of no advantage at all to a Socialist that private enterprise should be languishing.'[5]

The division in the Labour Party in the later days of the Attlee government have often been characterized as 'Consolidation versus Advance' – whether to take the nationalization programme even further or to build on what had already been achieved and try to increase private consumer affluence to win middle-class votes. The perception that nationalization was going too far crystallized when Labour promised to nationalize beet sugar manufacture and sugar refining for the 1950 general election: Tate and Lyle ran their famous 'Mr Cube' advertising campaign against it. The real division was on personality: Bevanites versus Gaitskellites characterized the history of the left–right struggles of the 1950s' Labour Party and not without good reason. Attlee's view was that there was 'no real difference of principle' between the two men and that difficulties were of a 'more personal nature'.[6] The real mystery of the resignations of March 1951 and the Bevan–Gaitskell clash was Attlee's failure to find compromise. Of all the Labour prime ministers, if the party faithful could have picked one to lead the party during this period and find a consensus position it would surely have been Attlee. In his leadership's greatest test, he apparently failed. How and why this happened, and whether it was a failure of his style of leadership or a failure to take any positive steps at all, is a central question in the overall assessment of Attlee's premiership.

By the start of 1949 it was clear that Cripps had been a successful chancellor. Unemployment, the perennial interwar problem, had been kept below 500,000 since 1945 (except during the 1947 fuel crisis when unemployment temporarily reached nearly two million). In contrast, by January 1922 the Lloyd George government had seen unemployment soar to over two million.[7] National income was rising, from around £8.5 billion in 1947 to just under £9.7 billion in 1948, and over £10.2 billion in 1949.[8] Cripps's policy of 'austerity' was to reduce consumption at home with tighter rationing and higher taxes. Bread rationing, introduced under Dalton in 1946, was supplemented by potato rationing in 1947. In 1948, a single man earning £10,000 could only expect to retain £3501[9] after income tax and surtax (the 'super-tax' added to one's personal income tax liability). The historian David Kynaston records that in the spring of 1948: 'Gallup revealed … as many as 42 per cent of people wanted to emigrate, compared with 19 per cent immediately after the end of the war.' 'Soon afterwards there were merciful signs that Cripps' strong medicine was starting to work, with a modest petrol ration for pleasure purposes being reinstated from 1 June, together with 12 extra clothing coupons.'[10] The balance of payments improved, with a £381 million deficit in 1947 turned into a surplus of £26 million in 1948, and only a small deficit of £1 million in 1949. In 1950, the balance of payments was in a healthy surplus of £307 million.[11]

Attlee also presided over the 1949 devaluation of the pound: the first of the three that have occurred in postwar twentieth-century Britain. This episode, unlike those of 1967 and 1992, did not lead to immediate defeat for the government at the next general election, but that was a small consolation when the government fell at the one shortly thereafter. Attlee had a marginal direct impact on events. However, unlike 1947, when a currency crisis had threatened his leadership, his personal position remained more secure. Devaluation had the positive impact the government sought. It was not that he had become an appropriate pilot in a hurricane, but, if the wind speed drops fairly quickly, demands to change the man at the controls recede. In January 1949 Hugh Gaitskell, still minister of fuel and power, prepared a detailed paper setting out starkly what the options were. The expected £300 million gap in the dollar account had widened to between £500 and £600 million; dollar expenditure had to be reduced and dollar earnings increased. There were two possible policies – deflation, which would reduce imports by reducing incomes and increase exports by cutting money costs (and accordingly prices); and devaluation. Gaitskell felt that deflation was the 'clumsier instrument' because it involved 'deliberately creating unemployment and that in this case it is the unemployed and those who suffer wage cuts who *pay* for the high exports, whereas with devaluation it is the people with fixed incomes who do the real paying – in the form of higher import prices.'[12]

Gaitskell put forward the following dates: 'August 28th, September 4th and September 18th. September 11th is excluded because on that day many Finance Ministers and Governors of Central Banks will be *en route* to the annual meeting of the International Bank and Fund which is due to open in Washington on September 13th.'[13] Gaitskell set out the arguments for both the two earlier dates and the later dates. In favour of the early dates was the ending of uncertainty, the avoidance of delay and risk of leaks, and, what Gaitskell regarded 'as of crucial importance', that the government 'had not given way to

American pressure'. The arguments in favour of 18 September 1949 generally related to being able to consult the Commonwealth and United States properly and the opportunity of 'an orderly realignment of currencies through simultaneous action by a large number of countries'. Gaitskell then stated not just his view but that of Morrison, Wilson, the then minister of fuel, Alf Robens, and the economic secretary, Douglas Jay: 'we are definitely inclined to prefer alternative (b) (August 28th or September 4th) as likely both to strengthen our position in Washington and with the British public.' However, he sought the views of Attlee and Bevin before a final decision could be made.[14] The first question is the extent to which this was a government decision at all: Morgan has argued that it was decided 'effectively ... by three young ministers, the thirty-three-year-old Harold Wilson, and Hugh Gaitskell and Douglas Jay.'[15]

There was no meeting of the cabinet between 29 August and 17 September. Attlee opened the meeting on 29 August with a strong statement in favour of devaluation:

> since the Cabinet's discussions in the last week of July he had discussed with the Ministers immediately concerned whether devaluation of the pound would mitigate the short-term difficulties of the dollar balance of payments. ... Opinion had hardened in favour of devaluation, although it was realised that this would not in itself provide a solution of the long-term problem. He recommended that the Foreign Secretary and Chancellor of the Exchequer should be authorised to discuss devalue-ation at Washington and to form a view, in the light of those discussions, on the amount and timing of the measure.[16]

Attlee's delegation of such a critical task exemplified his leadership style. Holding discussions in Washington also delayed devaluation until the very latest of dates envisaged – 19 September 1949. Cripps, who spoke after Attlee, did not really provide confidence in the proposed policy:

> It was impossible to show arithmetically that devaluation would prove to be an advantageous step to take, and it was doubtful whether any considerable benefits would accrue by way on increased dollar receipts. An atmosphere had, however, been created in this country, in the United States, and in other countries in which the pound could not reach stability without devaluation. If there was a reasonable prospect that stability could be secured by this means, and if assurances could be obtained from the United States Government that they would not take measures that would defeat the purpose of devaluation, then he believed devaluation would on balance be of advantage to this country.[17]

The air of desperation that hung over the Cabinet appears later in the same meeting:

> It was recognised that there was little prospect of persuading the United States Government to lessen, by the provision of dollars, the burden which these balances imposed on the United Kingdom's balance of payments. It was also recognised that it would be politically inexpedient to bring any undue pressure to bear on India and Pakistan to accept cancellation of their sterling balances.

But disussion with the United States 'would at least provide an opportunity for making clear to the United States authorities the extent to which the United Kingdom had already contributed, through the drawing down of sterling balances, to measures of economic reconstruction which the United States would otherwise have been called upon to finance'.[18]

In the midst of the crisis, Attlee found time to address the Trades Union Congress at Bridlington on 7 September: 'When I entrust important business to two colleagues in whom I have the most complete confidence [Bevin and Cripps], I like to leave the matter in their hands.'[19] He most certainly did, but was he right to do so with a policy of such importance as devaluation? As he had made an exception to his general approach with India, should he have done the same with devaluation, even though he admittedly knew less about financial matters?

Before Cripps left for Washington, he approved a report of a working party considering devaluation: 'The main purpose of devaluation is to increase the competitive power of our exports by cheapening them to dollar buyers.'[20] The flip side, of course, was the increase in the cost of raw materials and food bought from the dollar area. The working party set up at the suggestion of Johnson in the absence of Norman Brook consisted of Addison, Williams, Isaacs, Wilson, Gaitskell, Strachey, Jay and Attlee. It met on 14 September and Cripps's suggestion of a month's statutory standstill on prices was heavily criticized: it was felt that some prices (like those on fresh produce) varied from week to week, that the government was already accused of having created an 'over-rigid' economy, and that there were fears both of a rush on the shops and of traders increasing prices after the standstill was over.[21] By the time the cabinet met on Saturday 17 September, the discussion was limited to fine-tuning Cripps's broadcast. There was no disagreement on the principle of the decision itself.[22] The broadcast on 18 September set out the devaluation from $4.03 to $2.80, and the penny increase in the price of bread. Cripps finished with a rhetorical flourish, but Churchill's 'sunlit uplands' this was not: 'We thus start upon another stage in the magnificent struggle of our people to overcome the crushing difficulties imposed upon them by their sacrifices in the world war.'[23] *The Times* recorded: 'Even before the Washington talks began, it seems, the Government had decided, with great reluctance, that some reduction in the dollar exchange value of the pound was unavoidable;' and added that it was 'doubtful whether the people yet understand the real nature of the ordeal that has to be faced if the standard of life and welfare is itself to be saved'. 'Never were brave ... leadership and frank speech more needed.'[24] Attlee had not seen it as his role to provide such leadership. If he had, he would have been in Washington with Bevin and Cripps. He defended his position in a letter to Tom: 'The papers all seemed to suggest that I should have made some epoch making announcement, but this would obviously have been stupid with Stafford and Ernie in the midst of negotiations.'[25] He got away with it, principally because devaluation was successful: the gold reserves recovered, and by 1950 Britain no longer required Marshall aid.

Throughout 1949 Attlee faced the decision of when to hold the next general election. He had until July 1950 to seek a dissolution. On 18 August 1949 the increasingly prominent Gaitskell had sent Attlee his thoughts, in a document marked 'Political Strategy', giving what were in his view the viable options. He ruled out the months of December 1949 to March 1950 not only on the basis of cuts in electricity supply during peak hours but also because people often feel more depressed about their well-being during the winter months. He ruled out April to May because there would have to be a budget then that was likely to be unpopular: there might have to be cuts in public spending to keep taxes at the same level; there was no chance of tax cuts due to inflationary pressures. As there was to be a new electoral register to be published in early October, it would be difficult to argue that an election should be fought during the last weeks of the old one, so the two options were November 1949 or June/July 1950. Unless there were sound reasons to expect an improvement in the economic situation by June/July 1950, Gaitskell favoured the earlier date.[26]

With devaluation and the bread price increase, a 1949 election was ruled out. On 13 October 1949 Attlee ended speculation with a press notice: 'the Prime Minister thinks it right to inform the country of his decision not to advise His Majesty to dissolve Parliament this year.'[27] In a letter to the *Sunday Times* the historian G. M. Young criticized Attlee for verging on unconstitutional behaviour. His response to Lascelles's reply to him was that parliament could not simply be 'allowed' to expire. Lacscelles's answer was that Attlee might be 'violating an age-old *Custom* but surely not the *Constitution*'.[28] This was probably correct: Britain had no written constitution to violate, but Attlee was in uncharted territory. Since the coming of mass democracy in 1918, no parliament had gone its full five-year term. What should happen at the end of the five-year period – the prime minister calling an election or the simple expiration of parliament – was unclear.[29]

The timing of the 1950 general election, in February has often been laid at the door of Cripps who refused to construct a budget prior to a general election. Morrison was opposed to an election early in 1950 on the grounds that a lack of preparation time and winter weather would disproportionately harm turnout among Labour voters. He dismissed Attlee's view that the majority would be between 20 and 30 whatever the weather.[30] Bevin, ill in Eastbourne, offered no view and wrote in to say he was 'no politician'. In his absence, Attlee, Morrison, Cripps, Addison, Whiteley and Dalton put their views at Downing Street on 7 December 1949. Peter Clarke's view is that Cripps's 'pressure on Attlee to call an immediate General Election, a course which other economic ministers supported, was perhaps taken less seriously because his own judgement now seemed rather erratic'. (Bevan had allegedly told Dalton that Cripps had 'persecution mania, and was taking very hard charges of dishonourable conduct over devaluation', namely that he had lied to defend the currency prior to devaluation.)[31] This was possibly true, but it mattered little in any event since, of the ministers present at the meeting, only Morrison was opposed to a February election.[32]

Officials also pressed Attlee towards a February election. In a 'Note prepared in Cabinet Office in consultation with Treasury and Whips Office', the issue of the pros and cons for the timing of a general election in 1950 were considered.[33] It was noted that the spring register would be ready on 15 March 1950 and that, prior to that, the autumn register of 1 October 1949 would be a stale one. That point aside, the rest of the document pushes the reader towards an early election, on the basis, principally, of 'supply business' – the appropriate process for putting in place sufficient funds for the activities of government, bearing in mind the end of the financial year on 31 March and the end of the income tax year on 5 April. An early election in February would allow the 'supply procedure' to operate normally; and an 'intermediate election' in, say, March, would be 'very complicated', bringing forward the 'supply procedure': 'Whether the necessary figures could be prepared and published in time, it is difficult to say'; as regards a late election the necessary ways and means resolution on income tax had to be passed by 5 May, so there would have to be a mini-budget with an election taking place 'in the absence of any detailed knowledge of the Government's financial proposals for the year'. There was also the argument, put by Cripps, that the economic situation could get worse: he said he could not 'hold sterling beyond February'.[34] Attlee duly wrote to the king on 5 January 1950, asking for dissolution on 3 February, with polling day on 23 February. He felt that, given their talks over recent months, the king would not be surprised and cited 'a marked swing of public opinion towards an early General Election, and the continuance of the present suspense and uncertainty cannot be in the nation's interest'.[35] Attlee's personal reputation remained high throughout the campaign, which was remarkably short of controversy. On 16 February 1950 the Labour Party received many letters 'containing eulogistic reference to Mr Attlee' and Morgan Phillips drew this to the attention of J. L. Pumphrey, private secretary to the prime minister.[36] Violet drove Attlee around the country as usual; Morgan Phillips wrote almost casually to Attlee on 21 February 1950 that Transport House would be open on election night, and that if he 'would care to look in … it would be much appreciated'.[37]

Attlee's prediction of a majority of 20 to 30 proved optimistic. On polling day, Labour lost 78 seats, taking 315 seats in the House of Commons, with over 13.2 million votes, to the Conservatives' 298 seats, just over 12.5 million votes, and the Liberals' 9 seats, just over 2.6 million votes, 9.1 per cent. Attlee contested West Walthamstow, the Whitechapel and Limehouse divisions of Stepney having being combined into one seat, which he left to the Mile End MP Walter Edwards to contest. He won easily, with a majority of over 12,000. *The Times* noted that Labour's overall majority of five was 'far from being what Governments in these days regard as an effective working majority', adding: 'immediate difficulties might arise about the Iron and Steel Act' but the 'Government [was] expected to carry on'.[38] The cabinet met on Saturday 25 February at 11 a.m. and agreed to continue in office, while acknowledging the difficulties of carrying through controversial measures with such a small majority. Attlee felt that:

> the King's Government must be carried on, and, as Labour would have a majority, the proper course was for a Labour Administration to remain in office. It must, however, be recognised that, with so small a majority, there would be great difficulty in transacting Government business in the House of Commons. There could, in particular, be no question of attempting to carry through any of the major controversial legislation which had been promised in the Party's Election Manifesto. Very careful consideration would also have to be given to the content and presentation of the budget.[39]

Parliamentary work was extremely difficult. Attlee recalled that 'Opposition tactics were designed to wear out our members by keeping them late every night. This was done particularly by putting down "Prayers" against Orders. These come on after the ordinary business of the day.'[40] Attlee found the whole experience distasteful: 'It was not pleasant to have Members coming from hospital at the risk of their lives to prevent a defeat in the House.'[41] They were tough times. On 14 March 1950, Attlee wrote openly to Morgan Phillips to parachute Sir Frank Soskice back in as a candidate: 'our people in the Neepsend Division of Sheffield should accept the Solicitor General as their candidate so that he may return to the House of Commons to assist the Government during these difficult days.'[42] He was accepted, and won the subsequent by-election. Attlee's gamble of leaving him in office despite losing his seat had paid off.

Iron and steel nationalization went ahead. On 20 June 1949, cabinet had resolved that the government 'should decline to accept any amendment moved in the House of Lords with the object of providing that the Iron and Steel Bill could not be brought into effective operation until after the General Election'.[43] At cabinet on 27 October 1949, however, Attlee was invited to form a committee to look at the issues that had arisen from the passage of the bill through parliament.[44] This met on 31 October, with Morrison in the chair, and agreed, subject to Attlee's approval (which was given), to propose that a compromise be reached with the leader of the opposition whereby the bill would become operative on 1 October 1950, with vesting at the discretion of the minister within 18 months afterwards.[45] In fact, Salisbury, on behalf of the Conservatives in the Lords, was willing to agree to a more favourable compromise allowing the bill to become operative at the date of passing, provided companies would not vest within the corporation before 1 October 1950.[46] After its re-election, the government decided to proceed. On 14 September 1950 Churchill placed a motion on the order paper 'regretting that at this most critical period in our national safety [during the Korean War] we should be, by this act of the Government, plunged into the fiercest party controversy at home'.[47] He coruscated Attlee for a 'reckless, wanton and partisan act'.[48] Attlee pressed on and confirmed to Strauss on 6 October 1950 that he had no objection to 15 February 1951 as the 'first practicable date' for the 'transfer of securities to the Iron and Steel Corporation of Great Britain'.[49] Churchill's last-ditch attempt to scupper the bill came on 2 February with a motion to prevent the government giving effect to the nationalization,[50] but this was a gesture rather than an effective political move, and the industry was duly nationalized.

Post-devaluation, Cripps's final budget of 1950 contained few radical measures. On 17 March, the cabinet endorsed the policy Cripps had pursued since November 1947 – avoiding inflation while keeping employment high.[51] It had been suggested that there was 'no convincing reason' for his aim of providing a budget surplus; there was a call for tax cuts or borrowing, to make the budget balance. Cripps's major concern was inflation.[52] In the event, Cripps did cut income tax on the first £250 of earnings to benefit the low-paid, and those paid overtime; he also increased the duty on petrol while doubling the standard ration from 1 June. Attlee's speech on 3 October at the 1950 party conference began with the singing of 'For He's a Jolly Good Fellow' and three cheers. He declared that devaluation had proved to be 'wise and successful'. In terms of the new parliament, he felt that 'the only danger from the voting point of view in this House is not a question of opinion but a question of health'.[53] He declared that 'the General Election will come at the right time', but that the whole position was 'overshadowed by the increasing need for strengthening our defences'.[54] As the political situation worsened, Violet remained keen on Attlee performing at his best. Tony Benn, who entered the Commons at a by-election on 30 November 1950, was invited to tea with Attlee and Violet. Violet attacked Attlee for his failure to perform in the House of Commons to such an extent that Attlee left the room, leaving Benn to have tea with Violet alone.[55]

Defence spending was to become a central part of the dispute between Bevan and Gaitskell. Only days after Attlee's speech, the Chinese decided to intervene in the Korean War, escalating the conflict in the Far East. If there was ever a political dispute about personalities, not substance, this was it. Bevan's talents were certainly not lost on Attlee. After his 'vermin' comment in 1948, Attlee had written privately to him asking him to be more careful in his own interest. On 15 February 1951 Attlee wrote to Morgan Phillips about consideration being given to publishing Bevan's 'brilliant speech' on defence as it might 'do good in the party'.[56] Yet, it was Gaitskell who felt he was being carefully managed by Attlee. In his diary, Hugh Gaitskell recounts how, on his move from the Ministry of Fuel and Power to the Treasury in February 1950, ostensibly a demotion to being number two to Cripps, Attlee told him that he would have to accept a cut in salary from £5000 a year to £3000 a year. Gaitskell 'discovered from the Treasury that is was a pure mistake on the PM's part and that he had got muddled up'.[57] However, he ascribed ulterior motives to Attlee: 'I … thought the PM had tried it as a deliberate test of my loyalty – rather like the King and the good prince in the fairy stories.'[58]

It was hardly a demotion in any event. Gaitskell had been sent to the Treasury to deputize for the ailing Cripps, whose failing health eventually led to his resignation on 16 October. Gaitskell was ideally placed to succeed him and became chancellor for the final year of the Attlee premiership, just five years after becoming an MP. Dalton's view was that 'no one (ruling myself out) could face this job who was senior to the Young Economists, and that, of these, Hugh was incomparably the best, far ahead of either Harold Wilson or Douglas Jay.'[59] The existence of such a group within the government was an indication of Attlee's difficulty with economics; the possibility of Bevan as chancellor had not crossed Dalton's mind, though it almost certainly crossed Gaitskell's. Just a month before Cripps's resignation, he chatted to Dalton about Bevan, who recorded: 'Nye is absolutely fed up with the Ministry of Health. They have the most frightful wrangles on the Cabinet Committee on finance of Health Service. Gaitskell is sure he ought to be moved. What about Ministry of Labour? He thinks Nye would do that very well.'[60] Morrison thought the appointment of Gaitskell 'bold and wise', but noted that it 'displeased some of the old guard and infuriated a few of his own contemporaries, possibly including Nye Bevan and Harold Wilson'.[61] It is unclear who the 'old guard' were to whom Morrison was referring, but it was obvious that most of the 1945 intake were going to be jealous of Gaitskell. For Bevan, once the youngest member of the cabinet and an MP for over 20 years, it must have been difficult to stomach. He wrote to Attlee to protest about Gaitskell's appointment, only to be offered the Ministry of Labour in response, in line with Gaitskell's suggestion. Bevan delayed, fearing a Gaitskell attack on the health service budget, but eventually relented and accepted the post on 17 January 1950. With rearmament a priority in the light of fears over a third world war, it was obvious that the health service would be a target for any economies in public spending. Morrison's view was that Bevan's 'health expenditure was getting out of control'.[62] Departmental responsibility for health may have been taken away from Bevan, but from the moment Gaitskell was appointed, his first budget in the spring of 1951 was inevitably going to bring conflict. It would have helped if Attlee had sought to press Gaitskell during the early months of his appointment as chancellor, even to the minimal extent of urging him to speak to Bevan privately himself to try and head off a potential conflict, but he did not.

Attlee was relying increasingly on Gaitskell. Violet also liked him and, in a rare foray into Attlee's political life, commented that Gaitskell was so much Cripps's pupil that if she closed her eyes, she sometimes thought Gaitskell *was* Cripps.[63] In February 1951 Gaitskell spoke to Attlee about Bevin's successor at the Foreign Office on more than one occasion. Bevin was by now too ill to undertake his tasks properly and Attlee knew he had to be replaced. Gaitskell suggested Herbert Morrison, but Attlee 'disagreed … that … H. [Morrison] … had good judgement in foreign affairs'.[64] Attlee put forward Jim Griffiths; Gaitskell thought him 'far too weak as FS [Foreign Secretary]'.[65] Bevan was not seriously considered for the post at all, possibly because his appointment (with his known position that he opposed increased spending on rearmament at the expense of the NHS) would have sent out a bad signal to the United States regarding support for the Korean War. Gaitskell recorded that the candidates were, in addition to Morrison and Jim Griffiths, Hartley Shawcross, Hector McNeil and Patrick Gordon Walker.[66] This list of names is unsurprising. With the demise of Bevin and Cripps, Morrison was unquestionably the cabinet's dominant figure alongside Attlee. The other figures all had experience of foreign affairs: Griffiths was the current colonial secretary; Shawcross had been the UK's foremost prosecutor at Nuremberg and a UN delegate; McNeil, the current Scottish secretary, had been minister of state at the Foreign Office; and Gordon Walker was the Commonwealth relations secretary. Gaitskell, however, saw Morrison as 'the only person with the capacity to do it and be acceptable to the Party and the country'.[67] Dalton declared himself out of the running and recorded that Griffiths was Attlee's favourite, certainly as of 19 and 20 February.[68] Attlee was of course to change his mind and, on 10 March, Morrison became foreign secretary. His appointment has not been regarded as a successful one. He himself put it down to events: 'No one could deny that I had my share of unwelcome surprises during my comparatively brief term of office as Foreign Secretary.'[69] When the Persian government nationalized the British oil wells at Abadan, Morrison wanted to take military action, just as Eden did over Suez five years later, but was unable to persuade the cabinet, including Attlee. It did not help that, in May 1951, Donald Maclean and Guy Burgess, two Cambridge spies, very publicly defected to the Soviet Union. Morrison had to comfort himself with his 1951 Festival of Britain: a celebration in the heart of the capital city whose politics he had dominated in the 1930s. Bevin was horrified at the appointment: 'He would have preferred Jim Griffiths, and when Francis Williams expressed surprise, replied, "Well, Nye then. I'd sooner have had Nye that 'Erbert." He might have turned out quite good.'[70] Dalton recorded a story John Freeman recounted to him about Bevan:

CLEM, having asked NYE to come and see him: You're the only member of the Government who hasn't advised me yet who should be the next Foreign Secretary.

NYE: Oh, I'd like it myself.

CLEM: I've been looking up the records, and I find that the Foreign Office has never led on to the Premiership.

NYE: Oh, then give it to Herbert.[71]

Even allowing for the historical inaccuracy (the Earl of Rosebery had succeeded to the premiership from the Foreign Office in 1894), this is an indication of Bevan's ambition, and the extent to which he felt slighted by the time the crisis with Gaitskell broke in March 1951.

For a key period, Attlee was in hospital with a duodenal ulcer. However, the key protagonists regularly went to see him and he had the chance to make his influence felt. On 20 March 1951 Gaitskell set out his budget proposals to cabinet, which virtually doubled defence spending and contained a ceiling on health service expenditure of £400 million, together with charges for teeth and spectacles – the patient would now pay half the cost with the National Health Service paying the other half. Bevan argued that it was a matter of principle, but he had accepted legislative provision for prescription charges of up to a shilling in December 1949 (though in his resignation speech he argued that he knew the charge would never be introduced due to impracticability). Over the next six weeks the personal battle between Bevan and Gaitskell was so intense that Norman Brook did not initially include the discussions on the health service charges, which led to the resignations, in the cabinet minutes, but wrote patiently to Attlee on 28 May that he felt that the events leading to the resignations *should* be included, but that the descriptions were 'moderate in tone'.[72]

The division was neatly crystallized in a direct confrontation between Bevan and Gaitskell at a cabinet meeting on the morning of 9 April. Gaitskell records that, 'Morrison read out a message from the PM which in effect gave his vote to me and urged the Cabinet to stand by me.'[73] Bevan said that 'in a Budget totalling over £4000 million, there must be tolerances which would allow the Chancellor, if he wished, to forego his insistence on a saving of only £13 million on the Health Service.' He suggested increasing the contribution made to the NHS by the National Insurance Fund or reducing the £13 million surplus at which the budget was aimed. Gaitskell's response was clear:

He was not prepared to adopt either of the courses suggested by the Minister of Labour. They would both be inflationary in effect. Moreover, if he had such a sum at his disposal, he would certainly wish to consider to what purpose it could most usefully be applied. He was by no means satisfied that, even within the social services, the Health Service had the first claims on any additional money that might be available.

The minutes record sombrely: 'Several Ministers expressed the view that, if the Minister of Labour resigned from the Government on this issue, an acute political crisis would develop.' Morrison adjourned the meeting to later in the day in order to speak to the hospitalized Attlee.

This was Attlee's window of opportunity. When Morrison opened the meeting at 6.30 p.m. he passed on Attlee's views. The series of arguments read rather scientifically in the cabinet minutes and it is difficult to doubt that Morrison passed on the views accurately. Whiteley, who was present both at the meeting with Attlee and in Cabinet, did not correct Morrison in any way and, in any event, Morrison was fully aware that official minutes were being prepared. Several points were put, including the fact that, historically, only Lord Randolph Churchill had previously resigned over a budgetary issue (his 'political fortunes had never recovered thereafter'); that anyone disagreeing with the present proposals should consider not just himself in resignation but the effect on the Labour Party; and that provoking a general election at this time under these circumstances could put the Conservatives in office for a significant period. Such a responsibility would, in Attlee's view, lie with those who resigned. He expected support for Gaitskell. Bevan replied that he was 'not surprised that the Prime Minister took this view' and added, with reference to problems for the party, that 'It was not he who had taken the initiative in proposing charges under the Health Service.' He reiterated that the issue was 'relatively small' and put forward a number of compromise suggestions. These included delaying the introduction of charges for six months to see if they were actually needed; resuming the discussion 'at greater leisure under the Chairmanship of the Prime Minister himself'; having the chancellor simply announce that expenditure on the NHS had a ceiling of £400 million; introducing economies of administration; and adding a charge to prescriptions as opposed to dentures and spectacles (Bevan had himself conceded that prescription charges did not breach the principle of a free health service). Gaitskell was immovable: 'none of these gave him a sufficient assurance that the necessary savings would in fact be secured.' At the end of the meeting Bevan announced that he would submit his resignation the next day.

He did not do so and the next day, in hospital, Attlee saw Bevan and Wilson at 10.30 a.m., before seeing Gaitskell at 11.15 a.m. This was a critical moment, as Gaitskell's diary confirms:

> As I expected, he tried to get me to accept some form of words on the lines that I have already mentioned. He had something written down that he had done while talking to Bevan and Wilson and which they would accept, to the effect of a ceiling of £400 millions and if charges were necessary then they would have to be passed. ... But I had made up my mind that I would announce the charges and I refused to give way. I offered my resignation several times, and I thought as I listened to his arguments that he was going to accept it.[74]

The discussion concluded with the key defining moment of the struggle between Gaitskell and Bevan: 'Finally, he [Attlee] murmured what I took to be "Very well, you will have to go." In a split second I realized he had said, "I am afraid *they* will have to go".'[75] Gaitskell duly presented his budget that afternoon.

That same day James Callaghan and a number of other junior ministers – Alfred Robens, James Stewart, Arthur Blenkinsop and Fred Lee – wrote to Bevan to ask him to delay his resignation. Bevan summoned Callaghan on receipt of the letter and decried Gaitskell: 'Hugh is a Tory. Why do they put me up against it? They have known my position for weeks.' Callaghan's view was: 'I certainly did not go away from that conversation believing, as others have said, that Nye was looking for an excuse to resign. On the contrary, I felt he was tormented as to whether he was taking the right course.'[76] When Callaghan saw him later that day, in calmer mood, Bevan was talking of postponing the charges as a method of compromise.

12. Attlee's maypole, 30 April 1951.

At cabinet on 12 April Wilson appealed for postponement of further discussion until Attlee's return. But when Bevan confirmed he could not vote with the government on the National Health Service bill, Morrison indicated that the decision was acceptable to the majority of the parliamentary party; it would be introduced on 17 April, with second reading on the 23rd. The one minor concession Bevan extracted was the wish to find a form of words to indicate that the dentures and spectacles charge together with the £400 million ceiling was not a 'permanent feature' of the National Health Service. Bevan duly resigned on 23 April; his resignation speech was poisonous: 'If he finds it necessary to mutilate, or begin to mutilate, the Health Services for £13 million out of £4000 million, what will he do next year?' He added: 'I should like to ask my Right hon. and hon. Friends, where are they going? Where am I going? I am where I always was.'[77] Harold Wilson and John Freeman, the left-wing parliamentary secretary at the Ministry of Supply, also resigned.

Attlee's skills at finding compromise had apparently deserted him. Writing to Tom on 24 July, he knew there was trouble ahead: 'We are in for a good deal of bother with Nye Bevan – too much ego in his cosmos.'[78] Yet Bevan was right when he said that the amount was tiny, just £13 million. Gaitskell had made it a resignation issue and in doing so forced Bevan out of the government. Attlee knew the consequences of a Bevan resignation and, with all his skills of managing people, should have tried to head off the clash in advance. He had several months to do so and should have known that moving Bevan to the Ministry of Labour was no solution. In the crisis he should have spoken to Gaitskell *before* the meeting of 20 March, for once Gaitskell had put the health charges on the table he was always going to be unlikely to withdraw them. Once they were proposed, Attlee should have tried to find a way out. Postponement of the charges was clearly one option and, even in the final days after the budget had been presented, a realistic option. That he did not was not a failure of his *style* of leadership, but his own failure to apply the very style that should have succeeded. He gave Gaitskell great support without managing him properly: only perhaps Ernest Bevin had previously been given so much leeway and he was, after all, the rock upon which Attlee built his leadership. It was, quite simply a mistake and, as the next chapter will show, a costly one for the Labour Party.

In the midst of the crisis Ernest Bevin died on 14 April. Attlee was deeply upset. Of all people, Morrison paid a generous tribute to Bevin in the Commons on 16 April 1951: 'I ask the House to join me in paying a tribute to the memory of a truly great man.'[79] Bevin's ashes were interred at Westminster Abbey on Friday 8 June 1951, with the address given by Attlee. Attlee's broadcast tribute summed up his feelings for Bevin: 'For the last five years, save when he was out of the country, I saw him almost daily. ... I have lost in him a good and loyal comrade, and a very dear friend.'[80] Even in such troubled times, Attlee found time for a little light relief. On 29 June 1951, a young girl wrote to Attlee in poetry about having to spend an extra year at school. Attlee replied in kind, delighted to show off his own skills:

> I've not the least idea why
> They have this curious rule
> Condemning you to sit and sigh
> Another year at school ...
> George Tomlinson is ill, but I
> have asked him to explain
> And when I get the reason why
> I'll write to you again.[81]

Heavy political matters were, however, just around the corner. Attlee wrote privately on 19 September that he had decided to proceed to a general election.[82] Attlee's decision to call the 1951 general election for 25 October was a mistake because it meant that the tiny Liberal Party could not afford to run the same number of candidates as it did in 1950. As a consequence, it left a number of potential Liberal voters in many seats with a straight Conservative–Labour choice and, on balance, they tended to opt for the former, causing Labour to lose the election despite gaining more votes than the Conservatives. Churchill had been a Liberal himself for two decades prior to his return to the Conservative Party as chancellor under Baldwin in 1924. The Liberal leader, Clement Davies, was offered a seat in the Churchill cabinet (though he did not accept) and Lloyd George's son, Gwilym, served as Churchill's home secretary from 1954.

Attlee's constitutional conservatism and respect for the monarchy – present throughout his life – were at play here. He was also worried about ill MPs having to be wheeled in to keep the government afloat. The key intervention was from the king over his proposed trip to Australia in the autumn of 1951; he wanted the parliamentary situation resolved before his departure. In the event, he was too ill to go and the papers in the Public Record Office include a letter from Lascelles on behalf of the king, assuring historians of the future that the king had not deliberately misled Attlee.[83] Attlee was left with holding an election in unfavourable circumstances. Labour was behind in the opinion polls by 11 per cent.[84] Only John Major in 1992 has since called a general election at a time of his own choosing while his party was behind in the polls. By 1952 the balance of payments was back in surplus, after falling into a deficit in 1951 and, with a long stalemate in the Korean War, peace moves were afoot, reducing the need for rearmament. The Conservatives became associated with the 'Age of Affluence'; the Attlee government remained associated with austerity.

When it emerged that the king was too ill to travel, on 23 September 1951 Morrison sent a personal cipher telegram from on board the *Queen Mary* to Attlee. He had been to San Francisco for the signing of the Japanese Peace Treaty. In handwritten form now, there is some doubt over some of the words and phrasing, but the underlying message is very clear:

> Rumours on board the SS *Queen Mary* make Lord Chancellor and me anxious about the King's health. … We are also concerned (at the?) rush and conjunction of events (with the?) King all we consider that the inevitable rough and tumble of a General election may be out of place. … Whether possible to postpone in the light of development of His Majesty's illness we cannot tell from here but as executive members Minister of Defence and I would wish M. Phillips to be informed (so that?) (he can?) (enquire views?) of the Executive and take into account Monday. Thus the need for this telegram. When I left London I was under the impression move would not come quite so quickly.[85]

Morrison's point was that the king's illness could be used as political cover to postpone an election in which he feared the worst for Labour. The point was anathema to Attlee, who was terse in response:

> You will have heard of the success of the operation. Anxiety remains for the next few days, but hopes are good. Postponement of the election would, I am sure, be contrary to the King's wishes. It would appear to contemplate the worst. It is contrary to constitutional practice to allow illness of King to interfere with working of the constitution. A demise of the Crown is, of course, another matter.[86]

It was a triumph for Attlee's Victorian respect for the monarchy, but not for the interests of the Labour Party.

When the 1951 party conference took place at Scarborough from 1 October, Labour was in pre-election mode. Attlee defended the record of the 1950–51 parliament on 1 October: 'We have had to bat on a very sticky wicket and great progress has been made.'[87] He finished with the stirring quotation from William Blake:

> I will not cease from mental fight,
> Nor shall my sword sleep in my hand
> Till we have built Jerusalem
> In England's green and pleasant land.[88]

The chairman of the United Textile Factory Workers' Association, H. Earnshaw, presented Violet with a bouquet for her contribution in driving Attlee around the country. As the campaign progressed, with Churchill mocking Bevan, Attlee knew the difficulty posed was by the Liberal voters and wrote to Tom on 21 October: 'The result of the election is anybody's guess depending largely on which way the liberal cat jumps.'[89] He should have realized that waiting a few more months would have helped in what was a tight election.

At the election, Labour lost 20 seats, but gained over 13.9 million votes, 48.8 per cent, to the Conservatives' 321 seats, just over 13.7 million votes, 48.0 per cent. The Liberals won only six seats, just over 700,000 votes, 2.5 per cent. Numerically, the Labour vote had risen from just under 12 million in 1945, to just over 13.2 million in 1950, to the 1951 total, which has still not been surpassed. More voters voted Labour in 1951 than at any time before or since. Turnout was high, at 82.5 per cent, with *The Times* noting that polling day reduced attendance at the motor show.[90] The redrawing of electoral boundaries under the Representation of the People Act (1948) was unhelpful: Labour won safe seats with large majorities and lost narrowly in more marginal seats to the Conservatives. Crucially, the Liberals ran only 109 candidates, as opposed to the 475 that had run in 1950, and what potential Liberal voters did in the absence of a Liberal candidate was crucial. Attlee's view was that 'the Liberals tended in most areas to give two or three votes to the Conservative for every one they gave to Labour'.[91] As a consequence, *The Times* noted that Churchill 'for the first time in his life accepts the office of Prime Minister at the direct bidding of the electors – instead of, as eleven years ago, at the call of history itself.'[92] After 11 years in Downing Street, Attlee's years of power were at an end.

He was never to hold office again. At a stroke, his daily life changed dramatically. His years of reliance on civil servants were over. He lost his official residences, though Churchill was generous in victory, indicating that he would not be using Chequers for a month or Downing Street for at least a fortnight: 'On no account put yourself to any inconvenience.'[93] Indeed, the mutual respect between the two men endured. Clementine Churchill even attended the wedding of Martin Attlee in 1955.[94] Initially, Attlee was understandably disoriented: 'It seems quite odd to be free of heavy responsibilities and to look forward to a whole day without nothing particular to do.'[95] But he took his fall from power stoically. Evan Durbin's description of how Attlee adapted to being prime minister applied equally to when he returned to being leader of the opposition in 1951: 'He took that in his stride. It was just another hard job to do like the others he had done in the past.'[96] He wrote to Tom: 'I have had a very heavy correspondence. People have been very kind.' He added: 'We have been very busy getting settled into Cherry Cottage which looks very well now. It was a very heavy job unpacking and shelving books … 2000 or so volumes.'[97] Attlee enjoyed the additional time to himself. He particularly enjoyed having more time to read. In January 1954, he wrote an article, 'The Pleasure of Books': 'In moments of leisure I like to wander round and to pull out a book here and there, perhaps only for old times' sake; but there are some that I read again and again.'[98] He still loved history: 'I love to stray into the byways of history and to read of curious episodes, such as the Latin Kingdom of Jerusalem.'[99] He enjoyed biographies, local government works, maps and atlases, and war books: the 'ranks are led by the present Prime Minister's great series [Churchill's multi-volume *The Second World War*].'[100] His 'miscellaneous texts' included detective novelists such as Agatha Christie, though 'Science is hardly represented and there is little theology, except the Bible, or philosophy.'[101] Given his views on the 'mumbo-jumbo' of Christianity, this is hardly surprising. Attlee also found time to write his autobiography, *As It Happened*, published in 1954. With characteristic modesty he remarked to Tom that it was 'not very good'.[102] Dalton commented: 'Understatement exaggerates its emphasis. But he fitted with the requirements of the times; lacks all positive political vices, is honest and infused by rather drab goodwill.'[103] Put in a more positive way, the book was characteristically Clem Attlee.

Above all, Attlee enjoyed the opportunity to spend more time at home with his family. He worked on the garden at Cherry Cottage: in the autumn of 1953 'getting rid of a rather ugly bed and putting in new rose trees'.[104] In the summer of 1952, he visited Belgium Festival of Labour, then travelled to Rhodesia. Violet, having missed him while in Belgium, accompanied him to Africa.[105] When Violet was ill again in the summer of 1953, he could give her far more of his time, and was relieved when she recovered: 'Vi is better but had a good deal of trouble last week.'[106] But, even with an increased measure of freedom, Attlee still led the Labour Party. With the Bevan–Gaitskell division, the remaining four years of Attlee's leadership proved a major challenge of his skills of party management.

Chapter 22
MANAGING THE PARTY, 1951–55

The last four years of Attlee's leadership of the Labour Party were times of internal strife and discord. They marked the first four years of Labour's 13-year period in the wilderness as the so-called 'Bevanites' presented him with a significant problem in terms of party management. He had a group of MPs who sought to present a coherent alternative strategy of opposition, and a group on the right, including Morrison and Gaitskell, who wanted strong disciplinary measures taken against them. Was the difficulty *so* significant that it required Attlee to stay on as leader? Conventional wisdom has it that Attlee remained as leader because the obvious alternative, Herbert Morrison, would have taken such a tough line with the left of the party that it would have caused an irrevocable split. Whether this would have occurred can only be a matter of supposition – what can only be judged is the effectiveness of Attlee's leadership and the state of the party when he eventually retired in December 1955.

Churchill ignited the smouldering animosity in the Labour Party by referring to Bevan's resignation speech in the House of Commons on 6 December 1951. He conceded that the government would be unable to spend all the money that Gaitskell had allocated to rearmament in the 1951 budget, and mockingly congratulated Bevan: 'the right hon. Gentleman … it appears by accident, perhaps not for the best of motives, happened to be right.'[1] To add to Attlee's problems, Churchill announced in parliament on 18 February 1952 that Britain would be testing an atomic bomb later in the year in the Monte Bello archipelago just off the coast of Australia. Attlee's decision for Britain to have its own atomic weapon and to keep its development secret from parliament was out in the open.

Unsurprisingly, it was over defence that matters came to a head, in a parliamentary debate on 5 March 1952. The government had produced a defence White Paper setting out defence expenditure. Rearmament had, after all, been the policy of Labour in government, and the party in opposition would have lacked any credibility had it switched to deriding it when in opposition. The problem was that Bevan and his followers were not in favour of carrying out the rearmament programme. Attlee found a compromise: the defence White Paper was to be approved in principle, but no confidence would be expressed in the government to carry out the rearmament programme. He, together with Morrison and the chief whip Whiteley, sent a letter to each MP setting out the position to take in the vote. Procedurally, this meant that the party would put down an amendment to the government motion to approve the White Paper, and then abstain on the motion itself. The Labour amendment was defeated by 314 votes to 219: the Conservative majority, usually around 20, had vastly increased, meaning that a significant number of Labour MPs had not voted for the amendment; on the motion itself, 57 Labour MPs voted against.

Attlee was now faced with a disciplinary crisis. Some on the right of the party, such as Alf Robens and James Callaghan, wanted to take away the Labour whip from the 57 rebels.[2] Attlee could hardly expel all 57 members, which would have been over one-sixth of the parliamentary party; in any event Bevan and his followers were very popular in the constituency Labour parties. Gaitskell felt that there was something to be said for being able to attack Bevan if he left the party.[3] At the meeting of the parliamentary party the next week, on 10 March, Attlee proposed a motion that the 57 be criticized, standing orders (suspended in 1945 to encourage, as opposed to imposing, loyalty to the party line) be reintroduced, and all MPs sign to say they were accepted. However, it was not Attlee who had formulated the resolution. Gaitskell records a discussion the day after the defence debate within the parliamentary committee (the modern-day shadow cabinet) that came up with the approach.[4] Second, when Attlee proposed it at the full meeting of the parliamentary party, he, according to Gaitskell, 'made a fairly strong speech to start with but did not attempt to explain our resolution'. The debate seems to have got away from Attlee. A 'middle-way' option proposed by George Strauss, of the reintroduction of standing orders only, was passed by what Foot called the 'astonishing majority' of 162 to 73.[5] An admittedly hard-line Gaitskell bemoaned that the 'real blame for this must rest with Attlee who made a very weak speech indeed, and did not in the least give the impression that it was important to him to carry the Committee's resolution.'[6]

In trying to maintain unity, Attlee remained studiously objective. He doodled increasingly in meetings. At the start of April 1952, Bevan published *In Place of Fear*, his democratic socialist tract on society, declaring that its 'chief

13. Labour Party leader Attlee with papers and pipe.

enemy is vacillation'.[7] Attlee, tongue-in-cheek, placed his copy on his bookcase next to *Aesop's Fables*.[8]

The historian Eric Shaw had argued that the *overall* 'reaction seems quite disproportionate', but is explained by the troubled climate of the times with the Korean War ongoing, the fact that the parliamentary party had not had such discontent since the Independent Labour Party left in 1931, and the impression that the behaviour was an 'affront' to accepted standards of behaviour.[9] Either way, Attlee has to be judged by results. Vacillating or not – or even if the party was over-reacting – if his aims were limited simply to keeping the party together, and not to expel the Bevanites, then he succeeded. But it was his mismanagement of the Bevan–Gaitskell dispute while in government that *shaped* his aims. The division was so deep that party unity was an overriding consideration; returning Labour to power at the next general election became secondary.

In any event, Attlee only had temporary respite. The 1952 party conference took place from 29 September at Morecambe. Dalton thought it was 'the worst Labour Party Conference for bad temper and general hatred, since 1926, the year of the General Strike'.[10] If Attlee needed any confirmation that the Bevanites had significant support in the constituencies, the results of voting for the constituency section of the national executive committee confirmed this, with Bevan topping the poll, and other Bevanites Barbara Castle, Tom Driberg, Harold Wilson, Ian Mikardo and Richard Crossman all being elected. Only Jim Griffiths survived the Bevanite tide, with Morrison, Dalton, Gaitskell, Callaghan and Shinwell all failing to get elected.

On the second day of the conference, 30 September, Attlee proposed a document 'Facing the Facts', an interim statement of policy from the executive, which Attlee declared a 'sober, serious statement'.[11] It expressed deep concern about the foreign exchange difficulties. 'We are almost like a patient who is always taking his pulse and if there is a slight quickening of the pulse he gets violently excited. A slight change somewhere causes great difficulties.'[12] Morrison wound up the debate and Dalton noted that his 'speech was much written up in the press, and it is suggested that he should now become leader in place of Attlee who played a very passive part throughout'.[13] Dalton added, however, in parenthesis: 'But what *could* he have done? Hardly declared, or implied, that vote for the National Executive was wrong!'[14] The following day, however, matters went from bad to worse as both Will Lawther, president of the National Union of Mineworkers, and Arthur Deakin, who had replaced Bevin as general secretary of the Transport and General Workers' Union were 'very provocative' to the Bevanites, and there was 'continuous booing'.[15] The conference had brought matters to a head and, in October 1952, the shadow cabinet recommended to the parliamentary party that groups within the party ('the party within a party') be disbanded; this was passed by 188 votes to 51. Attlee had finally taken a hard line.

Bevan had in many senses created an ideal CV for a senior leadership position – dedicated followers, a book on his political philosophy, a mouthpiece for his views in *Tribune*, and a distance from the fall of the Attlee government brought about by his resignation. It was no surprise that he stood for the deputy leadership against Morrison in November 1952. However, the parliamentary party was noticeably not Bevanite and Morrison won by 194 votes to 82. Attlee's leadership was clearly damaged during 1952. Dalton felt that the 82 votes for Bevan represented a 'demonstrative vote, against [the] leadership, Attlee as much as Morrison'.[16] When Dalton spoke to Jim Griffiths on 3 November, Griffiths had said that he 'had pressed Attlee to go on, and [should] have pressed Vi. *She* had been frightened by the deaths of Ernie and Stafford and wanted Clem for a few years to herself.'[17]

Indeed, Attlee was ill at the start of 1953 and had to spend a few weeks away from active politics having an operation to have his appendix removed.[18] But, he soldiered on. Bevan noticeably did not attend Attlee's seventieth birthday celebration buffet tea at the House of Commons on 25 February 1953.[19] Attlee had been in the Far East on 3 January (at the Asian socialist conference in Rangoon and then in India), so his birthday celebration involving all sections of the Labour movement was held at this later time. If Bevan's snub was an old-fashioned timeless way of showing unhappiness with an individual, Attlee was also having to deal with more modern-day political tactics – leaks to the press. On 4 May 1953 Attlee wrote to Morgan Phillips about the 'very full report' appearing in the *Observer* of a conference of the executive: 'It is in my view obvious that there is someone deliberately feeding the *Observer* with inform-ation.'[20] Morgan Phillips replied the next day that he had 'raised it on many occasions but we have not been successful in tracing the source'.[21] The prob-lem of the Bevanite *Tribune* also remained. Gaitskell reflected the frustration of many on the right of the party when he declared that they were 'handicapped … *vis-à-vis* the Bevanites because of the *New Statesman* and *Tribune*'.[22] On 28 January 1953 the national executive committee met and ordered that the 'Tribune Brains Trust' be investigated by subcommittee to see if it, too, constituted a 'party within a party'. The 'Brains Trust' was made up of Bevan-ites who presented the political case around the constituency parties. However, on 18 February, the subcommittee criticized them as against the spirit of the recent Parliamentary Labour Party decisions, but did not impose a ban. Attlee went back to basics at the 1953 party conference in Margate from 28 Sep-tember to 2 October. Speaking on the final day, in an impassioned defence of his leadership style, he declared: 'It is principles and policy that count, not personalities. I am only here to carry out your will. Nye Bevan has told us how in the 1945 Government we worked as a team. … I have never known a team work better and more solidly together.'[23]

Bevan's personality continued to count a great deal and the Bevanites pro-voked controversy at the 1954 party conference, which took place from 27 September at Scarborough. The major difficulty was German rearmament, which provoked uproarious debate in the hall. Denis Healey neatly summed up the emergency resolution the national executive proposed and for which Attlee spoke on 28 September: 'It means that we shall be asking the National Executive to meet the European Socialists to try to find if we can agree on a common policy for controlling German rearmament and making sure that if Germany is rearmed she will be rearmed under control on our side.'[24] Attlee relied on his own experiences in both wars and set out the twin dangers, first that of giving Germany complete freedom to rearm, but second, if it did not rearm at all, the burden of defending West Germany. Moreover, if there was to be no rearmament, how could that be enforced? For him, the reintegration of Germany with the West was 'of very great importance'.[25] The Amalgamated Union of Foundry Workers proposed a different resolution: while agreeing about the need for a democratic and united Germany, German rearmament was opposed. The real division beneath this was the Bevanite support for this position and their opposition to German rearmament. The national executive emergency resolution was carried by 3,270,000 votes to 3,022,000, and the rival resolution narrowly defeated by 3,281,000 to 2,910,000. The Attlee line had narrowly held, but Bevan's behaviour was becoming increasingly unacceptable to the party right.

This said, Attlee presided over one of the more curious episodes in the history of the Labour Party – the attempt to expel Bevan in the early part of 1955. On 16 March 1955 the parliamentary party met to consider the parliamentary committee's recommendation to withdraw the whip from Bevan. Before the meeting Gaitksell sent Attlee a paper setting out the case against Bevan.[26] This related to three incidents, the first of which arose when Eden, as foreign secretary, made a statement on 13 April 1954 on Southeast Asian defence and atomic energy. Without there being an agreed line from the parliamentary committee, Bevan rose and condemned it, saying it would be seen as yielding to America. The next day Bevan resigned from the parliamentary committee. The second concerned a motion moved by Bevan in a special party meeting on 9 February 1955, in which he sought to reconfirm Attlee's Commons statement of 18 November 1954 that talks with Russia on Germany should take place, and wished to move such a motion in the House of Commons. However, the parliamentary committee had not agreed that placing such a motion on the order paper was the tactically preferred method, wanting more detail on any Soviet promise of elections, and Bevan's proposal was voted down by 93 votes to 70. Bevan nevertheless put down a motion on 15 February. On 24 February Attlee moved in a party meeting to condemn Bevan, which was carried by 132 votes to 72. The final problem, however, arose from the government debate on the nuclear bomb on 1 March 1955. The Labour Party put down an amendment recognizing the value of nuclear weapons as a

14. Attlee and Bevan in the boxing ring, 17 March 1955.

deterrent. Bevan deliberately confronted Attlee in the debate, asking whether the use of nuclear weapons was favoured in circumstances where the opponent was only using conventional weapons, and he was one of 62 MPs who abstained, rather than voting in favour of, the Labour Party amendment.

When the parliamentary committee had met on 7 March, the question of what could be done about Bevan was dominant. Gaitskell claimed he 'retained an open mind',[27] and it was actually Ede who proposed withdrawing the whip from Bevan. Attlee *did intervene*: he 'spoke and made it plain that he was against withdrawing the Whip, and preferred the censure motion'.[28] Yet, the parliamentary committee did vote to recommend to withdraw the whip, with only Jim Griffiths, Harold Wilson, Hugh Dalton and Alf Robens against. Gaitskell comments rather derisorily that 'I do not recall throughout this that Attlee said anything.'[29] On 9 March, the parliamentary committee considered whether the withdrawal of the whip should be a vote of confidence, and decided that it should be. Gaitskell noted that:

> Attlee, if I recollect rightly, first of all seemed doubtful as to whether we should announce that we should resign if we were not supported, and to everybody's surprise first of all Morrison also seemed doubtful; but everybody else – Jim Griffiths and Harold Wilson were away – said in the strongest terms that it must be made absolutely plain to the party that if we lost we would all resign.[30]

Since Bevan was ill, the party meeting was delayed until 16 March. It was finely balanced. Attlee's difficulty was that he was caught between the two stools of withdrawing the whip from Bevan and the resignation of the parliamentary committee. He wanted neither outcome. In the meeting, the 'middle way' motion put by Fred Lee, MP for Newton in Lancashire, that Bevan be censured rather than deprived of the whip, was lost by 138 to 124. However, the parliamentary committee's motion of withdrawal of the whip was carried by 141 to 112.

Attlee was disappointed. Of course, he received criticism for not putting the case for the parliamentary committee's resolution strongly enough. When Attlee was asked if he and his colleagues would resign if the motion were lost, Dalton noted that 'Attlee says, in a weak voice, "We should have to consider our position".'[31] Dalton added: 'Someone said, "He [Attlee] was weak this morning because he wasn't sure which way the vote would go, and was determined, whichever way it went, to stay on as Leader".'[32] Gaitskell was slightly more positive: 'Attlee made a fairly strong statement, better than the worst, though not as good as the best that was to be expected, but he carefully avoided any indication that this was an issue of confidence.'[33] That he did this is, however, unsurprising. Attlee wanted to avoid a schism in the party and was looking for a way out. When Robens went with Gaitskell to see Attlee the next day, Gaitskell records: 'Attlee appeared surprised when Alf criticized him for not pushing the issue of confidence sufficiently strongly. He thought he had done so, and did not agree that if in fact he had made it perfectly plain that we would resign there would have been a much more favourable vote.'[34] This quotation says it all – Attlee claiming he *had* put the issue sufficiently strongly, yet also conceding that he could have put it *more* strongly but denying any advantage in doing so. One can only imagine the surprise was somewhat feigned.

With the whip withdrawn, however, the question now was whether the national executive committee would expel Bevan. Gaitskell noted that Attlee 'refused to commit himself at all, but it was plain that he was rather against expulsion'.[35] When the NEC considered Bevan's expulsion on 23 March 1955, Attlee proposed a subcommittee to consider his conduct, which was carried by 14 votes to 13. Kenneth Harris records:

> When it began to look highly probable that Bevan would be expelled, Attlee broke off his doodling and proposed that Bevan should be asked to prepare a statement for the NEC, and submit to questioning on it by a subcommittee of the Executive, which would report back to the full body.[36]

The subcommittee met on 29 March, but was somewhat overtaken by events. In the meantime, Bevan had met Attlee and agreed on a statement of apology, which was put to the NEC on 30 March and accepted by 20 votes to 6; a warning of strong action of future breaches of party discipline was carried by 15 votes to 10, Attlee opposing. On 21 April the whip was restored to Bevan and the whole sorry episode had reached its conclusion.

Eric Shaw has set out a variety of reasons for the failure of the attempt to expel Bevan – Ian Mikardo's daughter changing her wedding plans to free her father to vote; Jean Mann, a right-wing opponent of Bevan, who for odd reasons did not vote to expel him; and an imminent general election and boundary changes meaning those searching for seats would not wish to incur the wrath of party members by opposing Bevan. Shaw concludes: 'Another decisive factor – which, alone, probably turned the table – was Attlee's opposition to expulsion.'[37] Foot concluded that 'the expulsion crisis of 1955 had merely been the classic, compressed example of how political understanding between the two men could be first ruptured and then repaired.'[38]

Attlee's final four years as party leader had a purpose after all, albeit a limited one. He kept the party together and prevented a schism that might have damaged the party to a far greater extent than the internal strife with which he had to deal. This analysis is, however, based on two assumptions. The first is that Attlee *was* the key factor in holding the party together. Weighing up his contribution against other factors is inevitably fraught with difficulty. One cannot unpick the importance given to the various factors in the minds of the various participants in the events. Attlee's critical contribution was the proposal of a subcommittee at the NEC meeting on 23 March 1955. The second assumption is that *another* leader who, had Attlee stepped down in the early 1950s, most probably would have been Herbert Morrison, would have been so draconian on party discipline that the Bevanites, and Bevan himself, would have been expelled from the party, while retaining such a level of support at the grass-roots level that the party would have been riven by division both within the parliamentary party, and between the parliamentary party and the wider party. Would Morrison really have been this politically short-sighted? Morrison's biographers Donoghue and Jones record that: 'At the Shadow Cabinet, when Attlee declined to give a lead, Morrison stepped in with a strong speech recounting Bevan's many past misdeeds and he swung the meeting firmly behind a resolution recommending the parliamentary party to withdraw the whip.'[39] Yet, in the parliamentary committee meeting on 9 February, it seems Morrison had initially been reluctant about withdrawing the whip. Morrison pays tribute to Bevan in his autobiography, admittedly published in the wake of Bevan's death in 1960: 'I am doubtful how well he knew the British temperament, but he certainly knew and understood Labour's left wing.'[40] Of Attlee's uniqueness in dealing with the problem one can only speculate.

On the negative side, the saga had spilled over into the 1955 general election campaign. On 6 April 1955 Eden had succeeded Churchill as Conservative prime minister and called a general election. This had an immediate impact on the opinion polls. Gallup had Labour at 44 per cent in both February and March 1955, with the Conservatives at 46 per cent for both months. In April 1955, the Conservatives rose to 48 per cent, with Labour remaining at 44 per cent; in May, the Conservatives rose to 51 per cent, with Labour only increasing its rating to 47 per cent.[41] Attlee was 72 years old and hardly in a position to offer change. Over the first 15 days of Eden's premiership, the Bevan expulsion controversy had raged on, hardly the best showcase for a party wishing to govern again. When Dalton spoke to Attlee about the election on 31 March, he actually considered who might occupy cabinet positions. Dalton told him 'I don't believe we can win, certainly if it's a quick one,' and that 'he *must* go on as Leader until Morrison is no longer an inevitable successor.'[42] Intriguingly, Attlee said 'he can't go on much longer, but is very critical of Morrison.'[43] Attlee certainly discussed many people and positions with Dalton, but, tellingly: 'This conversation took a long time. But it will be seen that we left many offices and persons undiscussed.'[44]

The 1955 general election took place on 26 May 1955. Labour lost 18 seats, gaining just over 12.4 million votes, 46.4 per cent, to the Conservatives' 344 seats, just under 13.3 million votes, 49.7 per cent. The Liberals remained with six seats, just over 700,000 votes, 2.7 per cent. For the third consecutive election, the party's parliamentary representation had decreased in size. Attlee's leadership of the party – now in its twentieth year – was coming to its natural end. Dalton wrote to him on 1 June stating that he was standing down from the shadow cabinet, and urged all others over 65 to do the same, exempting only Attlee himself.[45] This was a calculated attempt to undermine 67-year-old Herbert Morrison in favour of the right's new standard-bearer, Hugh Gaitskell. Attlee remained stubbornly – and needlessly – at the helm. The traditionalist in him waited until the end of the year when the parliamentary party usually elected its new leader. Dalton, however, recorded in October that 'it is becoming embarrassing that this uncertainty should continue.'[46]

Attlee, by contrast, ended on an optimistic note at his last party conference as party leader, at Margate on 11 October: 'I believe that the signs are more hopeful for getting agreement today on world disarmament than ever before, because I think all Governments are facing up to realities.'[47] This casting of himself as a multilateral disarmer was significant. Two years later, at the party conference in Brighton, Bevan famously abandoned the unilateral disarmament stance of the left and declared that simply to abandon Britain's nuclear deterrent would be to send a British foreign secretary 'naked into the conference Chamber' with nothing to negotiate with as regards other countries disarming.

15. British Labour Party election posters.

Attlee was also given a final chance to exhibit his leadership style. When Victor Yates, the MP for Birmingham Ladywood, raised the issue of the withdrawal of the whip from six Labour MPs, Attlee replied in characteristic fashion: 'The Party recognises the right of individual members to abstain from voting on matters of strictly held personal conscientious conviction … [but] … I believe that conscience is a still, small voice and not a loud-speaker.'[48]

His final words as leader at conference were simple but resolute: 'You can be sure that as soon as we get back again we shall put up a vigorous and, I hope, very united fight in the House.'[49]

Attlee eventually resigned from the leadership at a meeting of the parliamentary party on 7 December 1955. On 14 December 1955, on one ballot only, the Parliamentary Labour Party chose Hugh Gaitskell to succeed Attlee; there were 157 votes for Gaitskell, 70 for Bevan and 40 for Morrison. Morrison got fewer votes than he had in the much smaller parliamentary party in 1935. It has been argued that Attlee's 'secret hope had earlier been that Bevan would mend his ways and become the leader'[50] but Attlee's management of the Gaitskell–Bevan clash in March 1951 had made that improbable: it had made Gaitskell the sensible 'insider' candidate from the start. Attlee had left the party in one piece and only 18 seats below its 1951 position. By contrast, after the internal strife following the 1979 general election defeat, during which the party *did* split with Roy Jenkins, Shirley Williams, Bill Rodgers and David Owen – all to one degree or another Hugh Gaitskell devotees – forming the Social Democratic Party, the party found itself losing a further 60 seats at the polls. Overall, Attlee's lengthy leadership had been at the expense of neither his party nor his country. By the mid-1950s, it was starting to look as if Labour had built a solid economic base from which the Conservatives gained the electoral rewards. Attlee was able to write to the Labour candidate in the Gateshead West by-election, in a handwritten note dated 29 November 1955 (the contest was on 7 December 1955), that the Conservative government was 'taking advantage of the solid foundation laid by the Labour government'.[51]

Chapter 23
THE LAST YEARS, 1955–67

Attlee enjoyed his retirement. Violet finally had her wish of having her husband to herself, and he 'always seemed perfectly happy. When he wasn't responsible for anything any more, he was able to relax.'[1] Indeed, his material contribution to the political events of the day was minimal. There is no evidence that Hugh Gaitskell, or, from 1963, Harold Wilson, consulted him on matters of political strategy or party management. This may seem odd given Attlee's 20 years of experience as party leader – unparalleled in *any* major political party in Britain in the twentieth-century – but may also be explained by his decision to hold onto the leadership for so long after the general election defeat in October 1951. After such a long waiting for his departure, he was not welcome at the back door. A matter of days after he stood down as party leader, on 16 December 1955, he accepted a hereditary peerage and became Earl Attlee and Viscount Prestwood in Walthamstow in the County of Essex. When he became a Knight of the Garter in June 1956 he completed a quadruplet of gongs, having accepted a Companion of Honour in 1945, and an Order of Merit on his retirement as party leader. He very much enjoyed his garter ceremony, particularly the presence of his family, telling Tom: 'The Garter show went off very well. The children had seats in the chapel while Vi was present at all the ceremonies.'[2] He also wrote probably his most famous verse:

> Few thought he was even a starter
> There were many who thought themselves smarter
> But he ended PM
> CH and OM
> An earl and a knight of the garter.[3]

Attlee's acceptance of a peerage was not quite the betrayal of, say, Lloyd George, who accepted a seat in 1945 after having built a radical reputation by attacking the House of Lords and having seen the upper house reject his 1909 people's budget. Attlee was a conservative on constitutional change and his attitude of 'leave well alone' during the reform debate of 1948 and 1949 did not sit uncomfortably with his later peerage. The peerage did not change him. He travelled into the House of Lords on the tube. He would be recognized and would simply confirm to those who asked if he was Mr Attlee.[4] Violet, however, was protective of her husband and felt he should be given the respect he deserved. Tony Benn recalled a party at which a lady approached Attlee and said she had always wanted to meet *Mr* Attlee. Violet interjected immediately: 'It's *Lord* Attlee if you don't mind.'[5]

Lord Attlee was not slow to contribute in the House of Lords. On 26 July 1956, the Egyptian republic under Nasser nationalized the Suez Canal. As prime minister, Attlee's Middle Eastern policy had been predicated on the basis of a friendly Egypt to retain British influence. Attlee cautioned against an aggressive act in response; Eden, of course, ignored such calls. Attlee became a model elder statesman. His party honoured him and, on 10 February 1956, a dinner was held for Attlee and Violet at the Cooperative Wholesale Society Assembly Hall in the East End. Hugh Gaitskell paid him the warmest of tributes: 'as Prime Minister from 1945, he led a Government whose record we shall always be proud to remember. Clem would say it was a team job. And of course it was. But successful team work depends a lot on the captain.'[6] Attlee arrived late, having been in a car accident with Violet on the way, another vehicle striking their car. Attlee was 'very pleased' with the speech and must indeed have shown considerable commitment to attend at all, for he had broken a couple of ribs.[7] Later in the year, the Labour Party conference passed a resolution of thanks to Attlee for his long service and great leadership.

He concentrated on lectures and book reviews. In September 1956, he visited India and was accorded a civic reception in Madras together with an honorary degree from Madras University. He playfully deemed the second volume of Churchill's *A History of the English-Speaking Peoples* as 'Things in history which have interested me'.[8] His relationship with Churchill remained undamaged and, in December 1957, he and Violet lunched with Churchill and Clementine. Churchill 'recalled with satisfaction that he and I either as Allies or as Government and Opposition leaders covered fifteen years between us'.[9] When Dalton's *The Fateful Years: Memoirs, 1931–1945* appeared in 1957, Attlee declared that, while he 'wrote the Acts, Dalton wrote Revelations'.[10] Attlee was also drawn to defend his own actions several times. Writing on the role of the monarchy in 1959, he denied that the king's preference for Bevin's appointment as foreign secretary was a decisive factor in his decision in 1945.[11]

16. John Kennedy chatting to Clement Attlee.

Reviewing the first volume of Michael Foot's biography of Nye Bevan in 1960, he said he thought Bevan 'would have been a natural leader of the Labour Party if one was sure he would learn to keep his temper. Far from standing in his way, I tried to bring him on.' He denied Bevan ever asked to be foreign secretary in 1951, but said he would have tried him in that post had he won the general election of 1955. However, Attlee maintained that Bevan should not have been chancellor, for he lacked the economic expertise of Gaitskell or Cripps.[12] Over the same period, Attlee lectured. He visited America in early 1957, and again twice in 1959, arguing against the stockpiling of weapons. He gave the annual memorial lecture of May 1958 at the David Davies Memorial Institute of International Studies, arguing that the real distinction was not so much between conventional and nuclear weapons, but 'between weapons of mass destruction and weapons (comparatively light) suitable for police purposes'.[13] In October 1959, just after the general election in which he gave a number of speeches, he visited Australia for a lecture tour and spoke in favour of world government. He returned to Britain via the United States to deliver the Oxford University Chichele Lectures in May 1960, 'Empire into Commonwealth'.

By then, Hugh Gaitskell had launched his attack on Clause 4 of the Labour Party constitution. In the general election on 8 October 1959, Labour lost 19 seats, falling to 258 MPs in the House of Commons, with Harold Macmillan holding a majority of 100 seats. Gaitskell sought to reform the party, signalling his intent at the party conference at Blackpool in November 1959. At this time, Clause IV part 4 of the constitution actually stated:

> To secure for the workers by hand or by brain the full fruits of their industry and the control and the most equitable distribution thereof that may be possible, upon the basis of the common ownership of the means of production, distribution, and exchange, and the best obtainable system of popular administration and control of each industry or service.[14]

Attlee was not surprised when Gaitskell failed. He was attached to the old Clause IV – striving for the good of the community over and above the profit motive. His career was in many ways reflective of the Labour Party's attachment to nationalization. In the early 1930s, he had argued for common ownership against the national government, and he was the prime minister of a government that took a number of industries into public ownership and control. The problem was that Attlee, as so many others within the party, saw common ownership as the solution to the ills of capitalism and, when common ownership did not prove to be a panacea, the party struggled to find a coherent voice. But on this front Attlee was no guiltier than any other Labour politician of his generation.

Attlee was very ill in the later part of 1961, in fact so ill that Hugh Gaitskell prepared a tribute for him in the event of his death.[15] Violet sent a cautious letter to Gaitskell on 9 December from Amersham General Hospital: 'All one can really say is that Clem is holding his own.'[16] By 11 December Gaitskell was gratefully able to note that he was 'so terribly pleased that according to the latest news it does not seem that these arrangements will be necessary'.[17] By 1962 Attlee was well enough to visit Moscow and India, by which time Macmillan's government was losing its way. Macmillan subsequently resigned on 18 October 1963, to be replaced by Alec Douglas-Home, who restricted the Labour majority to just four in the general election of October 1964. Attlee, despite being over 80 years old, spoke in the campaign. By now, Harold Wilson was leader of the party; Gaitskell had died on 18 January 1963. With such a small majority, another election was inevitable and Wilson called it on 31 March 1966. Labour won comfortably, with a majority of close to 100.

Attlee's eightieth birthday was celebrated at the eve-of-conference rally on 29 September 1963 in Scarborough. Harold Wilson, Fred Hayday and Willie Brandt all spoke. His final years became very lonely when Violet died in June 1964 and he moved into a flat in central London with a manservant. Though physically weakening, he made it to Churchill's funeral in 1965. His political interest remained and he was vigorously opposed to Britain joining what was then the European Economic Community. Attlee remained a strong British patriot to the end. He also wrote to *The Times* on 11 April 1967 to reinforce the need to settle international disputes by peaceful means.[18] He suffered a stroke in late 1966 and, on 21 September 1967, his old parliamentary seat of Walthamstow West fell to the Conservatives in a by-election. He died in his sleep on 8 October 1967.

His funeral was held on 11 October at the Temple Church and his ashes buried on 7 November at Westminster Abbey. Attlee himself chose the psalm, lesson and hymns, including *I Vow to Thee My Country*.[19] Attlee's 'Orders and Decorations' were carried by Charles Griffiths, his erstwhile batman. On 13 October 1967 the Attlee Memorial Appeal was launched, with Lord Longford as chairman of the trustees. By April 1970 over £400,000 had been raised, and a community drugs project had been set up in Camberwell.[20] On 18 November 1971 the queen opened Attlee House in the grounds of Toynbee Hall, which housed a project to take in young people from 'disturbed backgrounds' to become 'useful citizens'.[21] The government of India provided stone, Pakistan a carpet for the Attlee Memorial Room, with furniture for that room from Ceylon and New Zealand.[22] Attlee would have warmly approved.

CONCLUSION

Clement Attlee bestrides the twentieth-century history of the Labour Party. Its greatest constructive achievements are his government's achievements. The British welfare state, including the National Health Service, the nationalizations, independence for India, and the Atlanticism of his government's foreign policy were all central pillars of British politics for many years after his government left office. His government's great legacy was the so-called 'postwar consensus' – the acceptance of the same central policy framework of a mixed economy and maintenance of high employment. His government sits among three peace-time administrations during the twentieth century that unquestionably changed the British political landscape. Alongside the Liberal government of 1905–15, his government represented the high point of progressive reform; only Margaret Thatcher's government of 1979–90 could argue from the right that it had truly changed society. In doing so, it reintroduced what Attlee's government had sought to minimize the effect of – the profit motive, through lower taxes and free markets, encompassing privatization and a reduction in trade union power.

Criticism of the 1945–51 Labour government has centred on two themes – whether it was too left wing or simply not left wing enough. Correlli Barnett leads the right-wing attack, commenting that the 'dream turned to a dank reality of a segregated, subliterate, unskilled, unhealthy and institutionalized proletariat hanging on the nipple of state materialism'.[1] From the other side of the political spectrum, the Marxist historian Ralph Miliband, father of David and Ed, has argued that the Attlee government simply did not do enough to create a socialist society: 'From the beginning the nationalization proposals of the Government were designed to achieve the sole purpose of improving the efficiency of a capitalist economy.'[2] These criticisms are, however, about political *direction*, not about the failure to carry out manifesto commitements.

As with all holders of high office, Attlee needed not just great talent, but significant luck. He was unquestionably a student of high ability. Contrary to popular belief, he was an outstanding pupil at Haileybury and held the rare distinction of being a prefect without excelling at sport. He read history at University College, Oxford and, despite studying for the Bar, was from a rich enough background to be able to choose to do what he wanted rather than having to work to earn money. He found socialism in the East End, but came from a family with a history of social work. He served his country bravely in the First World War and found himself in a great position to find a parliamentary seat: in Mile End, he was just the type of respectable pro-war middle-class army major that the Labour Party needed if it were to be taken seriously as a contender for government.

He gained ministerial experience in both Labour governments in interwar Britain and his work in ensuring that local authorities played a significant part in electricity provision, together with his place on the Simon Commission, proved excellent preparation for two major issues his government faced – nationalization and Indian independence. He was incredibly lucky in 1931, surviving as an MP by just 551 votes. Had he lost his seat, he would never have been Labour prime minister. As it was, he became part of a leadership triumvirate along with George Lansbury and Stafford Cripps, both of whom – for very different reasons – lacked long-term leadership potential. During the Second World War he grew into an effective manager of government business and proved to be an able administrator. He flourished as dominions secretary and deputy prime minister. But in no other 20-year period in the twentieth century would Attlee have survived as Labour leader. When he became leader in 1935, it was not with any expectation that he would become prime minister. When he fought the 1945 general election, the Labour landslide came as a surprise to many people. Even in victory, moves were afoot to try to find a replacement prime minister. The advantage he had, however, was incumbency. He was the man available to take the king's commission and he made this advantage tell. Also, as in the sterling crisis of 1947, he was buttressed by not just Ernest Bevin, but the rivalry between Bevin and Herbert Morrison. Had the two men ever agreed on *one* successor to Attlee, he would not have survived. Yet he was much more than a leader by default.

'Greatness' is a notoriously nebulous concept. *The Times* obituary of Attlee on 9 October 1967 declared him a 'successful if not a great Prime Minister', but it is not abundantly clear what the difference is. He was certainly not what would be understood by a 'celebrity' in the modern sense, and he did not thrive on public attention. Tony Benn recalled putting together a Labour Party political broadcast at Walthamstow town hall in the early 1950s. Knowing how laconic Attlee was, 15 questions had been drafted for a 15-minute slot to ensure that he filled the time. In the event, he rattled through all the questions within 13 minutes and the final, desperate question, 'Mr Attlee, gold and dollar reserves are lower now than when you became Prime Minister' did not yield the expected attack on the Conservative government, Attlee merely commenting: 'That may very well be so.'[3] Yet 'greatness' can come from great deeds, of which his government had a number, or from the ability to bring the best out of other great people, something Attlee accomplished for a significant period during his premiership. The historian Robert Pearce, writing in 1999, asked 'Who, for instance, would be best suited to presiding over an all-time, all-star Labour Cabinet? The answer is surely ... Attlee. Who else would survive such a titanic clash of principles, strategies and personalities ... who else would be likely to emerge with any agreed policies?'[4]

To understand Attlee and his leadership in the context of the other Labour prime ministers is difficult. At the time of writing, there have only been six – Ramsay MacDonald, Attlee, Harold Wilson, James Callaghan, Tony Blair and Gordon Brown. American political scholars often talk of the 'small N' problem in studies of US presidents: with only 45 to consider, there is a sparsity of evidence. With Labour prime ministers this problem is all the more acute. An obvious comparison is with Tony Blair, whose leadership also had many successes. Blair governed for ten years, a record matched by few prime ministers, let alone Labour ones. Over the past 100 years only Margaret Thatcher has lasted longer in Number 10. Blair was also a great election winner. Unlike Wilson, who won four times but only once with a majority of more than single figures, Blair secured two landslides in 1997 and 2001, and a further term with a comfortable majority of 70 in 2005. Blair presided over a period of growth and low inflation, invested in and reformed public services, and fought three wars on foreign soil – in Kosovo, Afghanistan and Iraq with the final one now widely criticised. His government also produced the widest swathe of constitutional reform, probably since the Glorious Revolution of 1688. Attlee would no doubt have approved of the national minimum wage.

Like Attlee, Blair is a product of public school, Fettes in Edinburgh. As leaders, however, Attlee and Blair were very different. Blair's early years were marked by a tendency towards central control. Famously, all ministerial speeches had to be cleared through Number 10 Downing Street. Attlee was a polar opposite, with his emphasis on the prime minister as a facilitator in decision-making. He saw efficiently-run committees as effective decision-making bodies. This contrasts with the Blair conception of a centralized Number 10, plus, in his later terms, a strong supporting 'Delivery Unit' driving policy through. Gordon Brown, who so dominated his government's economic policy response to the financial crisis of 2007–2008, is also in a different category from Attlee.

When Richard Crossman's *Diaries of a Cabinet Minister* covering the Wilson premiership of 1964–70 appeared from 1975, they painted a picture of prime ministerial dominance that gave the lie to the constitutionally-accepted doctrine of cabinet government. But Attlee's leadership style was not totally unique. James Callaghan held numerous cabinet meetings during the economic crisis of 1976, which ended with a loan from the International Monetary Fund to stabilize the British economy. On the Conservative side, Attlee's closest comparators probably include Stanley Baldwin, whose leadership was characterized by his biographer Philip Williamson as a 'matter of coordination, arbitration, and trouble-shooting'.[5] Just as Attlee was a reaction against MacDonald's personal style of leadership, so Baldwin was a reaction against the dominating, 'presidential' style of Lloyd George.

Above all, Attlee was authentic. Churchill's comment that he was a 'sheep in sheep's clothing' was revealing. He could compartmentalize – a key quality when prime minister, as a variety of different issues came across his desk demanding instant responses. Because of the way government records are organized in the Public Record Office – essentially by subject – it is too easy to see government as dealing with a series of policies in isolation. The prime minister has to deal simultaneously with issues across the board: in the summer of 1947, when Attlee was receiving the plaudits for Indian independence, his government was dealing with an economic crisis, seeking a compromise on the nationalization of iron and steel and negotiating Marshall aid.[7] When his brother Tom was a conscientious objector in the First World War, Attlee never let it damage his relationship with him, and this ability to be objective – he would no doubt claim it was a product of his public school education – was also critical to his success. When Cripps remarked to Dalton in September 1947 that he had taken his suggestion that he stand aside well, it was not just an indication that Attlee had manipulated Cripps into accepting the role of minister for economic affairs: Attlee had to have a constructive relationship with Cripps as the new chancellor from November 1947. Attlee was also a patriot. The Labour Party has often had its patriotism questioned. From its historic pacifism, embodied in the likes of MacDonald and Lansbury, to unilateral nuclear disarmament, and Margaret Thatcher famously dubbing Arthur Scargill and other militant trade union leaders the 'enemy within' working to subvert British society, the party has allowed itself to be portrayed as somehow anti-British. Attlee personified Britishness – understated, unemotional in public, practical, unfussy and with a deep pride in his country and its history.

Yet – as with all political leaders – Attlee's leadership style had its limitations as well as its strengths. If his greatness lay in getting the best out of other great people, the presumption is that there were *many* other great people within his cabinet. His management of Bevan in his negotiations with the British Medical Association showed him at his best; his trust in Shinwell over the advice of his civil servants on coal provision in the autumn of 1946 showed the weakness. His 'chairmanship' style of leaving matters in the hands of senior colleagues (or, at times, officials) was followed to the letter, even in times of crisis. Keynes was sent to Washington to negotiate the American loan in 1945; Wilfred Eady went in 1947 to suspend convertibility; and Cripps and Bevin went to deal with devaluation in 1949. His failure to meet Truman for five years between December 1945 and December 1950 was a reflection of this approach. It was not that he did not value the 'special relationship' but that he did not see it as the prime minister's role to personalize foreign affairs. His failure to understand the American president – or at times domestic American politics – was a major factor in failing to capitalize on the American involvement in Palestine that would surely have followed an agreement to allow 100,000 Jews into Palestine when there was an overwhelming moral argument to do so in 1945. In times of crisis, when colleagues looked to the top for leadership, little was forthcoming, which was a key factor in the plot to force him out in September 1947.

As with all political leaders, Attlee sometimes had to accept the inevitable. The general direction of Britain's postwar external relations, in terms of the special relationship with America and decolonization was made almost inevitable by Britain's financial dependence on the United States. Socialism at home came at a price abroad. Laski's proclamation of closeness to the Soviet Union in 1945 was a fantasy. However, there were other specific policy failures. The haste with which he left India came at a cost, particularly the decision to hold off the announcement of the Radcliffe partition line until after independence and the fate of Kashmir. It is most difficult to explain why certain issues but not others were chosen for what Philip Williamson terms 'troubleshooting'. He was, along with Cripps, the leading authority in the government on India, so there is little controversy there. Arguably, the issue of the development of a nuclear deterrent was by its nature top secret, particularly in its embryonic form. When he visited Truman to discuss the Korean War in December 1950, it was forced upon him as Bevin was too ill to fly. There were also political failures. The division in the party between Gaitskell and Bevan in March 1951, Bevan's resignation from the government, and the internal party strife that followed would seem an ideal dispute for the Attlee consensus – finding skills to work their magic. His failure to do so, which it has to be said was partly due to his being hospitalized during a key period, and to work harder on persuading

Hugh Gaitskell to find an alternative in relation to what was an insignificant amount of money, had far-reaching consequences. It was not a failure of his leadership style, but a failure to *apply* the style that had served him so well in the past: if Bevin and Morrison – or indeed Bevin and Bevan – could survive in government together for so long, why not Bevan and Gaitskell? Attlee's failure was to choose to make Gaitskell feel as if he was being managed and valued, rather than Bevan. Bevan did not *want* to resign; it was Gaitskell who offered no compromise. While Attlee cannot be held responsible for Bevan's behaviour thereafter, he can be held responsible for failing to find a compromise between the two men. In addition, holding a general election in October 1951 demonstrated Attlee's respect for the king, but was disadvantageous to the Labour Party. A delay – even of a few months – would have helped.

Would Attlee have succeeded as a leader in the modern day? The answer is probably not. It was not that he had no personality, but that he was slow to open up. As Lascelles put it: 'I find him excellent company when he thaws out; like most men with no natural presence, he seems to be fighting a continual rearguard action against his physical insignificance, but his mental stature is good enough.'[7] Attlee was too reserved, too unemotional in public and too formal to have survived the 24-hour media. He would have baulked at any intrusion into his family life and one cannot imagine him sitting at home with Violet and the children being filmed. Quite simply, he was what he was: a quieter chairman who for a significant period was able to read and manipulate others to the best advantage of the government. Perhaps the greatest lesson that the political life of Clement Attlee is this: if there is not a place for such a leader in modern politics, that may say more about the modern political system and media than it does about him.

NOTES

Preface

1. Roy Hattersley, *Guardian*, 31 July 2010, and Francis Beckett, *History Today*, 4 January 2011.
2. W. Golant, 'The Emergence of C. R. Attlee as Leader of the Parliamentary Labour Party in 1935.' *The Historical Journal*, vol. 13, no. 2, June 1970, pp. 318–32.
3. Philip Ziegler, *Spectator*, 31 July 2010.
4. 'The suggestion that he should have intervened personally in Kashmir when Mountbatten had failed to persuade the maharajah to accede either to India or Pakistan is frankly absurd.' Philip Ziegler, *Spectator*, 31 July 2010.

Introduction to the 2023 edition

1. Still available at: https://www.ipsos.com/en-uk/rating-british-prime-ministers.
2. Now Trafford General Hospital.
3. Francis Williams, *A Prime Minister Remembers* (London: William Heinemann Ltd, 1961), 83.
4. *The Times*, 15 June 1957.
5. Hansard, House of Commons, 23 October 1967, Volume 751 Column 1359.
6. *The Times*, 9 October 1967.
7. Clement Attlee, *As It Happened* (London: William Heinemann Ltd), 166.

Introduction

1. Kevin Theakston, 'Rating British Prime Ministers', IPSOS/MORI, available from <www.ipsos-mori.com/content/rating-british-prime-ministers1.ashx>, accessed 6 March 2009.
2. *The Times*, 9 October 1967.
3. Attlee produced a memorandum on the organization of government, which is reproduced in Kenneth Harris, *Attlee* (London: Weidenfeld & Nicolson, 1984) in Appendix 3, pp. 589–95, along with his autobiographical notes. Written in the 1930s, it was with a note dated 1948. This quotation is on p. 591.
4. Speech at Oxford, 14 June 1957, as quoted in Antony Jay (ed.) *The Oxford Dictionary of Political Quotations* (Oxford: Oxford University Press, 1996) p. 20.
5. Lord Morrison of Lambeth, *Herbert Morrison: An Autobiography* (London: Odhams Press Ltd, 1960) p. 295.
6. PREM 8/873, Memorandum by Attlee, 4 March 1948.
7. Letter to the author, 19 March 2009.
8. Just some examples of new material are from his Haileybury days, his involvement with the Stepney Boys' Club in London's East End, and the Indian Statutory Commission from 1927 to 1930.
9. Duff Hart-Davis (ed.) *King's Counsellor: Abdication and War – The Diaries of Sir Alan Lascelles* (London: Phoenix, 2007) p. 389, entry from 26 February 1946.

1. Growing Up in Victorian England, 1883–1901

1. 'Lineage', by 1st Earl Attlee, written for his daughter-in-law Anne, Countess Attlee (hereafter referred to as Lady Attlee) and in her possession.

2. A. N. Wilson, *The Victorians* (London: Hutchinson, 2002) pp. 442–3, quoting Mark Pattison.

3. Michael Kinnear, *The British Voter: An Atlas and Survey since 1885* (London: Batsford, 1968) p. 13, quoting N. Blewett.

4. 'Lineage', by 1st Earl Attlee.

5. Ibid.

6. Interview with Lady Attlee, 7 April 2009.

7. Harris, *Attlee*, p. 5.

8. The Rt. Hon. C. R. Attlee, 'The Pleasure of Books', *The National and English Review*, vol. 142, no. 851, January 1954, p. 17.

9. C. R. Attlee, *As It Happened* (London: Heinemann, 1954) p. 3.

10. 'Lineage', by 1st Earl Attlee.

11. Ibid.

12. Haileybury College Archive, Haileybury Admissions Book.

13. Extract from 'Haileybury Letter', 21 July 1905, in L. S. Milford, *Haileybury College: Past and Present* (London: T. Fisher Unwin, 1909).

14. Haileybury College Archive, Haileybury College, 'Blue Books', 1900–5, p. 12.

15. Attlee, *As It Happened*, p. 11.

16. Haileybury College Archive, Haileybury Records, 'The Shakespeare Society'.

17. Haileybury College Archive, Haileybury College Literary Society, third term of 1900, 384th meeting, 24 September. Attlee's name is at the top of a non-alphabetical list.

18. Stanley Mease Toyne, *History of the Haileybury College Debating Society* (Oxford: Blackwell, 1912) pp. 78–9. The coal tax debate was on 20 May 1900; professionalism in games was the topic on 7 October; state control of railways on 18 November, and press freedom on 9 December.

19. Haileybury College Archive, Lawrence House Records.

20. 'The Model Lance-Jack' author unknown, but with initials 'THEB' who attended a public school cadet corps camp at Aldershot with Attlee as lance corporal. The article was written after 1918, but has no precise date, and appears as a cutting in Bernard Attlee's scrapbook, now in the Attlee papers in Lady Attlee's possession.

21. Note from Lady Attlee to the author, 11 May 2009.

22. Interview with Lady Attlee, 7 April 2009.

23. Quoted in Harris, *Attlee*, p. 9.

24. Attlee, *As It Happened*, p. 12.

25. 'Lineage', by 1st Earl Attlee.

26. Haileybury College Archive, Lawrence House Records.

27. I am grateful to Haileybury's archivist, Mr Toby Parker, for pointing this out to me.

28. C. R. Attlee, *Early Poems*. Attlee brought out an edition of his collected works to date, probably soon after the First World War. A copy of this is in the possession of Lady Attlee. She made a later edition of the same poems herself to save the need to handle the fragile original. A copy of that edition is also in Lady Attlee's possession. Letter from Lady Attlee to the author, 8 June 2009.

2. From Oxford to the East End, 1901–14

1. Attlee, *As It Happened*, p. 14.

2. Ibid., p. 15.

3. Ibid., p. 15.

4. Ibid., pp. 15–16.

5. Hubert Picarda, 'Stick to a Stuff-Gown', in Theobald Mathew, *Forensic Fables by O* (London: Butterworths, 1961) p. vii.
6. Attlee, *As It Happened*, p. 17.
7. Picarda, 'Stick to a Stuff-Gown', p. viii.
8. Attlee, *As It Happened*, p. 17.
9. Picarda, 'Stick to a Stuff-Gown', p. viii.
10. Attlee, *As It Happened*, p. 17.
11. Ibid., p. 24.
12. Interview with Lady Attlee, 7 April 2009.
13. Attlee, *As It Happened*, p. 18.
14. Ibid., p. 19.
15. Ibid., p. 20.
16. Haileybury College Archive, 'Haileybury Stepney Boys Club Minute Books', meeting of 2 August 1907.
17. Ibid., meeting of 7 December 1907.
18. Attlee, *As It Happened*, p. 20.
19. Ibid., p. 21.
20. Attlee, *Early Poems*.
21. Ibid.
22. For example, see *The Haileyburian*, vol. 17, June 1908–March 1911 (Hertford: Simson Company Ltd, 1911) p. 617.
23. Haileybury College Archive, letter from Attlee to members of the Haileybury Club, 8 August 1945.
24. Haileybury College Archive, Haileybury Guild Council, The Haileybury Guild Stepney Boys Club Minute Books (Haileybury, 1965).
25. Attlee, *As It Happened*, p. 24.
26. And those, like the Local Government Board, which argued in favour of maintaining the system as it stood.
27. John Grigg, *Lloyd George: The People's Champion 1902–1911* (London: Penguin Books, 2002) pp. 325–6.
28. Ibid., p. 315.
29. David Marquand, *Ramsay MacDonald* (London: Jonathan Cape Ltd, 1977) pp. 140–1. In using the word 'simplified' Marquand was quoting from 'From Green Benches', *Leicester Pioneer*, 20 May 1911, footnote 18.
30. Marquand, *MacDonald*, p. 138.
31. Attlee, *As It Happened*, p. 31.
32. Ibid., p. 32.
33. Ibid., p. 36.

3. The First World War, 1914–18

1. Interview with Lady Attlee, 7 April 2009.
2. John Shepherd, *George Lansbury: At the Heart of Old Labour* (Oxford: Oxford University Press, 2004) pp. 159–60.
3. 'Experiences on Active Service: September 1914 to June 1916 in training, Gallipoli, Egypt and Mesopotamia', by Captain C. R. Attlee, 6 South Lancashires, 38th Brigade, 13th Division. Often referred to as Attlee's 'War Diary', this has been transcribed by Lady Attlee.
4. 'Experiences on Active Service' by Captain C. R. Attlee.

5. Attlee's 'Experiences on Active Service' fell into two parts, both probably written when he was in hospital – the first part when he was wounded in 1916 and the second when he was injured in 1918. Letter from Lady Attlee to the author, 8 June 2009.

6. Attlee, *Early Poems*.

7. Roy Jenkins, *Churchill* (London: Macmillan, 2001) p. 255. Churchill had also considered the invasion of Schelswig-Holstein to enable Denmark to join the war on the Allied side.

8. Attlee, *Early Poems*.

9. Peter Simkins, Geoffrey Jukes and Michael Hickey, *The First World War: The War to End All Wars* (Oxford: Osprey Publishing, 2003) p. 297.

10. 'Experiences on Active Service' by Captain C. R. Attlee.

11. Ibid.

12. C. R. Attlee papers. Letters from Clement Attlee to his brother Tom ('Letters to Tom') August 1915 to August 1960: Mb.Eng.C.4792 (August 1915–October 1939) Mb.Eng. C.4793 (January 1940–December 1949) and Mb.Eng.C.4794 (March 1950–August 1960).

13. Simkins et al., *First World War*, p. 300.

14. Attlee, *As It Happened*, p. 41.

15. Simkins et al., *First World War*, p. 298.

16. Jenkins, *Churchill*, p. 261.

17. C. R. Attlee papers, 'Letters to Tom'.

18. 'Experiences on Active Service: 1916 to 1919' by Major Attlee. This forms the second part of Attlee's 'War Diary' and is based on his service in Europe; it ends with his discharge from hospital in 1919. It has been transcribed by Lady Attlee.

19. Attlee, *As It Happened*, p. 43.

20. C. R. Attlee papers, 'Letters to Tom'.

21. Ibid.

22. Ibid.

23. Ibid.

24. Ibid.

25. As quoted in Harris, *Attlee*, p. 39.

26. C. R. Attlee papers, 'Letters to Tom'.

4. The Political Apprenticeship, 1918–22

1. Attlee, *As It Happened*, p. 47.

2. Ibid., p. 46.

3. Ibid.

4. Harris, *Attlee*, p. 43.

5. Ibid., p. 47.

6. Attlee, *As It Happened*, p. 50.

7. Ibid.

8. Clement Attlee, *The Social Worker* (London: G. Bell & Sons Limited, 1920) pp. 5–6.

9. Clement Attlee, 'Borough Councils: Their Constitution, Powers and Duties', *Fabian Tract*, no. 191 (London: The Fabian Society, 1920) p. 15.

10. Ibid., p. 14.

11. C. Northcote Parkinson, *Parkinson's Law* (London: Penguin Classics, 2002) p. 60.

12. Attlee, *Early Poems*.

13. Attlee, *As It Happened*, p. 51.

14. Harris, *Attlee*, p. 51.

15. Geoffrey Dellar (ed.) *Attlee As I Knew Him* (London: London Borough of Tower Hamlets Directorate of Community Services, Library Service, 1983). Contribution of Anne Attlee, p. 64.
16. Interview with Lady Attlee, 7 April 2009.
17. Interview with Tony Benn, 26 April 2009.
18. Attlee, *As It Happened*, p. 52.

5. A New Member of Parliament, 1922–24

1. Attlee, *As It Happened*, p. 57.
2. Hansard, HC 1922, vol. 159 (20 November–15 December) column 93, 96, 23 November 1922.
3. Hansard, HC 1923, vol. 160 (13 February–2 March) column 1713–14, 27 February 1923.
4. Hansard, HC 1923, vol. 161 (5–23 March) column 2373, 20 March 1923.
5. Hansard, HC 1923, vol. 160 (13 February–2 March) column 303, 15 February 1923.
6. Hansard, HC 1923, vol. 160 (13 February–2 March) columns 2087–93, 28 February 1923.
7. Hansard, HC 1923, vol. 161 (5–23 March) column 15, 5 March 1923.
8. Hansard, HC 1923, vol. 161 (5–23 March) column 459, 7 March 1923.
9. Hansard, HC 1923, vol. 161 (5–23 March) column 1595, 14 March 1923.
10. Hansard, HC 1923, vol. 161 (5–23 March) column 1897, 15 March 1923.
11. Hansard, HC 1923, vol. 161 (5–23 March) column 1898, 15 March 1923.
12. Hansard, HC 1923, vol. 161 (5–23 March) columns 482–3, 7 March 1923.
13. Hansard, HC 1923, vol. 161 (5–23 March) column 300, 6 March 1923.
14. David Butler and Gareth Butler, *Twentieth-Century British Political Facts 1900–2000* (London: Macmillan, 2000) p. 400.
15. Labour Party, *Report of the 23rd Annual Conference* (London: Labour Party, 1923) p. 232.
16. Ibid.
17. Hansard, HC 1923, vol. 166 (2–20 July) columns 128–9, 2 July 1923.
18. Hansard, HC 1923, vol. 166 (2–20 July) column 2086, 17 July 1923.
19. Hansard, HC 1923, vol. 167 (23 July–2 August) columns 437–8, 25 July 1923.
20. As quoted in Marquand, *Ramsay MacDonald*, p. 299.
21. Attlee, *As It Happened*, pp. 60–1.
22. Attlee, *As It Happened*, p. 61.
23. Hansard, HC 1924, vol. 171 (17 March–4 April) column 111, 17 March 1924.
24. Hansard, HC 1924, vol. 171 (17 March–4 April) column 114, 17 March 1924.
25. Hansard, HC 1924, vol. 170 (25 February–14 March) column 2712–13, 13 March 1924.
26. Hansard, HC 1924, vol. 171 (17 March–4 April) columns 2367–8, 2 April 1924.
27. Hansard, HC 1924, vol. 175 (23 June–11 July) column 1948, 8 July 1924.
28. Colin Cross, *Philip Snowden* (London: Barrie & Rockliff, 1966) p. 207.

6. Opposition and Indian Affairs, 1924–30

1. Hansard, HC 1925, vol. 181 (2–20 March) column 1924, 16 March 1925.
2. Hansard, HC 1925, vol. 185 (15 June–3 July) column 2963, 3 July 1925.
3. Hansard, HC 1925, vol. 188 (16 November–4 December) columns 1007–8, 23 November 1925.
4. Hansard, HC 1925, vol. 188 (16 November–4 December) column 1941, 30 November 1925.
5. Attlee, *As It Happened*, p. 55.
6. Hansard, HC 1925, vol. 180 (10–27 February) columns 2074–5, 25 July 1925.
7. Hansard, HC 1925, vol. 181 (2–20 March) column 178, 2 March 1925.

8. Hansard, HC 1925, vol. 183 (28 April–15 May) columns 2183–5, 14 May 1925.
9. Hansard, HC 1925, vol. 184 (18 May– 2 June) columns 769–70, 21 May 1925.
10. Attlee, *As It Happened*, p. 55.
11. Hansard, HC 1926, vol. 192 (22 February–12 March) column 167, 22 February 1926.
12. Hansard, HC 1926, vol. 193 (15 March–1 April) column 1324, 24 March 1926.
13. Hansard, HC 1926, vol. 193 (15 March–1 April) column 1795, 26 March 1926.
14. Hansard, HC 1926, vol. 199 (30 August–19 November) column 1441, 12 November 1926.
15. Hansard, HC 1927, vol. 207 (30 May–24 June) column 259, 31 May 1927.
16. Hansard, HC 1927, vol. 211 (28 November–16 December) columns 1924–5, 12 December 1927.
17. C. R. Attlee papers, 'Letters to Tom'.
18. Ibid.
19. Ibid.
20. Ibid.
21. Ibid.
22. India Office Records, Indian Statutory Commission: The Simon Commission. This consists of a series of 89 blue folders (except Q/ISC/89) containing additional files loose together with 42 bound volumes of evidence and memoranda – being catalogued by Mr John O'Brien at the India Records Office (Q/ISC/46). Note by Major Attlee on the Indian states, 10 April 1929.
23. India Office Records, Q/ISC/46. 'Note on the Central Government and the Problem of Federation'.
24. India Office Records, Q/ISC/44. 'Note on action in emergency by the Central Government by Major Attlee'.
25. India Office Records, Q/ISC/44. 'Note on normative by the Central Government by Major Attlee'.
26. Ibid.
27. Ibid.
28. India Office Records, Q/ISC/67 S.C./J.S. 61. 'Further memorandum by Major Attlee on the Central Government, 13 February 1930'.
29. India Office Records, Q/ISC/67. 'The Future of the Central Government: note on Major Attlee's further memorandum of the 13th February 1930'.
30. Ibid.
31. India Office Records, Q/ISC/82. 'Draft by Major Attlee on Provincial Re-distribution (vol. 2 of the Commission's Report) 22 November 1929'.
32. India Office Records, Q/ISC/82: D–7. 'Draft by Major Attlee on the North West Frontier Province (Part III of vol. 2 of the Commission's Report) 22 November 1929'.
33. India Office Records, Q/ISC/44. 'Note on the methods of election to Provincial Legislative Councils by Major Attlee, 23 July 1929'.
34. Ibid.
35. Ibid.
36. Ibid.
37. India Office Records, Q/ISC/44. 'Memorandum of the electoral system for Provincial Councils by Major Attlee, 19 September 1929'.
38. Ibid.
39. India Office Records, Q/ISC/46. 'Note by Major Attlee on the Indian States, 10 April 1929'.

40. Andrew Roberts, 'The Holy Fox': The Life of Lord Halifax (London: Phoenix, 2004) p. 25.
41. Labour Party, Report of the 31st Annual Conference (London: Labour Party, 1931) p. 216.

7. In Government, 1930–31

1. Attlee, As It Happened, p. 66.
2. Ibid., p. 58.
3. Hansard, HC 1929–30, vol. 232 (18 November–6 December) column 2416–17, 4 December 1929.
4. Butler and Butler, Twentieth-Century British Political Facts, p. 400.
5. Ross McKibbin, 'The Economic Policy of the Second Labour Government,' in Ross McKibbin, The Ideologies of Class: Social Relations in Britain, 1880–1950 (Oxford: Clarendon Press, 1994) pp. 197–228.
6. C. R. Attlee papers, 'Letters to Tom'.
7. Memorandum provided in Harris, Attlee, pp. 570–84; this extract is from p. 583.
8. C. R. Attlee papers, 'Letters to Tom'.
9. Hansard, HC 1930–31, vol. 244 (23 October–14 November) column 628, 3 November 1930.
10. Ibid.
11. C. R. Attlee papers, 'Letters to Tom'.
12. Hansard, HC 1929–30, vol. 235 (10–28 February) column 1786, 21 February 1930.
13. Hansard, HC 1930–31, vol. 245 (17 November–5 December) column 331, 18 November 1930.
14. Hansard, HC 1930–31, vol. 249 (2–20 March) column 2229, 19 March 1931.
15. Hansard, HC 1930–31, vol. 251 (14 April–1 May) column 882, 21 March 1931.
16. Hansard, HC 1930–31, vol. 255 (13–31 July) columns 2629–30, 31 July 1931.
17. Attlee, As It Happened, p. 71.
18. C. R. Attlee papers, 'Letters to Tom'.
19. As set out in the Report of the 31st Annual Conference (London: Labour Party, 1931) p. 5.
20. C. R. Attlee papers, 'Letters to Tom'.
21. Attlee, As It Happened, p. 72.

8. Back in Opposition, 1931–35

1. Hansard, HC 1930–31, vol. 257 (28 September–7 October) columns 705–6, 2 October 1931.
2. Labour Party, Report of the 31st Annual Conference (London: Labour Party, 1931) p. 3.
3. Attlee, As It Happened, p. 75.
4. Ibid., p. 77.
5. Henry Pelling, A Short History of the Labour Party (London: Macmillan & Company Ltd, 1962) p. 75.
6. Hansard, HC 1932–33, vol. 273 (12–22 December) columns 707–8, 16 December 1932.
7. Jack Lawson, 'The Rt. Hon. Clement Attlee, CH, MP, Prime Minister', 15-page typed manuscript in the possession of Lady Attlee.
8. Hansard, HC 1931–32, vol. 259 (3–20 November) columns 121–7, 11 November 1931.
9. C. R. Attlee papers, 'Letters to Tom'.
10. Ibid.
11. Hansard, HC 1931–32, vol. 260 (23 November–11 December) column 103, 23 November 1931.
12. Hansard, HC 1931–32, vol. 260 (23 November–11 December) column 416, 25 November 1931.

13. Hansard, HC 1931–32, vol. 260 (23 November–11 December) column 1118, 2 December 1931.
14. C. R. Attlee papers, 'Letters to Tom'.
15. Attlee, *As It Happened*, p. 77.
16. Hansard, HC 1931–32, vol. 261 (2–19 February) column 301, 4 February 1932.
17. Hansard, HC 1931–32, vol. 264 (5–22 April) column 1495, 20 April 1932.
18. C. R. Attlee papers, 'Letters to Tom'.
19. Hansard, HC 1931–32, vol. 265 (25 April–13 May) column 1681, 9 May 1932.
20. C. R. Attlee papers, 'Letters to Tom'.
21. Labour Party, *Report of the 32nd Annual Conference* (London: Labour Party, 1932) p. 167.
22. C. R. Attlee papers, 'Letters to Tom'.
23. Hansard, HC 1931–32, vol. 270 (7–17 November) columns 143–4, 7 November 1932.
24. Hansard, HC 1932–33, vol. 272 (22 November–9 December) columns 369–70, 25 November 1932.
25. Hansard, HC 1932–33, vol. 272 (22 November–9 December) column 1006, 1 December 1932.
26. C. R. Attlee papers, 'Letters to Tom'.
27. Hansard, HC 1932–33, vol. 274 (7–24 February) column 1302, 16 February 1933.
28. Hansard, HC 1932–33, vol. 277 (25 March–12 May) column 108, 26 April 1933.
29. Hansard, HC 1932–33, vol. 276 (20 March–13 April) column 2739–48, 13 April 1933.
30. Hansard, HC 1932–33, vol. 281 (7–17 November) columns 146–7, 7 November 1933.
31. Labour Party, *Report of the 33rd Annual Conference* (London: Labour Party, 1933) p. 162.
32. Hansard, HC 1933–34, vol. 286 (29 January–16 February) column 1067–8, 27 February 1934.
33. Hansard, HC 1933–34, vol. 288 (9–27 April) columns 929–30, 17 April 1934.
34. Hansard, HC 1933–34, vol. 289 (30 April–18 May) column 1723, 15 May 1934.
35. Hansard, HC 1933–34, vol. 290 (29 May–15 June) columns 958–62, 6 June 1934.
36. Hansard, HC 1933–34, vol. 290 (29 May–15 June) columns 1927–35, 14 June 1934.
37. Hansard, HC 1933–34, vol. 288 (9–27 April) column 850, 16 April 1934.
38. Hansard, HC 1933–34, vol. 293 (30 October–16 November) column 129, 30 October 1934.
39. Hansard, HC 1933–34, vol. 286 (29 January–16 February) column 2048, 8 March 1934.
40. Hansard, HC 1933–34, vol. 287 (12–29 March) column 470, 14 March 1934.
41. G. D. H. Cole, *A History of the Labour Party from 1914* (London: Routledge & Kegan Paul Ltd, 1948) p. 322.
42. Hansard, HC 1933–34, vol. 292 (9–31 July) column 686, 13 July 1934.
43. Though, in contrast, the 1930 London Naval Treaty had not been renewed, leaving Japan free to engage in building major ships from 1 January 1938.
44. Labour Party, *Report of the 34th Annual Conference* (London: Labour Party, 1934) p. 190.
45. Labour Party, *Report of the 35th Annual Conference* (London: Labour Party, 1935) p. 153.
46. Ibid., p. 173.
47. Ibid., p. 175.
48. Ibid., p. 177.
49. Ibid., p. 178.
50. Ibid., p. 180.
51. Iain Dale (ed.) *Labour Party General Election Manifestos, 1900–1997* (London: Routledge and Politico's Publishing, 2000) p. 45.
52. Ibid., p. 47.

53. Attlee, *As It Happened*, p. 80.
54. Harris, *Attlee*, p. 92.
55. C. R. Attlee papers, 'Letters to Tom'.
56. Ibid. Letters of 15 July 1932, 13 January 1933 and 3 April 1933.
57. Ibid. Letter of 18 October 1934.
58. Ibid. Letter of 20 April 1935.
59. Ibid. Letter of 8 August 1932 detailing a picnic in Norfolk.
60. Harris, *Attlee*, p. 110.
61. C. R. Attlee papers, 'Letters to Tom', letter of 26 October 1936.
62. Attlee, *As It Happened*, p. 81; Morrison presents the results slightly differently, giving Greenwood 33 votes on the first ballot and noting that on the second ballot 'all but four of Greenwood's supporters voted for Attlee' (Morrison, *An Autobiography*, p. 164). This concurs with Hugh Dalton's recollection of the numbers: Attlee 58, Morrison 44 and Greenwood 33 on the first ballot.
63. At the Bodleian Library, Oxford.
64. Morrison, *An Autobiography*, p. 164.
65. Hugh Dalton, *The Fateful Years: Memoirs, 1931–1945* (London: Frederick Muller Ltd, 1957) p. 82.
66. Ibid.
67. Ibid.
68. Ibid.
69. Harris, *Attlee*, p. 122. See also Bernard Donoughue and G. W. Jones, *Herbert Morrison: Portrait of a Politician* (London: Phoenix Press, 2001) pp. 238–43.
70. Morrison, *An Autobiography*, p. 164.
71. As quoted in Dalton, *The Fateful Years*, p. 82.
72. Morrison, *An Autobiography*, p. 164.

9. Labour Leadership, 1935–39

1. Poem in a collection of satirical verses by C. R. Attlee and others in the possession of Lady Attlee.
2. Attlee, *As It Happened*, p. 99.
3. Ben Pimlott, *Hugh Dalton* (London: Harper Collins, 1995) pp. 263–4.
4. Ibid., p. 264.
5. John Swift, *Labour in Crisis: Clement Attlee and the Labour Party in Opposition, 1931–40* (Basingstoke: Palgrave, 2001) pp. 160–1.
6. Matthew Worley, *Labour Inside the Gate: A History of the British Labour Party between the Wars* (London: I.B.Tauris & Co. Ltd, 2005) p. 170.
7. Butler and Butler, *Twentieth-Century British Political Facts*, p. 265.
8. Clement Attlee, *The Betrayal of Collective Security: 'National' Government's Surrender to Mussolini* (London: The Labour Publications Department, 1936) p. 7.
9. Morrison, *An Autobiography*, p. 165.
10. Labour Party, *Report of the 36th Annual Conference* (London: Labour Party, 1936) p. 182.
11. Ibid., p. 182.
12. Ibid., p. 186.
13. Ibid., p. 196.
14. Ibid., p. 204.
15. Ibid., p. 201.
16. Ibid., p. 201.

17. Ibid., p. 206.
18. Ibid., p. 207.
19. Attlee, *As It Happened*, p. 86.
20. Clement Attlee, *Labour Shows the Way: The Will and the Way to Socialism* (London: Methuen & Co. Ltd, 1935) pp. 54–5.
21. Ibid., pp. 54–84.
22. Ibid., p. 91.
23. Clement Attlee, *The Labour Party in Perspective* (London: Victor Gollancz Ltd, 1937) pp. 7–8.
24. Ibid., p. 286.
25. Ibid., p. 286.
26. Labour Party, *Report of the 37th Annual Conference* (London: Labour Party, 1937) p. 216.
27. Poem in a collection of satirical verses by C. R. Attlee and others in the possession of Lady Attlee.
28. Harris, *Attlee*, pp. 156–7.

10. From Opposition to Government, 1939–42

1. Attlee, *As It Happened*, p. 105.
2. Ibid.
3. Clement Attlee, *Labour's Peace Aims* (London: Peace Book Company (London) Ltd, 1940) pp. 12–13.
4. Edwards sat as a Conservative after 1948.
5. Ben Pimlott (ed.) *The Political Diary of Hugh Dalton, 1918–40, 1945–60* (London: Jonathan Cape in association with the London School of Economics and Political Science, 1986) p. 312.
6. Ibid., p. 312.
7. Ibid., p. 296. Maurice Webb, then a *Daily Herald* journalist but later a Labour MP, told Dalton about Greenwood's thinking.
8. Pimlott, *The Political Diary of Hugh Dalton*, p. 296.
9. Ibid., p. 312.
10. Attlee, *As It Happened*, p. 107.
11. Ibid., p. 110.
12. Jeanne MacKenzie and Norman MacKenzie (eds) *The Diary of Beatrice Webb*, vol. 4, *1924–1943, The Wheel of Life* (London: Virago in association with the London School of Economics and Political Science, 1984) p. 451.
13. Ibid., pp. 447–8.
14. Pimlott, *The Political Diary of Hugh Dalton*, pp. 343–4.
15. As quoted in Jenkins, *Churchill*, p. 576.
16. Roberts, *The Holy Fox*, p. 145.
17. Winston Churchill, *The Second World War*, vol. 1, *Gathering Storm* (London: Penguin Classics, 2005) p. 597.
18. Ibid.
19. Ibid.
20. Roberts, *The Holy Fox*, p. 203.
21. The historian Martin Gilbert, *Second World War* (London: Phoenix Press, 2000) p. 63 wrote: 'On the Western Front, the German commanders had vied with each other during May 11 on how far they could advance.'
22. Labour Party, *Report of the 39th Annual Conference* (London: Labour Party, 1940) p. 125.

23. Ibid., p. 134.

24. Pimlott, *The Political Diary of Hugh Dalton*, p. 348.

25. MacKenzie and MacKenzie, *The Diary of Beatrice Webb*, p. 451.

26. Ben Pimlott (ed.) *The Second World War Diary of Hugh Dalton, 1940–45* (London: Jonathan Cape in association with the London School of Economics and Political Science 1986) p. 28.

27. Jenkins, *Churchill*, p. 607.

28. Roberts, *The Holy Fox*, p. 224.

29. Jenkins, *Churchill*, p. 601.

30. CAB 65/7, WM (40) 142nd Conclusions, Monday 27 May 1940, at 4.30 p.m.

31. CAB 65/7, WM (40) 144th Conclusions, Tuesday 28 May 1940, at 11.30 a.m.

32. Roberts, *The Holy Fox*, p. 224.

33. Attlee, *As It Happened*, p. 117.

34. David Cannadine (ed.) The *Speeches of Winston Churchill* (London: Penguin Books, 1990) p. 178.

35. CAB 127/206, Dalton to Attlee, 2 July 1940.

36. CAB 127/206, Dalton to Halifax, 2 July 1940.

37. CAB 127/206, Dalton to Attlee, 2 July 1940.

38. CAB 127/206, Note by Dalton, 16 August 1940.

39. Gilbert, *Second World War*, p. 117.

40. Ibid., pp. 120–1.

41. Air Ministry, AIR 16/690.

42. Ms. Eng. Attlee dep 1, fol 215.

43. Trades Union Congress, *Report of Proceedings of the 72nd Annual Trades Union Congress, held at Southport October 7th to 9th 1940* (London: Cooperative Printing Society Ltd, 1940) p. 271.

44. Pimlott, *The Second World War Diary of Hugh Dalton*, p. 64.

45. CAB 120/774, 'Chemical Warfare: Report by the Lord Privy Seal', 18 November 1940.

46. Pimlott, *The Second World War Diary of Hugh Dalton*, p. 96.

47. David Dilks (ed.) *The Diaries of Sir Alexander Cadogan, 1938–1945* (London: Cassell & Company Ltd, 1971) p. 334.

48. Interview with the Third Earl Attlee, 26 March 2009.

49. Dalton, *The Fateful Years*, p. 467.

50. C. R. Attlee papers, 'Letters to Tom'.

51. Ibid.

52. Ms. Eng. Attlee dep 2, fol 58.

53. Trades Union Congress, *Report of Proceedings of the 73rd Annual Trades Union Congress, held at Edinburgh September 1st to 4th 1941* (London: Cooperative Printing Society Ltd, 1941) p. 268.

54. CAB 117/1, Prime Minister's Minute: Study of Post-war Problems, 30 December 1940.

55. Hansard, HC 1940–41, vol. 368 (21 January–13 February) columns 264–5, 22 January 1941.

56. CAB 87/1, War Cabinet: Reconstruction Problems Committee, RP (41) 1st meeting, Thursday 6 March 1941, at 2.30 p.m.

57. Ibid.

58. CAB 87/1, War Cabinet: Reconstruction Problems Committee, RP (41) 16th meeting, 23 June 1941.

59. Labour Party, *Report of the 40th Annual Conference* (London: Labour Party, 1941) p. 133.
60. Ms. Eng. Attlee dep 3, fol 11.
61. C. R. Attlee papers, 'Letters to Tom'.
62. Ms. Eng. Attlee dep 4, fol 69.
63. Ms. Eng. Attlee dep 4, fol 99.
64. Ms. Eng. Attlee dep 4, fol 172, interviews with Ritchie Calder.
65. CAB 127/206, Dalton to Attlee, 30 December 1941, 'Draft: Proposal for a Ministry of Economic and Political Warfare'.
66. CAB 127/206, Dalton to Attlee, 30 December 1941.
67. CAB 127/206, Dalton to Attlee, 30 December 1941, 'Draft: Proposal for a Ministry of Economic and Political Warfare'.

11. Deputy Prime Minister and Dominions Secretary, 1942–43

1. DO/121/10A, Cranborne to Churchill, 18 November 1941.
2. DO 121/10B, Attlee to Churchill, 16 June 1942.
3. DO 121/107, Lord Harlech to Attlee, 15 March 1943.
4. DO 121/107, Attlee to Lord Harlech, 30 April 1943.
5. DO 121/10B, Attlee to Churchill, 2 July 1942.
6. DO 121/10B, Attlee to Churchill, 27 April 1943.
7. DO 121/10B, Attlee to Churchill, 21 September 1943.
8. DO 121/10B, Attlee to Churchill, 11 February 1943.
9. DO 121/10B, Attlee to Churchill, 9 June 1942.
10. DO 121/10, Attlee to Churchill, 29 June 1942.
11. DO 121/107, Attlee to Lord Harlech, 10 April 1942.
12. DO 121/10B, Attlee to Churchill, 25 February 1942.
13. DO 121/10B, telegram to Commander-in-Chief, India, from Chiefs of Staff, undated, but must be 14–16 April, 1942.
14. DO 121/10B, Attlee to Churchill, 16 April 1942.
15. DO 121/10B, Prime Minister's Personal Minute, Serial No. 139/2, 16 April 1942.
16. DO 121/10B, Attlee to Churchill, 7 May 1942.
17. Dilks, *The Diaries of Sir Alexander Cadogan*, pp. 429–30.
18. Prime Minister's Office, PREM 4/48/8, Amery to Churchill: Secretary of State's Minute: Serial No. P. 2/42, 10 February 1942.
19. PREM 4/48/8, Telegram from Sir Stafford Cripps for Prime Minister, No. 81/S, 28 March 1942.
20. PREM 4/48/8, Telegram from Viceroy to Secretary of State for India, T. 492/2, 29 March 1942.
21. PREM 4/48/8, Telegram from Viceroy to Secretary of State for India, No. 8598, 1 April 1942.
22. PREM 4/48/8, Prime Minister to Sir Stafford Cripps, 2 April 1942.
23. Francis Williams, *A Prime Minister Remembers: The War and Post-War Memoirs of The Rt Hon. Earl Attlee KG, PC, OM, CH: Based on his Private Papers, and on a Series of Recorded Conversations* (London: Heinemann, 1961) pp. 205–6.
24. Quoted in Michael Foot, *Aneurin Bevan, 1897–1960* (London: Victor Gollancz, 1997) p. 185.
25. Labour Party, *Report of the 41st Annual Conference* (London: Labour Party, 1942) p. 59.
26. Ibid., p. 100.
27. Ibid., p. 139.

28. DO 121/10B, Attlee to Churchill, 1 March 1942.
29. DO 121/10B, Churchill to Auchinleck, 1 March 1942.
30. Sir William Beveridge, *Social Insurance and Allied Services*, CMND 6404 (London: His Majesty's Stationery Office, 1942).
31. DO 121/10B, Attlee to Churchill, 8 December 1942.
32. PREM 5/532, Prime Minister's Personal Telegram, Serial No. T 514, Lord Linlithgow to Churchill, 25 August 1941.
33. PREM 5/532, Amery to Churchill, 16 April 1943.
34. Ibid.
35. Hart-Davis, *King's Counsellor*, p. 125.
36. PREM 5/532, Churchill to the King, 24 April 1943.
37. PREM 5/532, The King to Churchill, 28 April 1943.
38. PREM 5/532, Prime Minister to Viceroy, 9 June 1943.
39. Labour Party, *Report of the 42nd Annual Conference* (London: Labour Party, 1943) p. 20.
40. Ibid., p. 122.
41. Ibid., pp. 136–42.
42. Ibid., p. 127.
43. Ibid., p. 130.

12. Deputy Prime Minister and Lord President of the Council, 1943–45

1. MS. Attlee, dep 11, Correspondence and Papers, 24 November–December 1943.
2. Ibid.
3. A Geo. Mathers from Edinburgh wrote to praise the 'excellent broadcast'; and John Simon wrote from Dowding in Surrey that he and his wife had 'exclaimed with one voice "It was very good!"' MS. Attlee, dep 11, Correspondence and Papers, 24 November–December 1943.
4. The only discordant notes were about the failure to mention agriculture specifically, and from a Catholic who was unhappy with the forthcoming Education Bill: MS. Attlee, dep 12, Correspondence and Papers, January–7 March 1944.
5. MS. Attlee, dep 12, Correspondence and Papers, January–7 March 1944.
6. Robert Rhodes James, *Anthony Eden* (London: George Weidenfeld and Nicolson Ltd, 1986) p. 293.
7. Quoted in Williams, *A Prime Minister Remembers*, p. 40.
8. Hansard, HC 1943–44, vol 395 (24 November–17 December) column 1771, 16 December 1943.
9. MS. Attlee, dep 12, Correspondence and Papers, January–7 March 1944.
10. The act actually set out a tripartite devision, but secondary technical schools, which were more geared towards preparation for trades, were not developed.
11. MS. Attlee, dep 14, Correspondence and Papers, May–August 1944.
12. MS. Attlee, dep 17, Correspondence and Papers, 15 February 1945–17 May 1945.
13. C. R. Attlee papers, 'Letters to Tom'.
14. MS. Attlee, dep 12, Correspondence and Papers, January–7 March 1944.
15. Ibid.
16. Ibid.
17. MS. Attlee, dep 13, Correspondence and Papers, 8 March–April 1944.
18. Ibid.
19. Attlee, *As It Happened*, p. 132.
20. MS. Attlee, dep 13, Correspondence and Papers, 8 March–April 1944.

21. Ibid.
22. Ibid.
23. Ibid. Theodore Besterman to Attlee.
24. MS. Attlee, dep 14, Correspondence and Papers, May–August 1944.
25. Anon, *Employment Policy: Presented by the Minister of Reconstruction in Parliament by Command of His Majesty* (London: His Majesty's Stationery Office, 1944).
26. PREM 4/93/1, War Cabinet: Reconstruction Committee: London Housing: Memorandum by the Home Secretary, R (44) 149, 30 August 1944.
27. PREM 4/93/1, War Cabinet: Reconstruction Committee, R (44) 59th meeting 8 September 1944.
28. MS. Attlee, dep 15, Correspondence and Papers, September–November 1944.
29. Ibid.
30. Ibid.
31. Ibid.
32. MS. Attlee, dep 16, Correspondence and Papers, December 1944–13 February 1945.
33. Labour Party, *Report of the 43rd Annual Conference* (London: Labour Party, 1944) p. 113.
34. Ibid., p. 115.
35. Ibid., p. 118.
36. Ibid., p. 133.
37. MS. Attlee, dep 16, Correspondence and Papers, December 1944–13 February 1945, Letter from Monsieur Jan Becko to Attlee.
38. The letter is set out in full in Harris, *Attlee*, pp. 241–3.
39. John Colville, *The Fringes of Power: Downing Street Diaries, 1939–1955* (London: Phoenix, 2005 edition) p. 526.
40. Jenkins, *Churchill*, p. 777.
41. Quoted in Williams, *A Prime Minister Remembers*, p. 45.
42. C. R. Attlee papers, 'Letters to Tom', letter of 19 May 1943.
43. Interview with the Third Earl Attlee, 26 March 2009.
44. Quoted in Williams, *A Prime Minister Remembers*, p. 45.
45. MS. Attlee, dep 16, Correspondence and Papers, December1944–13 February 1945.
46. Ibid.
47. Ibid.
48. PREM 4/6/5, WM (45) 24th Conclusions, Thursday 22 February 1945.
49. CAB 87/10, R (42) 1st Meeting, War Cabinet: Reconstruction Committee, 8 January 1945.
50. CAB 87/10, R (42) 4th Meeting, War Cabinet: Reconstruction Committee, 22 January 1945.
51. CAB 87/10, R (42) 12th Meeting, War Cabinet: Reconstruction Committee, 12 March 1945.
52. CAB 87/10, R (45) 18th Meeting, War Cabinet: Reconstruction Committee, 7 May 1945.
53. CAB 87/10, R (45) 47th Meeting, War Cabinet: Reconstruction committee: Industrial Injuries Bill: Miscellaneous Points: Memorandum by the Minister of National Insurance, 2 May 1945.
54. CAB 87/10, R (45) 14th Meeting, War Cabinet: Reconstruction Committee, 10 April 1945.
55. CAB 87/10, R (45) 17th Meeting, War Cabinet: Reconstruction Committee, 30 April 1945.

56. CAB 123/228: 'Supplies to Liberated Areas: Memorandum by the Lord President of the Council and Deputy Prime Minister,' 15 March 1945.
57. CAB 123/228, Duff Cooper to Eden, 12 March 1945.
58. MS. Attlee, dep 17, Correspondence and Papers, 15 February 1945–17 May 1945.
59. Ibid.
60. Ibid.
61. Ibid.
62. MS. Attlee, dep 18, Correspondence and Papers, 18 May 1945–13 August 1945.

13. The 1945 General Election

1. *The Times*, 5 July 1945.
2. Labour Party, Report of the 44th Annual Conference (London: Labour Party, 1945) p. 88. Churchill and Attlee's letters appear at pp. 86–8.
3. Paul Addison, 'By-elections of the Second World War', in Chris Cook and John Ramsden (eds) *By-elections in British Politics* (London: UCL Press Ltd, 1997) p. 141.
4. Ibid., p. 148.
5. Hart-Davis, *King's Counsellor*, p. 342.
6. Kenneth O. Morgan, *Labour in Power 1945–1951* (Oxford: Oxford University Press, 2002) p. 44.
7. Henry Pelling, *The Labour Governments, 1945–51* (London: Macmillan, 1984) pp. 30–2.
8. Paul Addison, *The Road to 1945: British politics and the Second World War* (London: Pimlico, 1994) pp. 270–9.
9. Cannadine, *The Speeches of Winston Churchill*, p. 274.
10. MS. Attlee, dep 18, Correspondence and Papers, 18 May 1945–13 August 1945.
11. H. Laski Correspondence, National Museum of Labour History Archive, Manchester, General Correspondence, 1938–50, LP/LAS/38/21ii.
12. This correspondence appears in PREM 4/7/7.
13. H. Laski Correspondence, LP/LAS/38/20.
14. H. Laski Correspondence, LP/LAS/38/22 (telegram from Geoffrey De Freitas, Nottingham Labour Candidate, to Laski) and LP/LAS/38/23 (Labour Party Press Release, 20 June 1945).
15. Hart-Davis, *King's Counsellor*, p. 343.
16. *The Times*, 27 July 1945.
17. Ibid.
18. Pelling, *The Labour Governments*, p. 31.
19. MS. Attlee, dep 18, Correspondence and Papers, 18 May–13 August 1945.
20. Dalton, *The Fateful Years*, p. 467.
21. MS. Attlee, dep 18, Correspondence and Papers, 18 May–13 August 1945.
22. Morrison of Lambeth, *Herbert Morrison*, p. 245.
23. Ibid.
24. Alan Bullock, *The Life and Times of Ernest Bevin*, vol. 2, *Minister of Labour 1940–1945* (London: Heinemann, 1967) pp. 392–3. Bullock footnotes that both Morgan Phillips and Attlee gave accounts to him for the events of the afternoon.
25. Dalton, *The Fateful Years*, p. 467.
26. Hart-Davis, *King's Counsellor*, p. 344.

14. Attlee as Prime Minister

1. Harold Wilson, *A Prime Minister on Prime Ministers* (London: Orion, 1977) p. 297.

2. Hart-Davis, *King's Counsellor*, p. 344.

3. Dalton, *The Fateful Years*, p. 468.

4. Ibid., p. 469.

5. Morrison of Lambeth, *Herbert Morrison*, pp. 246–7.

6. MS. Attlee, dep 18, Correspondence and Papers, 18 May–13 August 1945.

7. Ibid.

8. The five younger ones were Balfour (53), Asquith (55), Lloyd George (53), MacDonald (57) and Baldwin (55); Chamberlain and Churchill aside, the other two older were Campbell-Bannerman (69) and Bonar Law (64).

9. Evan Durbin, a five-page typed manuscript entitled 'CRA', which states: 'This essay was written by Evan Durbin in 1945 or 46; it is not known if it was published.' The author refers to a copy in the possession of Lady Attlee.

10. C. R. Attlee papers, 'Letters to Tom', letter of 18 October 1945.

11. Attlee, *As It Happened*, p. 91.

12. Peter Hennessy, *The Prime Minister: The Office and Its Holders Since 1945* (London: Penguin Books, 2000) p. 163.

13. Ibid., p. 164. The more traditional standing committees contained all ministers with a relevant departmental interest, while the *ad hoc* committees were more fluid, with membership and chairmanship within the prime minister's gift.

14. MS. Attlee, dep 18, Correspondence and Papers, 18 May–13 August 1945.

15. *The Times*, 28 July 1945.

16. Lord Moyle, 'Earl Attlee – The Man', *Labour Organiser*, November 1967, pp. 206–7.

17. Ibid.

18. Ibid.

19. James Callaghan, *Time and Chance* (Politico's Publishing: London, 2006) p. 95.

20. Moyle, 'Earl Attlee – The Man', pp. 206–7.

21. Lady Attlee's collection of private papers, Durbin, 'CRA'.

22. MS. Attlee, dep 18, Correspondence and Papers, 18 May–13 August 1945.

23. Interview with Lady Attlee, 7 April 2009. She mentioned Attlee's abilities at what would today be termed 'DIY'.

24. C. R. Attlee papers, 'Letters to Tom', letter of 23 February 1948.

25. Harris, *Attlee*, p. 412.

15. The Scale of the Challenge, July–November 1945

1. *The Times*, 28 July 1945.

2. MS. Attlee, dep 21, Correspondence and Papers, 1–9 September 1945.

3. *The Times*, 28 July 1945.

4. CAB 120/192, Top Secret Cypher Telegram from Foreign Office to Terminal, Onward No. 258, 28 July 1945.

5. A less extreme approach than the Morgenthau Plan to strip Germany of its industrial capacity; in the event, industrial capacity was limited, and plants surplus to the limits dismantled and transferred to other countries by way of reparations.

6. CAB 123/228; *The Times*, 2 March 1945.

7. Ministry of Agriculture and Food, MAF 128/8, File Note by G. R. P. Wall, 6 November 1945, appending list of foods.

8. CAB 120/192, Top Secret Cypher Telegram: Chiefs of General Staff from Foreign Office to Terminal, Onward No. 292, 30 July 1945.

9. CAB 120/192, Telegram from Foreign Office to Washington, No. 7991, 31 July 1945.

10. MS. Attlee, dep 22, Correspondence and Papers, 10–16 September 1945.

11. CAB 120/192, Telegram from Moscow to the Foreign Office, No. 3350, 29 July 1945; Sent as Onward No. 279, 29 July 1945.

12. Top Secret Cypher Telegram, Morrison to Attlee, Onward No. 252, 30 July 1945.

13. MS. Attlee, dep 18, Correspondence and Papers, 18 May–13 August 1945.

14. Ibid.

15. Trades Union Congress, *Report of Proceedings of the 77th Annual Trades Union Congress, held at Blackpool September 10th to 14th 1945* (London: Cooperative Printing Society Ltd, 1945) p. 315.

16. Ibid., p. 317.

17. MS. Attlee, dep 19, Correspondence and Papers, 14–17 August 1945.

18. MS. Attlee, dep 18, Correspondence and Papers, 18 May–13 August 1945.

19. On 1 September, *The Times* reported that the British Medical Students' Association demanded that 'a scheme to provide the country with the health centres should be begun without delay, the first to be placed where there is a shortage of doctors'.

20. MS. Attlee, dep 13, Correspondence and Papers, 8 March–April 1944, *The Economic Council Review of Books* (vol. 1, no. 9, 1 February 1944). The Economic Council is based in New York, Chicago, Utica and Washington.

21. PREM 8/35, Gen. 89/13, 'Cabinet: Washington Financial Talks: Memorandum by the Chancellor of the Exchequer', 22 November 1945.

22. PREM 8/35, Cypher from Foreign Office to Washington, 24 November 1945, No. 11789.

23. PREM 8/35, Prime Minister's Personal Telegram, T.211/45, 26 November, 1945.

24. Anon, *Financial Agreement between the Governments of the United States and the United Kingdom dated 6th December, 1945 CMD 6708* (London: His Majesty's Stationery Office, 1945).

25. Quoted in Williams, *A Prime Minister Remembers*, p. 183.

26. Ibid., p. 188.

27. Ibid., p. 190.

28. PREM 8/89, Telegram from Washington to Foreign Office, No. 6537, 29 September 1945.

29. PREM 8/89.

30. MS. Attlee, dep 19, Correspondence and Papers, 14–17 August 1945.

31. MS. Attlee, dep 22, Correspondence and Papers, 10–16 September 1945.

32. MS. Attlee, dep 23, Correspondence and Papers, 17 September–9 Oct 1945.

33. MS. Attlee, dep 18, Correspondence and Papers, 18 May–13 August 1945.

34. TNA, PRO, CAB 130/3, 'The Atomic Bomb: Memorandum by the Prime Minister', Gen 75/1, 28 August 1945.

16. Fulfilling the Party's Ambitions: National Insurance, National Health and Nationalization, 1945–48

1. PREM 8/290, CP (45) 315, 'Report by the Social Services Committee on the National Insurance Scheme', 1 December 1945.

2. PREM 8/290, CP (45) 323, 'National Insurance Scheme: Memorandum by the Chancellor of the Exchequer', 5 December 1945.

3. PREM 8/290, CM (45) 60th Conclusion, 6 December 1945.

4. PREM 8/290, CM (45) 63rd Conclusions, Thursday, 13 December 1945 at 10 a.m.

5. Ibid.

6. PREM 8/290, CP (46) 14 'National Insurance Scheme – Limitation of

Unemployment Benefit', Memorandum by the Minister of National Insurance, 15 January 1946.

7. PREM 8/290, Dalton to Attlee, 14 January 1946.

8. PREM 8/290, Attlee to Dalton, Prime Minister's Personal Minute, 13 January 1946.

9. PREM 8/290, CM (46) 6th Conclusions, 17 January 1946.

10. Hansard, HC 1945–46, vol. 418 (22 January–8 February) column 1896, 7 February 1946.

11. Though Bevan's Labour Party Conference speech of 1947 focused on the nurses rather than the doctors, referring to the improvement of their pay and conditions, and the need for sufficient numbers of them in order to run the NHS. A. Bevan, 'Speech to Conference', *Labour Party Annual Review*, 1947, p. 197, in MS. Attlee dep 138, GB 161, p. 4.

12. BMA Negotiation Committee Minutes Session, 1947–1948, 'The Profession and the National Health Service Act, 1946', vol. 1, 'The Negotiating Committee's Case', p. 12, para 66.

13. BMA Negotiation Committee Minutes Session, 1947–1948, NC178, Meeting Between the Negotiating Committee and the Minister of Health, Tuesday 2 December 1947 and Wednesday 3 December 1947.

14. Ibid.

15. These were the four issues that remained on the agenda in opposition to the BMA's cooperation line in the special representative meeting of Friday 28 May 1948, para 26, Special Representative Meeting Minutes, 1948.

16. BMA Negotiation Committee Minutes Session, 1947–1948, NC178, Meeting Between the Negotiating Committee and the Minister of Health, Tuesday 2 December 1947 and Wednesday 3 December 1947, p. 4.

17. Minutes of Special Representative Meeting of the BMA, 8 January 1948, para 39, in BMA, Minutes of Special Representative Meetings, 1948.

18. Ibid., paras 19–21.

19. Prime Minister's Minute M.14/48 dated 16 January 1948.

20. Previous cabinet opposition to Bevan's position had come principally from Herbert Morrison, Home Secretary Chuter Ede, and A. V. Alexander, and centred on voluntary and municipal hospitals remaining in local control (Morgan, *Labour in Power*, p. 155).

21. Hill served as chancellor of the Duchy of Lancaster from 1957 to 1961 under Harold Macmillan.

22. PREM 8/844, CP (48) 23, 19 January 1948.

23. Ibid., 'Prime Minister: National Health service: Attitude of the Medical Practitioner'.

24. PREM 8/844, Note from Ministry of Health to Graham-Harrison at No. 10 Downing Street.

25. Hansard, HC 1947–48, vol. 446 (20 January–6 February) column 1204, 29 January 1948.

26. PREM 8, CM (48) 9th Conclusions, 2 February 1948, Minute 2/Minute 3.

27. Ibid.

28. PREM 8/844, 'Suggested Notes for Prime Minister's Intervention in the Health Service Debate'.

29. PREM 8/844, Note from the Prime Minister dated 9 February 1948.

30. PREM 8/844, Note by Attlee's Private Secretary, Helsby, for the Prime Minister, 17 February 1948.

31. BMA Negotiation Committee Minutes Session, 1947–1948, Statement by BMA Council: The Plebiscite, 8 May 1948.

32. BMA, Minutes of Special Representative Meetings, para 53, 17 March 1948.

33. As quoted in Morgan, *Labour in Power*, p. 159.

34. *The Times*, 6 April 1948, available in PREM 8/844.

35. Note in PREM 8/844.

36. He confirmed this to Cabinet on 29 April 1948, PREM 8/844 CM (48) 30th Cons.

37. Statement by BMA Council: The Plebiscite, 8 May 1948, available in the BMA Negotiation Committee Minutes Session 1947–1948.

38. MS. Attlee, dep 72, Letter – Aneurin Bevan to Attlee, 2 July 1948, pp. 13–14.

39. As quoted in Harris, *Attlee*, p. 424.

40. Morrison of Lambeth, *Herbert Morrison*, pp. 263–4.

41. PREM 8/295, LP (45) 178, 'War Cabinet: Lord President's Committee: Statistical Report (Coal) by the Minister of Fuel and Power for August, 1945', 21 September 1945.

42. PREM 8/295, LP (45) 179, 'Lord President's Committee. Nationalisation of the Coal Industry: Memorandum by the Minister of Fuel and Power', undated.

43. PREM 8/295, LP (45) 35th Meeting, 'Lord President's Committee: Conclusions of a Meeting of the Committee held on Tuesday, 2nd October, 1945, at 3.15 p.m.'

44. PREM 8/295, a four-page note (from Edward Bridges?) simply had the words 'discuss them further' underlined in red pencil and the word 'Yes' added: Note to Prime Minister, 8 October 1945.

45. PREM 8/295, LP (45) 238, Coalmining Industry (Nationalisation) Bill: Memorandum by the Minister of Fuel & Power, 21 November 1945.

46. PREM 8/295, 'TLR'?, Note to Prime Minister, 11 December 1945.

47. PREM 8/295, CM (45) 62nd Conclusions, Thursday 13 December 1945 at 10 a.m.

48. Labour Party, *Report of the 45th Annual Conference* (London: Labour Party, 1946) p. 124.

49. Ibid.

50. Ibid., p. 127.

51. Ibid.

52. PREM 8/763, CP (47) 240, 25 August 1947, 'Balance of Payments: Increased Prices of Gas and Electricity: Memorandum by Minister of Fuel and Power'.

53. PREM 8/763, undated draft statement.

54. PREM 8/763, 'Prime Minister's Personal Minute' to the Minister of Fuel and Power, 28 July 1948.

55. PREM 8/621, CP (46) 149, 'Nationalisation of Transport: Memorandum by the Minister of Transport', 10 April 1946.

56. *The Times*, 8 April 1946.

57. PREM 8/621, CP (46) 225, 'Cabinet: Nationalisation of Transport: Memorandum by the Lord President of the Council', 1 July 1946.

58. PREM 8/621, CM (46) 64th Conclusions, 4 July 1946.

59. PREM 8/295, CP (46) 408, Cabinet: Transport Bill: Memorandum by the Minister of Transport', 1 November 1946.

60. PREM 8/621, Note to Prime Minister from Helsby (?) 23 December 1946.

61. PREM 8/621, CM (47) 28th Conclusions, 13 March 1947.

62. PREM 8/621, Minute from Attlee to the Minister of Transport and the Minister of Town and Country Planning, 19 April, 1947.

63. As quoted in Morgan, *Labour in Power*, p. 108. Morgan uses the Minutes of the Socialization of Industries Committee, 8 March, 9 May 1946 (CAB 134/687) and Proceedings of the Executive Committee of the National Union of Railwaymen,

December quarter 1951 (University of Warwick, Modern Records Centre, MS 127).

64. PREM 8/1040, CM (47) 37th Conclusions, 17 April 1947, Minute 8, Part I.

65. PREM 8/1040, CP (48) 14, 9 January 1948, 'Gas Bill: Memorandum by the Minister of Fuel and Power', Part I.

66. PREM 8/1040, CM (48) 3rd Conclusions, 13 January 1948, Minute 3, 13 January 1948, Part I. The assumption that organizations would necessarily pursue the public interest proved ill-founded. Gas (as consumer) was later to be at odds with the producer (the National Coal Board) until the switch to natural gas.

67. PREM 8/1040, EPC (49) 43rd Conclusions, Minute 5, 16 November 1949, Part II.

17. India

1. Peter Clarke, *The Last Thousand Days of the British Empire* (London: Allen Lane, 2007) p. 464.

2. CAB 21/3372, Political Situation in India, 'The Indian Situation: A Personal Note by Lord Ismay', 5 October 1947.

3. Philip Ziegler, *Mountbatten: The Official Biography* (London: Collins, 1985) p. 404.

4. *The Times*, 2 April 1946.

5. PREM 8/247.

6. Ibid.

7. PREM 8/554, Attlee to Wavell, 22 July 1946.

8. PREM 8/554, Wavell to Attlee, 1 August 1946.

9. PREM 8/554, Attlee to Wavell, 20 August 1946.

10. PREM 8/554, Wavell to Attlee, 28 August 1946.

11. PREM 8/554, Transcript of conversation between Vallabhbhai Patel (a leading member of Congress and later India's first deputy prime minister) and Sudhir Ghosh, Gandhi's emissary, talking of contact with Cripps, and Pethick-Lawrence enclosed with letter from Wavell to Attlee, 28 August 1946.

12. PREM 8/554, Telegram written by Gandhi, sent to Sudhir Ghosh in London by his wife, 28 August 1946.

13. PREM 8/554, Note to the Prime Minister, 6 September 1946.

14. India Office Records, IOR 19382: Photo EUR 212: Copies of selected papers of Clement Attlee relating to transfer of power in India 1946–47.

15. Ibid.

16. PREM 8/554, Wavell to Attlee, 30 October 1946.

17. Adrian Fort, *Archibald Wavell: The Life and Times of an Imperial Servant* (London: Jonathan Cape, 2009) p. 404.

18. Clement Attlee and Ernest Bevin, *Britain's Foreign Policy* (London: The Labour Publications Department, 1946) p. 2.

19. Ibid., p. 32.

20. CAB 127/108, 'Neither I nor the Governors nor any responsible officials'. 'Notes for discussion with PM and Ministers – 3 December 1946', unsigned, but apparently written by Wavell.

21. CAB 128/6, Cabinet Minutes (46) Confidential Annex, 10 December 1946.

22. Account of a conversation between Attlee and Harris (Harris, *Attlee*, p. 373).

23. India Office Records, IOR 19382: Photo EUR 212: Copies of selected papers of Clement Attlee relating to transfer of power in India, 1946–47.

24. Hart-Davis, *King's Counsellor*, p. 374.

25. Ibid.

26. Pamela Mountbatten, *India Remembered: A Personal Account of the Mountbattens During the Transfer of Power* (London: Pavilion Books, 2007). Copy of letter appears on p. 15.

27. India Office Records, IOR 19382: Photo EUR 212: Copies of selected papers of Clement Attlee relating to transfer of power in India, 1946–47.

28. Ibid.

29. Harris, *Attlee*, p. 377

30. Attlee, *As It Happened*, p. 183.

31. Mountbatten, *India Remembered*, p. 14.

32. PREM 8/564, Letter from Bevin to Attlee, PM/47/1.

33. Ibid.

34. Ibid.

35. Ibid.

36. Ibid.

37. Ibid.

38. Ibid.

39. PREM 8/564, Letter from Attlee to Bevin, 2 January 1947.

40. Ibid.

41. Ibid.

42. Ibid.

43. Ibid.

44. Ibid.

45. Lawrence James, *Raj: The Making and Unmaking of British India* (London: Abacus, 2003) pp. 608–39.

46. PREM 8/554, Attlee to Wavell, 6 January 1947.

47. PREM 8/554, Wavell to Attlee, 17 January 1947.

48. Ibid.

49. PREM 8/554, Attlee to Wavell, 31 January 1947.

50. PREM 8/554, Wavell to Attlee, 5 February 1947.

51. J. P. D. Dunbabin, *International Relations Since 1945: A History in Two Volumes: The Post-Imperial Age: The Great Powers and the Wider World* (London: Longman, 1994) p. 48. Attlee did not give the same leeway to Eire, which became a republic and left the Commonwealth.

52. C. R. Attlee papers, 'Letters to Tom', letter of 3 June 1947.

53. Email from Mrs Janet Shipton, eldest daughter of Attlee, to the author, 23 September 2009. Mountbatten, *India Remembered*, copy of handwritten letter appears on pp. 126–7.

54. Hansard, HC 1946–47, vol. 439 (23 June–11 July) column 2441, 10 July 1947.

55. Hansard, HC 1946–47, vol. 439 (23 June–11 July) column 2462–3, 10 July 1947.

56. *The Times*, 15 August 1947.

57. India Office Records, File L/I/1/1283, Hughes to A. H. Joyce at the India Office, 20 March 1947.

58. PREM 8/808, Letter from Rajagopalachari to Attlee, 23 June 1948.

59. PREM 8/543, Minister of State's Minute Serial No. 2/47 Prime Minister, Communication with Lord Mountbatten, 4 September 1947.

60. Hindus who converted to Islam in the fourteenth century.

61. James, *Raj*, p. 619.

62. *The Times*, 5 September 1947.

63. DO 142/24, inward telegram from UK High Commissioner in India to the Secretary of State for Commonwealth Relations, 7 October 1947.

64. Ibid.

65. Mountbatten, *India Remembered*, p. 26.

66. CAB 21/3372: Political Situation in India, 'The Indian Situation: A Personal Note by Lord Ismay', 5 October 1947.

67. India Office Records: Copies of Correspondence between Mohammed Ali Jinnah and Clement Attlee IOR/L/PJ/7/12508 – 1947.

68. PREM 8/585, CA (47) 11, 3 November 1947, 'Cabinet: Commonwealth Affairs Committee: The Indian Scene: Memorandum by the Lord Privy Seal'.

69. PREM 8/585, Bevin to Attlee, 13 November 1947.

70. PREM 8/585, handwritten note by Attlee in response to request for instructions, 20 November 1947.

71. DO 142/24, inward telegram from UK High Commissioner in India to the Secretary of State for Commonwealth Relations, sent 12 November 1947, received 13 November 1947.

72. Ziegler, *Mountbatten*, p. 413.

73. Jinnah also ordered a military response, but his commander General Gracey refused to move without the approval of the commander-in-chief Auchinleck (Ziegler, *Mountbatten*, p. 447).

74. PREM 8/1455/1, 1951 India (Policy) Kashmir, Prime Minister's Personal Telegram, Serial No. T.447/47, received 24 November 1947.

75. CAB 21/3372, 'Events in India and Pakistan during December 1947', Pol.6370/48: Political Situation in India.

76. PREM 8/1455/1, 1951 India (Policy) Kashmir, Prime Minister's Personal Telegram, Serial No. T.491/47, received 29 December 1947.

77. PREM 8/1455/2, 1951 India (Policy) Kashmir, Mountbatten to Attlee, 14 February 1948.

78. PREM 8/1455/2, 1951 India (Policy) Kashmir, Prime Minister's Personal Telegram, Serial No. T49/48, Sent 19 February 1948.

79. See Dunbabin, *The Post-Imperial Age*, pp. 44–5.

80. PREM 8/1455/8, 1951 India (Policy) Kashmir, MNB, Minute, Commonwealth Relations Office, 4 February 1950 Serial No. 4/50.

81. PREM 8/870, 1948 Parliament (Procedure), Churchill to Attlee, 27 July 1948.

82. PREM 8/1455/5, 1951 India (Policy) Kashmir, Note to Prime Minister from Sir Archibald Carter at Commonwealth Relations Office, 26 August 1948; Telegram from Commonwealth Relations Office to Acting UK High Commissioners in India and Pakistan, sent 26 August 1948; Note to Prime Minister by Helsby (?) 27 August 1948.

83. India Office Records: File POL 2037/49 – letter from S. C. Guha expressing satisfaction with Clement Attlee's attitude towards Kashmir IOR/L/PJ/7/14279 – 1948–9.

84. CAB 21/3372: Political Situation in India, Prime Minister's Personal Telegram, Serial No. T94/48, Sent 3 April 1948.

85. CAB 21/1782: Meeting of Commonwealth Prime Ministers (January 1951): Discussions on Kashmir: Attlee's Notes of Conversations on 9 and 14 January 1951.

86. Attlee, *As It Happened*, p. 182.

87. Aside from the Indo–Pakistani conflicts of 1947–49 and 1965 over the province, there has been the Indo–Chinese war in 1962 over the position of the Himalayan border to the northeastern part of the province. Today, Pakistan administers the northwestern part of the area; China occupies the northeastern portion, and India the rest. India also

intervened in the Pakistani civil war of 1971 which led to East Pakistan becoming a separate state, Bangladesh. India tested its first nuclear weapon in 1974, with Pakistan announcing successful tests in 1998.

18. Britain and America, 1945–51

1. Robert H. Ferrell (ed.) *Off the Record: the private papers of Harry S. Truman* (Middlesex: Penguin Books, 1982) p. 127.

2. Quoted in Williams, *A Prime Minister Remembers*, p. 192.

3. Ibid., p. 195.

4. Ibid., pp. 196–7.

5. Ibid., p. 197.

6. Ibid., p. 199.

7. Ibid., p. 200.

8. DO 35/1593, Prime Minister's Personal Telegram, Serial No. T.453/46, 4 October 1946.

9. DO 35/1593, Prime Minister's Personal Telegram, Serial No. T.460/46, 4 October 1946.

10. DO 35/1593, Prime Minister's Personal Telegram, Serial No. T.468/46, 10 October 1946.

11. *The Times*, 2 January 1947.

12. *The Times*, 10 January 1947.

13. PREM 8/859 Part II, E 4887/1078/G: 'Conversation With the United States Ambassador: Situation in Palestine: Mr Bevin to Lord Inverchapel (Washington)'.

14. CAB 128/9: Cabinet Meetings of 7, 14 and 18 February 1947.

15. PREM 8/859, Part I, Note to Prime Minister, 'Palestine', 28 April 1947.

16. *The Times*, 1 August 1947.

17. PREM 8/859 Part I, DO (47) 91 'Cabinet: Defence Committee: 'Palestine-Plan of Withdrawal: Memorandum by the Official Committee on Palestine'.

18. PREM 8/859 Part I, CM (47) 93rd Conclusions 4 December 1947, Minute 1.

19. Hansard, HC 1947–48, vol. 451 (25 May–11 June) column 1030, 2 June 1948.

20. Hansard, HL 1947–48, vol. 156 (31 May–24 June) column 528–529, 9 June 1948.

21. CM (48) 57th Conclusions, Minute 4, Confidential Annex (26 August 1948 – 3.0 p.m.).

22. PREM 8/859 Part I, DO (47) 85, 'Cabinet: Defence Committee: Withdrawal From Palestine: Relations With Arab Governments: Memorandum by the Official Committee on Palestine'.

23. Alan Bullock, *Ernest Bevin: Foreign Secretary* (London: Heinemann, 1983) p. 323.

24. Prime Minister's Personal Minute, M. 304/47, 10 August, 1947.

25. PREM 8/1049, Fraser to Attlee, 29 August 1949; Attlee to Fraser, 17 September 1949.

26. Gerald Kaufman, 'Review of Francis Beckett's *Clem Attlee*', *Independent*, 1 November 1997.

27. C. R. Attlee papers, 'Letters to Tom', 29 December 1946.

28. See, for example, Peter Hennessy, *Cabinets and the Bomb* (Oxford: Oxford University Press for the British Academy) p. 48.

29. TNA, PRO, CAB 130/16, Gen 163/1st Meeting, 8 January 1947, Note of Meeting and Confidential Annex, Minute 1.

30. Prime Minister's Personal Minute, Serial No. M.140c/51, 8 December 1951, TNA, PRO, PREM 11/297.

31. Labour Party, *Report of the 47th Annual Conference* (London: Labour Party, 1948) p. 161.

32. TNA, PRO, CAB 130/3, 'The Atomic Bomb: Memorandum by the Prime Minister', Gen 75/1, 28 August, 1945.
33. Ferrell, *Off the Record*, p. 203.
34. Attlee, *As It Happened*, p. 200.
35. PREM 8/1560, 'Top Secret – Record of Washington Talks – Atomic Weapon'.
36. Rhodes James, *Anthony Eden*, p. 339.

19. Coal and Currency: Attlee's Leadership Crisis of 1947

1. See http://www.metoffice.gov.uk/corporate/pressoffice/anniversary/winter1946–47.html
2. Emmanuel Shinwell, *Conflict Without Malice* (London: Odhams Press Ltd, 1955) p. 182.
3. Ibid., p. 183.
4. Ibid., p. 180.
5. PREM 8/729, Prime Minister's Personal Minute, 17.363/46.
6. PREM 8/729, Shinwell to Attlee.
7. PREM 8/729, Note by Brook on 'Winter Fuel Supplies for Industry' (CP (46) 419).
8. PREM 8/729, CP (46) 423 15 November 1946.
9. PREM 8/729, CM (46) 98th Conclusions, 19 November 1946, Minute 4.
10. PREM 8/729, CM (46) 100th Conclusions, 25 November 1946.
11. PREM 8/729, CP (47) 6, 3 January 1947, 'Coal and Electricity'.
12. PREM 8/729, CP (47) 17, 6 January 1947 'Coal and Electricity', Memorandum by the Lord President of the Council.
13. PREM 8/729, CM (47) 3rd Conclusions, 7 January 1947.
14. PREM 8/729, Cripps to Attlee, 10 January 1947.
15. PREM 8/729, Note to Prime Minister, 5 February 1947.
16. PREM 8/729, CM (47) 20th Conclusions, 11 February 1947.
17. PREM 8/729, CM (47) 21st Conclusions, Minute 1, 13 February 1947.
18. *The Times*, 20 February 1947.
19. PREM 8/729, Note to Prime Minister, 26 February 1948.
20. Morgan, *Labour in Power*, p. 48.
21. Labour Party, *Report of the 46th Annual Conference* (London: Labour Party, 1947) p. 119.
22. *The Times*, 2 January 1947.
23. Anon, *United Kingdom Balance of Payments 1946 and 1947* (London: His Majesty's Stationery Office, February 1948) Cmd. 7324
24. PREM 8/489, Part I, BP WP (47) 1 (Revise) 25 April 1947.
25. Ibid.
26. PREM 8/489, Part I, Gen. 179/1st Meeting: Note of Meeting of Ministers held at 10 Downing Street, SW1 on Monday, 5th May 1947, at 11 a.m.
27. PREM 8/489, Part I, Gen. 179/3 (Revise) 17 May 1947, 'Import Programme for 1947–48: Memorandum by the Steering Committee'.
28. PREM 8/489, Part I, Gen. 179, Import Programme 1947/48: Note of a Meeting with Ministers held at 10 Downing Street, SW1 on Monday 19 May 1947 at 11.0 a.m.
29. Ibid.
30. Ibid.
31. PREM 8/489, Part I, CP (47) 167 28 May 1947: 'Import Programme 1947–48: Memorandum by the Chancellor of the Exchequer'.
32. PREM 8/489, Part I, CP (47) 172, 2 June 1947: 'Textile Exports and the Clothes Ration: Memorandum by the President of the Board of Trade'.

33. Hansard, HC 1946–47, vol. 439 (23 June–11 July) column 2150, 8 July 1947.
34. PREM 8/489, Part I, Gen. 179/14 25 July, 1947, 'Balance of Payments: Note by the Chancellor of the Exchequer'.
35. PREM 8/489, Part I, CM (47) 65th Conclusions, Minute 2: Confidential Annex (29 July 1947 – 11 a.m.).
36. PREM 8/489, Part I, CP (47) 220, 30 July 1947, 'Cabinet: National Crisis Scheme for Increasing Production: Memorandum by the Minister of Labour and National Service'.
37. PREM 8/489, Part I, CP (47) 221, 30 July 1947, 'Cabinet: Balance of Payments: Memorandum by the Chancellor of the Exchequer'.
38. PREM 8/489, Part I, CM (47) 68th Conclusions: Confidential Annex: 1 August – 2.30 p.m.
39. PREM 8/489, Part 2, Telegram from Washington to the Foreign Office, No. 4,293, 4 August 1947.
40. Hansard, HC 1946–47, vol. 441 (28 July–20 October) column 1488, 6 August 1947.
41. Hansard, HC 1946–47, vol. 441 (28 July– 20 October) column 1491, 6 August 1947.
42. PREM 8/489, Part 2.
43. PREM 8/489, Part II, CM (47) 71st Conclusions, Minute 1: Confidential Annex (17th August 1947 – 5 p.m.).
44. PREM 8/489, Part II, Prime Minister's Personal Minute, M316/47, 18 August, 1947.
45. PREM 8/489, Part II, Prime Minister's Personal Minute, M318/47, 18 August, 1947.
46. *The Times*, 19 August 1947.
47. Ibid.
48. Ibid.
49. PREM 8/489, Part II, CM (47) 72nd Conclusions, Minute 1: Confidential Annex (19 August 1947 – 12 noon).
50. *The Times*, 20 August 1947.
51. Nigel Nicolson (ed.) *The Harold Nicolson Diaries: 1907–1963* (London: Weidenfeld & Nicolson, 2004 edition) p. 182.
52. *The Times*, 21 August 1947.
53. PREM 8/489, Part II, 'Notes on the Present Situation' to the Lord President, signed by Hugh Weeks.
54. PREM 8/489, Part II, Note from Cabinet Office to Attlee, 19 August 1947, together with handwritten note, 19 August 1947, on the face of it from Helsby to Attlee.
55. PREM 8/489, Part II, Prime Minister's Personal Minute, M321/47 to the Lord President, 20 August 1947.
56. PREM 8/489, Part II, From Washington to Foreign Office, No. 4567, 20 August 1947.
57. Subject to an additional paragraph about the requirement to consult for Article XIV of the International Monetary Fund, without which there would be no further proposals to 'notify any further withdrawals', PREM 8/489, Part II, CM (47) 73rd Conclusions of a Meeting of the Cabinet held at 10 Downing Street, SW1, on Wednesday 20 August 1947 at 12.15 p.m.
58. PREM 8/489, Part I, 'Exchange of Letters between His Majesty's Government and the United States Government dated 20th August, 1947' (London: His Majesty's Stationery Office, September 1947).
59. PREM 8/489, Part II, Gen. 179/14th Meeting: 'Balance of Payments': Note of a Meeting held at 10 Downing Street, SW1, on Wednesday 20 August 1947, at 5.0 p.m.
60. PREM 8/489, Part II, Strachey to Attlee, 21 August 1947.

61. PREM 8/489, Part II, CM (47) 74th Conclusions 25.8.47 Min. 2.

62. *The Times*, 25 August 1947.

63. *The Times*, 26 August 1947.

64. *The Times*, 28 August 1947.

65. *The Times*, 1 September 1947.

66. *The Times*, 3 September 1947.

67. Pimlott, *The Political Diary of Hugh Dalton*, p. 652.

68. Hugh Dalton, *High Tide and After: Memoirs 1945–1960* (London: Frederick Muller Ltd, 1962) p. 240.

69. Morrison of Lambeth, *Herbert Morrison*, p. 260.

70. Dalton, *High Tide and After*, p. 242.

71. Ibid., p. 245.

72. Harris, *Attlee*, p. 349.

73. Anon, *Report from the Select Committee on the Budget Disclosure Together With the Proceedings of the Committee, Minutes of Evidence and Appendices* (London: HMSO, 11 December 1947) p. iv.

74. PREM 8/435, CM (47) 88th Conclusions, Minute 1, 17 November 1947.

75. Anon, *Report from the Select Committee on the Budget Disclosure*, p. x.

76. Wilson, *A Prime Minister on Prime Ministers*, p. 295.

77. *The Times*, 16 July 1947.

20. Missed Opportunities? 1948–49

1. Butler and Butler, *Twentieth-Century British Political Facts*, p. 266. The poll findings are from Gallup – November 1947 Conservative 50.5 per cent, Labour 38 per cent; May 1948 Conservative 45 per cent, Labour 41 per cent.

2. Labour Party, *Report of the 47th Annual Conference* (London: Labour Party, 1948) p. 161.

3. Ed 147/45: National Society 1945–51: Letter dated 2 November 1946.

4. PREM 8/1059, Part I, CP (46) 376, Cabinet: Amendment of the Parliament Act: Memorandum by the Lord Chancellor, 11 October 1946.

5. PREM 8/1059, Part I, handwritten note by Attlee, 13 October 1946, on paper dated 12 October 1946.

6. PREM 8/1059, Part I, CM (46) 90th Conclusions, 24 October 1946.

7. PREM 8/1059, Part I, handwritten note by Attlee, 20 November 1946, on paper dated 19 November 1946.

8. PREM 8/1059, Part I, CM (47) 80th Conclusions, Minute 1: Confidential Annex, 14th October 1947.

9. Ibid.

10. Ibid.

11. PREM 8/1059, Part I, Prime Minister's Personal Telegram Serial No. T406/47.

12. PREM 8/1059, Part I, CP (47) 292, 18 October 1947.

13. PREM 8/1059, Part I, CM (47) 81st Conclusions, Minute 2, 20 October 1947.

14. PREM 8/1059, Part I, Draft of a Bill to Amend the Parliament Act, 1911, 11 Geo. 6, 28 October 1947.

15. PREM 8/1059, Part I, CM (47) 83rd Conclusions, Minute 3, 30 October 1947.

16. Attlee, Morrison, Addison, Jowitt and Whiteley for the government; Eden (when ill replaced by Stanley) Maxwell-Fyfe and Lords Salisbury and Swinton for the Conservatives; Samuel and Clement Davies for the Liberals.

17. PREM 8/1059, Part I, CP (48) 79, Cabinet: Parliament Bill: Memorandum by the Prime Minister, 9 March 1948.

18. PREM 8/1059, Part I, House of Lords Reform: Parliament Bill, Party Leaders' Conference: Record of the fourth preliminary Meeting between Party Leaders which took place in the Prime Minister's Room at the House of Commons, on Thursday 11 March 1948, at 5.15 p.m.

19. PREM 8/1053, Attlee to Jowitt, 29 July 1949.

20. PREM 8/739, CM (47) 55th Conclusions, 19 June 1947.

21. PREM 8/739, CM (47) 61st Conclusions, 15 July 1947.

22. PREM 8/739, CP (47) 217, 28 July 1947.

23. PREM 8/739, CM (47) 84th Conclusions, 3 November 1947.

24. PREM 8/739, CP (47) 306, 13 November 1947: Criminal Justice Bill: Capital Punishment.

25. PREM 8/739, CM (47) 89th Conclusions, Minute 4, 18 November 1947.

26. PREM 8/739, draft of proposed statement at Second Reading, Ede to Attlee, 25 November 1947.

27. PREM 8/739, CM (48) 27th Conclusions, 8 April 1948.

28. PREM 8/739, CM (48) 28th Conclusions, 15 April 1948.

29. PREM 8/739, CP (48) 174, 2 July 1948, Criminal Justice Bill: Capital Punishment Memorandum by the Home Secretary.

30. PREM 8/739, CM (48) 47th Conclusions, Minute 4, 5 July 1948.

31. PREM 8/739, B. A. Gould, J. Paton, G. Benson and S. Silverman to Attlee, 13 July 1948.

32. PREM 8/739, CM (48) 47th Conclusions, Minute 2, 15 July 1948.

33. PREM 8/739, CM (48) 53rd Conclusions, 22 July 1948.

34. PREM 8/739, CP (48) 252, 3 November 1948, 'Inquiry into Capital Punishment': Memorandum by the Home Secretary and the Secretary of State for Scotland.

35. PREM 8/739, Brook to Attlee, Capital Punishment: CP (48) 252.

36. PREM 8/739, CM (48) 73rd Conclusions, Minute 5, 15 July 1948.

37. PREM 8/231, CP (46) 161, 6 May 1946, 'Cabinet: Progress Report on Housing: March 1946: Memorandum by Minister of Health'.

38. PREM 8/226, CP (46) 417, 8 November 1946, 'Cabinet: Timber for Housing: Memorandum by the Minister of Health'.

39. PREM 8/226, CP (46) 417, 8 November 1946, 'Cabinet: Timber for Housing: Memorandum by the Minister of Health'.

40. PREM 8/226, HG (46) 7, 10 December 1946, 'Housing: Housing Programme for 1947: Memorandum by the Minister of Health'.

41. *The Times*, 22 April 1947.

42. Ibid.

43. CAB 139/386, 'House-building before and after the two wars', signed B. N. Davies, 27 April 1948. These figures may not, however, be entirely reliable: another estimate is that between 1920 and 1930 around 1.5 million houses were built in England and Wales, two in three state-assisted. See C. L. Mowat, *Britain Between the Wars, 1918–1940* (London: Methuen & Co Ltd, 1968).

44. Butler and Butler, *Twentieth-Century British Political Facts*, pp. 356–7.

45. CAB 124/452, Gaitskell to Morrison, 8 August 1947.

46. Cmd. 7004.

47. PREM 8/761, CP (47) 74, 28 February 1947, Electoral Legislation: Memorandum by the Home Secretary and the Secretary of State for Scotland.

48. PREM 8/761, CM (47) 26th Conclusions, 6 March 1947.

49. PREM 8/761, CP (47) 193, 3 July 1947, Electoral Legislation: Memorandum by the Home Secretary.
50. PREM 8/761, CP (47) 333, 12 December 1947, Electoral Legislation: Memorandum by the Home Secretary.
51. PREM 8/761, CM (47) 96th Conclusions, 18 December 1947.
52. Dartford, Leyton, Twickenham and others where the existing seat distribution gave an average electorate of over 70,000 per seat who could also argue for more represent-tation: Bradford, Leicester and Nottingham (three seats each) Hackney and Stoke Newington and Plymouth (two seats each). PREM 8/761, CP (48) 3, 3 January 1948.
53. PREM 8/761, Brook to Attlee, 'Redistribution of Seats,' 17 January 1948.
54. PREM 8/761, CM (48) 5th Conclusions, Minute 6, 19 January 1948.
55. PREM 8/761, CP (48) 64, 4 March 1948, 'Redistribution of Seats: Memorandum by the Home Secretary'.
56. PREM 8/761, CM (48) 20th Conclusions, Minute 6, 8 March 1948.
57. Hansard, HC 1947–48, vol. 449 (6–23 April) column 162, 1948.
58. Labour Party, *Report of the 34th Annual Conference* (London: Labour Party, 1934) p. 201.
59. PREM 1489/Part I, LP (45) 228, 7 November 1945, 'Future of the Iron and Steel Industry: Memorandum by the Minister of Supply and of Aircraft Production'.
60. Ibid.
61. PREM 1489/Part I, *British Iron and Steel Federation: Report to the Ministry of Supply on the Iron and Steel Industry* (London: The Fanfare Press, 1945) pp. 21–4.
62. PREM 1489/Part I, SI (M) 46, 4th Meeting, Cabinet: Committee on the Socialisation of Industries, 14 March 1946.
63. PREM 1489/Part I, Bridges to Attlee, 28 March 1946, reflecting points put to Attlee in discussion.
64. PREM 1489/Part I, Bridges to Rowan, 28 March 1948.
65. PREM 1489/Part I, Cab:Cons: 30 (46) 4 April 1946.
66. Hansard, HC 1945–46, vol. 421 (25 March–18 April) column 2693, 17 April 1946.
67. Hansard, HC 1945–46, vol. 421 (25 March–18 April) column 2707, 17 April 1946.
68. PREM 1489/Part I, CM (46) 76th Conclusions, 1 August 1946.
69. PREM 1489/Part I, SI (M) (47) 13, Cabinet: Committee on Socialisation of Industries: Proposed Scheme for Public Ownership of Sections of the Iron and Steel Industry: Memorandum by the Minister of Supply, 12 March 1947.
70. Ibid.
71. PREM 1489/Part I, CP (47) 123, 14 April 1947: 'Proposed Scheme for Public Ownership of Sections of the Iron and Steel Industry: Memorandum by the Minister of Supply'.
72. PREM 1489/Part I, CM (47) 44th Conclusions, 6 May 1947.
73. PREM 1489/Part I, Notes of a Meeting held on Wednesday 21 May 1947.
74. Ibid.
75. PREM 1489/Part I, Rowan to Attlee, 22 May 1947.
76. PREM 1489/Part I, SI (M) 47, 6th Meeting, 18 June 1947.
77. Ibid.
78. PREM 1489/Part I, CM (47) 57th Conclusions, Minute 5, Confidential Annex, 26 June 1947.
79. PREM 1489/Part I, Prime Minister's Personal Minutes, M 260/47(to Wilmot) and M 261/47 (to Morrison) both 28 June 1947.

80. PREM 1489/Part I, Note of a Meeting held in the Lord President's Room, No. 11 Downing Street, 10 July 1947.

81. PREM 1489/Part I, CP (47) 212, 21 July 1947: Reorganisation of the Iron and Steel Industry: Joint Memorandum by the Lord President of the Council and the Minister of Supply.

82. Ibid.

83. PREM 1489/Part I, CM (47) 64th Conclusions, 24 July 1947.

84. PREM 1489/Part I, CM (47) 66th Conclusions, Minute 4, 31 July 1947, Confidential Annex.

85. Ibid.

86. PREM 1489/Part I, Douglas to Attlee, 23 August 1947.

87. Hansard, HC 1946–47, vol. 443 (21 October– 7 November) column 33, 21 October 1947.

88. PREM 1489/Part I, Morrison, Herbert Morrison, p. 296.

89. PREM 1489/Part II, CP (48) 123, 20 May 1948, 'Iron and Steel Bill: Memorandum by the Minister of Supply'.

90. PREM 1489/Part II, Brook to Attlee, 29 May 1948.

91. PREM 8/1059, Part I, CP (48) 147 Cabinet: Amendment of the Parliament Act, 1911: Memorandum by the Lord President of the Council, 11th June 1948.

92. Hansard, HC 1947–48, vol. 452 (14 June–2 July) column 1570, 24 June 1948.

93. PREM 1489/Part II, CP (48) 181, 15 July 1948, 'Iron and Steel Bill: Note by the Lord President of the Council: Iron and Steel Bill: Review of Arguments'.

94. PREM 1489/Part II, Bevin to Morrison, 17 July 1948.

95. PREM 1489/Part II, 'Iron and Steel Bill: Note by the Prime Minister,' 22 July 1948.

96. PREM 1489/Part II, CM (48) 66th Conclusions, Minute 2, 25 October 1948.

97. Hansard, HC 1948–49, vol. 458 (15 November–3 December) column 226, 16 November 1948.

21. Political Troubles, 1949–51

1. Labour Party, *Report of the 48th Annual Conference* (London: Labour Party, 1949) p. 134.

2. Ibid., p. 137.

3. Ibid., p. 153.

4. Ibid., p. 153.

5. Ibid., p. 171.

6. Attlee, *As It Happened*, p. 206.

7. Butler and Butler, *Twentieth-Century British Political Facts*, p. 400.

8. Ibid., p. 411. Neither Cripps nor Dalton used monetary policy, with the bank rate remaining at 2 per cent throughout Labour's period in office.

9. Ibid., p. 411.

10. David Kynaston, *Austerity Britain* (London: Bloomsbury Publishing House, 2007) p. 249.

11. Butler and Butler, *Twentieth-Century British Political Facts*, p. 417.

12. Gaitskell Papers, C26, 'Note by HG, January 1949'.

13. Ibid.

14. Ibid.

15. Morgan, *Labour in Power*, p. 59.

16. PREM 8/973, CM (49) 53rd Conclusions, Monday 29 August 1949, at 11 a.m.

17. Ibid.

18. Ibid.
19. Trades Union Congress, *Report of Proceedings of the 81st Annual Trades Union Congress, held at Bridlington September 5th to 9th 1949* (London: Cooperative Printing Society Ltd, 1949) p. 388.
20. PREM 8/973, 'Report of a Working Party on Wages Policy and Devaluation', 8 September 1949.
21. PREM 8/973, Gen. 298/1st Meeting: Minutes of a Meeting of Ministers, 14 September 1949.
22. PREM 8/973, CM (49) 55th Conclusions, 17 September 1949.
23. PREM 8/973, CM (49) 55th Conclusions, 17 September 1949, Annex: Draft of Broadcast by the Chancellor of the Exchequer.
24. *The Times*, 19 September 1949.
25. C. R. Attlee papers, 'Letters to Tom', letter of 11 September 1949.
26. Gaitskell Papers, C26, 'Political Strategy': Marked 'Top Secret', by Hugh Gaitskell, 18 August 1949.
27. PREM 8/963, Press Notice, 13 October 1949.
28. PREM 8/963, Young to Lascelles, 11 November 1949; Lascelles to Young, 17 November 1949.
29. The ten-year parliament of 1935 was brought about by the advent of the Second World War.
30. Morrison, *Herbert Morrison*, p. 268.
31. Peter Clarke, *The Cripps Version: The Life of Sir Stafford Cripps* (London: Allen Lane, 2002) p. 52, based on Pimlott, *The Political Diary of Hugh Dalton*, p. 459.
32. Pimlott, *The Political Diary of Hugh Dalton*, p. 462.
33. PREM 8/1256.
34. Pimlott, *The Political Diary of Hugh Dalton*, p. 462.
35. PREM 8/1256, Letter from Attlee to the King, 5 January 1950.
36. National Museum of Labour History Archive, Manchester. General Secretary's Papers, Box 17, Clement Attlee, Document GS/CRA/3.
37. Ibid., Document GS/CRA/4.
38. *The Times*, 25 February 1950.
39. PREM 8/1166, CM 50, 5th Conclusions Cabinet 5 (50).
40. Attlee, *As It Happened*, pp. 206–7.
41. Ibid., p. 206.
42. National Museum of Labour History Archive, Manchester. General Secretary's Papers, Box 17, Clement Attlee, Document GS/CRA/13.
43. PREM 1489/Part II, CM (49) 41st Conclusions, Minute 2, 20 June 1949.
44. PREM 1489/Part II, CM (49) 62nd Conclusions, Minute 4, 27 October 1949.
45. PREM 1489/Part II, Gen. 302/1st Meeting, Cabinet: Iron and Steel Bill: Minutes of a Meeting of Ministers held at 11 Downing Street, 31 October, 1949.
46. PREM 1489/Part II, CM (49) 65th Conclusions, Minute 2, Confidential Annex, 10 November 1949.
47. Hansard, HC 1948–49, vol. 478 (24 July–26 October) column 1254, 14 September 1950.
48. Ibid., column 1255, 14 September 1950.
49. PREM 1489/Part II, Letter from Strauss to Attlee dated 5 October 1951, marked by Attlee on 6 October 1951.

50. PREM 1489/Part II, 'Text of an Opposition Motion dictated over the telephone by Mr C. J. Harris, 2 February 1951', with Churchill, Eden, Butler, Lyttelton and Maclay in support.
51. PREM 8/1188, CM (50) 12th Conclusions, 17 March 1950.
52. PREM 8/1188, 'Budget Policy' 15 March 1950.
53. Labour Party, *Report of the 49th Annual Conference* (London: Labour Party, 1950) p. 98.
54. Ibid., p. 99.
55. Interview with Tony Benn, 26 April 2009.
56. National Museum of Labour History Archive, Manchester. General Secretary's Papers, Box 17, Clement Attlee, Document GS/CRA/14.
57. Philip M. Williams, (ed.) *The Diary of Hugh Gaitskell* (London: Jonathan Cape, 1983) p. 173.
58. Ibid.
59. Pimlott, *The Political Diary of Hugh Dalton*, p. 489.
60. Ibid., p. 485.
61. Morrison, *Herbert Morrison*, p. 271.
62. Ibid., p. 263.
63. Clarke, *The Cripps Version*, p. 534. Attlee passed on the comment to Cripps.
64. Williams, *The Diary of Hugh Gaitskell*, p. 235.
65. Ibid.
66. Ibid., p. 238.
67. Ibid.
68. Pimlott, *The Political Diary of Hugh Dalton*, p. 506.
69. Morrison, *Herbert Morrison*, p. 281.
70. Bullock, *Ernest Bevin: Foreign Secretary*, p. 834.
71. Pimlott, *The Political Diary of Hugh Dalton*, p. 510.
72. PREM 8/1480, Note from Brook to Attlee, 28 May 1951.
73. Williams, *The Diary of Hugh Gaitskell*, pp. 246–7.
74. Ibid., p. 246.
75. Ibid.
76. Callaghan, *Time and Chance*, p. 110.
77. Hansard, HC 1950–51, vol. 487 (23 April–1 May) columns 41–2, 23 April 1951.
78. C. R. Attlee papers, 'Letters to Tom', 24 July 1951.
79. Hansard, HC 1950–51, vol. 486 (3–20 April) column 1471, 16 April 1951.
80. Attlee, *As It Happened*, p. 205.
81. Poem to a schoolgirl, in the possession of Lady Attlee.
82. PREM 8/1391, Attlee to Arthur Henderson, 19 September 1951.
83. PREM 8/1392.
84. In September 1951, Gallup placed the Conservatives on 52 per cent, with Labour on 41 per cent. Quoted in Butler and Butler, *Twentieth-Century British Political Facts*, p. 267.
85. PREM 8/1392, Prime Minister's Personal Telegram from the *Queen Mary* to the Foreign Office, 23 September 1951.
86. PREM 8/1392, Prime Minister's Personal Telegram to Foreign Secretary and Cabinet Colleagues.
87. Labour Party, *Report of the 50th Annual Conference* (London: The Labour Party, 1951) p. 87.
88. Ibid., p. 89.
89. C. R. Attlee papers, 'Letters to Tom', 21 October 1951.

90. *The Times*, 27 October 1951.
91. Attlee, *As It Happened*, p. 208.
92. *The Times*, 27 October 1951.
93. PREM 8/1391, Churchill to Attlee, 26 October 1951.
94. Interview with Lady Attlee, 7 April 2009.
95. C. R. Attlee papers, 'Letters to Tom', Letter of 14 November 1951.
96. Lady Attlee's collection of private papers, Durbin, 'CRA'.
97. C. R. Attlee papers, 'Letters to Tom', Letter of 14 November 1951.
98. Attlee, 'The Pleasure of Books', p. 17.
99. Ibid., p. 19.
100. Ibid.
101. Ibid., p. 20.
102. C. R. Attlee papers, 'Letters to Tom', letter of 8 April 1954.
103. Pimlott, *The Political Diary of Hugh Dalton*, p. 621.
104. C. R. Attlee papers, 'Letters to Tom', letter of 13 October 1953.
105. Ibid., letter of 9 August 1952.
106. Ibid., letter of 8 June 1953.

22. Managing the Party, 1951–55

1. Hansard, HC 1951–52, vol. 494 (19 November–7 December) column 2602, 6 December 1951.
2. Williams, *The Diary of Hugh Gaitskell*, p. 312.
3. Ibid., p. 313.
4. Ibid., p. 312.
5. Foot, *Aneurin Bevan*, p. 439.
6. Williams, *The Diary of Hugh Gaitskell*, p. 313.
7. Aneurin Bevan, *In Place of Fear* (London: Quartet Books Ltd, 1978) p. 202.
8. Interview with Tony Benn, 26 April 2009.
9. Eric Shaw, *Discipline and Discord in the Labour Party: The Politics of Managerial Control in the Labour Party, 1951–87* (Manchester: Manchester University Press, 1988) p. 32.
10. Williams, *The Diary of Hugh Gaitskell*, p. 598.
11. Labour Party, *Report of the 51st Annual Conference* (London: Labour Party, 1952) p. 87.
12. Ibid., p. 88.
13. Pimlott, *The Political Diary of Hugh Dalton*, p. 599.
14. Ibid.
15. Ibid.
16. Ibid., p. 601.
17. Ibid.
18. C. R. Attlee papers, 'Letters to Tom', letter of 28 March 1953.
19. National Museum of Labour History Archive, Manchester, General Secretary's Papers, Box 17, Clement Attlee, Document GS/CRA/30: list of names with 'Yes' or 'No' alongside. Only G. Brinham, S. Watson and A. Bevan have 'No' alongside their names.
20. Ibid., Document GS/CRA/40.
21. Ibid., Document GS/CRA/41.
22. Williams, *The Diary of Hugh Gaitskell*, p. 337.
23. Labour Party, *Report of the 52nd Annual Conference* (London: Labour Party, 1953) p. 207.
24. Labour Party, *Report of the 53rd Annual Conference* (London: Labour Party, 1954) p. 101.
25. Ibid., p. 93.

26. Williams, *The Diary of Hugh Gaitskell*, pp. 375–82.
27. Ibid., p. 368.
28. Ibid.
29. Ibid., p. 369.
30. Ibid., p. 370.
31. Pimlott, *The Political Diary of Hugh Dalton*, p. 653.
32. Ibid.
33. Williams, *The Diary of Hugh Gaitskell*, p. 372.
34. Ibid., p. 383.
35. Ibid.
36. Harris, *Attlee*, pp. 530–1.
37. Shaw, *Discipline and Discord in the Labour Party*, p. 43.
38. Foot, *Aneurin Bevan*, p. 506.
39. Donoghue and Jones, *Herbert Morrison*, p. 533.
40. Morrison, *An Autobiography*, p. 323.
41. Butler and Butler, *Twentieth-Century British Political Facts*, p. 160.
42. Pimlott, *The Political Diary of Hugh Dalton*, p. 655.
43. Ibid.
44. Ibid., p. 657.
45. Ibid., p. 672.
46. Ibid., p. 675.
47. Labour Party, *Report of the 54th Annual Conference* (London: Labour Party, 1955) p. 138.
48. Ibid., p. 210.
49. Ibid.
50. Harris, *Attlee*, p. 543.
51. H. Gaitskell Papers, C276. Draft message prepared by the Labour Party Press Department from the Rt. Hon. C. R. Attlee, OM, CH, MP, Leader of the Parliamentary Labour Party, to Mr H. E. Randall, Labour candidate in the Gateshead West Parliamentary by-election.

23. The Last Years, 1955–67

1. Interview with Lady Attlee, 7 April 2009.
2. C. R. Attlee papers, 'Letters to Tom', letter of 24 June 1956.
3. Ibid., letter of 8 April 1956.
4. Interview with Tony Benn, 26 April 2009.
5. Ibid.
6. H. Gaitskell Papers, A117. Copy of speech issued by the Labour Party Press and Publicity Department, Transport House, Smith Square, London, 10 February 1956.
7. Williams, *The Diary of Hugh Gaitskell*, p. 440.
8. Clement Attlee, 'England My England', *Observer*, 25 November 1956, in Frank Field (ed.) *Attlee's Great Contemporaries: The Politics of Character* (London: Continuum, 2009) p. 33.
9. C. R. Attlee papers, 'Letters to Tom', letter of 26 December 1957.
10. As quoted in Harris, *Attlee*, p. 549.
11. Clement Attlee, 'From Victorian to Elizabethan: The Role of the Monarchy', *Observer*, 23 August 1959, in Field, *Attlee's Great Contemporaries*, p. 75.
12. Clement Attlee, 'Bevan as Hero', *Observer*, 6 November 1960, in Field, *Attlee's Great Contemporaries*, pp. 139–40.

13. Earl Attlee, *Collective Security under the United Nations* (London: David Davies Memorial Institute of International Studies, 1958) p. 7.
14. Labour Party, *Report of the 44th Annual Conference* (London: Labour Party, 1945) p. 154.
15. H. Gaitskell Papers, A117. Tribute prepared by HG on Lord Attlee at time of his illness, December 1961.
16. Ibid. Letter from Countess Attlee at Amersham General Hospital, 9 December 1961.
17. Ibid. Letter from Hugh Gaitskell to George Gretten, Head of European Talks and English Service.
18. *The Times*, 11 April 1967.
19. Lewisham Archives A81/6/3/7, Clement Richard, 1st Earl Attlee KG, PC, OM, CH, FRS, 1883–1967 Prime Minister 1945–1951: Service of Memorial and Burial, Tuesday 7 November 1967, 11.30 a.m.
20. National Museum of Labour History Archive, Manchester, Attlee Memorial Appeal: Second Progress Report, April 1970.
21. Ibid. Second Progress Report, April 1970 and Director's Report, 6 August 1971.
22. Ibid. Second Progress Report, April 1970.

Conclusion

1. Correlli Barnett, *The Audit of War: The Illusion and Reality of Britain as a Great Nation* (London: Macmillan, 1987).
2. Ralph Miliband, *Parliamentary Socialism: A Study in the Politics of Labour* (London: Merlin Press, 1972) pp. 288–9.
3. Interview with Tony Benn, 26 April 2009.
4. Robert Pearce, 'Clement Attlee 1935–55', in Kevin Jefferys (ed.) *Leading Labour: From Keir Hardie to Tony Blair* (London: I.B.Tauris & Co. Ltd, 1999) pp. 94–5.
5. Philip Williamson, *Stanley Baldwin* (Cambridge: Cambridge University Press, digitally printed version, 2007) p. 67.
6. And passing the Town and Country Planning Act, the foundation of, *inter alia*, the modern-day system of planning permission.
7. Hart-Davis, *King's Counsellor*, p. 354.

FURTHER READING

Two interim biographies were written during Attlee's time as prime minister. The American Cyril Clemens's *The Man from Limehouse: Clement Richard Attlee* appeared in 1946, and Roy Jenkins's *Mr Attlee: An Interim Biography* was published in 1948. However, initial interest surrounded other members of his cabinet. Alan Bullock's *Life and Times of Ernest Bevin: Volume One: Trade Union Leader: 1881 to 1940* appeared in 1960 and Michael Foot's *Aneurin Bevan: Volume 1: 1897–1945* was published in 1962. Bernard Donoghue and G. W. Jones's *Herbert Morrison: Portrait of a Politician* appeared in 1973. It was not until 1982 that the first major biography of Attlee – Kenneth Harris's *Attlee* – appeared. Harris knew Attlee and could use a number of conversations with him to produce a sympathetic appraisal, standing both as a biography and primary research tool for historians. Trevor Burridge brought out a further study of Attlee's life in 1985, which was also very sympathetic. Jerry H. Brookshire's thematic *Clement Attlee*, published in 1995, was also very positive about Attlee, and a further positive biography, *Clem Attlee* by Francis Beckett, was published in 1997. Shorter biographies include Robert Pearce's *Attlee* for Longman's Profiles in Power Series of 1997 and David Howell's *Attlee* in Haus Publishing Ltd's *The 20 Prime Ministers of the 20th Century* of 2006. Contrary to the accepted view, Attlee's autobiography, *As It Happened*, published in the final years of his leadership of the Labour Party, in 1954, does contain useful material, but avoids controversy and omits so much that as a piece it is not illuminating. John Swift's *Labour in Crisis: Clement Attlee and the Labour Party in Opposition, 1931–40* of 2001 advances a positive case for Attlee's leadership in the 1930s. Giles Radice's *The Tortoise and the Hares* of 2008 charts the rivalry of Attlee as the tortoise with Bevin, Cripps, Dalton and Morrison as the hares. *Attlee's Great Contemporaries: The Politics of Character*, a collection of the articles he wrote in the 1950s and 1960s, edited by Frank Field, appeared in 2009. More recently, John Bew's *Citizen Clem* was published in 2016.

BIBLIOGRAPHY

Primary sources

Public Records

Air Ministry (AIR) 16/690
Cabinet (CAB)
Dominions Office (DO)
Hansard, Parliamentary Debates, Fifth Series.
India Office Records (IOR)
Ministry of Agriculture and Food (MAF)
Prime Minister's Office (PREM)

Private Papers

C. R. Attlee papers (Bodleian Library, Oxford): these include the 'Letters to Tom' from August 1915 to August 1960: Mb.Eng.C.4792 (August 1915–October 1939), Mb.Eng.C.4793 (January 1940–December 1949) and Mb.Eng.C.4794 (March 1950–August 1960) MS. Attlee, dep. 2–23

Lady Attlee's collection: private papers which include: Evan Durbin, 'CRA', five-page typed manuscript; Jack Lawson, 'The Rt Hon. Clement Attlee, CH, MP, Prime Minister', 15-page typed manuscript

H. Laski Correspondence (National Museum of Labour History, Manchester)
H. Gaitskell papers (University College, London)
A. Greenwood papers (Bodleian Library, Oxford)

Other Papers

BMA Negotiation Committee Minutes Session, 1947–1948
Haileybury College Archive, which include 'Blue Books'; Haileybury Admissions Book; Haileybury College Literary Society; Haileybury Guild Council; Haileybury Records, 'The Shakespeare Society'; 'The Haileybury Stepney Boys' Club Minute Books'; Lawrence House Records

Lewisham Archives (A81/6/3/7)
National Museum of Labour History Archive, Manchester. General Secretary's
papers; Attlee Memorial Appeal

Newspapers and Periodicals

Economic Council Review of Books
Haileyburian, The
Independent
Observer
The Times

Reports

Labour Party, Reports of Annual Conferences; Annual Reviews
Trades Union Congress, Reports of Annual Conferences

Secondary sources

Addison, Paul, *The Road to 1945: British politics and the Second World War* (London:
  Pimlico, 1994)
  'By-elections of the Second World War', in Chris Cook and John Ramsden
  (eds) *By-elections in British Politics* (London: UCL Press Ltd, 1997) pp. 130–51
Anon, *Employment Policy: Presented by the Minister of Reconstruction in Parliament by
  Command of His Majesty* (London: His Majesty's Stationery Office, 1944).
Anon, *Financial Agreement between the Governments of the United States and the United
  Kingdom dated 6th December, 1945* (London: His Majesty's Stationery Office,
  1945) CMD 6708
Anon, *Report from the Select Committee on the Budget Disclosure Together With the
  Proceedings of the Committee, Minutes of Evidence and Appendices* (London: His
  Majesty's Stationery Office, 11 December 1947)
Anon, *United Kingdom Balance of Payments 1946 and 1947* (London: His Majesty's
  Stationery Office February 1948) Cmd. 7324
Attlee, Clement, *The Social Worker* (London: G. Bell & Sons Limited, 1920)
  'Borough Councils: Their Constitution, Powers and Duties', *Fabian Tract*, no.
  191 (London: The Fabian Society, 1920)
  Labour Shows the Way: The Will and the Way to Socialism (London: Methuen &
  Co. Ltd, 1935)
  The Betrayal of Collective Security: 'National' Government's Surrender to Mussolini
  (London: The Labour Publications Department, 1936)
  The Labour Party in Perspective (London: Victor Gollancz Ltd, 1937)
  Labour's Peace Aims (London: Peace Book Company (London) Ltd, 1940)
  As It Happened (London: Heinemann, 1954)
  'The Pleasure of Books', *The National and English Review*, vol. 142, no. 851,
  January 1954, pp.17–21

Collective Security under the United Nations (London: David Davies Memorial Institute of International Studies, 1958)

Attlee, Clement and Ernest Bevin, *Britain's Foreign Policy* (London: The Labour Publications Department, 1946)

Barnett, Correlli, *The Audit of War: The Illusion and Reality of Britain as a Great Nation* (London: Macmillan, 1987)

Beckett, Francis, *Clem Attlee* (London: Politico's Publishing Ltd, 1997)

Bevan, A., 'Speech to Conference', *Labour Party Annual Review*, 1947
In Place of Fear (London: Quartet Books Ltd, 1978)

Beveridge, Sir William, *Social Insurance and Allied Services*, CMND 6404 (London: His Majesty's Stationery Office, 1942)

Brookshire, Jerry H., *Clement Attlee* (Manchester: Manchester University Press, 1995)

Bullock, Alan, *Ernest Bevin: Foreign Secretary* (London: Heinemann, 1983)
Life and Times of Ernest Bevin: Volume One: Trade Union Leader: 1881 to 1940 (London: Heinemann)
The Life and Times of Ernest Bevin, vol. 2, *Minister of Labour 1940–1945* (London: Heinemann, 1967)

Burridge, Trevor, *Clement Attlee* (London: Jonathan Cape Ltd, 1985)

Butler, David and Gareth Butler, *Twentieth-Century British Political Facts 1900–2000* (London: Macmillan, 2000)

Callaghan, James, *Time and Chance* (London: Politico's Publishing, 2006)

Cannadine, David (ed.) *The Speeches of Winston Churchill* (London: Penguin Books, 1990)

Churchill, Winston, *The Second World War*, vol. 1, *Gathering Storm* (London: Penguin Classics, 2005)

Clarke, Peter, *The Cripps Version: The Life of Sir Stafford Cripps* (London: Allen Lane, 2002)
The Last Thousand Days of the British Empire (London: Allen Lane, 2007)

Clemens, Cyril, *The Man from Limehouse: Clement Richard Attlee* (Missouri: International Mark Twain Society, 1946)

Cole, G. D. H., *A History of the Labour Party from 1914* (London: Routledge & Kegan Paul Ltd, 1948)

Colville, John, *The Fringes of Power: Downing Street Diaries, 1939–1955* (London: Phoenix, 2005)

Cook, Chris and John Ramsden (eds) *By-elections in British Politics* (London: UCL Press Ltd, 1997)

Cross, Colin, *Philip Snowden* (London: Barrie & Rockliff, 1966)

Dale, Iain (ed.) *Labour Party General Election Manifestos, 1900–1997* (London: Routledge and Politico's Publishing, 2000)

Dalton, Hugh, *The Fateful Years: Memoirs, 1931–1945* (London: Frederick Muller Ltd, 1957)
High Tide and After: Memoirs 1945–1960 (London: Frederick Muller Ltd, 1962)

Dellar, Geoffrey (ed.) *Attlee As I Knew Him* (London: London Borough of Tower Hamlets Directorate of Community Services, Library Service, 1983)

Dilks, David (ed.) *The Diaries of Sir Alexander Cadogan, 1938–1945* (London: Cassell & Company Ltd, 1971)

Donoughue, Bernard and G. W. Jones, *Herbert Morrison: Portrait of a Politician* (London: Phoenix Press, 2001)

Dunbabin, J. P. D., *International Relations Since 1945: A History in Two Volumes: The Post-Imperial Age: The Great Powers and the Wider World* (London: Longman, 1994)

Ferrell, Robert H. (ed.) *Off the Record: The Private Papers of Harry S. Truman* (Middlesex: Penguin Books, 1982),

Field, Frank (ed.) *Attlee's Great Contemporaries: The Politics of Character* (London: Continuum, 2009)

Foot, Michael, *Aneurin Bevan: Volume 1: 1897–1945* (London: Victor Gollancz 1997)

Fort, Adrian, *Archibald Wavell: The Life and Times of an Imperial Servant* (London: Jonathan Cape, 2009)

Gilbert, Martin, *Second World War* (London: Phoenix Press, 2000)

Grigg, John, *Lloyd George: The People's Champion 1902–1911* (London: Penguin Books, 2002)

Harris, Kenneth, *Attlee* (London: Weidenfeld & Nicolson, 1984)

Hart-Davis, Duff (ed.) *King's Counsellor: Abdication and War – The Diaries of Sir Alan Lascelles* (London: Phoenix, 2007)

Hennessy, Peter, *Cabinets and the Bomb* (Oxford: Oxford University Press for the British Academy, 2007)

The Prime Minister: The Office and Its Holders Since 1945 (London: Penguin Books, 2000)

Howell, David, *Attlee* (London: Haus Publishing Ltd, 2006)

James, Lawrence, *Raj: The Making and Unmaking of British India* (London: Abacus, 2003)

Jay, Anthony, *The Oxford Dictionary of Political Quotations* (Oxford: Oxford University Press, 1996)

Jefferys, Kevin (ed.) *Leading Labour: From Keir Hardie to Tony Blair* (London: I.B.Tauris & Co. Ltd, 1999)

Jenkins, Roy, *Mr Attlee: An Interim Biography* (London: Heinemann, 1948)

Churchill (London: Macmillan, 2001)

Kaufman, Gerald, 'Review of Francis Beckett's *Clem Attlee*', *Independent*, 1 November 1997.

Kinnear, Michael, *The British Voter: An Atlas and Survey since 1885* (London: Batsford, 1968)

Kynaston, David, *Austerity Britain* (London: Bloomsbury Publishing House, 2007)

MacKenzie, Jeanne and Norman MacKenzie (eds) *The Diary of Beatrice Webb*, vol. 4, *1924–1943, The Wheel of Life* (London: Virago in association with the London School of Economics and Political Science, 1984)

McKibbin, Ross, 'The Economic Policy of the Second Labour Government,' in Ross McKibbin, *The Ideologies of Class: Social Relations in Britain, 1880–1950* (Oxford: Clarendon Press, 1994)

Marquand, David, *Ramsay MacDonald* (London: Jonathan Cape Ltd, 1977)

Mathew, Theobald, *Forensic Fables by O* (London: Butterworths, 1961)

Milford, L. S., *Haileybury College: Past and Present* (London: T. Fisher Unwin, 1909)

Miliband, Ralph, *Parliamentary Socialism: A Study in the Politics of Labour* (London: Merlin Press, 1972)

Morgan, Kenneth O., *Labour in Power, 1945–1951* (Oxford: Oxford University Press, 2002)

Morrison of Lambeth, Lord, *Herbert Morrison: An Autobiography* (London: Odhams Press Ltd, 1960)

An Autobiography (London: The Hollen Street Press Ltd, 1960)

Mountbatten, Pamela, *India Remembered: A Personal Account of the Mountbattens During the Transfer of Power* (London: Pavilion Books, 2007)

Mowat, C. L., *Britain Between the Wars, 1918–1940* (London: Methuen & Co Ltd, 1968)

Moyle, Lord, 'Earl Attlee – the Man', *Labour Organiser* [Labour Party publication], November 1967

Nicolson, Nigel (ed.) *The Harold Nicolson Diaries: 1907–1963* (London: Weidenfeld & Nicolson London: Weidenfeld & Nicolson, 2004)

Parkinson, C. Northcote, *Parkinson's Law* (London: Penguin Classics, 2002)

Pearce, Robert, *Attlee* (London: Longman Profiles in Power Series, 1997

'Clement Attlee 1935–55', in Kevin Jefferys (ed.) *Leading Labour: From Keir Hardie to Tony Blair* (London: I.B.Tauris & Co. Ltd, 1999) pp. 80–96

Pelling, Henry, *A Short History of the Labour Party* (London: Macmillan & Company Ltd, 1962)

The Labour Governments, 1945–51 (London: Macmillan, 1984)

Picarda, Hubert, 'Stick to a Stuff-Gown', in Theobald Mathew, *Forensic Fables by O* (London: Butterworths, 1961)

Pimlott, Ben (ed.) *The Political Diary of Hugh Dalton, 1918–40, 1945–60* (London: Jonathan Cape in association with the London School of Economics and Political Science, 1986)

The Second World War Diary of Hugh Dalton, 1940–45 (London: Jonathan Cape in association with the London School of Economics and Political Science, 1986)

Hugh Dalton (London: Harper Collins, 1995)

Radice, Giles, *The Tortoise and the Hares: Attlee, Bevin, Cripps, Dalton, Morrison* (London: Politico's, 2008)

Rhodes James, Robert, *Anthony Eden* (London: George Weidenfeld and Nicolson Ltd, 1986)

Roberts, Andrew, *'The Holy Fox': The Life of Lord Halifax* (London: Phoenix, 2004)

Shaw, Eric, *Discipline and Discord in the Labour Party: The Politics of Managerial Control in the Labour Party, 1951–87* (Manchester: Manchester University Press, 1988)

Shepherd, John, *George Lansbury: At the Heart of Old Labour* (Oxford: Oxford University Press, 2004)

Shinwell, Emmanuel, *Conflict Without Malice* (London: Odhams Press Ltd, 1955)

Simkins, Peter, Geoffrey Jukes and Michael Hickey, *The First World War: The War to End All Wars* (Oxford: Osprey Publishing, 2003)

Swift, John, *Labour in Crisis: Clement Attlee and the Labour Party in Opposition, 1931–40* (Basingstoke: Palgrave, 2001)

Kevin Theakston, 'Rating British Prime Ministers', IPSOS/MORI, available from <http://www.ipsos-mori.com/content/rating-british-prime-ministers1.ashx >, accessed 6 March 2009.

Toyne, Stanley Mease, *History of the Haileybury College Debating Society* (Oxford: Blackwell, 1912)

Williams, Francis, *A Prime Minister Remembers: The War and Post-War Memoirs of The Rt Hon. Earl Attlee KG, PC, OM, CH: Based on his Private Papers and on a Series of Recorded Conversations* (London: Heinemann, 1961)

Williams, Philip M. (ed.) *The Diary of Hugh Gaitskell* (London: Jonathan Cape, 1983)

Williamson, Philip, *Stanley Baldwin* (Cambridge: Cambridge University Press, digitally printed version, 2007)

Wilson, A. N., *The Victorians* (London: Hutchinson, 2002)

Wilson, Harold, *A Prime Minister on Prime Ministers* (London: Orion, 1977)

Worley, Matthew, *Labour Inside the Gate: A History of the British Labour Party between the Wars* (London: I.B.Tauris & Co. Ltd, 2005)

Ziegler, Philip, *Mountbatten: The Official Biography* (London: Collins, 1985)

INDEX